Fuzzy Decision Support Systems for Efficient Energy Management

Fuzzy Decision Support Systems for Efficient Energy Management

Guest Editors

Jelena Kilić Pamuković
Katarina Rogulj

MDPI

Basel • Beijing • Wuhan • Barcelona • Belgrade • Novi Sad • Cluj • Manchester

Guest Editors
Jelena Kilić Pamuković
Faculty of Civil Engineering,
Architecture and Geodesy
University of Split
Split
Croatia

Katarina Rogulj
Faculty of Civil Engineering,
Architecture and Geodesy
University of Split
Split
Croatia

Editorial Office
MDPI AG
Grosspeteranlage 5
4052 Basel, Switzerland

This is a reprint of the Special Issue, published open access by the journal *Energies* (ISSN 1996-1073), freely accessible at: www.mdpi.com/journal/energies/special_issues/14P6P82G8R.

For citation purposes, cite each article independently as indicated on the article page online and as indicated below:

Lastname, A.A.; Lastname, B.B. Article Title. *Journal Name* **Year**, *Volume Number*, Page Range.

ISBN 978-3-7258-4460-9 (Hbk)
ISBN 978-3-7258-4459-3 (PDF)
https://doi.org/10.3390/books978-3-7258-4459-3

Contents

About the Editors

Jelena Kilić Pamuković

Jelena Kilić Pamuković is an Assistant Professor at the Faculty of Civil Engineering, Architecture and Geodesy, University of Split. She earned her PhD in Geodesy in 2019 from the University of Zagreb with a dissertation on spatial decision support systems for urban land consolidation. Since 2013, she has worked in academia and research, contributing to several EU-funded projects such as Erasmus+ BESTSDI and GEOBIZ, COST Action 18126, Interreg ITA-CRO DEEP-SEA, and PRAG. She teaches geodesy and geoinformatics courses and has served as a Guest Editor for Special Issues of *Energies* and *Applied Sciences*. She has published over 30 scientific papers.

Katarina Rogulj

Katarina Rogulj is an Assistant Professor at the Faculty of Civil Engineering, Architecture and Geodesy, University of Split. She earned her PhD in 2018 with a dissertation on decision support systems for the restoration of historical road bridges. Between 2013 and 2019, she worked in the private construction sector on various design and execution projects. She has been employed at the University of Split since 2019, teaching courses in construction management, project planning, operations research, and decision systems. She has participated in international scientific and professional projects and has served as a Guest Editor for Special Issues of *Energies* and *Applied Sciences*. She has co-authored more than 30 scientific papers.

Preface

One of the most essential resources for continuous development and comfort in everyday life is energy. Throughout the decades, energy demand has been constantly rising due to improvements in living standards, population growth, and economic expansion worldwide. On the other hand, the reserves of fossil fuels are steadily decreasing, which progressively increases their cost. Nowadays, decision-makers are dealing with great challenges in distributing energy resources within systems of efficient energy management. There are many parameters included in these systems that are mainly uncertain, complex, and stochastically valued, such as technology efficiencies, resource properties, and location characteristics. These parameters demand certain skills and experiences from decision-makers. For that reason, it is necessary to create effective and useful tools for managing efficient energy systems under multiple scales of socio-economic and ecological environments. Decision support systems are well-known and often used as a tool for solving various problems that involve energy efficiency and energy management. Recently, decision support systems have been frequently developed under fuzzy logic theory when dealing with complex, vague, uncertain, and multi-objective problems such as system management of efficient energy.

This Special Issue aims to present and disseminate the most recent advances related to the numerical modelling of efficient energy management using fuzzy decision support systems (FDSSs). Topics of interest presented here are the development of FDSSs for energy efficiency and energy management in construction, mobility, industrial processes, materials, manufacturing, environmental processes that include water, air, and soil resources, exploration, exploitation, conversion, supply of energy resources, etc.

Jelena Kilić Pamuković and Katarina Rogulj
Guest Editors

energies

MDPI

Article

Renewable Energy from Solid Waste: A Spherical Fuzzy Multi-Criteria Decision-Making Model Addressing Solid Waste and Energy Challenges

Nattaporn Chattham [1], Nguyen Van Thanh [2,*] and Chawalit Jeenanunta [3]

1 Department of Physics, Faculty of Science, Kasetsart University, Bangkok 10900, Thailand; nattaporn.c@ku.ac.th
2 Department of Logistics and Supply Chain Management, School of Technology, Van Lang University, Ho Chi Minh City, Vietnam
3 School of Management Technology, Sirindhorn International Institute of Technology, Thammasat University, Pathum Thani 12120, Thailand; chawalit@siit.tu.ac.th
* Correspondence: thanh.nguyenvan@vlu.edu.vn

Abstract: With rapid urbanization and industrialization, Vietnam is facing many challenges in solid waste management and increasing energy demand. In this context, the development of renewable energy from solid waste not only solves the problem of environmental pollution but also makes an important contribution to energy security and sustainable economic development. Solid waste to energy is a system of solid waste reatment by thermal methods, in which the heat generated from this treatment process is recovered and utilized to produce energy. Site selection is one of the biggest challenges for renewable energy projects. In addition to technical factors, this decision must also consider environmental impacts, including protecting ecosystems, minimizing noise, and limiting impacts on public health. To solve this problem, multi-criteria decision making (MCDM) methods combined with fuzzy numbers are often used. These methods allow planners to evaluate and balance competing factors, thereby determining the most optimal location for the project. In this study, the authors proposed a Spherical Fuzzy Multi-Criteria Decision-making Model (SFMCDM) for site selection in solid waste-to-energy projects. In the first stage, all criteria affecting the decision-making process are defined based on literature review, experts and triple bottom line model (social, environmental, and economic), and analytic hierarchy process (AHP), and fuzzy theory is applied for calculating the weights in the second stage. The weighted aggregated sum product assessment (WASPAS) method is utilized for ranking four potential locations in the final stage. The contribution of the proposed process is its structured, systematic, and innovative approach to solving the location selection problem for renewable energy projects. Choosing the right location not only ensures the success of the project but also contributes to the sustainable development of renewable energy.

Keywords: renewable energy; MCDM model; fuzzy theory; location selection; environment issue

1. Introduction

Renewable energy is becoming a prominent field in the global energy system, playing a crucial role in sustainable development worldwide. It meets the demands of economic growth while utilizing clean and safe energy sources. Renewable energy is projected to grow at an annual rate of 7.1% over the next 2 decades, eventually surpassing coal to become the world's leading energy source by 2040 [1]. In this context, Vietnam must effectively leverage its potential and strengths in renewable energy to achieve the goal of net-zero carbon emissions by 2050, fostering rapid and sustainable development while enhancing its economic competitiveness [2].

Renewable energy sources such as solar, wind, biomass, small hydropower, and solid waste energy all have great potential for development in Vietnam. Vietnam is currently facing an increasing amount of domestic and industrial waste, putting great pressure on the waste treatment system. Converting solid waste into energy not only helps solve the problem of environmental pollution and reduces the burden on landfills but also creates a sustainable energy source for economic development. Waste-to-energy incineration technology is a modern solution that Vietnam can apply to turn challenges into opportunities, while contributing to the implementation of national sustainable development goals.

However, the development of renewable energy projects often faces many challenges such as feasibility assessment, selection of appropriate technology, cost optimization, and risk management. To address these challenges, managers need to consider various factors, ranging from investment costs, technical performance, and environmental impacts to community acceptance. In this context, multi-criteria decision-making (MCDM) models have been applied to provide a systematic and transparent approach to identifying and selecting optimal solutions. The Multi-Criteria Decision-Making Model (MCDM) emerged in the early 1970s as an important research area in the field of decision science, helping to solve complex decision-making problems when considering many different criteria. MCDM has been widely applied in fields such as supply chain management, environmental and energy management, finance, healthcare, etc [3]. Nowadays, with the development of new methods and the integration of advanced techniques such as fuzzy set theory, MCDM models are becoming increasingly important and can be widely applied in many different fields. Fuzzy set theory combined with MCDM models helps to handle ambiguity and uncertainty in the decision-making process. Through fuzzy set theory, subjective and unclear assessments are presented flexibly, increasing the accuracy of the decision-making model and supporting better decision-making. From here, MCDM models are improved in adaptability and can be widely applied in many fields, from supply chain management to choosing the optimal solution in renewable energy development projects, thanks to the ability to integrate information from many different sources [4].

This research proposes a spherical fuzzy multi-criteria decision-making model (SFMCDM) for selecting solid waste energy plant locations. Combining the Spherical Fuzzy Analytic Hierarchy Process (SFAHP) and Weighted Aggregated Sum Product Assessment (WASPAS), the model uses Spherical Fuzzy Numbers (SFNs) to enhance uncertainty representation. This integration provides detailed analysis, improving efficiency and addressing the limitations of traditional MCDM models. At the same time, SFMCDM models support decision-makers in weighing both quantitative and qualitative factors.

In this study, the authors identify the criteria that influence the decision-making process based on the Triple Bottom Line (TBL) model. The Triple Bottom Line (TBL) model is a framework for evaluating the performance of an organization or projects, focusing on three main aspects: economic (profit), social (people), and environmental (planet). Developed by John Elkington in 1994, the model encourages businesses to expand their goals beyond financial profit to consider social and environmental impact [5]. This approach helps to comprehensively evaluate options, balancing financial benefits with environmental protection requirements and social consensus. In addition, clearly defining criteria helps to increase transparency, minimize conflicts of interest, and improve the acceptability of stakeholders. This is especially important in long-term projects, such as renewable energy, where sustainability criteria play a decisive role in the overall success of the project. A structure of the Triple Bottom Line (TBL) model is shown in Figure 1 [6,7].

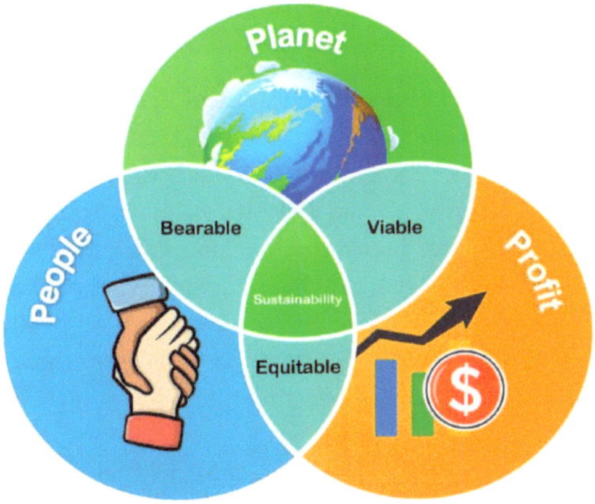

Figure 1. Triple Bottom Line (TBL) model.

The main objective of this study is to develop a decision support model to assist in the assessment and selection of optimal locations for solid waste-to-energy plants, ensuring comprehensive consideration of economic, environmental, and social factors in a complex and uncertain context. The study not only provides a scientific and systematic approach to solving the problem of site selection in waste-to-energy projects, but also contributes to promoting sustainable development, reducing negative impacts on the environment, and optimizing the use of resources.

The structure of this paper is divided into five parts including Section 1 Introduction: presents the research context, the problem to be solved, and the objectives and significance of the research; Section 2 Literature review: provides an overview of previous studies related to the selection of renewable energy plant locations and MCDM methods, especially Spherical Fuzzy AHP and WASPAS; Section 3 Research method: describes in detail the process of building the SFMCDM model, including how to calculate the criteria weights using SFAHP and evaluate the options using WASPAS; Sections 4 and 5 Case study and Discussion: applies the model to the problem of selecting the location of a solid waste-to-energy plant in a specific locality, including actual data, and analysis of results and discussion; Finally, Section 6 Conclusions: summarizes the results achieved, clearly states the contributions of the research and limitations and suggests future development directions.

2. Literature Review

MCDM models are regarded by researchers as one of the most popular approaches to complex decision-making problems in existing pieces of literature. The term MCDM refers to the process of picking the best choice from a group of possibilities. Different models have been developed to handle this decision process, some of which are based on MCDM methods, which have been employed alone or in conjunction with other MCDM methods and/or other strategies [8,9].

There has been much research on the application of MCDM models in the field of sustainable energy development. Most of these revolve around decision-making problems such as supplier evaluation and selection, location selection, project evaluation, technology evaluation and selection, etc. Qingpeng Cao et al. [10] proposed a three-stage MCDM model including the Stepwise Weight Assessment Ratio Analysis (SWARA), Full Consistency

Method (FUCOM), and Evaluation based on Distance from Average Solution (EDAS) methods for evaluation of contractors for the installation of solar panels. Tien-Chin Wang et al. [11] introduced a hybrid MCDM model for evaluation and selection of solar panel supplier for a photovoltaic system design. In this study, the authors combined several MCDM model as FAHP and Data Envelopment Analysis (DEA) model. The result of this study lies in the evolution of a new model that is flexible and practical to the decision-maker in renewable energy sector. Pablo Aragonés Beltrán et al. [12] introduced a decision-making model based on the AHP and the Analytic Network Process (ANP) model. There are three phases in their decision approach. This research analyzed the factors that should be considered before accepting or rejecting proposals for investment in solar thermal power plants. Wang et al. [13] presented a MCDM model for risk ranking of energy performance contracting project under fuzzy environment. In this work, the authors applied Multi-Attributive Border approximation Area Comparison (MABAC) method with fuzzy theory for ranking the risks and identifying the priority of risks by reflecting the decision-maker's bounded rationality and behavior psychology.

Over the years, many studies have investigated the application of MCDM techniques in solving location evaluation and selection problems of renewable energy projects (Table 1). Most of these studies considered multiple evaluation factors and criteria. In some cases where qualitative criteria are considered, fuzzy logic is often used to convey the ambiguity of a human's decision-making process. Lijian Sun et al. [14] combined the MCDM model and Geographic Information System (GIS) for the site selection of large-scale solar plants. In this study, the weight of all factors is calculated by the AHP model. A proposed model is illustrated by China. As a result, their model can be used for the selection of the potential location for solar power plant installation. Seda Ozdemira and Gokhan Sahin [15] used the AHP model for electricity production locations; the authors took into consideration both quantitative and qualitative characteristics that play an effective role in electricity production. Majid Vafaeipour et al. [16] proposed a hybrid MCDM model for ranking 25 scattered cities all around the country with the goal of constructing solar power plants. The SWARA and the Weighted Aggregated Sum Product Assessment (WASPAS) models are used in this research. Eventually, by considering the ranked cities, a comprehensive GIS map of their country was also presented.

Younes Noorollahi et al. [17] applied fuzzy Boolean logic, AHP model, and GIS to select the optimal location for constructing solar power plants. The authors considered both qualitative and quantitative factors. Meryem Tahri et al. [18] combined a hybrid MCDM model including GIS tools and the AHP method to assess the suitability of a certain set of locations. As a result, the most suitable sites are those where the ground is flat and oriented towards the south. Olayinka S. Ohunakin and Burak Omer Saracoglu [19] used several MCDM approaches including the AHP model, Consistency-Driven Pairwise Comparisons (CDPC) model, Decision EXpert (DEX), ELECTRE III and IV for location selection of very large concentrated solar power plants. Graciele Rediske et al. [20] combined AHP and Technique for Order Preference by Similarity to Ideal Solution (TOPSIS) methods with GIS for evaluation and classification of the best locations for the implantation of solar photovoltaic power plants. Wang et al. [21] developed a hybrid FAHP-TOPSIS model to support the location selection process of wind power plant development projects in Vietnam. A real-world case study was performed to validate the feasibility of the proposed model where seven alternatives were evaluated based on 12 criteria. Wang et al. [22] proposed an integrated methodology of Fuzzy AHP, Data Envelopment Analysis (DEA), and Fuzzy TOPSIS for evaluating and selecting optimal locations for building a solar power plant. The authors considered both quantitative and qualitative criteria including social, environmental, technological, economic, and site characteristics factors. Wang et al. [23] introduced a FANP-TOPSIS model to solve the solid waste power plant location selection problem. In the associated case study, the authors evaluated eight potential locations across 13 quantitative and qualitative criteria. Gil-García et al. [24] utilized a hybrid fuzzy AHP-TOPSIS in combination with GIS for optimal off-shore wind location evaluation process.

Table 1. Overview of studies of MCDM and renewable energy plant location selection problem.

No.	Authors	Project Type	MCDM Techniques	Location	Main Findings
1	Lijian Sun et al. [14]	Solar energy	AHP	China	Utilized a combination of AHP and Geographic Information System (GIS). Considered quantitative factors only (Climate, Orography, Water availability, and Location). Case study results are validated via sensitivity analysis.
2	Seda Ozdemira and Gokhan Sahin [15]	Solar energy	AHP	Turkey	Utilized a combination of AHP and Photovoltaic Geographic Information System (GIS). Considered quantitative and qualitative factors (Potential energy production, Environmental criteria, Safety, Distance to existing transmission line, and Topographical properties).
3	Majid Vafaeipour et al. [16]	Solar energy	SWARA, WASPAS	Iran	Considered 14 qualitative and quantitative criteria, divided into Economical, Environmental, Social, and Risk factors. Economic factors are considered as the most important.
4	Younes Noorollahi et al. [17]	Solar energy	Fuzzy AHP	Iran	Utilized a combination of Fuzzy AHP and Photovoltaic Geographic Information System (PVGIS). Considered qualitative factors (Climatic, Economic, Orography, and Environment).
5	Meryem Tahri et al. [18]	Solar energy	AHP	Morocco	Utilized a combination of Fuzzy AHP and GIS. Considered qualitative factors (Climate, Location, Orography, and Land use). The most important factors are Climate factors, specifically, potential solar radiation and land surface temperature.
6	Olayinka S. Ohunakin and Burak Omer Saracoglu [19]	Solar energy	AHP, CDPC, DEX, ELECTRE III and IV	Nigeria	A comparative study where multiple MCDM techniques were applied. Considered Technological, Environmental, Legal, Political, and Social factors. While there is some inconsistency between the results of different techniques, the overall result can be used as the basis for further study.
7	Graciele Rediske et al. [20]	Solar energy	AHP, TOPSIS	Brazil	Utilized the combination of AHP and TOPSIS techniques with GIS. Considered qualitative factors: Environmental, Location, Climate, and Orographic. The most important factors are Location factors, followed by Environmental factors. The case study results were verified using sensitivity analysis.
8	Wang et al. [21]	Wind energy	Fuzzy AHP, TOPSIS	Vietnam	The authors considered qualitative and quantitative factors (Environmental, Economic, Social, and Technological). The most important factors are Economic factors.
9	Wang et al. [22]	Solar energy	Fuzzy AHP, TOPSIS, DEA	Vietnam	The authors considered qualitative and quantitative factors (Environmental, Economic, Social, Technological, and Site characteristics). The most important factors in this case are Environmental factors (Sunshine hours and Temperature).
10	Wang et al. [23]	Solid waste power	Fuzzy ANP, TOPSIS	Vietnam	The authors considered qualitative and quantitative factors (Environmental, Economic, Social, and Technological). The most important factors in this case are Economic factors.
11	García et al. [24]	Wind energy	Fuzzy AHP, TOPSIS	USA	Fuzzy AHP-TOPSIS models are applied in combination with GIS. The use of GIS allows a more graphical solution in comparison with traditional MCDM models.

In recent years, there have been several MCDM models developed to support location selection problems in wave energy projects (Table 2). Many of these pieces of literature employed fuzzy theory in combination with classical and novel MCDM techniques. Wang et al. [25] presented a FAHP-WAPAS-based approach to the wave energy plant location selection project. A case study was performed where 10 potential locations were evaluated across 15 criteria. Le et al. [26] developed an AHP-TOPSIS model in combination with

GIS to identify optimal wave energy locations around the coast of Tasmania, Australia. Eda Bolturk and Cengiz Kahraman [27] developed an Intuitionistic Fuzzy Combinative Distance-based Assessment (CODAS) model to evaluate the potential location of a wave energy farm in Turkey. Abaei et al. [28] introduced a novel Bayesian Network and Influence Diagram-based MCDM model to identify optimal wave energy converter locations in Tasmania. Wang et al. [29] combined Fuzzy Best-Worst Method (BWM) and Fuzzy TODIM to develop a comprehensive approach to the wave energy location evaluation problem.

The aim of this research is to develop a comprehensive and applicable SFMCDM model to support the solid waste-to-energy power plant location selection under a fuzzy decision-making environment. To avoid omitting expert opinion, spherical fuzzy logic is applied in conjunction with classical MCDM methods.

The primary contributions of this research include advancing the theoretical framework for addressing complex site selection challenges in renewable energy projects by integrating economic, environmental, and social criteria. The study introduces an innovative Spherical Fuzzy Multi-Criteria Decision-Making (SFMCDM) model, offering enhanced decision-making capabilities under uncertainty and ambiguity, with more detailed analysis than traditional fuzzy methods. Additionally, it provides a structured and systematic approach to support stakeholders in identifying optimal locations for solid waste-to-energy plants, thereby improving project feasibility, and promoting sustainability.

3. Methodology

3.1. Research Process

This study introduces a Spherical Fuzzy MCDM framework to determine the optimal site for constructing a renewable energy plant powered by solid waste. The research process is divided into three main stages, as illustrated in Figure 2.

Stage 1: Identifying Evaluation Criteria and Potential Locations

In this phase, key evaluation criteria are established based on insights from the literature, the Triple Bottom Line (TBL) framework, and expert opinions. These criteria encompass economic, environmental, and social dimensions. Concurrently, potential locations are selected to undergo assessment.

Stage 2: Determining Criteria Weights with the Spherical Fuzzy AHP Method

Next, the relative importance of each criterion is quantified using the Spherical Fuzzy AHP method. This approach incorporates expert judgment and accounts for uncertainty, employing a fuzzy data set to objectively and flexibly prioritize the criteria.

Stage 3: Evaluating and Ranking Locations using the WASPAS Method

With criteria weights established, the WASPAS method is then applied to evaluate the potential locations. This step calculates an overall efficiency score for each location, integrating all criteria to produce a final ranking. The outcome identifies the most suitable site for constructing the renewable energy plant.

The key difference between SF-AHP and FAHP lies in the distinction between Spherical Fuzzy Numbers (SFNs) and Triangular Fuzzy Numbers (TFNs). Theoretically, SFNs are superior to TFNs in capturing the vagueness of human decision-making, as TFNs are part of the Type-1 Fuzzy Sets family with two-dimensional membership functions, while SFNs belong to the Hesitant Type-2 Fuzzy Sets family with three-dimensional membership functions.

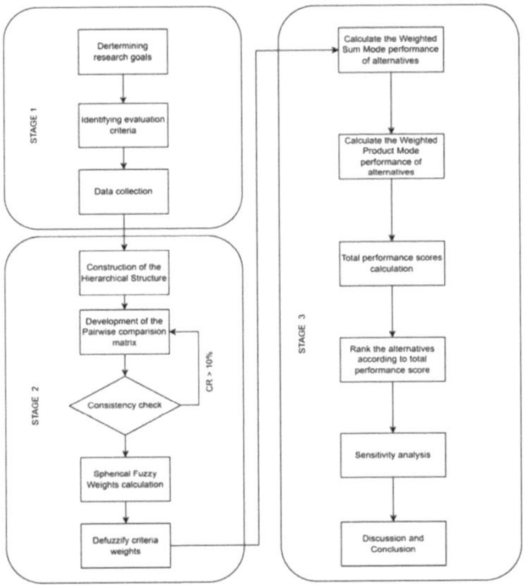

Figure 2. Research process.

TFN-based decision-making models often emphasize the lower bound, upper bound, and median values while overlooking membership and possibility degrees. In contrast, SFNs account for these aspects, offering a more comprehensive representation of decision-makers' opinions in MCDM models [30]. Consequently, the application of the SF-AHP model presents theoretical advantages over the conventional FAHP approach.

3.1.1. Spherical Fuzzy Sets Theory

Spherical fuzzy set theory was recently introduced by Gundogdu et al. [31] as a conceptual fusion of Pythagorean fuzzy sets [32] and Neutrosophic sets [33]. The core idea behind this theory is that a decision maker's hesitancy can be represented independently from both membership and non-membership degrees. By defining a membership function on a spherical surface, spherical fuzzy sets provide a framework to generalize other extensions of fuzzy sets, thereby offering greater flexibility in handling uncertain and imprecise information.

Spherical fuzzy sets $\widetilde{A}_S$ defined over the universe U_1 can be represented as

$$\widetilde{A}_S = \left\{ x, (\mu_{\widetilde{A}_S}(x), v_{\widetilde{A}_S}(x), \pi_{\widetilde{A}_S}(x)) | x \epsilon U_1 \right\} \quad (1)$$

where:

$$\begin{gathered} \mu_{\widetilde{A}_S}(x) : U_1 \to [0,1], v_{\widetilde{A}_S}(x) : U_1 \to [0,1], \textit{and } \pi_{\widetilde{A}_S}(x) : U_1 \to [0,1] \\ \text{and } 0 \leq \mu^2_{\widetilde{A}_S}(x) + v^2_{\widetilde{A}_S}(x) + \pi^2_{\widetilde{A}_S}(x) \leq 1 \text{with } \forall x \in U_1 \end{gathered} \quad (2)$$

$\mu_{\widetilde{A}_S}(x)$ is the degree of membership, $v_{\widetilde{A}_S}(x)$ is the degree of non-membership, and $\pi_{\widetilde{A}_S}(x)$ is the hesitancy of x to $\widetilde{A}_S$.

Gundogdu and Kahraman [33] established and illustrated the fundamental arithmetic operations for spherical fuzzy sets in their work.

3.1.2. Spherical Fuzzy Analytic Hierarchy Process (SF-AHP) Model

The Spherical Fuzzy AHP (SF-AHP) method, introduced by Gundogdu and Kahraman [34], extends the traditional AHP approach using spherical fuzzy sets. In this study, SF-AHP is applied to determine the weights of the DC selection criteria. Gundogdu and Kahraman's SF-AHP methodology consists of seven steps:

Step 1: Constructing the Hierarchical Structure: Begin by developing a hierarchical model comprising at least three levels. At the top (Level 1) is the overarching goal, represented by a score index. Level 2 enumerates the nnn criteria influencing the score index. Finally, Level 3 identifies a set of m alternatives A, where m $\geq$ 2, to be evaluated against these criteria.

Step 2: Develop pairwise comparison matrices for the criteria using spherical fuzzy judgments. These judgments rely on the linguistic terms proposed by Gundogdu and Kahraman [34,35]:

Table 2. Linguistic measures of importance [34].

	(μ, v, π)	**Score Index**
Absolutely more importance (AM)	(0.9, 0.1, 0.0)	9
Very high importance (VH)	(0.8, 0.2, 0.1)	7
High importance (HI)	(0.7, 0.3, 0.2)	5
Slightly more importance (SM)	(0.6, 0.4, 0.3)	3
Equally importance (EI)	(0.5, 0.4, 0.4)	1
Slightly lower importance (SL)	(0.4, 0.6, 0.3)	1/3
Low importance (LI)	(0.3, 0.7, 0.2)	1/5
Very low importance (VL)	(0.2, 0.8, 0.1)	1/7
Absolutely low importance (AL)	(0.1, 0.9, 0.0)	1/9

Equations (3) and (4) are then used to determine the score indices (SI) for each alternative.

$$SI = \sqrt{\left|100 * \left[\left(\mu_{\tilde{A}_s} - \pi_{\tilde{A}_s}\right)^2 - \left(v_{\tilde{A}_s} - \pi_{\tilde{A}_s}\right)^2\right]\right|} \tag{3}$$

For AM, VH, HI, SM, and EI.

$$\frac{1}{SI} = \frac{1}{\sqrt{\left|100 * \left[\left(\mu_{\tilde{A}_s} - \pi_{\tilde{A}_s}\right)^2 - \left(v_{\tilde{A}_s} - \pi_{\tilde{A}_s}\right)^2\right]\right|}} \tag{4}$$

For SL, LI, VL, and AL.

Step 3: Convert the linguistic terms in each pairwise comparison matrix into their corresponding score indices. After this conversion, conduct a traditional consistency check. Ensure that the Consistency Ratio (CR) value does not exceed the 10% threshold:

$$CR = \frac{CI}{RI} \tag{5}$$

Here, the Consistency Index (CI) is computed as:

$$CI = \frac{\lambda_{max} - n}{n - 1} \tag{6}$$

where λ_{max} is the largest eigenvalue of the comparison matrix and nnn is the number of criteria. The Random Index (RI) is selected based on the number of criteria, following Gundogdu and Kahraman [34].

Step 4: Determine the spherical fuzzy weights for both the criteria and the alternatives.

The weight of each alternative relative to each criterion is calculated using the following equation:

$$\begin{aligned} SWM_w(A_{S1}, \ldots, A_{Sn}) &= w_1 A_{S1} + \ldots + w_n A_{Sn} \\ &= \left\langle \left[1 - \prod_{i=1}^{n}\left(1 - \mu^2_{A_{Si}}\right)^{w_i}\right]^{1/2}, \prod_{i=1}^{n} V^{w_i}_{A_{Si}}, \left[\prod_{i=1}^{n}\left(1 - \mu^2_{A_{Si}}\right)^{w_i} - \prod_{i=1}^{n}\left(1 - \mu^2_{A_{Si}} - \pi^2_{A_{Si}}\right)^{w_i}\right]^{1/2} \right\rangle \end{aligned} \quad (7)$$

where $w = 1/n$.

Step 5: Determine the global weights through hierarchical layer sequencing.

The final ranking of the alternatives is determined by aggregating the spherical weights across all levels of the hierarchical structure. This can be achieved using one of two methods: The first method involves employing the score function in Equation (8) to defuzzify the criteria weights.

$$S\left(\tilde{w}^S_j\right) = \sqrt{\left|100 \times \left[\left(3\mu_{\tilde{A}_s} - \frac{\pi_{\tilde{A}_s}}{2}\right)^2 - \left(\frac{v_{\tilde{A}_s}}{2} - \pi_{\tilde{A}_s}\right)^2\right]\right|} \quad (8)$$

Next, the criteria weights are normalized using Equation (9), followed by the application of spherical fuzzy multiplication as outlined in Equation (10):

$$\overline{w}^s_j = \frac{S\left(\tilde{w}^S_j\right)}{\sum_{j=1}^{n} S\left(\tilde{w}^S_j\right)} \quad (9)$$

$$\tilde{A}_{S_{ij}} = \overline{w}^s_j \times \tilde{A}_{S_i} = \left\langle \left(1 - \left(1 - \mu^2_{\tilde{A}_S}\right)^{\overline{w}^s_j}\right)^{1/2}, v^{\overline{w}^s_j}_{\tilde{A}_S}, \left(\left(1 - \mu^2_{\tilde{A}_S}\right)^{\overline{w}^s_j} - \left(1 - \mu^2_{\tilde{A}_S} - \pi^2_{\tilde{A}_S}\right)^{\overline{w}^s_j}\right)^{1/2} \right\rangle \quad (10)$$

With $\forall i$.

The final ranking score $(\tilde{F})$ for each alternative A_i is computed using Equation (11):

$$\tilde{F} = \sum_{j=1}^{n} \tilde{A}_{S_{ij}} = \tilde{A}_{S_{i1}} + \tilde{A}_{S_{i2}} + \ldots + \tilde{A}_{S_{in}} \quad (11)$$

With $\forall i$.

The second approach involves proceeding with the calculation without defuzzifying the criteria weights. In this method, the spherical fuzzy global weights are determined as follows:

$$\prod_{j=1}^{n} \tilde{A}_{S_{ij}} = \tilde{A}_{S_{i1}} \times \tilde{A}_{S_{i2}} \times \ldots \times \tilde{A}_{S_{in}} \quad (12)$$

Subsequently, the final ranking score $(\tilde{F})$ for each alternative is computed using Equation (11).

3.1.3. Weighted Sum Method of Evaluation for Products

The Weighted Sum Model (WSM) is a widely used and effective multicriteria decision-making method for evaluating multiple alternatives across various criteria. Initially, s alternatives and c criteria are considered. The importance of each criterion, x_{sc}, is represented by w_c, while the performance level of alternative s with respect to criterion c

is assessed. Ultimately, the relative significance of an alternative, y, is calculated using $L_y^{(1)}$ [36]:

$$L_y^{(1)} = \sum_{c=1}^{n} \overline{x}_{sc} w_c \tag{13}$$

For each initial criterion value, linear normalization is performed as follows:

$$\overline{x}_{sc} = \frac{x_{sc}}{max_s x_{sc}} \tag{14}$$

when $max_s x_{sc}$ indicates that cost is prioritized over value, or:

$$\overline{x}_{sc} = \frac{min_s x_{sc}}{x_{sc}} \tag{15}$$

when $min_{sc} x_{sc}$ signifies that minimizing cost is prioritized over maximizing value.

The Weighted Product Model (WPM) is another commonly used approach for evaluating multiple alternatives y based on their overall relative value, $L_y^{(2)}$:

$$L_y^{(2)} = \prod_{c=1}^{n} (\overline{x}_{sc})^{w_c} \tag{16}$$

The weights representing the overall relative importance are evenly distributed between the WSM and WPM values to calculate the total score. This approach integrates both methodologies for a comprehensive analysis of the evaluation of the alternatives:

$$L_y = 0.5L_y^{(1)} + 0.5L_y^{(2)} \tag{17}$$

The outcomes from the WSM and WPM models can be further analyzed and adjusted to align with the specific environmental requirements identified in the research. This process aims to enhance the accuracy and effectiveness of decision-making. Such modifications are encapsulated in the Weighted Aggregate Sum Product Assessment (WASPAS) model, which was utilized in this study to rank the alternatives. If the decision-maker has no specific preference, λ is set to 0.5:

$$L_y = \lambda \sum_{c=1}^{n} \overline{x}_{sc} w_c + (1 - \lambda) \prod_{j=1}^{n} (\overline{x}_{sc})^{w_c} \tag{18}$$

3.2. The Subject of Analysis

Vietnam is currently among the top 20 countries generating the largest amounts of waste worldwide. On average, each Vietnamese person produces about 1.2 kg of waste per day, amounting to nearly 70,000 tons nationwide. Of this, more than 70% is buried, while only 13% is incinerated for energy recovery. In the context of increasingly scarce land resources, power plants utilizing waste as a resource are considered an effective solution to harmonize environmental preservation with economic development. Here is a revised version with improved grammar and clarity.

The thermal energy generated during the waste incineration process is recovered by the boiler system inside the incinerator. This system converts the heat into high-temperature and high-pressure steam, which is then transformed into electricity using a water turbine generator. The ash produced after the incineration process is collected and stabilized before being disposed of in landfills.

Additionally, this ash can be recycled to recover metals, produce construction materials, and more. By applying this technology, the volume of waste is significantly reduced (by approximately 90%) compared to its original volume. The closed treatment process effectively prevents odors, water leakage, and other environmental impacts. Furthermore, the treatment process generates electricity to support the plant's operations and allows surplus electricity to be connected to and sold on the grid. The process of solid waste-to-energy technology is illustrated in Figure 3.

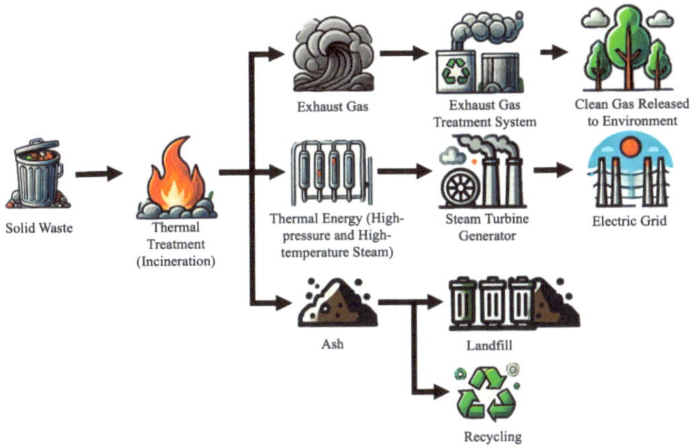

Figure 3. Solid waste-to-energy technology.

Choosing the location of a solid waste-to-energy plant is a strategic decision that directly affects economic efficiency, environmental impact, and social acceptance. This is a complex decision that requires comprehensive consideration of many related aspects, from the ability to provide stable raw materials and technical feasibility, to the long-term impact on the environment and surrounding community. Moreover, the construction of a solid waste-to-energy plant not only solves the problem of waste treatment but also contributes to promoting sustainable development through the production of renewable energy. Therefore, this decision is not simply a technical problem, but also a complex challenge that requires coordination among stakeholders, and a scientific and transparent assessment process. In this study, the authors develop a decision support model to assist in the assessment and selection of optimal locations for solid waste-to-energy plants, ensuring comprehensive consideration of economic, environmental, and social factors in a complex and uncertain context. A list of criteria affecting the decision-making process is shown in Table 3.

Table 3. List of criteria.

Criteria	Subcriteria	Symbol
Economic factors	Initial investment cost	THAI01
	Operating and maintenance costs	THAI02
	Potential access to the energy market	THAI03
Social	Job creation	THAI04
	Impact on local communities	THAI05
	Community acceptance	THAI06
Environmental factors	Impact on ecosystems	THAI07
	Ability to manage and reduce pollution	THAI08
	Proximity to sensitive areas	THAI09

4. Case Study

The proposed method is applied to a case study where four potential locations are considered for building a solid waste-to-energy plant in Ho Chi Minh City, the economic center of Vietnam.

The spherical fuzzy AHP model offers a flexible approach for calculating weights under uncertainty, aiding decision-makers in making accurate choices. Data is gathered through expert surveys, where criteria are evaluated via pairwise comparisons expressed as spherical fuzzy numbers. These are aggregated into a consistent matrix, and weights are calculated, accounting for uncertainty in judgments. In this case, input for the SF-AHP model was gathered from four industry experts and four academic experts, all possessing extensive experience in renewable energy development. The weights of the nine criteria are shown in Table 4.

Table 4. Initial Comparison Matrices.

Criteria	Left Criteria Is Greater				Equally Importance	Right Criteria Is Greater				Criteria	Number of Experts
	AMI	VHI	HI	SMI	EI	SLI	LI	VLI	ALI		
A				4	3	1				B	8
A			3	2	2	1				C	8
A				4	3		1			D	8
A					5	2		1		E	8
A					4	2	1	1		F	8
A					3	3	1	1		G	8
A					5	1	1	1		H	8
A				2	3	1	1	1		I	8
B					2	4	2			C	8
B					4	1	3			D	8
B					4	3	1			E	8
B						5	2	1		F	8
B					2	2	3	1		G	8
B					2	2	3	1		H	8
B					4	3	1			I	8
C				2	2	2	2			D	8
C					5	2	1			E	8
C					1	3	3	1		F	8
C					2	3	2	1		G	8
C					3	2	2	1		H	8
C						3	4	1		I	8
D						1	3	4		E	8
D					3	4	1			F	8
D				2	3	1	2			G	8
D						3	3	1	1	H	8
D					3	4	1			I	8
E				5		3				F	8
E					4	4				G	8
E				2	3	1	2			H	8
E					4	2	1	1		I	8
F					4	2	1	1		G	8
F					5	2		1		H	8
F			2	3	1	2				I	8
G					3	4		1		H	8
G			2	2	2	1		1		I	8
H				1	2	3	1	1		I	8

The pairwise comparison evaluation matrix of experts is summarized in Table 4.

The geometric mean of experts' evaluations is calculated to check the consistency of the data (Consistency Ratio—CR) as shown in Table 5:

Normalized matrix of Table 5 as shown in Table 6.

The matrix weights are normalized as shown in Table 7.

$$\text{Lamda max} = \frac{9.7948 + 9.7034 + 9.6217 + 9.96807 + 10.0239 + 9.6995 + 9.7266 + 9.8883 + 9.8662}{9} = 9.7783$$

Using Formulas (5) and (6), CI and CR are calculated as follows:

$$\text{CI} = \frac{9.7783 - 9}{9 - 1} = 0.0973$$

Since the problem involves a total of nine criteria, n = 9. According to Saaty, RI = 1.45

$$\text{CR} = \frac{0.0973}{1.45} = 0.0671 \text{ satisfies the condition CR} \leq 0.1$$

Since the condition CR is satisfied, the spherical fuzzy weights are determined by using the conversion scale in Table 2 to transform the pairwise comparison matrix in Table 4 and calculate the geometric mean weights in spherical fuzzy numbers as shown in Tables 8 and 9.

Determine the spherical fuzzy weight using Formula (7) as shown in Tables 10 and 11.

Table 5. Geometric mean of all experts.

Criteria	THAI01	THAI02	THAI03	THAI04	THAI05	THAI06	THAI07	THAI08	THAI09
THAI01	1.000	1.510	2.098	1.416	0.596	0.487	0.425	0.559	0.736
THAI02	0.662	1.000	0.386	0.477	0.542	0.264	0.326	0.326	0.542
THAI03	0.477	2.590	1.000	0.669	0.621	0.284	0.347	0.398	0.232
THAI04	0.706	2.098	1.495	1.000	0.180	0.472	0.767	0.216	0.472
THAI05	1.678	1.846	1.609	5.550	1.000	1.316	0.577	0.767	0.487
THAI06	2.053	3.789	3.521	2.118	0.760	1.000	0.487	0.596	1.715
THAI07	2.355	3.069	2.879	1.303	1.732	2.053	1.000	0.453	1.345
THAI08	1.789	3.069	2.510	4.634	1.303	1.678	2.209	1.000	0.487
THAI09	1.359	1.846	4.306	2.118	2.053	0.583	0.743	2.053	1.000

Table 6. Normalized matrix.

Criteria	THAI01	THAI02	THAI03	THAI04	THAI05	THAI06	THAI07	THAI08	THAI09	MEAN
THAI01	0.083	0.073	0.106	0.073	0.068	0.060	0.062	0.088	0.105	0.0796
THAI02	0.055	0.048	0.019	0.025	0.062	0.032	0.047	0.051	0.077	0.0463
THAI03	0.039	0.124	0.050	0.035	0.071	0.035	0.050	0.063	0.033	0.0556
THAI04	0.058	0.101	0.076	0.052	0.021	0.058	0.111	0.034	0.067	0.0642
THAI05	0.139	0.089	0.081	0.288	0.114	0.162	0.084	0.120	0.069	0.1273
THAI06	0.170	0.182	0.178	0.110	0.086	0.123	0.071	0.094	0.244	0.1398
THAI07	0.195	0.147	0.145	0.068	0.197	0.252	0.145	0.071	0.192	0.1570
THAI08	0.148	0.147	0.127	0.240	0.148	0.206	0.321	0.157	0.069	0.1739
THAI09	0.113	0.089	0.217	0.110	0.234	0.072	0.108	0.322	0.143	0.1563

Table 7. Normalized weighted matrix.

Criteria	WSV	CV
THAI01	0.7800	9.7948
THAI02	0.4494	9.7034
THAI03	0.5354	9.6217
THAI04	0.6215	9.6807
THAI05	1.2764	10.0239
THAI06	1.3555	9.6995
THAI07	1.5269	9.7266
THAI08	1.7191	9.8883
THAI09	1.5420	9.8662

Table 8. Geometric mean in spherical fuzzy.

	THAI01			THAI02			THAI03			THAI04			THAI05			THAI06			THAI07			THAI08			THAI09		
THAI01	0.500	0.400	0.400	0.533	0.812	0.695	0.577	0.837	0.744	0.514	0.789	0.682	0.422	0.706	0.593	0.396	0.663	0.567	0.385	0.641	0.552	0.407	0.686	0.582	0.426	0.686	0.596
THAI02	0.421	0.703	0.587	0.500	0.400	0.400	0.394	0.647	0.558	0.401	0.673	0.577	0.431	0.713	0.600	0.341	0.563	0.500	0.348	0.585	0.517	0.348	0.585	0.517	0.431	0.713	0.600
THAI03	0.378	0.633	0.549	0.563	0.833	0.733	0.500	0.400	0.400	0.436	0.693	0.603	0.444	0.737	0.616	0.339	0.566	0.503	0.361	0.602	0.527	0.371	0.623	0.541	0.318	0.532	0.481
THAI04	0.429	0.710	0.598	0.519	0.818	0.703	0.509	0.778	0.678	0.500	0.400	0.400	0.254	0.441	0.414	0.420	0.689	0.584	0.448	0.717	0.619	0.277	0.470	0.429	0.420	0.689	0.584
THAI05	0.483	0.796	0.665	0.499	0.802	0.678	0.475	0.790	0.658	0.734	0.925	0.892	0.500	0.400	0.400	0.515	0.759	0.668	0.447	0.733	0.612	0.448	0.717	0.619	0.396	0.663	0.567
THAI06	0.518	0.815	0.698	0.646	0.871	0.802	0.626	0.868	0.793	0.525	0.813	0.698	0.466	0.709	0.618	0.500	0.400	0.400	0.396	0.663	0.567	0.422	0.706	0.593	0.551	0.801	0.712
THAI07	0.545	0.827	0.719	0.595	0.856	0.769	0.584	0.847	0.755	0.484	0.767	0.658	0.490	0.794	0.665	0.518	0.815	0.698	0.500	0.400	0.400	0.399	0.660	0.563	0.494	0.745	0.664
THAI08	0.492	0.804	0.677	0.595	0.856	0.769	0.555	0.835	0.733	0.693	0.898	0.846	0.484	0.767	0.658	0.483	0.796	0.665	0.534	0.819	0.706	0.500	0.400	0.400	0.394	0.641	0.559
THAI09	0.492	0.772	0.666	0.499	0.802	0.678	0.672	0.889	0.832	0.525	0.813	0.698	0.518	0.815	0.698	0.412	0.660	0.576	0.427	0.685	0.599	0.545	0.811	0.713	0.500	0.400	0.400

Table 9. Intergrated Spherical Fuzzy Comparison matrix.

	THAI01			THAI02			THAI03			THAI04			THAI05			THAI06			THAI07			THAI08			THAI09		
THAI01	0.500	0.400	0.400	0.533	0.434	0.341	0.577	0.404	0.304	0.514	0.459	0.328	0.422	0.542	0.335	0.396	0.580	0.311	0.385	0.599	0.299	0.407	0.560	0.323	0.426	0.560	0.300
THAI02	0.421	0.545	0.340	0.500	0.400	0.400	0.394	0.594	0.299	0.401	0.572	0.311	0.431	0.536	0.336	0.341	0.661	0.251	0.348	0.644	0.262	0.348	0.644	0.262	0.431	0.536	0.336
THAI03	0.378	0.606	0.290	0.563	0.409	0.316	0.500	0.400	0.400	0.436	0.554	0.300	0.444	0.513	0.349	0.339	0.659	0.250	0.361	0.631	0.274	0.371	0.614	0.286	0.318	0.684	0.226
THAI04	0.429	0.539	0.334	0.519	0.427	0.339	0.509	0.471	0.316	0.500	0.400	0.400	0.254	0.748	0.165	0.420	0.558	0.324	0.448	0.532	0.313	0.277	0.728	0.202	0.420	0.558	0.324
THAI05	0.483	0.452	0.362	0.499	0.445	0.352	0.475	0.458	0.364	0.734	0.273	0.182	0.500	0.400	0.400	0.515	0.491	0.302	0.447	0.517	0.349	0.448	0.532	0.313	0.396	0.580	0.311
THAI06	0.518	0.430	0.342	0.646	0.359	0.264	0.626	0.364	0.274	0.525	0.432	0.339	0.466	0.540	0.301	0.500	0.400	0.400	0.396	0.580	0.311	0.422	0.542	0.335	0.551	0.446	0.299
THAI07	0.545	0.416	0.328	0.595	0.380	0.294	0.584	0.391	0.303	0.484	0.482	0.330	0.490	0.454	0.358	0.518	0.430	0.342	0.500	0.400	0.400	0.399	0.584	0.311	0.494	0.505	0.284
THAI08	0.492	0.443	0.355	0.595	0.380	0.294	0.555	0.406	0.320	0.693	0.319	0.230	0.484	0.482	0.330	0.483	0.452	0.362	0.534	0.426	0.336	0.500	0.400	0.400	0.394	0.599	0.287
THAI09	0.492	0.477	0.327	0.499	0.445	0.352	0.672	0.333	0.239	0.525	0.432	0.339	0.518	0.430	0.342	0.412	0.583	0.289	0.427	0.561	0.293	0.545	0.435	0.312	0.500	0.400	0.400

Table 10. Calculations to obtain spherical fuzzy weights.

	THAI01			THAI02			THAI03			THAI04			THAI05			THAI06			THAI07			THAI08			THAI09		
THAI01	0.750	0.400	0.590	0.716	0.434	0.600	0.667	0.404	0.574	0.736	0.459	0.629	0.822	0.542	0.710	0.843	0.580	0.747	0.852	0.599	0.763	0.835	0.560	0.730	0.819	0.560	0.729
THAI02	0.823	0.545	0.707	0.750	0.400	0.590	0.845	0.594	0.755	0.839	0.572	0.742	0.814	0.536	0.701	0.883	0.661	0.821	0.879	0.644	0.810	0.879	0.644	0.810	0.814	0.536	0.701
THAI03	0.857	0.606	0.773	0.683	0.409	0.583	0.750	0.400	0.590	0.810	0.554	0.720	0.803	0.513	0.682	0.885	0.659	0.823	0.870	0.631	0.794	0.862	0.614	0.780	0.899	0.684	0.848
THAI04	0.816	0.539	0.704	0.731	0.427	0.616	0.741	0.471	0.641	0.750	0.400	0.590	0.936	0.748	0.908	0.824	0.558	0.719	0.799	0.532	0.701	0.923	0.728	0.882	0.824	0.558	0.719
THAI05	0.767	0.452	0.636	0.751	0.445	0.627	0.775	0.458	0.642	0.461	0.273	0.428	0.750	0.400	0.590	0.734	0.491	0.643	0.800	0.517	0.678	0.799	0.532	0.701	0.843	0.580	0.747
THAI06	0.732	0.430	0.615	0.582	0.359	0.512	0.608	0.364	0.532	0.724	0.432	0.609	0.783	0.540	0.692	0.750	0.400	0.590	0.843	0.580	0.747	0.822	0.542	0.710	0.697	0.446	0.608
THAI07	0.703	0.416	0.596	0.645	0.380	0.559	0.659	0.391	0.567	0.766	0.482	0.657	0.760	0.454	0.631	0.732	0.430	0.615	0.750	0.400	0.590	0.841	0.584	0.744	0.756	0.505	0.675
THAI08	0.758	0.443	0.631	0.645	0.380	0.559	0.692	0.406	0.589	0.519	0.319	0.467	0.766	0.482	0.657	0.767	0.452	0.636	0.715	0.426	0.602	0.750	0.400	0.590	0.845	0.599	0.763
THAI09	0.758	0.477	0.651	0.751	0.445	0.627	0.549	0.333	0.492	0.724	0.432	0.609	0.732	0.430	0.615	0.830	0.583	0.747	0.818	0.561	0.732	0.703	0.435	0.606	0.750	0.400	0.590

Table 11. Spherical Weighted Fuzzy Mean (SWM).

Criteria		SWM	
THAI01	0.469	0.499	0.330
THAI02	0.406	0.565	0.318
THAI03	0.422	0.554	0.308
THAI04	0.432	0.540	0.316
THAI05	0.517	0.452	0.327
THAI06	0.527	0.449	0.320
THAI07	0.517	0.445	0.330
THAI08	0.537	0.428	0.325
THAI09	0.519	0.450	0.324

Defuzzify the criteria weights (calculate the crisp weights) using Formula (8) as presented in Table 12.

Table 12. Crisp Weights.

Criteria	Calculations to Obtain Crisp Weights			Crisp Weights
THAI01	1.546	0.006	12.408	0.107
THAI02	1.121	0.001	10.583	0.091
THAI03	1.239	0.001	11.127	0.096
THAI04	1.297	0.002	11.381	0.098
THAI05	1.923	0.010	13.829	0.120
THAI06	2.023	0.009	14.191	0.123
THAI07	1.922	0.012	13.822	0.119
THAI08	2.099	0.012	14.444	0.125
THAI09	1.947	0.010	13.919	0.120

The final priority weights among the criteria are presented in Table 13.

Table 13. Weight of criteria.

Criteria	Symbol	Weight
Initial investment cost	THAI01	0.1072
Operating and maintenance costs	THAI02	0.0915
Potential access to the energy market	THAI03	0.0962
Job creation	THAI04	0.0984
Impact on local communities	THAI05	0.1195
Community acceptance	THAI06	0.1227
Impact on ecosystems	THAI07	0.1195
Ability to manage and reduce pollution	THAI08	0.1248
Proximity to sensitive areas	THAI09	0.1203

In the next stage, the weighted aggregated sum product assessment (WASPAS) method is applied to rank four potential locations. The greatest option is the one that has the highest relative weights among the alternatives. The results of the WASPAS model are shown in Table 14.

Table 14. Results of WASPAS model.

Alternatives	L_{i1}	L_{i2}	L_i
WATHAI01	0.9569	1.0000	0.9784
WATHAI02	0.9123	0.9875	0.9499
WATHAI03	0.7852	0.9734	0.8793
WATHAI04	0.8045	0.9575	0.8810

Based on the WASPAS model in Table 15 and Figure 4, four locations were ranked, and the potential location with the symbol WATHAI01 was found to be the most appropriate. The WASPAS model considers several factors and rates each location according to how well it meets these requirements. Although WATHAI01 performed the best overall in this instance, the model acknowledges that other providers might also be a good choice in some circumstances. To evaluate the robustness of the results of the proposed process, a sensitivity analysis is conducted. Various approaches can be used for robustness testing and sensitivity analysis. In this study, the rankings of alternatives are assessed under different values of λ, which represents the level of compromise between the WSM and WPM methods. Since λ can take any value between 0 and 1 based on the decision-makers' preferences, the process is repeated using 10 different λ values. The performance scores of the alternatives corresponding to each λ value are presented in Table 15 and Figure 5.

Table 15. Alternatives' performance scores with changing λ value.

Alternatives	Performance Scores										
	λ = 0.0	λ = 0.1	λ = 0.2	λ = 0.3	λ = 0.4	λ = 0.5	λ = 0.6	λ = 0.7	λ = 0.8	λ = 0.9	λ = 1.0
A1	1.0000	0.9957	0.9914	0.9871	0.9827	0.9784	0.9741	0.9698	0.9655	0.9612	0.9569
A2	0.9875	0.9799	0.9724	0.9649	0.9574	0.9499	0.9424	0.9349	0.9274	0.9198	0.9123
A3	0.9734	0.9546	0.9358	0.9169	0.8981	0.8793	0.8605	0.8416	0.8228	0.8040	0.7852
A4	0.9575	0.9422	0.9269	0.9116	0.8963	0.8810	0.8657	0.8504	0.8351	0.8198	0.8045

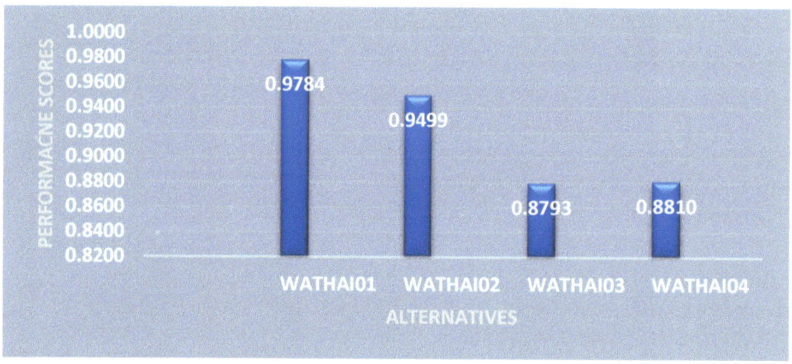

Figure 4. Final ranking of WASPAS model.

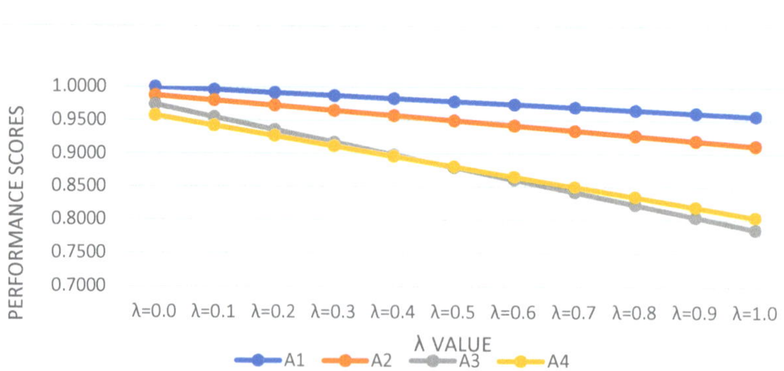

Figure 5. Alternatives' performance scores with changing λ value.

Consequently, the rankings of the alternatives are as shown in Table 16.

Table 16. Alternatives' rankings with changing λ value.

Alternatives	Ranking										
	λ = 0.0	λ = 0.1	λ = 0.2	λ = 0.3	λ = 0.4	λ = 0.5	λ = 0.6	λ = 0.7	λ = 0.8	λ = 0.9	λ = 1.0
A1	1	1	1	1	1	1	1	1	1	1	1
A2	2	2	2	2	2	2	2	2	2	2	2
A3	3	3	3	3	3	4	4	4	4	4	4
A4	4	4	4	4	4	3	3	3	3	3	3

From Table 16 and Figure 6, The rankings of alternatives WATHAI01 and WATHAI02 remain unchanged regardless of the value of λ. This suggests that these alternatives perform consistently well under both the WSM and WPM methods, implying a strong overall performance across all criteria.

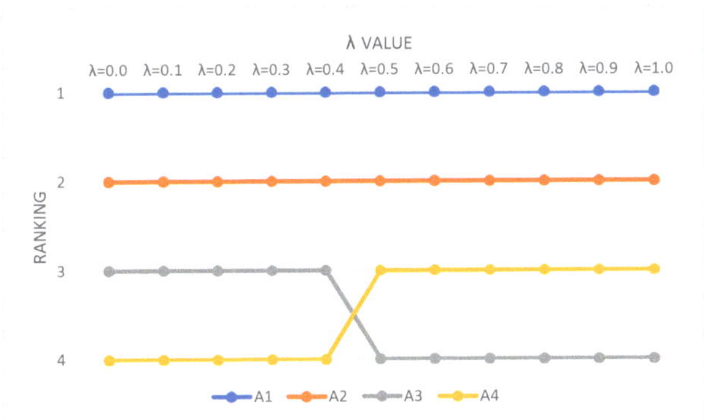

Figure 6. Alternatives' rankings with changing λ value.

The rankings of WATHAI03 and WATHAI04 are reversed when λ reaches 0.5 or higher. This is likely due to the following inherent differences between the WSM and WPM methods:

- WSM aggregates criteria in a linear manner, emphasizing additive contributions of criteria weights and scores. Alternatives that perform moderately well across most criteria tend to be favored in WSM, as such, WATHAI03 with consistent performance across criteria leads to a higher rank.
- WPM is multiplicative, making it more sensitive to variation across criteria. It penalizes alternatives with low scores in any criterion but rewards those with high scores in specific criteria. A4's higher performance in specific criteria (THAI05 and THAI09) outweighs its weaker performance in others, causing it to surpass A3.

The consistent rankings of WATHAI01 and WATHAI02 suggest robustness in their performance, making them reliable choices regardless of decision-maker preferences.

5. Discussion

The results of the study highlight the effectiveness of the proposed SFMCDM model in identifying optimal locations for solid waste-to-energy plants. Among the evaluated alternatives, WATHAI01 consistently ranked as the most suitable location, demonstrating superior performance across key economic, environmental, and social criteria. This outcome underscores the importance of considering a balanced set of criteria in location selection to achieve sustainable development objectives. The sensitivity analysis further validates the robustness of the proposed model. Regardless of the value of λ, WATHAI01 and WATHAI02 maintained their rankings, indicating their strong performance across different decision-maker preferences. The reversal in rankings between WATHAI03 and WATHAI04 at higher λ values highlights the model's adaptability to prioritize criteria differently under changing conditions. This flexibility ensures the reliability of the results, supporting informed decision-making tailored to varying stakeholder priorities.

This study underscores the importance of a structured and systematic approach in addressing the complexities of selecting suitable locations for solid waste-to-energy plants. The integration of the Spherical Fuzzy Multi-Criteria Decision-Making (SFMCDM) model enhances the ability to accommodate uncertainty and ambiguity, offering a comprehensive evaluation framework that balances economic, environmental, and social factors. The application of the Spherical Fuzzy Analytic Hierarchy Process (SFAHP) to calculate criteria weights, combined with the Weighted Aggregated Sum Product Assessment (WASPAS) method for ranking alternatives, demonstrates the effectiveness of this approach in decision-making. Key criteria, such as community acceptance, pollution management, and proximity to sensitive areas, were identified as critical to the selection process. The robustness of the model was validated through sensitivity analysis, ensuring the reliability of the results under varying decision-maker preferences.

6. Conclusions

Rapid urbanization, industrialization, and lifestyle changes have led to the generation of large amounts of waste in urban and industrial areas worldwide. To address the issue of domestic waste, countries have implemented various technologies, notably waste-to-energy technology, which enables waste to be treated and recycled before disposal. This study presents a novel Spherical Fuzzy Multi-Criteria Decision-Making (SFMCDM) framework to support the selection of optimal locations for solid waste-to-energy plants, addressing the pressing challenges of renewable energy development in a complex and uncertain environment. By integrating the Spherical Fuzzy Analytic Hierarchy Process (SFAHP) and Weighted Aggregated Sum Product Assessment (WASPAS) methods, the proposed framework effectively balances economic, environmental, and social criteria, providing a comprehensive and systematic solution to the site selection problem.

The key contributions of this research include advancing the theoretical application of spherical fuzzy sets in MCDM and demonstrating its robustness through a sensitivity analysis that validates the consistency of results across various decision-maker preferences. The study also highlights critical insights into the role of criteria such as community acceptance, pollution management, and proximity to sensitive areas in determining optimal locations, contributing valuable knowledge to the field of renewable energy project planning. The impact of this research extends beyond its immediate application, offering policymakers, businesses, and stakeholders a transparent and adaptable tool to support strategic decision-making in renewable energy projects. By promoting sustainable development and efficient resource utilization, the framework aligns with global efforts to address environmental challenges and energy security.

Future research should explore potential enhancements to the SFMCDM framework, such as incorporating additional models specialized in handling quantitative data to further enhance the model's precision. Additionally, expanding the framework's application to other renewable energy technologies or diverse geographical contexts could further validate its versatility and practical relevance. By bridging theoretical advancements with practical implementation, this study lays a foundation for informed decision-making in renewable energy projects, contributing to sustainable energy transitions and fostering environmental resilience.

Author Contributions: Conceptualization, N.C., N.V.T. and C.J.; Methodology, N.C., N.V.T. and C.J.; Software, N.C. and N.V.T.; Validation, N.C. and N.V.T.; Formal analysis, N.C., N.V.T. and C.J.; Investigation, N.V.T.; Resources, N.V.T.; Data curation, N.C. and N.V.T.; Writing—original draft, N.V.T. and C.J.; Writing—review & editing, N.C.; Visualization, C.J.; Supervision, C.J.; Project administration, C.J.; Funding acquisition, N.C. All authors have read and agreed to the published version of the manuscript.

Funding: This research has received funding support from NSRF via the Program Management Unit for Human Resources and Institutional Development, Research, and Innovation [grant numbers B11F670109] and Kasetsart University Research and Development Institute [grant number FF(KU)53.67]. This research is fully supported by the Center of Excellence in Logistics and Supply Chain Systems Engineering and Technology (LogEn Tech) and Sirindhorn International Institute of Technology, Thammasat University. This research also received support from Van Lang University, Ho Chi Minh City, Vietnam.

Data Availability Statement: No new data were created or analyzed in this study.

Conflicts of Interest: The authors declare no conflicts of interest.

References

1. Nguyen, T.D.; Ngo, T.B. Xu Hướng Phát Triển Năng Lượng Mới Trên thế Giới và vị trí, vai trò của Ngành dầu khí Việt Nam. Tạp Chí Cộng Sản Điện Tử. Available online: https://www.tapchicongsan.org.vn/web/guest/tap-oan-dau-khi-viet-nam/-/2018/813406/xu-huong-phat-trien-nang-luong-moi-tren-the-gioi-va-vi-tri,-vai-tro-cua-nganh-dau-khi-viet-nam.aspx (accessed on 20 November 2024).
2. Phan, T.S.T.; Nguyen, T.T. Một số Vấn đề về Phát Triển Năng Lượng tái tạo ở Việt Nam Hiện Nay: Thực Trạng, Tiềm Năng và Hàm ý Giải Pháp. Available online: https://www.tapchicongsan.org.vn/web/guest/nghien-cu/-/2018/906102/mot-so-van-de-ve-phat-trien-nang-luong-tai-tao-o-viet-nam-hien-nay--thuc-trang,-tiem-nang-va-ham-y-giai-phap.aspx (accessed on 12 November 2024).
3. Azhar, N.A.; Radzi, N.A.; Wan Ahmad, W.S.H.M. Multi-criteria decision making: A systematic review. *Recent Adv. Electr. Electron. Eng. (Former. Recent Pat. Electr. Electron. Eng.)* **2021**, *14*, 779–801. [CrossRef]
4. Djenadic, S.; Tanasijevic, M.; Jovancic, P.; Ignjatovic, D.; Petrovic, D.; Bugaric, U. Risk Evaluation: Brief Review and Innovation Model Based on Fuzzy Logic and MCDM. *Mathematics* **2022**, *10*, 811. [CrossRef]
5. Correia, M.S. Sustainability: An overview of the triple bottom line and sustainability implementation. *Int. J. Strateg. Eng. (IJoSE)* **2019**, *2*, 29–38. [CrossRef]
6. Anh, C. 6 Mô Hình lý Thuyết Phát Triển bền Vững bạn cần Biết. Available online: https://www.dearourcommunity.com/post/6-mo-hinh-ly-thuyet-phat-trien-ben-vung-ban-can-biet (accessed on 12 November 2024).
7. Żak, A. Triple bottom line concept in theory and practice. *Soc. Responsib. Organ. Dir. Changes* **2015**, *387*, 251–264. [CrossRef]
8. Schramm, V.; Cabral, L.; Schramm, F. Approaches for supporting sustainable supplier selection—A literature review. *J. Clean. Prod.* **2020**, *273*, 123089. [CrossRef]
9. Stojčić, M.; Zavadskas, E.; Pamučar, D.; Stević, Ž; Mardani, A. Application of MCDM Methods in Sustainability Engineering: A Literature Review 2008–2018. *Symmetry* **2019**, *11*, 350. [CrossRef]
10. Cao, Q.; Esangbedo, M.; Bai, S.; Esangbedo, C. Grey SWARA-FUCOM Weighting Method for Contractor Selection MCDM Problem: A Case Study of Floating Solar Panel Energy System Installation. *Energies* **2019**, *12*, 2481. [CrossRef]
11. Wang, T.; Tsai, S. Solar Panel Supplier Selection for the Photovoltaic System Design by Using Fuzzy Multi-Criteria Decision Making (MCDM) Approaches. *Energies* **2018**, *11*, 1989. [CrossRef]
12. Aragonés-Beltrán, P.; Chaparro-González, F.; Pastor-Ferrando, J.; Pla-Rubio, A. An AHP (Analytic Hierarchy Process)/ANP (Analytic Network Process)-based multi-criteria decision approach for the selection of solar-thermal power plant investment projects. *Energy* **2014**, *66*, 222–238. [CrossRef]
13. Wang, L.; Peng, J.; Wang, J. A multi-criteria decision-making framework for risk ranking of energy performance contracting project under picture fuzzy environment. *J. Clean. Prod.* **2018**, *191*, 105–118. [CrossRef]

14. Sun, L.; Jiang, Y.; Guo, Q.; Ji, L.; Xie, Y.; Qiao, Q.; Huang, G.; Xiao, K. A GIS-based multi-criteria decision-making method for th potential assessment and suitable sites selection of PV and CSP plants. *Resour. Conserv. Recycl.* **2021**, *168*, 105306. [CrossRef]
15. Ozdemir, S.; Sahin, G. Multi-criteria decision-making in the location selection for a solar PV power plant using AHP. *Measuremen* **2018**, *129*, 218–226. [CrossRef]
16. Vafaeipour, M.; Hashemkhani Zolfani, S.; Morshed Varzandeh, M.; Derakhti, A.; Keshavarz Eshkalag, M. Assessment of region priority for implementation of solar projects in Iran: New application of a hybrid multi-criteria decision making approach. *Energ Convers. Manag.* **2014**, *86*, 653–663. [CrossRef]
17. Noorollahi, Y.; Ghenaatpisheh Senani, A.; Fadaei, A.; Simaee, M.; Moltames, R. A framework for GIS-based site selection an technical potential evaluation of PV solar farm using Fuzzy-Boolean logic and AHP multi-criteria decision-making approac *Renew. Energy* **2022**, *186*, 89–104. [CrossRef]
18. Tahri, M.; Hakdaoui, M.; Maanan, M. The evaluation of solar farm locations applying Geographic Information System and Mult Criteria Decision-Making methods: Case study in southern Morocco. *Renew. Sustain. Energy Rev.* **2015**, *51*, 1354–1362. [CrossRef]
19. Ohunakin, O.; Saracoglu, B. A comparative study of selected multi-criteria decision-making methodologies for location selectio of very large concentrated solar power plants in Nigeria. *Afr. J. Sci. Technol. Innov. Dev.* **2018**, *10*, 551–567. [CrossRef]
20. Rediske, G.; Siluk, J.C.M.; Michels, L.; Rigo, P.D.; Rosa, C.B.; Cugler, G. Multi-criteria decision-making model for assessment c large photovoltaic farms in Brazil. *Energy* **2020**, *197*, 117167. [CrossRef]
21. Wang, C.; Huang, Y.; Chai, Y.; Nguyen, V. A Multi-Criteria Decision Making (MCDM) for Renewable Energy Plants Locatio Selection in Vietnam under a Fuzzy Environment. *Appl. Sci.* **2018**, *8*, 2069. [CrossRef]
22. Wang, C.; Nguyen, V.; Thai, H.; Duong, D. Multi-Criteria Decision Making (MCDM) Approaches for Solar Power Plant Locatio Selection in Viet Nam. *Energies* **2018**, *11*, 1504. [CrossRef]
23. Wang, C.; Nguyen, V.; Duong, D.; Thai, H. A Hybrid Fuzzy Analysis Network Process (FANP) and the Technique for Order c Preference by Similarity to Ideal Solution (TOPSIS) Approaches for Solid Waste to Energy Plant Location Selection in Vietnan *Appl. Sci.* **2018**, *8*, 1100. [CrossRef]
24. Gil-García, I.; Ramos-Escudero, A.; García-Cascales, M.; Dagher, H.; Molina-García, A. Fuzzy GIS-based MCDM solution for th optimal offshore wind site selection: The Gulf of Maine case. *Renew. Energy* **2022**, *183*, 130–147. [CrossRef]
25. Wang, C.; Chen, Y.; Tung, C. Evaluation of Wave Energy Location by Using an Integrated MCDM Approach. *Energies* **202** *14*, 1840. [CrossRef]
26. Le, P.; Fischer, A.; Penesis, I.; Rahimi, R. Aggregating GIS and MCDM to Optimize Wave Energy Converters Location in Tasmani Australia. In *Advances in Environmental Engineering and Green Technologies*; IGI Global: Hershey, PA, USA, 2015; pp. 141–164.
27. Bolturk, E.; Kahraman, C. Interval-valued intuitionistic fuzzy CODAS method and its application to wave energy facility locatio selection problem. *J. Intell. Fuzzy Syst.* **2018**, *35*, 4865–4877. [CrossRef]
28. Abaei, M.; Arzaghi, E.; Abbassi, R.; Garaniya, V.; Penesis, I. Developing a novel risk-based methodology for multi-criteria decisio making in marine renewable energy applications. *Renew. Energy* **2017**, *102*, 341–348. [CrossRef]
29. Wang, C.; Nhieu, N.; Nguyen, H.; Wang, J. Simulation-Based Optimization Integrated Multiple Criteria Decision-Makin Framework for Wave Energy Site Selection: A Case Study of Australia. *IEEE Access* **2021**, *9*, 167458–167476. [CrossRef]
30. Wang, F. Preference Degree of Triangular Fuzzy Numbers and Its Application to Multi-Attribute Group Decision Making. *Exper Syst. Appl.* **2021**, *178*, 114982. [CrossRef]
31. Kutlu Gündoğdu, F.; Kahraman, C. Spherical Fuzzy Sets And Spherical Fuzzy TOPSIS Method. *J. Intell. Fuzzy Syst.* **2019**, *36* 337–352. [CrossRef]
32. Yager, R.R. Pythagorean fuzzy subsets. In Proceedings of the 2013 Joint IFSA World Congress and NAFIPS Annual Meetin (IFSA/NAFIPS), Edmonton, AB, Canada, 24–28 June 2013; pp. 57–61.
33. Smarandache, F. *A Unifying Field in Logics Neutrosophy: Neutrosophic Probability, Set and Logic*; American Research Press: Rehobot DE, USA, 1999; pp. 1–141.
34. Kutlu Gündoğdu, F.; Kahraman, C. A Novel Spherical Fuzzy Analytic Hierarchy Process And Its Renewable Energy Applicatior *Soft Comput.* **2019**, *24*, 4607–4621. [CrossRef]
35. Kusumadewi, S.; Hartati, S.; Harjoko, A.; Wardoyo, R. Fuzzy Multi-Attribute Decision Making (Fuzzy MADM). *J. Transform* **2006**, *14*, 78–79.
36. Triantaphyllou, E.; Mann, S.H. An examination of the effectiveness of multi-dimensional decision-making methods: A decision making paradox. *Decis. Support Syst.* **1989**, *5*, 303–312. [CrossRef]

energies MDPI

Article

Fuzzy Decision-Making Valuation Model for Urban Green Infrastructure Implementation

Samanta Bačić [1,*], Hrvoje Tomić [2], Katarina Rogulj [1] and Goran Andlar [3]

1 Faculty of Civil Engineering, Architecture and Geodesy, University of Split, Matice Hrvatske 15, 21000 Split, Croatia; krogulj1@gradst.hr
2 Faculty of Geodesy, University of Zagreb, Kačićeva 26, 10000 Zagreb, Croatia; htomic@geof.hr
3 Faculty of Agriculture, University of Zagreb, Svetošimunska Cesta 25, 10000 Zagreb, Croatia; gandlar@agr.hr
* Correspondence: sbacic@gradst.hr

Abstract: Urban green infrastructure plays a significant role in sustainable development and requires proper land management during planning. This study develops a valuation model for urban green infrastructure in land management, focusing on Zagreb's 17 city districts. The fuzzy AHP method was used to calculate the weighting coefficients for a suitable set of criteria, and the TOPSIS method was used to select the priority city districts for implementing green infrastructure. The research results are relevant to decision makers, who can utilize them to prioritize areas for the development and implementation of green infrastructure. The green infrastructure index calculated in this study can be compared with other spatial and land data for effective spatial planning.

Keywords: green infrastructure; the city of Zagreb; decision making; fuzzy AHP; TOPSIS

1. Introduction

Most of the world's population lives in urban areas, and that number is increasing every day. Accelerated urbanization leads to overbuilding, air and environmental pollution, increasing climate change, and increased consumption of energy and natural resources. One of the ways to solve these problems is to plan green infrastructure. Urban green infrastructure is considered an essential structural part of cities. It plays a key role in strengthening the resilience and transformation of urban areas and in the sustainable development of Planet Earth [1,2].

Urban green infrastructure was introduced within the framework of the approach to sustainability and resilience of primarily urban areas. Investing in green infrastructure makes sound economic sense because an area can offer multiple benefits, provided its ecosystems are in a healthy condition. Such healthy ecosystems provide society with many valuable economically, socially, and ecologically important goods and services [3]. In the strategic document on green infrastructure, the European Commission defines green infrastructure as a strategically planned network of natural and semi-natural areas with other environmental features, designed and managed to deliver a wide range of ecosystem services and preserve biodiversity in urban and rural areas. It means that green infrastructure is not just any green area, but those green areas that realize at least one of the ecosystem services, provisioning, regulating, cultural, and supporting services [4]. Green infrastructure can mitigate the risks of climate change, helping to reduce the urban heat island effect and reduce the risk of flooding [5–8]. It improves air quality, and various scientific studies prove that in this way it affects a higher quality of life, and better physical and mental health [9–13]. It also helps preserve biological diversity through the preservation and restoration of natural habitats [14–16]. Green infrastructure also supports renewable energy. By integrating it with renewable energy, green infrastructure helps build a sustainable and energy-efficient future [17]. Unlike gray infrastructure, which usually has only one goal, green infrastructure is multifunctional and brings many social, ecological, and economic benefits [18,19], both in rural and urban environments. If properly planned, green infrastructure can result in a wide variety of benefits for both people and nature. Individual elements of green infrastructure may not necessarily provide all the desired benefits, but if they are well connected, then the entire network of green infrastructure can provide most of the benefits [20].

To obtain all the benefits from green infrastructure, the World Health Organization recommends that when planning and designing urban green areas, attention should be paid to the fact that green areas need to be located near people and their places of residence. Green infrastructure must be diverse, multifunctional, and adaptable to people's needs. Additionally, it is essential to pay attention to its subsequent maintenance [21]. This is why Cecil Konijnendijk [22,23] proposed the 3–30–300 rule for urban green infrastructure. The goal of this rule is to enable equal access to trees and green areas in such a way that every citizen should see at least 3 trees from his home, that in every neighborhood there should be at least 30% tree canopy coverage, and that everyone within a radius of 300 m has access to at least one green area surface. Applying the 3–30–300 rule will improve and expand urban green infrastructure and thus promote cities' health, well-being, resilience, and sustainable development. Many cities around the world have already adopted the 3–30–300 rule as part of their urban programs [24], and the implementation of the rule is also recommended in the UNECE document, which provides guidelines for green recovery and sustainable, healthy, and resilient cities [25]. The fact that it is included in the 2030 Agenda, which defines 17 global goals of sustainable development, speaks of the importance of green infrastructure for sustainable development. More precisely, one of the seven sub-goals for achieving goal 11, which is aimed at developing inclusive, safe, resilient, and sustainable cities, is providing access to safe and inclusive green and public spaces [26]. Special emphasis on access to green public spaces was brought by the New Urban Agenda emphasizing the importance and multifunctionality of green infrastructure [27]. Green infrastructure is continuously recognized and included in numerous other global and European strategies for sustainable development. The importance of green infrastructure is also recognized in Croatia. Based on the European Recovery Plan, the Government of the Republic of Croatia presented the National Recovery and Resilience Plan, in which the strategy of green urban renewal and development of green infrastructure was included as one of the goals [28]. The importance of green infrastructure in Croatia was highlighted by the adoption of the Program for the Development of Green Infrastructure in Urban Areas for the period from 2021 to 2030. This program outlines goals and measures for the development of green infrastructure in urban areas for the establishment of sustainable, resilient, and safe cities and settlements through increasing the energy efficiency of buildings and construction areas, the development of green infrastructure, and urban transformation and rehabilitation. The program intends to provide all stakeholders with a framework for the implementation of green infrastructure development in urban areas by identifying measures and activities, necessary frameworks and prerequisites for implementation, expected effects of measures, and anticipated sources of funding. The ultimate goal is to increase green infrastructure in urban areas [29].

From the above, green infrastructure plays a significant role in sustainable development and it is necessary to take care of the implementation of green infrastructure during spatial planning.

Analysis of previous research has established that there is a lot of research on green infrastructure, such as combating climate change [5,8,30], reducing flooding [31,32], improving air quality [33,34], improving water and soil quality [35], preserving biodiversity [16,36], and promoting physical and mental health [11,37,38]. However, there is significantly less research focused on the evaluation of green infrastructure in land management [39]. The analysis indicates that most research emphasizes the ecological and social benefits of green infrastructure, with less emphasis on the economic benefits. The same conclusion was reached by several other authors in their systematic literature reviews of green infrastructure [40–42]. The lack of appropriate spatial data infrastructure is considered the main challenge in evaluating green infrastructure in land management.

Some of the authors specifically used the fuzzy AHP (Analytic Hierarchy Process) multi-criteria evaluation method in their research on green infrastructure [43–47], as well as the TOPSIS (Technique for Order of Preference by Similarity to Ideal Solution) method of multi-criteria evaluation [36,48,49].

The structure of this article is organized as follows: Section 2 discusses the materials and methods of this research. It shows the spatial data required for the development of a valuation model of urban green infrastructure. It also explains the criteria for determining the green infrastructure index and the method of calculating the green infrastructure index using the fuzzy AHP and TOPSIS methods in detail. Section 3 discusses the Croatian (city of Zagreb) case study, which demonstrates the implementation of the proposed model. In Section 4, the results were summarized and the advantages of the developed model are presented. Finally, Section 5 provides conclusions and highlights potential directions for future research in this area.

2. Materials and Methods

To more easily evaluate green infrastructure and to examine which areas are more prioritized for its implementation, a model for the evaluation of urban green infrastructure in land management was developed. The developed model was implemented in the area of the city of Zagreb. The area of the city of Zagreb was chosen because it is the capital of Croatia, it has problems with construction at the expense of green areas, and because of the availability of spatial data.

Several different types of spatial data were collected from the city of Zagreb, which were used to conduct this research. The City Office for Economy, Environmental Sustainability, and Strategic Planning in the city of Zagreb has provided data on the planned purpose and actual use of the city of Zagreb's areas for the year 2020. From the City Office for Renovation, Construction, Spatial Planning, Construction, Communal Affairs, and Traffic in the city of Zagreb, data from the Green Cadastre on elements of green infrastructure were taken. All data are stored in the official projection coordinate reference system of the Republic of Croatia, that is, in the Croatian Terrestrial Reference System for the epoch 1995.55–HTRS96. All the above data can be viewed through the geoportal of the Zagreb Spatial Data Infrastructure (ZG Geoportal). ZG Geoportal is the access point of the Zagreb spatial data infrastructure and contains spatial data of the city's administrative bodies, companies, and institutions [50]. Via ZG Geoportal, it is only possible to view the data that the city of Zagreb has, but it is not possible to download and manage the data.

To develop a valuation model for urban green infrastructure in land management, all analyses were carried out for residential and mixed-use zones. From the data on actual land use, only those lands whose purpose is residential and mixed were filtered, and for the area of the city of Zagreb, there are 16,251 residential and mixed-use zones located in the area of 17 city districts (Brezovica, Črnomerec, Donja Dubrava, Donji Grad, Gornja Dubrava, Gornji Grad–Medveščak, Maksimir, Novi Zagreb–istok, Novi Zagreb–zapad, Peščenica–Žitnjak, Podsljeme, Podsused–Vrapče, Sesvete, Stenjevec, Trešnjevka–jug, Trešnjevka–sjever, and Trnje). In this research, an analysis was made for each city district.

Several different analyses of the availability of green infrastructure were carried out, namely, an analysis of the availability of trees, an analysis of the availability of recreational facilities, an analysis of the availability of public green areas, an analysis of the availability of water surfaces, and an analysis of the land surface temperature, and an analysis of brownfield areas were also carried out. These analyses were chosen because they can be conducted using available spatial data and compared with other spatial and land information, making them applicable to land management. Additionally, all analyses can be performed within a specific time interval, allowing for the monitoring of changes over time. They were automated and performed in QGIS using a combination of spatial and attribute queries. At the end, a cross-section analysis was made, and an index of green infrastructure was determined using fuzzy AHP and TOPSIS multi-criteria methods.

Due to the unavailability of data, only green infrastructure located in public areas was analyzed, that is, private green areas were not included in the analysis. Also, the final data should be able to be used in land management systems; therefore, all analyses should be feasible based on existing official data. That is, by using the proposed analyses, the data can be calculated in certain time intervals, and in this way, it is possible to determine the current and desired states.

2.1. Analysis of the Availability of Green Infrastructure

According to the World Health Organization, residents in urban areas should have access to green infrastructure and public green areas of at least 0.5–1 hectare within 300 m of air distance from their homes [21,51]. Therefore, in this paper, analyses of the availability of green infrastructure were carried out within a radius of 300 m from individual residential and mixed-use zones, and an average value was determined for each city district. For each residential and mixed-use zone, it was determined how many trees, recreational facilities, and public green areas larger than 0.5 hectares are within 300 m of air distance from that residential and mixed-use zone, and whether it is within 300 m of air distance from some residential and mixed-use zones and some water surface. Due to the multi-functionality and connectivity of green infrastructure, individual analyses inevitably overlap with each other, but concerning the available data, the previously mentioned accessibility analyses were defined and the valuation model for urban green infrastructure was defined.

2.1.1. Analysis of the Availability of Trees

The analysis of the availability of trees is based on data from the Green Cadastre managed by Zagreb holding–Zrinjevac, which includes green infrastructure elements transferred from the City Office for Renovation, Construction, Spatial Planning, Construction, Communal Affairs, and Traffic. However, these data do not cover green infrastructure elements in areas managed by other institutions. To address this gap, the average number of trees per square meter was calculated for parks, forest parks, and forests using available data. Additionally, data on land use from the City Office for Economy, Environmental Sustainability, and Strategic Planning were used to determine the number of trees in parks, forest parks, and forests not under the jurisdiction of Zrinjevac. After identifying the trees included in the analysis, we determined the total number of trees within 300 m of each residential and mixed-use zone in the city of Zagreb.

2.1.2. Analysis of the Availability of Recreational Facilities

The analysis of the availability of recreational facilities is limited to green infrastructure elements that were obtained from the City Office for Renovation, Construction, Spatial Planning, Construction, Communal Affairs, and Traffic. These data are from the Green Cadastre under the jurisdiction of the Zagreb holding–Zrinjevac, which means that they do not contain data of green infrastructure elements located in areas under the jurisdiction of other institutions or private owners. Among the available elements of green infrastructure, recreational facilities include playgrounds and paths, and the analysis was carried out based on these elements and on the areas for which data are available.

2.1.3. Analysis of the Availability of Public Green Areas

In its document on urban green areas, the World Health Organization emphasizes that people living in urban and rural areas should have access to public green areas larger than 0.5 hectares within 300 m of their homes [21]. Therefore, only green areas larger than 0.5 hectares are considered in the analysis of the availability of public green areas. In the city of Zagreb, 1660 such areas have been identified, including botanical gardens, zoos, parks, forest parks, or forests. City gardens are not included in this analysis, because they are given for the use of individual citizens or households and therefore are not accessible to the general public [52]. After identifying the public green areas included in the analysis, the availability of public green areas larger than 0.5 hectares within a 300 m radius of each residential and mixed-use zone was determined.

2.1.4. Analysis of the Availability of Water Surfaces

Water surfaces are an important part of the urban green infrastructure, also known as blue infrastructure. Blue infrastructure includes natural or artificial, permanent or temporary water surfaces found in urban areas. These can be rivers, lakes, banks, wetlands, coastal waters like estuaries, deltas, coastal tidal areas, and other water bodies [53]. To analyze the availability of water surfaces in the city of Zagreb, water and water assets in the form of polygons were included. These were filtered from the vector layer "land use" obtained from the City Office for Economy, Environmental Sustainability, and Strategic Planning. The analysis determined whether there is at least one water surface within a 300 m radius of each residential and mixed-use zone or none.

2.2. *Analysis of Land Surface Temperature*

Due to increasing urbanization and significant changes in land use, there are global climate changes and an increase in the land surface temperature, which leads to the formation of urban heat islands [54]. Many studies have confirmed that urban green infrastructure plays an important role in mitigating the effect of urban heat islands and reducing the land surface temperature [55], which is especially important in the summer months. Part of the urban green infrastructure creates a shadow and thus limits the heating of the soil and absorbs part of the solar radiation, and evapotranspiration increases the air humidity and thus reduces the temperature in the city [56]. Therefore, it is necessary to recognize the urban green infrastructure as one of the important tools for the fight against climate change and temperature increase. The land surface temperature can be determined in different ways, and in the framework of this research, it was determined by semi-automatic classification in QGIS.

Using a raster containing data on the land surface temperature, we determined the land surface temperature of individual residential and mixed-use zones, in such a way that each residential and mixed-use zone was assigned to the value of the raster cell that covers that specific area. After the analysis of land surface temperature by residential and mixed-use zones, these data were grouped, and by using them, we determined the average land surface temperature for each city district.

2.3. *Analysis of Brownfield Areas*

Brownfield areas are areas that were influenced by the previous use of that location and the surrounding land abandoned and underutilized areas, areas that may have real or possible problems with contamination and are mostly located in developed urban areas and require intervention to return them to beneficial use [57]. From the data on actual land use in the city of Zagreb, 146 brownfield areas were identified in the city of Zagreb, and it was determined how many brownfield areas are located within each city district and what their total area is.

2.4. *Green Infrastructure Index*

The previously explained analyses are defined as criteria for determining the green infrastructure index. To calculate the final green infrastructure index, it is necessary to use the fuzzy AHP method to determine the weights of all criteria and then to calculate the green infrastructure index using the TOPSIS method.

2.4.1. The Fuzzy AHP Method

Fuzzy sets, introduced by Zadeh [58], are an extended form of the classical sets where sets are binary determined, while fuzzy sets have a degree of membership. The mathematical expression of the fuzzy set can be described as presented in Equation (1) [59].

A fuzzy number $\tilde{A}$ on $\mathbb{R}$ is triangular fuzzy number if it has membership function $\mu_{\tilde{A}}(x) : \mathbb{R} \rightarrow [0,1]$ equal to the following:

$$\mu_{\tilde{A}}(x) = \begin{cases} \frac{x-l}{m-l}, & l \leq x \leq m \\ \frac{u-x}{u-m}, & m \leq x \leq u \\ 0, & otherwise \end{cases} \quad (1)$$

where l and u are upper and lower bounds of the fuzzy number $\tilde{A}$, and m is the middle value. Thus, triangular fuzzy number can be marked as $\tilde{A} = (l, m, u)$.

Furthermore, fuzzy AHP will be briefly explained in few steps [59].

Step 1. Matrices pairwise comparison of all criteria by assigning them linguistic terms with belonging fuzzy sets as follows:

$$\tilde{A} = \begin{bmatrix} 1 & \tilde{a}_{12} & \cdots & \tilde{a}_{1n} \\ \tilde{a}_{21} & 1 & \cdots & \tilde{a}_{2n} \\ \vdots & \vdots & \ddots & \vdots \\ \tilde{a}_{n1} & \tilde{a}_{n2} & \cdots & 1 \end{bmatrix} = \begin{bmatrix} 1 & \tilde{a}_{12} & \cdots & \tilde{a}_{1n} \\ 1/\tilde{a}_{12} & 1 & \cdots & \tilde{a}_{2n} \\ \vdots & \vdots & \ddots & \vdots \\ 1/\tilde{a}_{1n} & 1/\tilde{a}_{2n} & \cdots & 1 \end{bmatrix} \quad (2)$$

Step 2. Defining geometric mean using geometric mean operator. This way, experts' compromised fuzzy weights are denoted by geometric mean of lower, middle, and upper values of triangular fuzzy set [60].

$$\tilde{G}_i = (l_i, m_i, u_i) = [(l_{i1} \otimes l_{i2} \otimes \ldots \otimes l_{ik})^{\frac{1}{k}}, (m_{i1} \otimes m_{i2} \otimes \ldots \otimes m_{ik})^{\frac{1}{k}}, (u_{i1} \otimes u_{i2} \otimes \ldots \otimes u_{ik})^{\frac{1}{k}}] \quad (3)$$

where $i = 1, 2, \ldots n$ and $j = 1, 2, \ldots, k$, n is the number of criteria and k is the number of experts.

Then, to normalize fuzzy criteria weights, following expression is used:

$$\tilde{w}_j = \frac{(l_i, m_i, u_i)}{(\sum_{i=1}^{n} u_i, \sum_{i=1}^{n} m_i, \sum_{i=1}^{n} l_i)} = \left[\frac{l_i}{\sum_{i=1}^{n} u_i}, \frac{m_i}{\sum_{i=1}^{n} m_i}, \frac{u_i}{\sum_{i=1}^{n} l_i}\right] \quad (4)$$

Step 3. The defuzzyfied and normalized crisp criteria weights are obtained as follows:

$$w_j' = \frac{\frac{l_i}{\sum_{i=1}^{n} u_i} + \frac{m_i}{\sum_{i=1}^{n} m_i} + \frac{u_i}{\sum_{i=1}^{n} l_i}}{3} \quad (5)$$

$$w_j = \frac{w_j'}{\sum_{j=1}^{n} w_j'} \quad (6)$$

The linguistic values of fuzzy numbers and their fuzzy sets are shown in Table 1 and are used in mutual comparison of criteria weights.

Table 1. Linguistic value and belonging numerical value of membership functions [60].

Linguistic Value	Numerical Value
Equal importance	(1,1,1)
Low importance	(1,2,3)
Moderate importance	(2,3,4)
Moderate to strong importance	(3,4,5)
Strong importance	(4,5,6)
Strong to very strong importance	(5,6,7)
Very strong importance	(6,7,8)
Very strong to extreme importance	(7,8,9)
Extreme importance	(8,9,9)

2.4.2. The TOPSIS Method

The TOPSIS method was proposed by Hwang and Yoon [61], and further developed by Chen and Hwang [62], and Hwang, Lai, and Liu [63]. It is a technique for order of preference by similarity to ideal solution. It is based on the concept that the chosen alternative should have the shortest geometric distance from the positive ideal solution and the largest geometric distance from the negative ideal solution [61]. The TOPSIS method assumes that each criterion has a monotonically increasing or decreasing utility, making it easier to locate positive ideal and negative ideal solutions. The positive ideal solution is formed as the combination of the best criteria values, and the negative ideal solution is the combination of the worst criteria values. Euclidean distances are used to measure the distance of each alternative from the positive ideal solution and negative ideal solution, and the order of preferences of alternatives is achieved by comparing Euclidean distances [64].

To determine the order of alternatives using the TOPSIS method, it is first necessary to calculate the normalized decision matrix, and the value of r_{ij} is normalized according to the following expression [61,62]:

$$r_{ij} = \frac{x_{ij}}{\sqrt{\sum_{i=1}^{m} x_{ij}^2}}, i = 1,2,\ldots,m;\ j = 1,2,\ldots,n. \quad (7)$$

The next step is to determine the weighted normalized decision matrix. Weighted normalized value v_{ij} is calculated according to the following expression [61,62]:

$$v_{ij} = w_j \times r_{ij},\ i = 1,2,\ldots,m;\ j = 1,2,\ldots,n \quad (8)$$

where w_j is the relative weight of the jth criterion, and $\sum_{j=1}^{n} w_j = 1$.

Then, it is necessary to determine the positive and negative ideal solution. For benefit criteria, the best values are maximum, and for cost criteria, the best values are minimum [64]. Accordingly, the positive and negative ideal solution will be as follows [62]:

$$A^* = \{v_1^*,\ldots,v_n^*\} = \{(max_i v_{ij} \mid j \in J),\ (min_i v_{ij} \mid j \in J')\} \quad (9)$$

$$A^- = \{v_1^-,\ldots,v_n^-\} = \{(min_i v_{ij} \mid j \in J),\ (max_i v_{ij} \mid j \in J')\} \quad (10)$$

where J is the set of benefit criteria, and J' is the set of cost criteria.

The distance between each alternative can be measured by the n-dimensional Euclidean distance. The distance of each alternative from the positive ideal solution is given as follows [62]:

$$S_i^* = \sqrt{\sum_{j=1}^{n} \left(v_{ij} - v_j^*\right)^2}, i = 1,2,\ldots,m. \quad (11)$$

Respectively, the distance of each alternative from the negative ideal solution is given as follows [62]:

$$S_i^- = \sqrt{\sum_{j=1}^{n} \left(v_{ij} - v_j^-\right)^2}, i = 1,2,\ldots,m. \quad (12)$$

Then, it is necessary to calculate the relative coefficient of closeness of each alternative to the positive ideal solution. The relative closeness coefficient of the alternative A_i with respect to A^* is defined as follows [62]:

$$C_i^* = \frac{S_i^-}{S_i^* + S_i^-},\ 0 < C_i^* < 1, i = 1,2,\ldots,m. \quad (13)$$

The last step is to order the alternatives according to the relative closeness coefficient in such a way that the best option is the alternative that has the highest relative closeness coefficient, and the worst is one with the smallest relative closeness coefficient [61].

3. Results

This section presents the results obtained by implementing the proposed model in the area of the city of Zagreb. At the beginning, six valuation criteria were defined according to which the green infrastructure index was determined using multi-criteria methods. The criteria weights are obtained by the fuzzy AHP method, and the final green infrastructure index was determined using the TOPSIS method. The result of the proposed methodology is the determination of the priority areas for the implementation of green infrastructure. In this way, the proposed model can help final decision makers to more easily decide about future activities related to urban green renewal.

3.1. Valuation Criteria

Six valuation criteria are defined: (C1) analysis of the availability of trees, (C2) analysis of the availability of recreational facilities, (C3) analysis of the availability of public green areas, (C4) analysis of the availability of water surfaces, (C5) analysis of the land surface temperature, and (C6) analysis of brownfield areas. As mentioned in the previous section, all analyses were performed in QGIS 3.28.15 "Firenze" software using a combination of spatial and attribute queries. Given that we are interested in green infrastructure near the place of residence, an analysis was made for each residential and mixed-use zone, and at the end, an average value was determined for each city district in the area of the city of Zagreb. Figure 1 shows all the criteria analyzed at the city district level. Figure 1a shows an analysis of the availability of trees and the average availability of trees for each city district within a radius of 300 m from residential and mixed-use zones located within the same city district. Figure 1b,c show the same, only for recreational facilities and for public green areas larger than 0.5 hectares. Figure 1d shows whether, on average for all residential and mixed-use zones in a particular city district, there is an accessible or inaccessible water surface within a radius of 300 m. Figure 1e shows the average land surface temperature of all residential and mixed-use zones within the same city district, and Figure 1f shows brownfield areas by city districts.

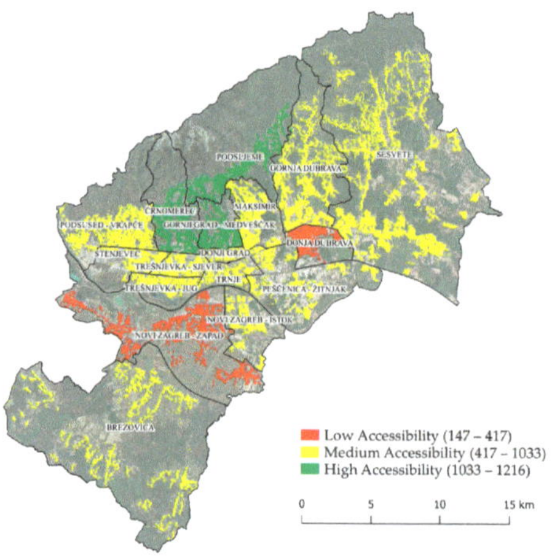

(a)

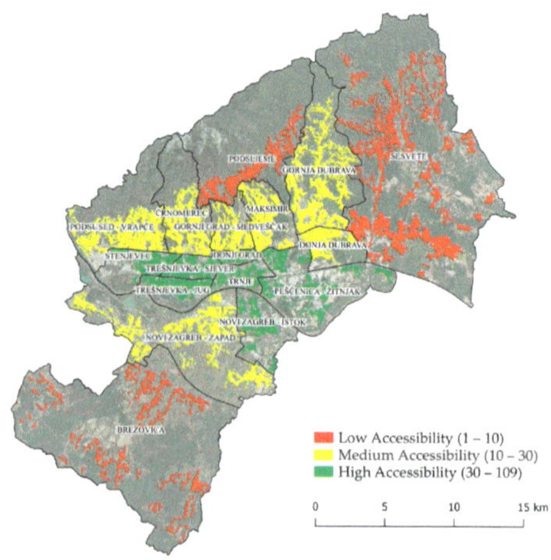

(b)

Figure 1. *Cont.*

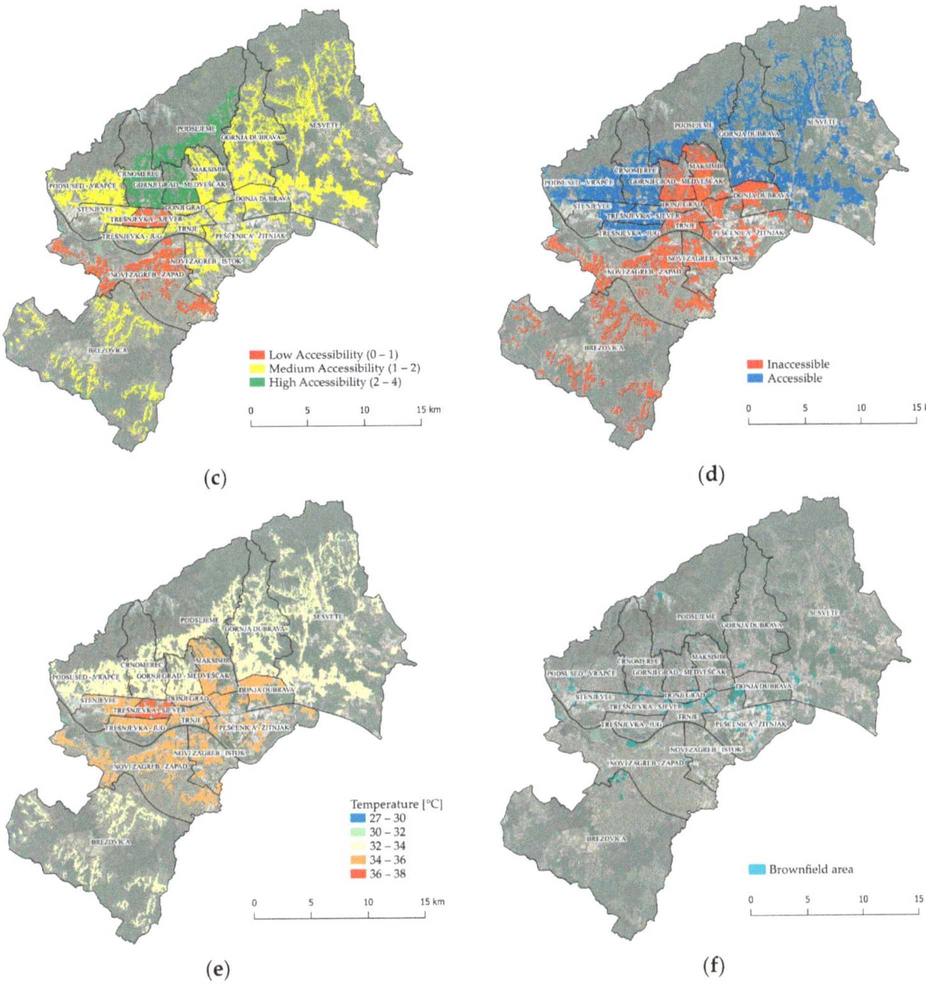

Figure 1. Valuation criteria: (**a**) analysis of the availability of trees; (**b**) analysis of the availability of recreational facilities; (**c**) analysis of the availability of public green areas; (**d**) analysis of the availability of water surfaces; (**e**) analysis of the land surface temperature; (**f**) analysis of brownfield areas.

3.2. Green Infrastructure Index

To determine the index of green infrastructure, we utilized previously explained valuation criteria, and the multi-criteria methods fuzzy AHP and TOPSIS. First, it is necessary to determine the weights of the criteria using the fuzzy AHP method. A team of experts compared the valuation criteria using Saaty's scale of relative importance. The team of experts consisted of an urban planner, landscape architect, surveyor, civil engineer, and a representative from the city of Zagreb administration. Along with the team of experts, interviews were also conducted with the end users, citizens of the city of Zagreb. Based on the assessments of experts and users, and the application of the arithmetic mean, the final assessments of the relative importance of the criteria were determined using triangular fuzzy numbers (Table 2).

Table 2. Pairwise comparison matrix, triangular fuzzy numbers.

Criteria	C1	C2	C3	C4	C5	C6
C1	1,1,1	1/3,1/2,1	1/5,1/4,1/3	1/4,1/3,1/2	1,1,1	4,5,6
C2	1,2,3	1,1,1	1/4,1/3,1/2	2,3,4	1,1,1	5,6,7
C3	3,4,5	2,3,4	1,1,1	2,3,4	1,1,1	5,6,7
C4	2,3,4	1/4,1/3,1/2	1/4,1/3,1/2	1,1,1	1,1,1	5,6,7
C5	1,1,1	1,1,1	1,1,1	1,1,1	1,1,1	4,5,6
C6	1/6,1/5,1/4	1/7,1/6,1/5	1/7,1/6,1/5	1/7,1/6,1/5	1/6,1/5,1/4	1,1,1

After the final assessments of the relative importance of the criteria have been made, it is possible to determine the weights of the criteria. First, the fuzzy weights of the criteria were calculated (see Table 3), based on which we obtained the normalized and final weight of each valuation criterion (see Table 4).

Table 3. Fuzzy weights.

Criteria	Fuzzy Weights		
C1	0.103	0.104	0.114
C2	0.189	0.204	0.213
C3	0.321	0.331	0.328
C4	0.150	0.152	0.158
C5	0.204	0.177	0.154
C6	0.034	0.032	0.032

Table 4. Normalized weights.

Criteria	Weights of Criteria
C1	0.107
C2	0.202
C3	0.327
C4	0.153
C5	0.178
C6	0.033

After defining the weights of the criteria using the TOPSIS method, the relative closeness coefficient was calculated. In this research, it represents the final green infrastructure index. The green infrastructure index ranges from zero to one. The higher in rank position of the green infrastructure index the better value of green infrastructure in that area compared to other investigated areas. In other words, a smaller green infrastructure index means there is less green infrastructure in that area compared to others. Therefore, these are the areas where the development and implementation of green infrastructure should be started first.

According to the formulas explained in Section 2.4.2 and using the criteria weights determined by the fuzzy AHP method (Table 4), the green infrastructure index was calculated for each city district in the area of the city of Zagreb using the TOPSIS method. The green infrastructure index of city districts was determined based on analyses carried out for each city district. The area of the city of Zagreb is divided into 17 city districts, and for each, the average value of an individual criterion was calculated based on residential and mixed-use zones (Figure 1). Positive and negative ideal solutions were determined using the TOPSIS method, to calculate the distance from the positive and negative ideal solutions and finally calculate the green infrastructure index. Table 5 shows the green infrastructure index for all city districts, and along with the green infrastructure index, the table also shows the values of positive and negative ideal solutions. The presentation of the index of green infrastructure by city districts is also given in Figure 2, where the index of green infrastructure is divided into five classes according to the given scale.

Table 5. Green infrastructure index for city districts.

City District	S_i^*	S_i^-	GI Index	Rank
Brezovica	0.158	0.055	0.258	14
Črnomerec	0.097	0.165	0.630	1
Donja Dubrava	0.174	0.032	0.155	16
Donji Grad	0.097	0.114	0.540	5
Gornja Dubrava	0.112	0.104	0.482	6
Gornji Grad–Medveščak	0.097	0.149	0.605	2
Maksimir	0.124	0.086	0.410	9
Novi Zagreb–istok	0.158	0.063	0.286	13
Novi Zagreb–zapad	0.186	0.025	0.118	17
Peščenica–Žitnjak	0.159	0.054	0.253	15
Podsljeme	0.111	0.134	0.547	4
Podsused–Vrapče	0.124	0.091	0.424	7
Sesvete	0.129	0.094	0.420	8
Stenjevec	0.145	0.083	0.364	11
Trešnjevka–jug	0.106	0.131	0.553	3
Trešnjevka–sjever	0.155	0.079	0.338	12
Trnje	0.135	0.090	0.401	10

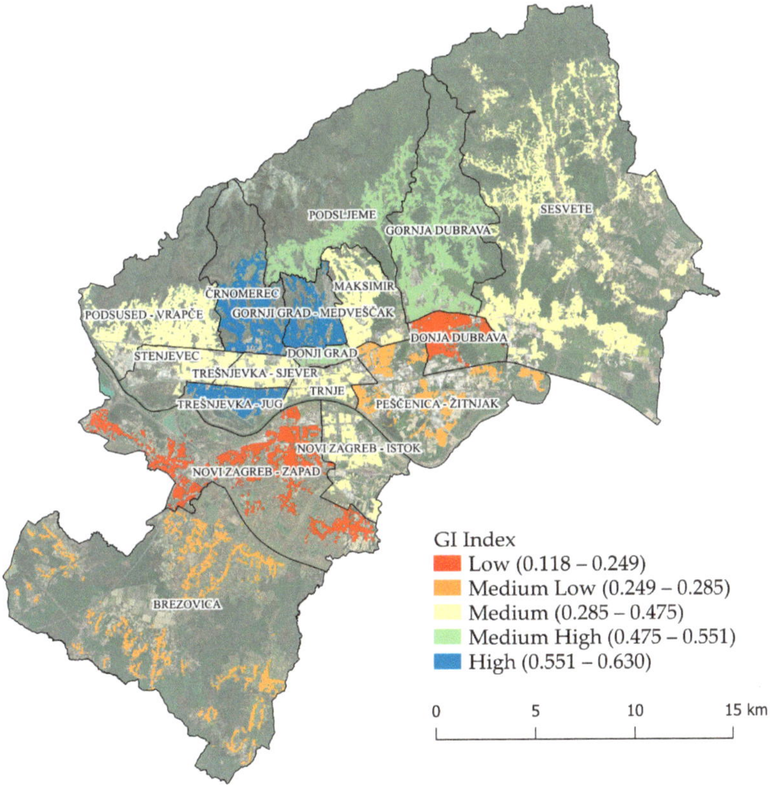

Figure 2. Green infrastructure index for city districts.

In Table 5 and Figure 2, we see that the city districts of Črnomerec and Gornji Grad–Medveščak have the highest green infrastructure index, which is quite expected considering their location next to Medvednica and the large parks located near the residential and mixed-use zones in these city districts. Also, the city district Trešnjevka–jug, situated along the river Sava and within which the Jarun Recreational Sports Center is located, also has a high green infrastructure index. Meanwhile, the city districts of Donja Dubrava and Novi Zagreb–zapad have the lowest green infrastructure index, which stands out significantly with a small green infrastructure index compared to other city districts. The city district of Donji Grad, as the narrowest center of the city, has a relatively high green infrastructure index, which is more than satisfactory considering the construction of that part of the city. Such a high green infrastructure index is mainly due to the large number of public green areas located near residential and mixed-use zones in that area.

4. Discussion

By applying the proposed valuation model for urban green infrastructure in land management, it is possible to valuate green infrastructure in an area with mathematical formulas and measurable parameters. However, to apply the model, spatial data on planned purpose and actual use, as well as data from the Green Cadastre on green infrastructure, should be available for that area.

As part of this research, the valuation model for urban green infrastructure in land management was examined and implemented in the area of the city of Zagreb. Based on the analyses, the analysis of the availability of trees, the analysis of the availability of recreational facilities, the analysis of the availability of public green areas larger than 0.5 hectares, the analysis of the availability of water surfaces, the analysis of land surface temperature, and the analysis of brownfield areas, the green infrastructure index was calculated. The green infrastructure index was calculated for city districts in the city of Zagreb using the fuzzy AHP and TOPSIS methods. The green infrastructure index calculates the value of green infrastructure in a particular area. A higher green infrastructure index indicates a better value of the green infrastructure in that area compared to other areas.

This study found that the city districts of Črnomerec, Gornji Grad–Medveščak, and Trešnjevka–jug have the highest index of green infrastructure. Črnomerec performed excellently in most criteria, except for the availability of recreational facilities, which resulted in the highest index of green infrastructure for this city district. Gornji Grad–Medveščak followed with a slightly lower index of green infrastructure due to the unavailability of water surfaces. Trešnjevka–jug did not excel in all criteria but had the largest number of recreational facilities and water surfaces, resulting in one of the highest indexes of green infrastructure. On the other hand, Novi Zagreb–zapad has the worst results for most criteria and therefore the lowest index of green infrastructure compared to other city districts.

All the proposed methods involve computer processing, and it is possible to evaluate the green infrastructure consecutively in a relatively short time and at the required time intervals to determine the trend of the green infrastructure index. The ultimate goal is to have the same services everywhere and to have the same density of green infrastructure in all areas. The model developed in this way provides support in land management because it is possible to determine the green infrastructure index and evaluate the current state, plan the ideal future state, and see how the implementation of green infrastructure progresses in a certain time interval. In this way, it is possible for the ultimate decision makers to more easily decide which areas are more prioritized for the development and implementation of green infrastructure. The green infrastructure index determined in this way can be compared with other spatial and land data during spatial planning.

5. Conclusions

Green infrastructure is gaining more and more importance today, especially after the adoption of the 2030 Agenda for Sustainable Development. There is a large body of research highlighting its benefits. However, there is a lack of research studies on green infrastructure for land management purposes. While green infrastructure is important for achieving sustainable development goals, it is also important to pay attention to sustainable land management [39]. When planning green infrastructure, it is necessary to pay more attention to land management to achieve a greater benefit and value of the land and potentially to standardize all available services in the areas where green infrastructure is planned. Therefore, in this research, the valuation model of urban green infrastructure in land management was developed, which can be used to determine the index of green infrastructure and thus enable planners and final decision makers to better plan green infrastructure and decide which areas are more prioritized for its implementation.

The test model evaluated the elements of green infrastructure that are available in the Green Cadastre. However, as we can see in the example of the city of Zagreb, these are not all publicly available elements of green infrastructure that exist in the city of Zagreb. Thus, the unavailability of some spatial data may prevent the full implementation of the developed model. This problem can be solved by additional field collection of data that are not available to us within the existing databases.

In future research, we will compare the green infrastructure index and land value and demonstrate the influence of green infrastructure on total land value. It is recommended that in future research, the number of the population be included in the development of the model and that the obtained data be compared with the population density to provide a more detailed representation of the percentage of green infrastructure relative to the number of inhabitants in a specific area. Also, it is possible to introduce additional criteria that could also affect the final green infrastructure index of the examined area.

Author Contributions: Conceptualization, S.B., H.T., K.R. and G.A.; methodology, S.B. and H.T.; software, S.B.; validation, S.B.; formal analysis, S.B.; investigation, S.B.; resources, S.B.; data curation, S.B.; writing—original draft preparation, S.B.; writing—review and editing, S.B., H.T., K.R. and G.A.; visualization, S.B.; supervision, H.T., K.R. and G.A. All authors have read and agreed to the published version of the manuscript.

Funding: This research received no external funding.

Data Availability Statement: Data available on request due to restrictions, e.g., privacy or ethical. The data presented in this study are available on request from the corresponding author. The data are not publicly available due to further research to be published.

Acknowledgments: This research is partially supported through project KK.01.1.1.02.0027, a project co-financed by the Croatian Government and the European Union through the European Regional Development Fund–the Competitiveness and Cohesion Operational Programme.

Conflicts of Interest: The authors declare no conflicts of interest.

References

1. Gelan, E.; Girma, Y. Sustainable Urban Green Infrastructure Development and Management System in Rapidly Urbanized Cities of Ethiopia. *Technologies* **2021**, *9*, 66. [CrossRef]
2. Hanna, E.; Comin, F.A. Urban Green Infrastructure and Sustainable Development: A Review. *Sustainability* **2021**, *13*, 11498. [CrossRef]
3. European Commission. *Building a Green Infrastructure for Europe*; European Commission: Brussels, Belgium, 2014.
4. European Commission. *Green Infrastructure Strategy*; European Commission: Brussels, Belgium, 2013.
5. Garcia, A.M.; Sante, I.; Loureiro, X.; Miranda, D. Spatial Planning of Green Infrastructure for Mitigation and Adaptation to Climate Change at a Regional Scale. *Sustainability* **2020**, *12*, 10525. [CrossRef]
6. Hobbie, S.E.; Grimm, N.B. Nature-Based Approaches to Managing Climate Change Impacts in Cities. *Philos. Trans. R. Soc. B Biol. Sci.* **2020**, *375*, 20190124. [CrossRef]
7. Reynolds, H.L.; Brandt, L.; Fischer, B.C.; Hardiman, B.S.; Moxley, D.J.; Sandweiss, E.; Speer, J.H.; Fei, S. Implications of Climate Change for Managing Urban Green Infrastructure: An Indiana, US Case Study. *Clim. Chang.* **2020**, *163*, 1967–1984. [CrossRef]
8. Shade, C.; Kremer, P.; Rockwell, J.S.; Henderson, K.G. The Effects of Urban Development and Current Green Infrastructure Policy on Future Climate Change Resilience. *Ecol. Soc.* **2020**, *25*, 37. [CrossRef]
9. Engemann, K.; Pedersen, C.B.; Arge, L.; Tsirogiannis, C.; Mortensen, P.B.; Svenning, J.-C. Residential Green Space in Childhood Is Associated with Lower Risk of Psychiatric Disorders from Adolescence into Adulthood. *Proc. Natl. Acad. Sci. USA* **2019**, *116*, 5188–5193. [CrossRef]
10. Kim, G.; Miller, P.A. The Impact of Green Infrastructure on Human Health and Well-Being: The Example of the Huckleberry Trail and the Heritage Community Park and Natural Area in Blacksburg, Virginia. *Sust. Cities Soc.* **2019**, *48*, 101562. [CrossRef]
11. Mansor, M.; Said, I.; Mohamad, I. Experiential Contacts with Green Infrastructure's Diversity and Well-Being of Urban Community. *Procedia-Soc. Behav. Sci.* **2012**, *49*, 257–267. [CrossRef]

12. Nawrath, M.; Guenat, S.; Elsey, H.; Dallimer, M. Exploring Uncharted Territory: Do Urban Greenspaces Support Mental Health i Low- and Middle-Income Countries? *Environ. Res.* **2021**, *194*, 110625. [CrossRef]
13. Sandifer, P.A.; Sutton-Grier, A.E.; Ward, B.P. Exploring Connections among Nature, Biodiversity, Ecosystem Services, and Huma Health and Well-Being: Opportunities to Enhance Health and Biodiversity Conservation. *Ecosyst. Serv.* **2015**, *12*, 1–15. [CrossRe
14. Brunbjerg, A.K.; Hale, J.D.; Bates, A.J.; Fowler, R.E.; Rosenfeld, E.J.; Sadler, J.P. Can Patterns of Urban Biodiversity Be Predicte Using Simple Measures of Green Infrastructure? *Urban For. Urban Green.* **2018**, *32*, 143–153. [CrossRef]
15. Roggema, R.; Tillie, N.; Keeffe, G. Nature-Based Urbanization: Scan Opportunities, Determine Directions and Create Inspirin Ecologies. *Land* **2021**, *10*, 651. [CrossRef]
16. Salomaa, A.; Paloniemi, R.; Kotiaho, J.S.; Kettunen, M.; Apostolopoulou, E.; Cent, J. Can Green Infrastructure Help to Conserv Biodiversity? *Environ. Plan. C-Polit. Space* **2017**, *35*, 265–288. [CrossRef]
17. Privitera, R.; Evola, G.; La Rosa, D.; Costanzo, V. Green Infrastructure to Reduce the Energy Demand of Cities. In *Urba Microclimate Modelling for Comfort and Energy Studies*; Palme, M., Salvati, A., Eds.; Springer International Publishing: Cham Switzerland, 2021; pp. 485–503. ISBN 978-3-030-65421-4.
18. Hansen, R.; Pauleit, S. From Multifunctionality to Multiple Ecosystem Services? A Conceptual Framework for Multifunctionalit in Green Infrastructure Planning for Urban Areas. *AMBIO* **2014**, *43*, 516–529. [CrossRef]
19. Korkou, M.; Tarigan, A.K.M.; Hanslin, H.M. The Multifunctionality Concept in Urban Green Infrastructure Planning: A Systemati Literature Review. *Urban For. Urban Green.* **2023**, *85*, 127975. [CrossRef]
20. Kambites, C.; Owen, S. Renewed Prospects for Green Infrastructure Planning in the UK 1. *Plan. Pract. Res.* **2006**, *21*, 483–49 [CrossRef]
21. WHO. *Urban Green Spaces: A Brief for Action*; WHO: Geneva, Switzerland, 2017.
22. Konijnendijk, C.C. Evidence-Based Guidelines for Greener, Healthier, More Resilient Neighbourhoods: Introducing the 3–30–30 Rule. *J. For. Res.* **2022**, *34*, 821–830. [CrossRef]
23. Konijnendijk, C.C. Promoting Health and Wellbeing through Urban Forests: Introducing the 3-30-300 Rule. *J. For. Res.* **2023**, *3* 821–830.
24. Browning, M.; Locke, D.; Konijnendijk, C.; Labib, S.M.; Rigolon, A.; Yeager, R.; Bardhan, M.; Berland, A.; Dadvand, P.; Helbich, M et al. Measuring the 3-30-300 Rule to Help Cities Meet Nature Access Thresholds. *Sci. Total Environ.* **2024**, *907*, 167739. [CrossRef
25. UNECE. *Policy Brief: Sustainable Urban and Peri-Urban Forestry-An Integrative and Inclusive Nature-Based Solution for Green Recover and Sustainable, Healthy and Resilient Cities (EFR)*; United Nations Economic Commission for Europe: Geneva, Switzerland, 202
26. UN General Assembly. *Transforming Our World: The 2030 Agenda for Sustainable Development*; UN General Assembly: New York NY, USA, 2015.
27. UN. *The New Urban Agenda*; United Nations: San Francisco, CA, USA, 2017.
28. Vlada Republike Hrvatske. *Nacionalni Plan Oporavka i Otpornosti 2021–2026*; Vlada Republike Hrvatske: Zagreb, Croatia, 2021.
29. Republika Hrvatska. Ministarstvo Prostornog Uređenja, Graditeljstva i Državne Imovine Program Razvoja Zelene Infrastruktur u Urbanim Područjima Za Razdoblje 2021. Do 2030. Godine 2021. Available online: https://mpgi.gov.hr/UserDocsImages/1415 (accessed on 10 January 2024).
30. Jones, S.; Somper, C. The Role of Green Infrastructure in Climate Change Adaptation in London. *Geogr. J.* **2014**, *180*, 191–19 [CrossRef]
31. EEA Green Infrastructure and Flood Management: Promoting Cost-Efficient Flood Risk Reduction via Green Infrastructure Solutions 2017. Available online: https://environmentalrisks.danube-region.eu/mdocs-posts/green-infrastructure-and-flood management-14-2017/ (accessed on 7 April 2024).
32. Li, L.; Uyttenhove, P.; Van Eetvelde, V. Planning Green Infrastructure to Mitigate Urban Surface Water Flooding Risk–A Methodology to Identify Priority Areas Applied in the City of Ghent. *Landsc. Urban Plan.* **2020**, *194*, 103703. [CrossRef]
33. Anderson, V.; Gough, W.A. Evaluating the Potential of Nature-Based Solutions to Reduce Ozone, Nitrogen Dioxide, and Carbor Dioxide through a Multi-Type Green Infrastructure Study in Ontario, Canada. *City Environ. Interact.* **2020**, *6*, 100043. [CrossRef
34. Bottalico, F.; Chirici, G.; Giannetti, F.; De Marco, A.; Nocentini, S.; Paoletti, E.; Salbitano, F.; Sanesi, G.; Serenelli, C.; Travaglini, D Air Pollution Removal by Green Infrastructures and Urban Forests in the City of Florence. *Agric. Agric. Sci. Procedia* **2016**, *8* 243–251. [CrossRef]
35. Morash, J.; Wright, A.; LeBleu, C.; Meder, A.; Kessler, R.; Brantley, E.; Howe, J. Increasing Sustainability of Residential Areas Using Rain Gardens to Improve Pollutant Capture, Biodiversity and Ecosystem Resilience. *Sustainability* **2019**, *11*, 3269. [CrossRef]
36. Chen, J.; Wang, S.; Wu, R. Optimization of the Integrated Green-Gray-Blue System to Deal with Urban Flood under Multi-Objective Decision-Making. *Water Sci. Technol.* **2024**, *89*, 434–453. [CrossRef]
37. Tzoulas, K.; Korpela, K.; Venn, S.; Yli-Pelkonen, V.; Kazmierczak, A.; Niemela, J.; James, P. Promoting Ecosystem and Humar Health in Urban Areas Using Green Infrastructure: A Literature Review. *Landsc. Urban Plan.* **2007**, *81*, 167–178. [CrossRef]
38. Venkataramanan, V.; Packman, A.; Peters, D.R.; Lopez, D.; McCuskey, D.J.; McDonald, R.; Miller, W.M.; Young, S.L. A Systematic Review of the Human Health and Social Well-Being Outcomes of Green Infrastructure for Stormwater and Flood Management. *J Environ. Manag.* **2019**, *246*, 868–880. [CrossRef]
39. Bačić, S.; Tomić, H.; Andlar, G.; Roić, M. Towards Integrated Land Management: The Role of Green Infrastructure. *ISPRS Int. J Geo-Inf.* **2022**, *11*, 513. [CrossRef]

0. Ersoy Mirici, M. The Ecosystem Services and Green Infrastructure: A Systematic Review and the Gap of Economic Valuation. *Sustainability* **2022**, *14*, 517. [CrossRef]
1. Van Oijstaeijen, W.; Van Passel, S.; Cools, J. Urban Green Infrastructure: A Review on Valuation Toolkits from an Urban Planning Perspective. *J. Environ. Manag.* **2020**, *267*, 110603. [CrossRef]
2. Ying, J.; Zhang, X.; Zhang, Y.; Bilan, S. Green Infrastructure: Systematic Literature Review. *Ekon. Istraz.* **2022**, *35*, 343–366. [CrossRef]
3. Dai, Y.; Solangi, Y.A. Evaluating and Prioritizing the Green Infrastructure Finance Risks for Sustainable Development in China. *Sustainability* **2023**, *15*, 7068. [CrossRef]
4. Tan, J.; Solangi, Y.A. Assessing Impact Investing for Green Infrastructure Development in Low-Carbon Transition and Sustainable Development in China. *Environ. Dev. Sustain.* **2023**, *26*, 25257–25280. [CrossRef]
5. Wang, R. Fuzzy-Based Multicriteria Analysis of the Driving Factors and Solution Strategies for Green Infrastructure Development in China. *Sust. Cities Soc.* **2022**, *82*, 103898. [CrossRef]
6. Park, Y.; Lee, S.-W.; Lee, J. Comparison of Fuzzy AHP and AHP in Multicriteria Inventory Classification While Planning Green Infrastructure for Resilient Stream Ecosystems. *Sustainability* **2020**, *12*, 9035. [CrossRef]
7. Ustaoglu, E.; Aydinoglu, A.C. Land Suitability Assessment of Green Infrastructure Development a Case Study of Pendik District (Turkey). *TeMA* **2019**, *12*, 165–178. [CrossRef]
8. Jayasooriya, V.M.; Muthukumaran, S.; Ng, A.W.M.; Perera, B.J.C. Multi Criteria Decision Making in Selecting Stormwater Management Green Infrastructure for Industrial Areas Part 2: A Case Study with TOPSIS. *Water Resour. Manag.* **2018**, *32*, 4297–4312. [CrossRef]
9. Zeng, J.; Lin, G.; Huang, G. Evaluation of the Cost-Effectiveness of Green Infrastructure in Climate Change Scenarios Using TOPSIS. *Urban For. Urban Green.* **2021**, *64*, 127287. [CrossRef]
0. GeoPortal Zagrebačke Infrastrukture Prostornih Podataka. Available online: https://geoportal.zagreb.hr/ (accessed on 25 July 2024).
1. WHO. *Urban Green Space Interventions and Health: A Review of Impacts and Effectiveness*; WHO: Bonn, Germany, 2016.
2. O Projektu: Organizacija Gradskih Vrtova. Available online: https://www.zagreb.hr/o-projektu/84060 (accessed on 2 October 2024).
3. Haase, D. Reflections about Blue Ecosystem Services in Cities. *Sustain. Water Qual. Ecol.* **2015**, *5*, 77–83. [CrossRef]
4. Ahmad, M.; Shao, Z.; Yaseen, A.; Javed, A.; Khalid, M. The Simulation and Prediction of Land Surface Temperature Based on SCP and CA-ANN Models Using Remote Sensing Data: A Case Study of Lahore. *Photogramm. Eng. Remote Sens.* **2022**, *88*, 783–790. [CrossRef]
5. Zhou, H.; Wang, Q.; Zhu, N.; Li, Y.; Li, J.; Zhou, L.; Pei, Y.; Zhang, S. Optimization Methods of Urban Green Space Layout on Tropical Islands to Control Heat Island Effects. *Energies* **2023**, *16*, 368. [CrossRef]
6. Bowler, D.E.; Buyung-Ali, L.; Knight, T.M.; Pullin, A.S. Urban Greening to Cool Towns and Cities: A Systematic Review of the Empirical Evidence. *Landsc. Urban Plan.* **2010**, *97*, 147–155. [CrossRef]
7. CLARINET. Brownfields and Redevelopment of Urban Areas; Version Austria 2002. Available online: https://www.commonforum.eu/fileadmin/inhalte/commonforum/pdf/clarinet/clarinet_brownfields_2002.pdf (accessed on 21 March 2024).
8. Zadeh, L.A. Fuzzy Sets. *Inf. Control* **1965**, *8*, 338–353. [CrossRef]
9. Sun, C.-C. A Performance Evaluation Model by Integrating Fuzzy AHP and Fuzzy TOPSIS Methods. *Expert Syst. Appl.* **2010**, *37*, 7745–7754. [CrossRef]
0. Kilić, J.; Jajac, N.; Rogulj, K.; Mastelić-Ivić, S. Assessing Land Fragmentation in Planning Sustainable Urban Renewal. *Sustainability* **2019**, *11*, 2576. [CrossRef]
1. Hwang, C.-L.; Yoon, K. Methods for Multiple Attribute Decision Making. In *Multiple Attribute Decision Making: Methods and Applications A State-of-the-Art Survey*; Hwang, C.-L., Yoon, K., Eds.; Lecture Notes in Economics and Mathematical Systems; Springer: Berlin/Heidelberg, Germany, 1981; pp. 58–191. ISBN 978-3-642-48318-9.
2. Chen, S.-J.; Hwang, C.-L. *Fuzzy Multiple Attribute Decision Making: Methods and Applications*; Lecture Notes in Economics and Mathematical Systems; Springer: Berlin/Heidelberg, Germany, 1992; Volume 375, ISBN 978-3-540-54998-7.
3. Hwang, C.-L.; Lai, Y.-J.; Liu, T.-Y. A New Approach for Multiple Objective Decision Making. *Comput. Oper. Res.* **1993**, *20*, 889–899. [CrossRef]
4. Mateo, J.R.S.C. *Multi Criteria Analysis in the Renewable Energy Industry*; Springer Science & Business Media: Berlin/Heidelberg, Germany, 2012; ISBN 978-1-4471-2346-0.

energies

MDPI

Review

A Systematic Review on Fuzzy Decision Support Systems and Multi-Criteria Analysis in Urban Heat Island Management

Majda Ćesić [1], Katarina Rogulj [1], Jelena Kilić Pamuković [1,*] and Andrija Krtalić [2]

[1] Faculty of Civil Engineering, Architecture and Geodesy, University of Split, 21000 Split, Croatia; mivic@gradst.hr (M.Ć.); krogulj1@gradst.hr (K.R.)
[2] Faculty of Geodesy, University of Zagreb, 10000 Zagreb, Croatia; kandrija@geof.hr
* Correspondence: jkilic@gradst.hr

Abstract: The phenomenon known as urban heat islands (UHIs) is becoming more common and widespread, especially in large cities and metropolises around the world. The main cause of these temperature variations between the city center and the suburbs is the replacement of large tracts of natural land with artificial (built-up) surfaces that absorb solar heat and radiate it back at night. UHIs have been the subject of numerous studies, most of which were about defining the main characteristics, factors, indexes, etc., of UHIs using remote sensing technologies or about determining mitigating activities. This paper provides a comprehensive overview of the literature, as well as a bibliometric analysis, to discover research trends related to the application of decision support systems and multi-criteria decision-making for UHI management, with a special emphasis on fuzzy theory. Data collection is conducted using the Scopus bibliographic database. Throughout the literature review, it was found that there were not many studies on multi-criteria analysis and decision support system applications regarding UHIs. The fuzzy theory application was also reviewed, resulting in only a few references. However, this topic is current, with an increase in published papers, and authors see this as an opportunity for improvement and further research.

Keywords: urban heat islands; decision support system; fuzzy theory; multi-criteria decision-making; bibliometric analysis; mitigation techniques

1. Introduction

The urbanization and changes in lifestyle and the environment that have taken place in recent decades have brought many benefits, provided new opportunities, and, in some aspects, raised the quality of life. However, in addition to the positive aspects, there are also some drawbacks to replacing the natural environment with a built-up one, among which is the appearance of urban heat islands (UHIs). This phenomenon can be defined as increased air and land temperatures in the built-up area compared to the surrounding rural areas. According to Yamamoto [1], it is a phenomenon that affects almost every major city and it primarily occurs when extensive natural land is substituted with artificially constructed surfaces that absorb solar radiation or heat during the day and emit it at night [2,3]. The difference in air temperature between the city's center and the suburbs can be from 1 to more than 10 degrees Celsius [4–6]. The biggest temperature differences occur in cities with populations exceeding 100,000 residents in lowland areas or valleys and in the summer period [7]. For the time being, the main and most effective option for mitigating the effects of UHIs is an increase in vegetation areas [8,9]. Urban vegetation can, to some extent, regulate the microclimate, mainly through shading [10] and evapotranspiration [11].

To make it easier to follow the review of the literature and comprehend the complexity of the issue, the introduction includes a detailed explanation of all the basic terms related to UHIs; factors that contribute to their occurrence; and UHI types, detection methods, and methods of mitigation.

1.1. Basic Concepts of UHIs

In addition to solar heating and current weather conditions, several factors affect the creation of UHIs. As already mentioned, urbanization leads to the loss of vegetation and the replacement of natural materials with metallic, asphaltic, and concrete substances, each possessing distinct thermal conductivities [12–14]. As a result of the removal of natural surfaces and vegetation during city development and expansion, there are lower levels of evaporation and humidity, which leads to the retention of heat during the day and its subsequent release at night [15–18]. Additionally, chopping down trees eliminates the cooling effect that trees' crowns provide, which is crucial for maintaining human comfort. Furthermore, artificial building materials have a high absorption of solar radiation, due to their low albedo [16–18]. Albedo indicates the proportion of shortwave radiation that a surface material reflects [19], which means that materials with a low albedo store more solar energy and directly contribute to the rise in urban temperature, i.e., the creation of a microclimate [20]. Materials with a low albedo and a high absorption of solar radiation include dark materials such as asphalt, while, for example, white roofs do not absorb much solar radiation. An important physical property of a material is its thermal diffusivity. For materials with a high heat diffusivity (which is a combination of thermal conductivity and heat capacity), such as concrete, heat penetrates deeper into their layers and is retained for longer. Natural materials and rural areas generally have a lower thermal diffusivity than built-up areas [15].

The development of UHIs is also influenced by the geometry of the built-up area. Tall buildings create a canyon geometry that causes heat to be trapped in the bottom layers. Due to the reduced sky view, heat release via longwave radiation is reduced and is captured by taller buildings, creating an urban canopy [15,21,22]. Due to the densely distributed tall buildings, less heat is convected from the surface to the air, since the buildings reduce the speed of the wind, which would otherwise cool the area [15,23]. The UHI effect is greatest during calm, clear weather when there is no wind [24]. The increase in temperature is influenced by both the arrangement of vegetation and built-up areas. According to Kazak [25], smaller urban development cores are more favorable to UHIs, while large urban clusters have a greater exposure to UHIs. Part of the reason for the increase in temperature is anthropogenic heat, which is caused by traffic, electrical energy consumption (air conditioning), industrial processes, and human and animal biological metabolism [15,20]. These activities also contribute to air pollution, which negatively affects air temperature. Exhaust gases released by cars or industry, in particular mineral and carbon aerosols, retain solar radiation in the Earth's atmosphere and thereby influence the creation of a microclimate, causing the greenhouse effect [26]. The UHI effect is most pronounced in summer, due to the prevalence of solar radiation. Other current weather conditions also influence the creation of a microclimate; for example, anticyclone conditions increase the UHI effect, while wind speed and cloud cover are negatively correlated with UHIs [2,27].

There are several UHI types—Atmospheric Urban Heat Islands (AUHIs), Surface Urban Heat Islands (SUHIs), and Subsurface Urban Heat Islands. AUHIs occur when the air temperature is higher in urban areas compared to rural areas and can be split into two groups, as follows: canopy layer urban heat islands, representing the zone amidst the urban surface and the height of the trees or buildings, and boundary layer heat islands, which encompass the space extending from the top of the canopy layer to approximately one mile above the surface, reaching an area where urban landscapes cease to impact the atmosphere. Canopy layer urban heat islands are indicative of the near-surface temperature, i.e., the temperature recorded using a shielded thermometer at a two meter height above the ground. SUHIs are measured using land surface temperature (LST), which is higher in urban areas than in the adjacent rural areas, and are present throughout both the day and the night. Subsurface UHIs are indicative of the difference in temperature between the soil beneath the urban area and the soil in the neighboring rural area [2,28,29].

A conventional measure of the UHI's magnitude is urban heat island intensity (UHII), which is determined as the difference between the maximum urban temperature, T_U, and a representative temperature of the rural area, T_R, over a specified period [28], as follows:

$$UHII = \Delta T_{U-R} = T_U - T_R \quad (1)$$

The choice of temperature (air, LST, or soil) depends on the type of heat island whose magnitude is being determined.

Stewart and Oke [30] introduced the local climate zones (LCZs) scheme, which is now a standard and is used in many research studies, to make it easier to distinguish between what belongs in an urban and a rural area. The LCZs scheme enables the objective determination of UHIs and includes 17 classes, 10 types of built environment, and 7 land types [30].

Urban heat islands can be identified using various techniques, including both the direct and indirect measurement of temperature and physical modeling [31]. The conventional method of measuring air temperature at stationary meteorological stations situated 1.5–2 m above ground is one form of direct measurement [18]. The primary drawbacks of this method are its high cost and the restricted coverage of meteorological stations; the meteorological stations that are currently in place are frequently located in remote areas, are insufficient in number, and are situated at elevations and locations that are not appropriate for identifying heat islands [15,29]. Another way of directly determining UHIs is via temperature measurement using moving sensors, mounted, for example, on a moving vehicle or a balloon for vertical measuring the changes in air temperature. The problem with such measurements is the high price of achieving simultaneous measurements at multiple locations. Indirect ways of determining UHIs include remote sensing techniques that use satellites and aircraft to measure LST. Satellites provide a good spatial resolution, but their problem is temporal resolution, since their data are only available at the time of satellite passage over a certain part of the Earth [15,31]. A new method of determining heat islands that would circumvent the shortcomings of satellite observations is the determination of AUHIs using a Global Navigation Satellite System, which uses precise point positioning measurements and temperatures are determined using the Zenith tropospheric refraction [32].

The urban microclimate plays a crucial role in determining the standard of living within a city and UHI effects have a substantial impact on both the physical environment and the socioeconomic sphere [33–35]. The emergence of UHIs in urban areas has the capacity to worsen the negative impacts of global warming, which are harmful to human health, water consumption, and the ecosystem itself. Cities are experiencing higher temperatures, particularly during the summer, which increases the demand for air conditioners and, consequently, energy consumption. Due to changes in local wind patterns and increased energy consumption, there are also increased levels of air pollution and greenhouse gas emissions, which enhance the ground-level ozone generation. SUHIs adversely affect the quality of water, causing its thermal pollution by increasing the temperature of storm water runoff, which then flows into rivers, seas, and lakes. All this affects human comfort and health, causing respiratory difficulties, heat stress, non-fatal heat stroke, and increasing mortality attributed to heat-related causes, which particularly applies to vulnerable groups with certain health issues, elderly people, and small children [29,35–37].

Recent studies have demonstrated that changes in momentum, mass, and heat transfer surrounding urban structures, which are caused by urban morphology, have a major effect on the urban outdoor environment [38]. The street canyon's poor anthropogenic heat removal and dilution is a result of stagnant airflow surrounding densely populated, towering buildings. Thus, in order to lessen the severity of UHIs, efficient methods for anthropogenic heat removal and dilution are essential. Numerous studies have been conducted on air flow in densely populated metropolitan areas. However, estimating the anthropogenic heat dispersion simply from the information of the air flow may be challenging, if not incorrect [38,39]. In order to assess the impact of human heat on air temperature, a microscale Computational Fluid Dynamics (CFD) simulation is often used to produce precise and high-resolution modeling results of heat transfer and dispersion in the street canyon [40].

There are several different techniques for the mitigation of the UHI effect and Santamouris et al. [41] classified these, as concerns cooling mechanisms, into the following: cool material, urban greenery, evaporative techniques, and underground cooling. Using vegetation, particularly trees, is one of the best strategies for mitigating UHIs [42]. By creating shady area and facilitating evapotranspiration, trees and other vegetation help to cool urban microclimates [37]. Green strategies include urban forests (parks), street trees, private green gardens, and green roofs (GRs) or facades [43]. Cool materials reduce temperatures by improving solar reflection and reducing solar absorption and their advantages are their low cost and easy implementation [44]. Various kinds of cool roofs and cool pavements are being used [37]. Evaporation methods, which include water bodies and sprinklers, can enhance the release of latent heat [45]. Urban water bodies (including lakes and rivers) are considered urban cooling islands [46], whose cooling effects can be felt up to 800 m away [47]. Underground cooling refers to reducing the temperature in the indoor area, in order to reduce both the anthropogenic heat that affects the outdoor temperature and to reduce energy consumption [45].

1.2. Decision Support Systems with Fuzzy Theory and Multi-Criteria Decision-Making

In order to make the right decisions for environmental and ecological purposes, as well as for the prediction of outcomes, computer science can assist and support ecologists, engineers, urban planners, and other experts in the formulation of ecological assessments. As a result, computer science has become an essential tool for environmental scientists and urban planners to solve complex ecological problems. The often-used tools in the environmental sector are decision support systems (DSSs), which are computer programs that support ecologists and urban planners in decision-making [48]. By demonstrating advanced reasoning abilities, DSSs can enhance environmental decision-making and encourage more effective practices. With the intention of giving computers the ability to "think" like experts, expert systems researchers create the majority of DSSs [49]. There are various DSS tools available to support decision-making and most of them rely on models and algorithms for data and information analysis and elaboration. Some of them are based on Analytical Hierarchy Processes and other multi-criteria decision-making techniques, or they are combined with different management strategies [50,51]. In environmental DSSs, trade-offs between socio-political, environmental, and economic aspects must be taken into account. Multiple stakeholder perspectives frequently complicate this process. Decisions in various sectors can be supported by multi-criteria decision-making (MCDM), a formal methodology that arose to address existing technical knowledge and stakeholder values. Environmental decision-making can particularly benefit from MCDM [52].

A distinguishing feature of a DSS is its knowledge, which enables the system to intelligently and specifically give information on an observed problem to increase efficacy. There are, in fact, two kinds of DSSs—knowledge-based and non-knowledge-based. The second applies machine learning, via neural networks or genetic algorithms, to artificial intelligence principles [53], while fuzzy logic-based DSSs (FDSSs) are a type of knowledge-based system [54,55]. These systems primarily rely on rules in the form of if–then statements and the data are typically linked to these rules.

Soft computing plays a major role in the development of fuzzy principles, which have roots in a variety of previous studies, including Zadeh's papers on fuzzy sets [56] and the analysis of complex systems and decision processes [57]. When dealing with fuzzy concepts, it is necessary to create fuzzy sets (with defined membership functions) and applied logical operations to those sets. The foundation for creating models of fuzzy systems is fuzzy logic, which offers guidelines for operations on fuzzy sets. To begin with, one must acknowledge that fuzzy logic is really an extension of conventional Boolean logic. Stated differently, fuzzy logic reduces to normal binary logic if fuzzy values remain at the extremes of 1 (totally true) and 0 (absolutely false) [58]. Fuzzy logic is more advantageous and effective for handling expert judgments and decision-making because, in contrast to other methods, it can handle the ambiguity and uncertainty of data.

1.3. Research Focus

Since the 1950s, the urban population has been growing rapidly and, according to [59], worldwide, a greater number of people live in urban areas compared to rural settlements. In 2018, this percentage was 55% and it is projected to reach 68% by the year 2050 [59]. As a result of this urbanization, there is a decrease in green space, an expansion of cities, and an increase in artificial material use, all of which have a negative impact on the development of UHIs. When such actions are taken without planning, the issue is even more serious. Thankfully, the problem of UHIs has become more widely acknowledged in recent years and, as a result, environmental policies and strategies have taken it into account, while increased research on the subject is being conducted. The problem is not easily solvable; it is necessary to develop a strategy and, according to [60], no UHI mitigation method is ideal; but, to solve the problem, several methods should be combined. This is where multi-criteria decision-making (MCDM), decision support systems (DSSs), and fuzzy theory found their role.

The aim of this research was to determine the incidence of the decision-making approaches and fuzzy theory in the management of UHIs. Research focus, thus, began with the formation of the following research questions:

a. What are the research trends in using DSSs and MCA for UHI decision-making?
b. How is fuzzy theory used?
c. Does the theme develop over time?
d. What are the most relevant authors and sources in the research field?

The first part of this paper provides an overview of the literature and the second part presents a bibliometric analysis to discover research trends in the use of the mentioned techniques for UHI mitigation, with a special emphasis on DSSs, MCDM, and fuzzy theory. An in-detail review is given for the remote sensing, mitigation, and management of UHIs; then, an application of multi-criteria analysis (MCA) and DSSs is presented as a support in various mitigation and management activities in evaluating and lowering the impact of UHIs. Finally, a discussion and the authors' conclusions are presented, as well as further research directions.

2. Literature Review

In this section, a thorough review is given regarding both general and review studies, remote sensing, and the mitigation of UHIs. Furthermore, studies on the application of MCDM on UHIs and DSSs are presented. All of the cited literature is obtained from internationally renowned databases and reputable scientific journals. It addresses the issue of UHIs in a manner that is scientifically representative and also covers the identification and addressing of UHI effect, as well as choosing mitigation strategies. Table 1 is a part of the table that presents a summary of the studies reviewed, while the entire table (Table A1) is presented in Appendix A.

Table 1. Summary of the studies reviewed.

Author(s)	Title	Year	Study Location	Methodology	Findings
Nuruzzaman, M. [20]	Urban heat island: causes, effects and mitigation measures-a review	2015	Not specified	Review of various measures used to encounter UHI effects.	The most effective measures are green vegetation, high albedo materials, and pervious pavements.
Duplančić Leder, T. et al. [31]	Split Metropolitan area surface temperature assessment with remote sensing method	2016	Split, Croatia	Landsat thermal channels have been used to determine the LST.	Microclimate changes and severe changes in LST and UHI effects.
Amani-Beni, M. et al. [46]	Impact of urban park's tree, grass and waterbody on microclimate in hot summer days: A case study of Olympic Park in Beijing, China	2018	Beijing, China	Observation of the greenery impact on the park during summer days.	The park was 0.48–1.12 °C cooler during the day; increased air humidity was observed at 2.39–3.74%; and a reduced human comfort index was used to generate a more comfortable thermal environment.
Nwakaire, C. M. et al. [61]	Urban Heat Island Studies with emphasis on urban pavements: A review	2020	Not specified	Literature review of UHIs, with emphasis on urban pavements.	One of the main findings included using creative designs that can provide cooling without compromising the structural integrity of the pavement, which is a key component of effective UHI mitigation techniques for highway pavements.
. . .					
Werbin, Z. et al. [62]	A tree-planting decision support tool for urban heat island mitigation	2020	Boston, USA	Development a Boston-specific Heat Vulnerability Index (HVI).	Researchers from Boston University examined the City of Boston's strategy for expanding the urban canopy because the City has encountered challenges in establishing a long-lasting growth. They determined what barriers there were to applying scientific information to tree-planting decisions and collaborated with the city to create a tool that would help with the process. The tool itself is replicable or adaptable to other cities, and the process of development offers a model of a fruitful collaboration between academia and the public sector.
Acosta, M. P. et al. [63]	How to bring UHI to the urban planning table? A data-driven modeling approach	2021	Montreal, Canada	Development of the decision support tool for the modeling of UHI at the street-level.	The methodology for creating a decision assistance tool for street-level UHI modeling was described in this research study. Urban planners can utilize this simple-to-use tool to look at how their design decisions will affect street-level traffic. There are five levels of UHI potential, ranging from low to high, represented by the UHI evaluation matrix.
Qi, J. et al. [64]	Planning for cooler cities: A framework to support the selection of urban heat mitigation techniques	2020	Sidney, Australia	Development decision-making framework to UHI mitigation	One of the study's contributions is the creation of a method that can determine the best combinations of UHMTs and planning and design elements with the greatest potential for cooling in a particular urban setting. The framework can support high-performance production and sustainable development in addition to giving decision-makers the best UHMTs for creating a workable policy for mitigating urban heat.

2.1. Remote Sensing and Mitigation of UHIs

In a study from Nwakaire et al. [61], a literature review on UHIs was provided, focusing specifically on urban pavements. Reports were provided on the state-of-the-art in UHI measurement, assessment, and mitigation. Kim and Brown [65] conducted a comprehensive systematic literature review, selecting 51 papers through a rigorous five-step filtering process. Their study focuses on examining the spatial extent of UHIs, the conceptual frameworks employed for UHI estimation, and the methodologies utilized for UHI estimation and analysis. A comprehensive assessment of records in Scopus and Web of Science (WOS), related to UHI analysis utilizing LST and remote sensing data and techniques, was reported by Almeida, Teodoro, and Gonçalves [66]. The review encompassed the years 2000–2020. A paper by Deilami, Kamruzzaman, and Liu [67] conducted a comprehensive and methodical review of the many temporal and spatial aspects influencing the UHI effect. In addition to examining the types of satellite images used, the methods for categorizing changes in land use and cover, the models for assessing the correlation between spatiotemporal factors and the UHI effect, and the impacts of these factors on UHIs, the paper systematically identified 75 eligible studies for review, specifically focusing on the UHI effect.

Nimac, Buli, and Uvela-Aloise [68] introduced a methodology for evaluating the impact of changes in land use/land cover and climate conditions on the total change in urban heat load in Zagreb from the 1960s to the present. Four modeling experiments were executed, involving the integration of two different city scenarios and two 30-year periods, which did not overlap. This approach allowed for a separate evaluation of the impacts of changes in land use/land cover and climate conditions.

The overall goal of Chen, Zheng, and Hu's research [60] was not restricted to examining the impact of a single variable on the microclimate results; rather, they examined and assessed the impact of various cooling technique combinations in each open LCZ. This information was useful for optimizing urban development programs at both the neighborhood and street levels. Finding the best cooling combinations to reduce air temperature in LCZ-4 (open high-rise), LCZ-5 (open middle-rise), and LCZ-6 (open low-rise) were the main challenges. The examination of individual factors (such as vegetation, ground albedo, and GRs) on pedestrian air temperature within the same LCZ type and under identical LCZ conditions was another challenge. Finally, it was crucial to ascertain whether the cooling effects of a similar intervention differed across various LCZs.

LST is a crucial variable for many different Earth processes. Duplančić Leder, Leder and Hećimović [31] and Duplančić Leder and Leder [69], in their research, gathered data on LST thanks to satellite thermal data. Using Landsat thermal channels, the LST in the Split metropolitan region [31] and Mostar area [69] was ascertained. The findings suggested that the observed climatic changes and the intense urbanization that has occurred in the Split metropolitan region and Mostar area are causing UHIs. Another study by Duplančić Leder and Bačić [70] used the well-known LCZ classification system in the Split metropolitan region and matched it with the zones that had the highest urban temperatures. Additionally, the research identified important issues and offered possible solutions to lower the impact of UHIs. In order to make it easier to determine the border between built-up and non-built-up areas and to calculate the intensity of the UHI, Estacio et al. [71] proposed an automated geographic information system (GIS)-based methodology for determining LCZs. Although the methodology was developed in the Quezon City, Philippines, it can also be applied to other cities by modifying the input data. Using Landsat TM satellite imagery, Bokaie et al. [72] explored the correlation between LST and land use/land cover (LULC) in Tehran Metropolitan City. For this, the LULC map was created using the supervised classification approach [73] and the LST was determined using the algorithm. UHI locations were identified, based on the LST map that was produced by analyzing the satellite image's thermal band, and their status, in connection to the population density and current LULC classes, was assessed. The findings demonstrated that the causal agent of the UHI produced in Tehran is distinct. To determine the LST and the UHI and to research their relationships with LULC and air pollution in Tabriz, Iran, Feizizadeh and Blaschke [74] proposed integrating Spectral Mixture Analysis and Endmember Remote Sensing Indices.

After researching 32 urban parks in Jinan, China, Zhu et al. [75] developed absolute and relative indices to illustrate the distinct characteristics of the parks' cooling islands. The land cover of parks was determined using high-spatial-resolution GF-2 pictures, while the thermal environment was examined using buffer analysis on Landsat 8 TIR photos. LST, remote sensing-based ecological index, and biophysical composition index data were used by Firozjaei et al. [76] to predict the land surface's ecological state. Zhang et al. [77] used heat, wetness, dryness, and greenness to evaluate the quality of the urban eco-environment. Zhang et al.'s [78] main focus was using land use data to assess how natural ecological land has changed. The retrieval of LST based on remote sensing data was the main emphasis of Jiang et al. [79]. Peng et al. [80] concentrated on using anthropogenic heat flux to study the impact of UHIs. However, evaluating the ecological environment solely on the basis of one criterion is incomplete and prejudiced. Several criteria are used in various studies to assess the ecological environment. A study by You et al. [81] used hot-spot analysis and Moran's I to explain the geographical distribution of UHIs in the central area of Fuzhou, China. The study separated the drivers into socio-economic factors and physical geographic factors. Geodetector software was used to conduct the factor interaction analysis and the influence study of a single factor on LST.

The aim of the research from Despini et al. [82] was to examine the potential of surface albedo, one of the qualities that contributes the most to the creation of UHIs. Remote sensing data were utilized to examine urban surfaces, while solar reflective materials were used to create hypotheses for various scenarios. To evaluate UHI mitigation, energy conservation, and economic savings, multiple parameters were calculated for every scenario.

Santos et al. [83] created a brand-new framework that offers a statistical evaluation of models of urban climate in a Singaporean urban environment. The climate model converts high-dimensional data into a low-dimensional ranking system, based on statistical measures that represent stakeholders' intended objectives. An analysis is conducted on various urban morphologies, taking into account operational energy costs and calculating their environmental impact on UHIs and population allocation potential.

In order to mitigate the UHI effect, Amani-Beni et al. [46] examined the effects of urban parks on microclimates and offered a point of reference for the management and planning requirements of urban green spaces. In their study, the researchers examined the cooling impacts of trees, grass, and water features in urban parks in Beijing's built-up areas. They also examined the variations in air temperature, humidity, and thermal comfort across different types of urban green spaces, as well as their management approaches. Also, in another study by the same authors [84], they identified the urban park's cooling effect on the neighborhood and made a contribution to the design, scientific planning, and management of urban green spaces. Using satellite imagery and the functionalities of Google Earth Engine—a robust geospatial analysis platform—Pritipadmaja, Garg, and Sharma [85] aimed to evaluate the cooling impact of blue–green spaces in Bhubaneswar. Their objective was to explore the implications of these features in mitigating UHI effects. The purpose of this study was to add to the body of knowledge already available on UHI mitigation techniques and to offer insightful information about the unique circumstances of Bhubaneswar. In particular, the links between the city's built-up, water, and vegetation indices, as well as fluctuations in LST, were examined.

In their study, Dong et al. [86] measured the cooling effect in high-density metropolitan areas at the city level, taking into account actual GR projects. The range of the effective cooling buffer zone and the quantitative link between the area of GRs and their LST were of special interest to them. In order to do this, the cooling effect of urban GRs was statistically analyzed using geographic information systems and data from Landsat 8 remote sensing images taken between 2014 and 2017. Imran et al. [87] assessed the potential benefits of cool roofs and GRs for decreasing the impact of UHIs, as well as how these strategies affected people's thermal comfort during one of the worst heatwaves ever recorded in Melbourne, southeast Australia, in January 2009. Due to the extremely dry and warm weather, this study demonstrates that convective rolls are more significant in the extreme heatwave event than the advection of moist air from rural areas, which has been reported to be a major mechanism in earlier studies. This study also demonstrated that UHIs are not greatly impacted by the initial soil wetness for GRs. In their research, Sanchez and Reames [88] examined how accessible GRs are to low-income and deprived groups in Detroit, Michigan, taking into account the UHI effect and the city's existing cooling center infrastructure. Sections of the city were assessed for their susceptibility to the UHI effect; because GRs increase surface albedo and evaporative cooling, they can mitigate this effect. In order to ascertain if GRs have been installed where there is the greatest need for ecosystem services and to ascertain how socioeconomic features may be connected to the sites of green infrastructure mitigating UHIs, existing GR initiatives were mapped. On the other hand, appropriate building- and urban-scale solutions are needed to reduce the energy demand for space cooling and to mitigate the UHI effect. Specifically, it has been determined that building roofs represent a potential area of intervention, with the ability to deliver substantial environmental benefits and energy savings. Within this context, cool roofs and GRs represent two highly intriguing options that could potentially achieve the dual goals of lowering energy use and enhancing interior and outdoor comfort levels. Therefore, a numerical comparison of the energy and environmental performance of three different types of roofs—a standard roof, a cool roof, and a GR—was made by Gagliano et al. [89]. Thus, it is discovered that cool, green roofs offer more environmental advantages and energy savings than typical, heavily insulated roofs.

Considering the realms of city planning, urban climatology, and climate science, Gunawardena, Wells, and Kershaw [90] provided a meta-analysis of the main ways that green and blue space affect urban canopy and boundary layer temperatures. According to their study, when it comes to mitigating heat stress, tree-dominated greenspace is the most effective. Additionally, the evapotranspiration-based cooling effect of both green and blue space is most significant for conditions pertaining to the urban canopy layer. In order to address difficulties, Guo, Wu, and Chen [91] conducted a comparative study between four highly urbanized Chinese cities that were comparable in terms of geography, but differed in terms of urban planning and ecological surroundings. The premise of this study was that complicated mechanisms exist between LST and spatial patterns of greenspace and that these links can be inferred by determining the relative contributions of landscape metrics related to greenspace under various conditions. By combining stepwise regression with hierarchical partitioning, they created a novel method to examine the regional differences in greenspace contributions to urban heat reduction.

He [92] examined the relationships between building and urban heat fluxes, the parameters that could influence the application of UHI mitigation approaches on building components, and the boundaries of the green building-based UHI mitigation system. Some of the aspects of UHIs that influenced the benefits of green building, as well as the theory behind heat mitigation are examined in more detail, along with the potentials for setting up the green building-based UHI mitigation system. All things considered, this research provided a theoretical and practical basis for the creation of a green building-based UHI mitigation system, which is a noteworthy response from the building industry to rising temperatures.

Semenzato and Bortolini [93] examined the model's applicability and created a technique that would yield temperature predictions that could be evaluated against the real temperature, in order to confirm the model's accuracy. The sole application of this model in Europe, at the moment, exists in the Po Valley climate area, where numerous cities are severely impacted by the UHI phenomena and its associated pollution. In addition, this study used locally obtained datasets, as opposed to conventional satellite-derived land cover data, and applied the model at a finer resolution than previous investigations.

In order to identify the most efficient method for preserving urban energy, Zheng et al. [94] examined the relation between UHI mitigation strategies and urban energy consumption.

Based on the theory of grey-box models and an urban energy consumption modeling tool, an inventive and thorough workflow is suggested. The procedure takes into account the mutual influences of urban energy consumption and UHIs by merging city object information with created urban microclimates. Nuruzzaman [20] made an attempt to evaluate several approaches to combat the impact of UHIs; the mechanisms by which these tactics work are depicted with diagrams. The potential UHI mitigation measures discussed in this research included the use of high albedo materials and pavements, as well as pervious pavements; green vegetation; GRs; shade trees; urban design; and the presence of water bodies in city areas.

2.2. Multi-Criteria Decision-Making and Fuzzy Theory Application in UHI Management

Using a mixed-method research approach, Sangkakool et al. [95] determined and measured the primary elements influencing the adoption of GRs. A qualitative content analysis was used to identify the important variables; internal/external and positive/negative elements were included in the structure; and an Analytical Hierarchy Process, based on expert judgments, was used to quantitatively assess the components. Three primary factors impacting Thailand's potential for GR dissemination are identified using the analysis. In their study, Qi, Ding, and Ling [96] suggested a framework for decision-making to aid in the choice of urban heat mitigation techniques. The study's particular objectives were to provide a tool that can adapt appropriate mitigation techniques to urban situations and to determine the best combination of urban heat mitigation techniques for a given urban context. Sangiorgio, Bruno, and Fiorito [97] used the current multi-criteria index-based approach to offer various strategies to reduce the UHI issue in Bari, Puglia, Italy's core district. First, the UHII index is used to create an intensity map of Bari's 17 urban areas. Second, for a total of 344 examined urban areas, the results are contrasted with those of five other significant European cities. The suggested method needed to gather a lot of data in order to create the database and generate the index. Temizkan, Merve, and Kayili [98] proposed a top cover for mitigating the UHI effect in KBU Social Life Center square, as well as to enable the collection of rainwater in the campus' vast area. An MCDM method, PROMETHEE, was used to determine the optimum cover material. The most acceptable material to be utilized for the recommended top cover is a polycarbonate panel, which was selected due to its cost, roof efficiency, and albedo coefficient properties. In Qureshi and Rachid's study [99], the application of several MCDM strategies was used to determine an intervention to mitigate outdoor urban heat stress. A total of eight established and traditional methods were calculated to assess the order of importance of the interventions. Teixeira and Amorim [100] used a multi-criteria model utilizing multiple linear regression to integrate primary air temperature data with spatial information, such as land use and terrain, in order to study AUHIs. The model studied in the Brazilian city of Presidente Prudente demonstrates that vegetation lowers atmospheric temperatures and it emphasizes that urban surface materials serve as the primary sources of energy, influencing heat transfer to the atmosphere.

In a study by Turhan et al. [101], the authors provided an integrated framework for decision-making that will assist in the reduction in the influence of UHIs on residential buildings' energy efficiency. The model combines an MCDM model with simulations of building energy performance and urban microclimates. Real-time measurement data from one of the Urban GreenUP project's case study areas in Izmir, Turkey, are used in the research.

Tabatabaee et al. [102] proposed a framework for evaluating the key benefits, opportunities, costs, and risks of GR installation and the mutual dependence between these factors. The Enhanced Fuzzy Delphi Method is employed in the first section of the methodology to identify the specified key parameters unique to the Malaysian region. These are first determined using the literature review and subsequently by interviewing experts. The fuzzy-DEMATEL method is used in the second part of the model to determine the inner dependencies among the key parameters that were previously determined. In their study,

Sturiale and Scuderi [103] developed a methodological framework to assess residents' social perceptions of urban green spaces. The suggested method is designed to help the city's government to implement a new, strong urban development by utilizing an integrated approach between participatory planning and social multi-criteria evaluation methodologies, in the context of Catania's "urban green system". Rosasco and Perini [104] compared a traditional solution with a greening system, in order to study the factors influencing designers in their choice of building roof systems. The study's conclusions determine their importance and the part that each factor had in the decision-making process using an MCA based on sustainability. Since plants naturally purify the air and trap carbon, a widespread installation of GRs in metropolitan areas offers the chance to enhance air quality [105]. It was possible to address other environmental problems that are specific to urban regions, like mitigating the UHI effect [106], which are indicative of higher temperatures in the cities than in the nearby rural areas.

The land suitability evaluation of the urban greenbelt and the estimation of the environmental appropriateness and change indicators, with relation to the current and future urban sprawl, were the primary research goals in the study by Rabbani, Madanian, and Daneshvar [107]. When evaluating land suitability, multiple criteria were applied in order to determine the geographical priority and appropriateness for a certain subject in a specific location. Ten essential factors were selected as raster data layers and were then combined to create a land suitability map that could be used to assess potential greenbelt sites. The agglomeration of UHIs was taken into account in this study, as a direct result of urbanization on the local climate and environment.

In order to determine what causes UHIs, Mushtaha et al. [108] divided the factors into the following three categories: the general urban surroundings, specific buildings around them, and the wider environment. This was carried out by reviewing prior research on the topic. In order to identify the most significant causes of UHIs, this study developed an approach using two research techniques, in an effort to corroborate earlier studies on the topic. The Analytical Hierarchy Process (AHP) was utilized in the first stage of the study to rank the UHI factors and, consequently, to determine the most significant factor of each category, based on the opinions of experts. This procedure was extended to examine the hierarchy of UHI components in an existing surrounding, which had most of the pertinent factors in its design and construction, during the study's second phase. Moradi et al. [109] presented a scenario-based spatial MCDM approach for assessing urban environment quality as the primary objective of their study. As proposed in the research, it was acceptable to use the suggested method to learn more about the detrimental effects of climate change on people's quality of life in marginalized communities, as well as the important role that climate-resilient urban design may play.

Green infrastructure is being expanded by cities in order to improve ecosystem services and resilience. Despite being praised for their versatility, green infrastructure projects are typically located to maximize a single benefit, such as a reduction in storm water, rather than a variety of other advantages. This is partly due to the dearth of city-scale, stakeholder-informed methods for methodically identifying ecosystem service tradeoffs, synergies, and "hotspots" related to the location of green infrastructure. In order to close this gap, Meerow and Newell [110] provided the Green Infrastructure Spatial Planning model, a multi-criteria, GIS-based strategy that incorporates the following six advantages: storm water management, air quality, green space, social vulnerability, UHI mitigation, and landscape connectedness.

The ability to meet the material and spiritual requirements of residents is referred to as quality in the urban setting. Urban planners and managers work to raise the living standard and life quality for residents by improving the urban environment. Therefore, Mahmoudzadeh et al. [111] used the spatial analysis of an MCDM method, CRITIC, to evaluate the quality of the urban environment. The Tabriz Metropolis Municipality's districts 2 and 4 were the sites of the study.

A new methodological framework for evaluating a building's capacity to withstand rising temperatures, taking into account the consequences on nearby metropolitan areas, was proposed by Lassandro and Turi [112]. They concentrated on the resilient retrofitting techniques required to develop buildings, based on three major macro-categories, as follows: mitigation ability, adaptability, and reliability. To deal with heat waves, a collection of indicators was established, in order to achieve a Response Index. The reference building and its surrounding area are used to test the method. Using an MCA based on the observed indicators, the final comparative analysis was conducted. The greenest solutions with the highest albedo were the most responsive ones. Furthermore, Kotharkar, Bagade, and Singh [113] investigated the main LCZs in Nagpur, India, which have a larger coverage area. To determine the criticality of the LCZs, they used The Order of Preference by Similarity to Ideal Solution (TOPSIS) method. Applying the ENVI met tool, they determined the key LCZs and assessed various measures, including greening and the use of reflective surfaces, such as cool pavement and CRs.

An example of a built-up area's development activity is that of Searang City, which has increased dramatically due to the city's rapid population growth. Due to the increased development, the occurrence of UHIs in Serang City is growing. Serang City is advised to continue developing, in the meantime, to create space for neighborhood events. In light of this, Januadi Putra et al. [114] offered a spatial analysis utilizing Spatial Multi-Criteria Evaluation to ascertain the development of built-up areas, based on the sustainability concept. The distribution of UHIs, the distance from the road, the distance from the river, the land use data, and the physiographic data were all analyzed using a specific weighting system to determine the built-up area's suitability.

Yan et al. [115] suggested an ecological environment assessment technique for remote sensing that relies on the projection pursuit model. First, remote sensing technology is used to gather a number of ecological parameters for the urban ecological environment. Then, the projection pursuit model, a practical multi-criteria evaluation technique, is used to assess the natural environment in its entirety. An analysis of Shanghai City's ecological environment changes over the last five years is conducted using the evaluation results. Teotónio et al. [116] adapted existing multi-criteria decision models for the setting of GR installations. The goal of the methodology they developed was to find a GR with an optimal cost–benefit ratio in accordance with the interests of investors; it was based on the Measuring Attractiveness by a Categorical-Based Evaluation Technique (MACBETH). The method was tested on an example in Lisbon for choosing among six types of GRs on a parking lot and the intensive GR turned out to be the best.

A new index has been proposed by Sangiorgio et al. [117] to measure the hazard of the absolute maximum intensity of UHIs in urban districts during the summer, by accounting for all the factors influencing the phenomenon. The methodology allows for the holistic assessment of UHIs. The suggested index was established by analyzing the parameters using the AHP method, a comprehensive data acquisition process that includes state-of-the-art techniques, optimization procedures for index calibration, and two validation tests involving a Jackknife resampling procedure.

A technique for mapping the UHIs, based on regional climate zones, has also been proposed by Phillips et al. [118]. The approach uses vector data, which is more time-consuming and requires a lot of data, but it produces better results than raster classification. The following two additional criteria were added to the classification in order to improve it: the compactness index and the vegetation parameter. LCZ polygons were digitized from cadastral data and their classification was carried out using a trapezoidal fuzzy logic model, which was determined using a decision tree.

Mostafa et al. [119] studied the urbanization trend, the changes in land use and cover that go along with it, and how these changes affected the LST and the UHI effect in Gharbia City, Egypt. In order to do this, they tracked the dynamics of LULC change using multi-temporal Landsat images from 1991 to 2018; then, they used the CA–Markov chain and the FAHP–CA–Markov chain to predict the LULC change. While both approaches yield good results, the integration of the FAHP and CA–Markov chains improves the prediction and identifies high-urbanization potential locations.

2.3. Decision Support System and Fuzzy Logic in UHIs

A few studies gave contributions to UHI mitigation and optimization using DSSs. Mostofi et al. [120] presented a spatial DSS in Tehran, Iran, to examine the influence of the type of roof covering on SUHI values and their variation, at the neighborhood scale. Another DSS is developed by Bathaei [121] and its purpose was to help the decision maker choose the most suitable method to mitigate UHIs, based on resiliency and sustainability concerns. The best mitigation strategy was chosen using the Weighted Scoring method (WSM). The proposed DSS has a Graphical User Interface and it was validated on a hypothetical example. Kazak, J. [25] proposed the use of a DSS to assess urban areas for potential exposure to the UHI effect. In the research by Metronamica [122], a spatial DSS, based on cellular automata, was used to analyze three different scenarios of possible future land use changes in the Wrocław Larger Urban Zone (Poland). Scenarios were created with regard to different spatial planning documents—local policy, regional policy, and national policy. The analysis showed that more scattered, smaller urban development cores are more favorable in relation to UHIs, while large urban clusters have a greater exposure to UHIs. Tuczek et al. [123] developed a DSS for mitigating the UHI effect; it was intended for city planners and policymakers, in order to support the planning process. This optimization tool helps to achieve balance between economy and ecology, by maximizing revenue from selling lands, while keeping the UHI intensity within appropriate limits.

Qureshi and Rachid [124] contributed to the UHI problem by reviewing the decision support toolss used for UHI mitigation and identifying their most important key factors. They reviewed existing spatial and non-spatial decision support toolss and analyzed, categorized, and ranked these tools, as well as their advantages and disadvantages, to help decision-makers in selecting heat resilience measures from the design phase to the heat mitigation phase. Mahdiyar et al. [125] developed a DSS for determining the best form of GR for residential buildings in Kuala Lumpur, enabling decision-makers to select the best alternative, by taking into account all significant financial and non-financial decision elements. The criteria were identified in two rounds using the Enhanced Fuzzy Delphi method (EFDM).

Further studies developed approaches based on decision-making or decision trees, for managing UHIs. A web application named "Right place, right tree—Boston" was created by Werbin et al. [62] to aid in decision-making when planting new trees in an effort to lower UHIs. To assist in identifying priority areas, the Boston Heat Vulnerability Index was created. Authors stated that HVIs are rarely used in decision-making and, according to them, the main reason for this is that a unique index should be created for that region, rather than using one that was created for a larger area, because of the inconsistent results. Acosta et al. [63] have developed an easy-to-use methodology for street-level UHI modeling to help governments and urban planners, taking UHIs into account when creating plans. In order to determine which features would be included in the model, supervised methods of decision trees and random forests were used to evaluate the significance or influence of particular features on UHIs. Qi et al. [64] proposed a five-step methodology to help in the decision-making process when choosing a combination of UHI mitigation strategies for a particular urban context.

3. Materials and Methods

The research methodology used is based on the methods of [126,127]. The selection of keywords and their analysis, which has not previously been conducted in this manner, represents the research's innovation and contribution. To the best of the authors' knowledge, there has not been a thorough literature review and bibliometric analysis of how multi-criteria analysis and decision support systems are used to address urban heat islands in this manner, particularly when it comes to fuzzy theory, which has not been covered by many authors in this field. This kind of study has shown that there is interest in using these techniques, but it also leaves room for more research, particularly in the area of applying fuzzy theory or creating fuzzy DSSs for UHI mitigation.

According to [126], the standard workflow of scientific in-depth research consists of the following five stages: study design, data collection, data analysis, data visualization, and interpretation. The process of study design involves formulating research questions and selecting bibliometric techniques to address them. Selecting the database for a search, filtering the results, and exporting the information are all included in the data collection phase. Data analysis refers to the selection of software and the analysis of the collected data itself, while data visualization refers to choosing the preferred visualization methods and selecting the appropriate software. The description and interpretation of the results are both included in the last phase.

The workflow of this study is presented in Figure 1. The study design can be found in the chapter entitled Research focus, while data collection, analysis, visualization, and interpretation are described in detail below.

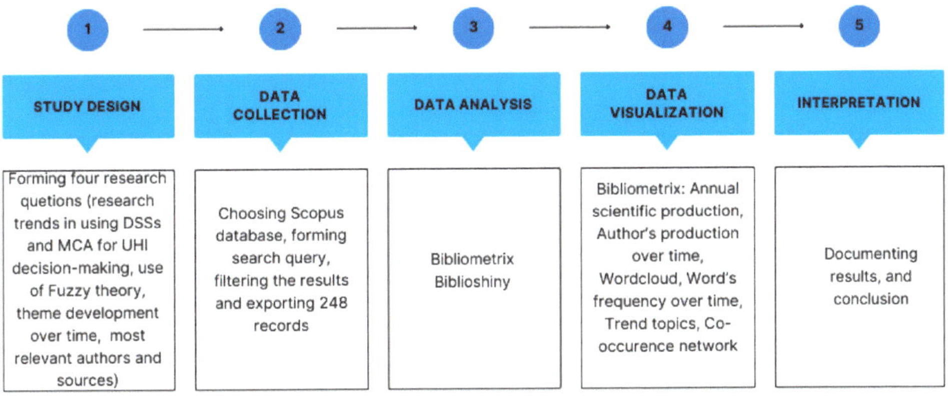

Figure 1. Workflow of bibliometric analysis on Fuzzy Decision Support and Multi-Criteria Analysis in UHI management.

After the research questions were formed, the data collection phase began with a keyword search in several bibliographic databases—Scopus, WoS, and IEEE explore. Using the same search criteria, the largest number of documents was found in the Scopus database. As many relevant papers contained in the other two databases were also found in this one, the research continued with a further and more detailed search exclusively of the Scopus database (https://www.scopus.com/ (accessed on 10 November 2023)). According to the Scopus Fact Sheet from 2022 [128], it contains 84+ million records, which date from as far back as 1788, from 7+ thousand publishers. Publications in Scopus are divided into the following four major subject areas: life sciences (15%), physical sciences (27%), health sciences (23%), and social sciences (35%) [128].

The final search query resulted in 248 records and was performed in November 2023; therefore, the analysis includes documents that were available at that time. The initial search began with the use of different keywords and their combinations within "All fields". However, such a research query resulted in a large number of articles that are not thematically related to the search topic and are not usable for analysis. Since these papers dealt with entirely different topics and would have only mentioned one of the search terms somewhere in the text or references, the search has been reduced to the fields "Article title, Abstract, Keywords." A similar methodology can be found in papers [129,130]. The search conducted within fields "Article title, Abstract, Keywords" consisted of several keyword combinations ("urban heat island" AND "decision support system", "urban heat island" AND "multi-criteria decision making", "urban heat island" AND "multi-criteria analysis", "urban heat island" AND "decision making"), which were interconnected with the operator OR. The above expression yielded 271 records, which were further reduced by excluding reviews (18) and conference reviews (2), as well as limiting the language to English (which excluded 4 documents), so that the final number of analyzed records was 248. The timespan was not limited, given that the development of the topic is being analyzed.

To conduct a parallel analysis of the papers that contain fuzzy theory, additional filtering was tried on the found documents to separate them. The search query only yielded four papers when the keywords "fuzzy" or "fuzzy theory" were added. As a result, a separate bibliometric analysis was not conducted for this small sample of papers, but they were included in the 248 papers that were mentioned. The details of the papers found on "fuzzy theory" are contained in Table 2.

Table 2. Research results on fuzzy theory search query.

Authors	Title	Year	Source Title	Cited by	Author's Keywords	Ref.
Lissner T.K.; Holsten A.; Walther C.; Kropp J.P.	Towards sectoral and standardised vulnerability assessments: The example of heatwave impacts on human health	2012	Climatic Change	33	/	[131]
Borri D.; Camarda D.; Pluchinotta I.	Planning urban microclimate through multiagent modelling: A cognitive mapping approach	2013	Lecture Notes in Computer Science	11	Behavioural knowledge; Decision support system; Fuzzy cognitive mapping; Multiple agents; Urban microclimate planning	[132]
Tabatabaee S.; Mahdiyar A.; Durdyev S.; Mohandes S.R.; Ismail S.	An assessment model of benefits, opportunities, costs, and risks of green roof installation: A multi criteria decision making approach	2019	Journal of Cleaner Production	55	Cleaner production; Fuzzy DEMATEL; Green roof; Multi criteria decision making (MCDM); Sustainability	[102]
Mostafa E.; Li X.; Sadek M.	Urbanization Trends Analysis Using Hybrid Modeling of Fuzzy Analytical Hierarchical Process-Cellular Automata-Markov Chain and Investigating Its Impact on Land Surface Temperature over Gharbia City, Egypt	2023	Remote Sensing	8	CA-Markov chain; fuzzy AHP; Gharbia governorate; hybrid models; LULCC dynamics; UHI	[119]

The data on the selected records were exported in csv format, in order to perform a bibliometric analysis. Bibliometric analysis is a favored and thorough method for analyzing scientific data, the popularity of which has recently grown, due to the development and availability of scientific databases (such as Scopus and Web of science) and tools for conducting the analysis itself (such as VOSviewer, Bilbiometrix, and Gephi). Bibliometrics uses large volumes of scientific data and provides insight into the global research trends in a particular field [133,134]. The review process is based on the statistical measurement of science and it is transparent and reproducible; hence, it offers more objective and reliable analyses than other literature review methods [127,135–137].

In the next step, the exported data were loaded into the bibliometrics tool. This study used the open-source bibliometrix R-package (R 4.3.2) to conduct bibliometric analysis. bibliometrix is a unique tool for quantitative research in scientometrics and bibliometrics, which provides all the instruments necessary to pursue a complete bibliometric analysis; its web application—biblioshiny—is easy to use for those with no coding skills [138].

4. Results

4.1. Descriptive Analysis

The main information regarding the collection process is presented in Table 3. The described search strategy resulted in 248 documents from 144 sources. The oldest record dates from 1996 (Table 3, Figure 2) and, as previously mentioned, the time period was not limited when filtering the documents. It can be noted that the time span is from 1996 to 2024. The papers that were accessible as of 15 November 2023, were examined; however, one of them was located in a journal volume from 2024. Since that paper was already available in November, when it was included in the analyses, the authors did not want to exclude it.

Table 3. Main information about the 248 publications collected from the Scopus database.

Description	Results
MAIN INFORMATION ABOUT DATA	
Timespan	1996:2024
Sources (Journals, Books, etc.)	144
Documents	248
Document Average Age	4.4
Average citations per doc	21.88
References	12,584
DOCUMENT CONTENTS	
Keywords Plus (ID)	1797
Author's Keywords (DE)	797
AUTHORS	
Authors	902
Authors of single-authored docs	17
AUTHORS COLLABORATION	
Single-authored docs	18
Co-Authors per Doc	4.03
International co-authorships %	25
DOCUMENT TYPES	
Article	183
Book	1
Book chapter	17
Conference paper	47

The majority of the documents were articles (183), followed by conference papers (47) and books (17), while there was only one book among the records. The average number of citations per document was 21.88 and the total number of cited documents was 12,584. There were only 18 single-authored documents, while the average number of co-authors per document was 4.03.

Figure 2 shows the Annual Scientific production of papers related to the use of MCA and DSSs in UHI management. The horizontal axis represents years, while the vertical axis represents the number of publications.

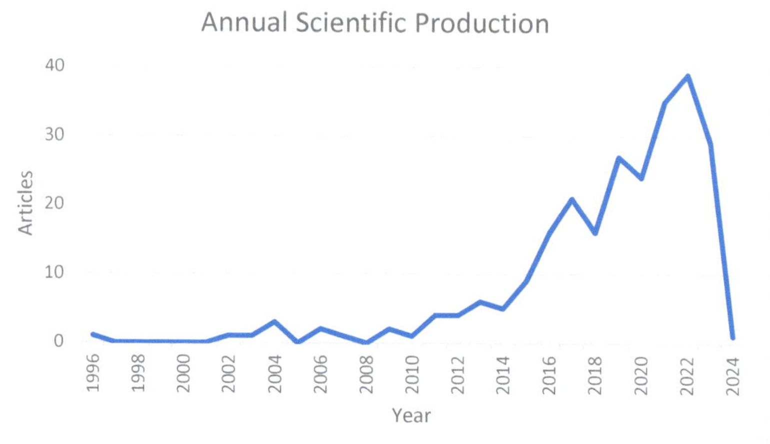

Figure 2. Annual scientific production on DSSs and MCA in UHI management. The figure was created according to bibliometrix data.

4.2. Sources and Authors Analysis

The most relevant sources, according to the number of published records, were Science of the Total Environment and Sustainable Cities and Society, with 11 published articles. The list of the first ten sources, according to the number of published records, arranged in descending order, is shown in Table 4.

Table 4. Most relevant sources according to the number of published records.

Sources	Articles
Science of the Total Environment	11
Sustainable Cities and Society	11
Sustainability (Switzerland)	9
Remote Sensing	8
Urban Climate	8
Urban Forestry and Urban Greening	7
Energy and Buildings	6
International Archives of the Photogrammetry, Remote Sensing and Spatial Information Sciences—Isprs Archives	6
Building and Environment	5
Journal of Cleaner Production	5

Table 5 shows the 10 most local cited sources, arranged in descending order. As expected, among the 10 most cited sources, there are also a good number of sources from the list of those with the most published records. The most cited journal is Remote sensing applications: society and environment, with 207 local citations, followed by Building and environment, with 186 citations and Energy and buildings, with 129 citations.

Table 6 presents statistics about the 20 most relevant authors, according to the total number of citations, sorted in descending order. The most cited author was Chen L., with 405 citations and 4 publications, followed by Zhang H., with 306 citations and 6 published documents and Sun R., with 271 citations and 2 publications. After them, there were several authors with 263 citations and 1 publication. According to [14], the H-index, or Hirsch index, is the number of articles (H) published by an author, each of which has been cited in other publications at least h times. The M-index is obtained when the h-index is divided by the number of years since the author published the first paper (n). The G-index provides an assessment of the global citation of a set of articles, giving more weight to highly cited articles. This is obtained by ranking the articles in descending order, with regard to the number of citations; then, the g-index represents the largest number, so that the first g articles received (together) at least g2 citations [139].

Table 5. Most local cited sources, according to the number of local citations.

Sources	Number of Local Citations
Remote Sensing Applications: Society and Environment	207
Building and Environment	186
Energy and Buildings	177
Landscape and Urban Planning	129
Remote Sensing	117
Science of the Total Environment	115
Energy and Buildings	109
Remote Sensing of Environment	106
Landscape and Urban Planning	104
Sustainable Cities and Society	100

Table 6. Most relevant authors, sorted by total number of citations.

Author	h-Index	g-Index	m-Index	Total Citations	Number of Publications	First Publication Year
Chen, L.	4	4	0.308	405	4	2011
Zhang, H.	5	6	0.455	306	6	2013
Sun, R.	2	2	0.167	271	2	2012
Cai, Y-B	1	1	0.091	263	1	2013
Chen, M-N	1	1	0.091	263	1	2013
Ma, W-C	1	1	0.091	263	1	2013
Qi, Z-F	1	1	0.091	263	1	2013
Ye, X-Y	1	1	0.091	263	1	2013
Maderspacher, J.	1	1	0.125	231	1	2016
Pauleit, S.	1	1	0.125	231	1	2016
Wamsler, C.	1	1	0.125	231	1	2016
Zölch, T.	1	1	0.125	231	1	2016
Yu, Z.	3	3	0.6	187	3	2019
Corburn, J.	1	1	0.067	184	1	2009
Wang, X.	2	2	0.4	169	2	2019
Qi, J.	2	2	0.286	162	2	2017
Vejre, H.	2	2	0.4	154	2	2019
Yang, G.	2	2	0.4	154	2	2019
Ben-Dor, E.	1	1	0.05	140	1	2004
Chudnovsky, A.	1	1	0.05	140	1	2004

Chen L. and Zhang H. are perhaps some of the most sonorous names in the searched area, since they were also among the 10 most productive authors (Figure 3). Moreover, Zhang H. was the most productive author and, from Figure 3, it can be seen that he has been dealing with this topic for a long time, with his first publication dating from 2013. Figure 3 shows the authors' production over time for the first 10 authors, by the number of their published articles. The line represents author's timeline, the size of the circle corresponds to the number of published papers, and the level of transparency indicates the number of total citations per year. Chen L. is also among the authors who have been publishing in this field for a long time, with their first publication hailing from the year 2011 and the last hailing from the year 2020; Li X. is also among these authors, with their first publication originating from 2014 and their last publication dating from 2023.

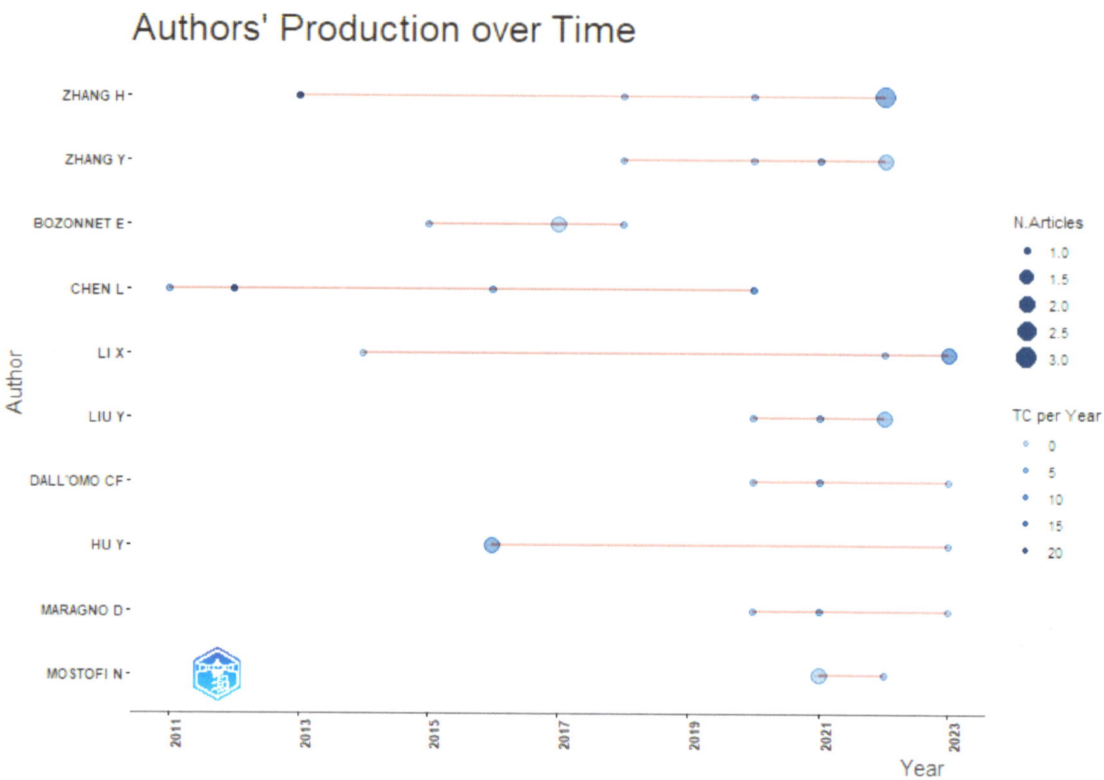

Figure 3. Authors' production over time of the first ten authors, according to their productivity. The figure was created using the bibliometrix R-package [127,138].

4.3. Topic Development Analysis

There was a total of 797 author's keywords among the collection of records (Table 3). Figure 4 presents a word cloud of the 50 most frequent keywords, where the words that appear more often are more prominent, displayed in a larger font size, while words that appear less frequently are shown in a smaller font size. When creating the world cloud, the keywords "urban heat island", "UHI", and similar were excluded, since they dominate the appearance and, considering that the entire research revolves around UHIs, it is not necessary to show them in order to see trends in the research papers.

Figure 5 presents words' frequency over time for the 10 most common keywords, plus words according to their cumulative occurrences. Similar to creating a word cloud, when creating this graph, the words "urban heat island", "urban heat islands", "urban heat island (UHI)", "UHI", "heat island", and "China" were excluded from the set of words. It is interesting to note that the term "decision making" recorded the greatest growth.

Figure 6 shows the development of the researched topic in the last 10 years, with regard to the keywords that appear most often in the titles of papers. When creating the graph, trivial words such as "research" and "study", as well as geographical names such as "China", "Germany", "Arizona", and "Hong Kong", were excluded. The line presents the timeline of the appearance of each word, while the circle size presents the term frequency.

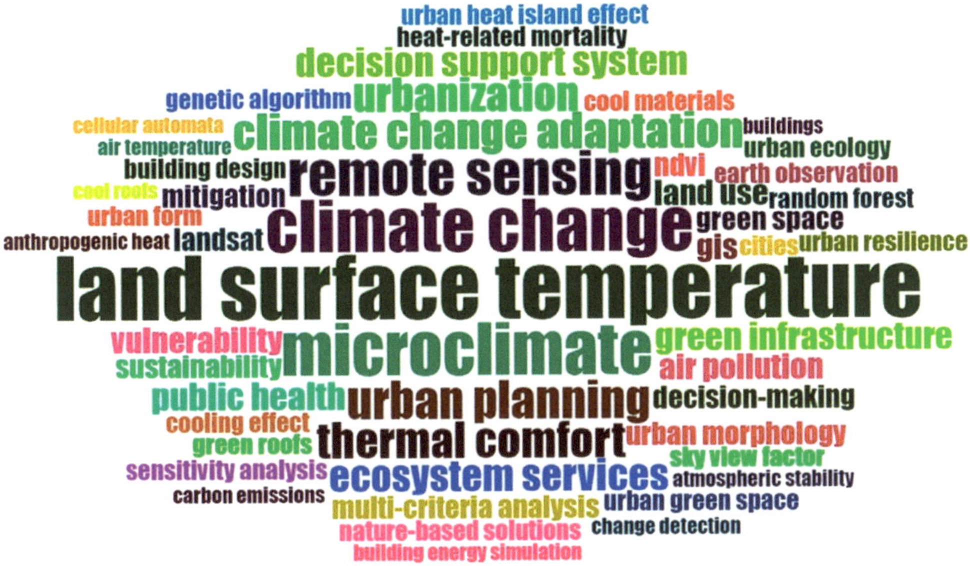

Figure 4. Word cloud of the 50 most frequent keywords on DSSs and MCA in UHI management. The figure was created using the bibliometrix R-package [127,138].

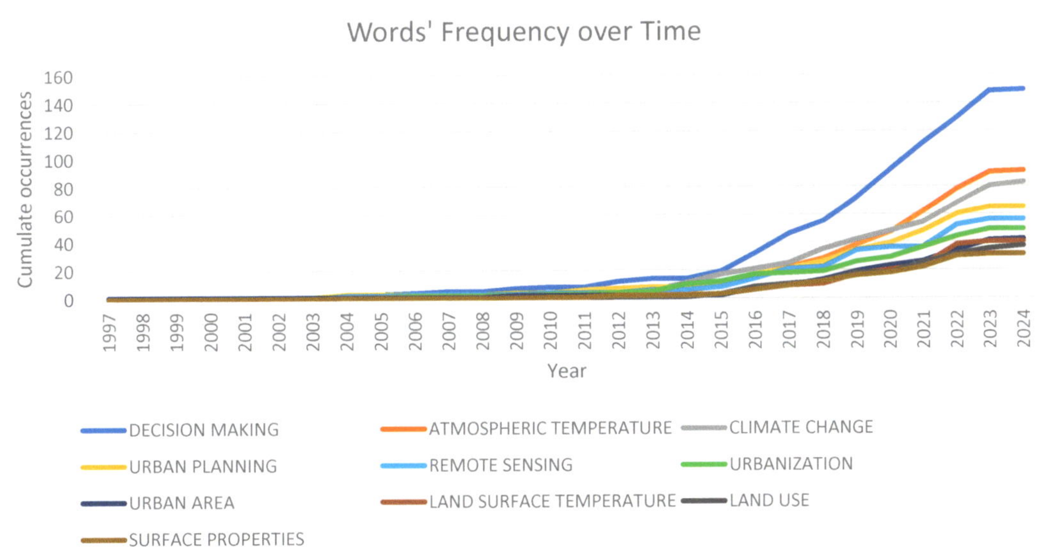

Figure 5. Words' frequency over time for the 10 most common keywords. The figure was created according to bibliometrix data.

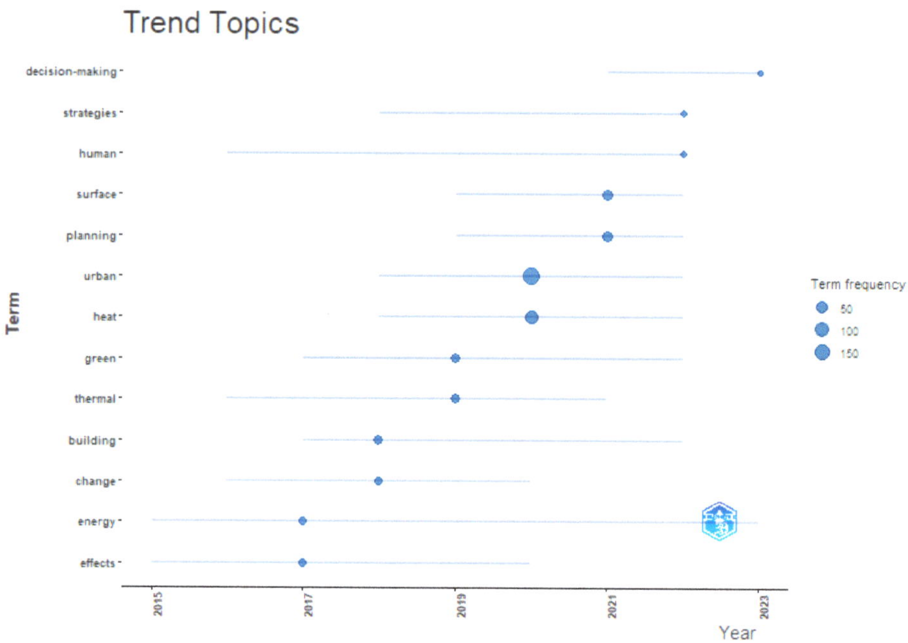

Figure 6. Trend topics in the last 10 years, with regard to the keywords that appear most often in the titles of papers. The figure was created using the bibliometrix R-package [127,138].

Figure 7 shows the co-occurrence network of the 50 most common keywords; the nodes represent the keywords, and their size is proportional to the number of occurrences of that word. The lines connecting the nodes show the co-occurrence of words, while the thickness of the line suggests the occurrence of that co-occurrence. Thus, it can be seen that the terms "urban heat island", "decision making", and "atmospheric temperature", with the highest mutual co-occurrence, are particularly prominent. It can also be noticed that there are three thematic clusters that are shown in different colors and that these three terms are in the same cluster.

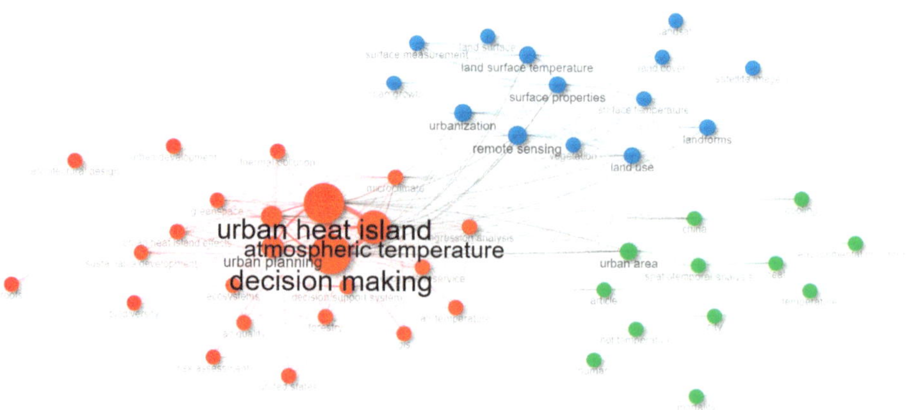

Figure 7. Co-occurrence network of the 50 most common keywords on DSSs and MCA in UHI management. The figure was created using the bibliometrix R-package [127,138].

5. Discussion

The literature is thoroughly reviewed in Chapter 2, with a summary available in Table A1, in Appendix A. To systematically represent the reviewed literature, Table 1 includes information on authors, titles, year of publication, study location, methodology, and main findings. Three subchapters make up Chapter 2, as follows: the first reviews the use of remote sensing in UHI management; the second reviews multi-criteria decision-making and the application of fuzzy theory in UHI mitigation; and the third reviews Decision Support Systems and fuzzy logic in UHIs. Since remote sensing is the fundamental technique for identifying and analyzing AUHIs, the chapter on this subject has the highest number of cited articles. Among the literature, there are several articles that provide an overview of the literature related to the emergence of UHIs [65,67] or the UHI mitigation method [20], but the authors did not find an overview and analysis such as this one. From the analysis of UHI mitigation techniques, it can be concluded that the best results are obtained when vegetation is applied [101]. While some research has focused on specific UHI mitigation strategies, like green roofs [86,88], only a few studies have combined multiple strategies to obtain the best possible solution, because doing so might be complex and it is a field that requires further investigation.

The bibliometric analysis aimed to answer research questions related to the use of MCA methods, DSSs, and fuzzy theory in UHI management. Initially, it was intended that two parallel bibliometric analyses would be conducted, but only four papers were found for the second analysis, related to fuzzy theory, and, as a result, a unified bibliometric analysis was performed. Since each of these four papers was written by a different author and was published in a different journal, it is impossible to identify the author or journal that prevails. After the first two papers were published in 2012 and 2013, there was a big time gap, but it seems that fuzzy theory still finds its application in dealing with UHIs, since two more recent papers were published in 2019 and 2023. This sequence is very interesting; it shows that there are strongholds and also opens up a lot of space for future research.

An analysis of the papers retrieved from the Scopus database revealed that the use of these methods began relatively late, only in 1996; however, the annual scientific production on the use of MCA methods and DSSs for dealing with the UHI effect grows over time (Figure 2). As it can be seen from Figure 2, the number of published documents in the first few years varied around zero or slightly above zero, while, from 2011, it started to grow exponentially. The peak occurred in 2022, when a total of 39 documents were published. There is a decrease in 2023, as compared to 2022, but this may be because some of the 2023 papers were not available when the study was conducted. Given that the year 2023 was not yet over at the time of data collection, it remains to be seen whether the number of records will exceed 2022 or not, since the positive growth trend shows that more and more researchers are dealing with this topic.

Table 3 shows that the average age of the documents is 4.4 years, indicating how current the topic is. Moreover, it is evident from the graph displaying the words' frequency over time (Figure 5), which displays the ten most common keywords, that the term "decision making" has grown the most over the past ten years. The co-occurrence network (Figure 7) shows that the terms "urban heat island", "decision making", and "atmospheric temperature" have the highest mutual co-occurrence. Among all the pictures and graphs that deal with the most common concepts, there is no fuzzy theory, which is expected, considering the number of papers.

With 11 published articles, "Science of the Total Environment" and "Sustainable Cities and Society" are the sources with the most published works (Table 4), while "Remote Sensing Applications: Society and Environment" and "Building and Environment" are the sources with the most local citations (Table 5). As might be expected given the topic, the majority of the articles were published in journals that dealt with environmental issues and sustainability.

"Remote Sensing Applications: Society and Environment" is the journal with the highest number of local citations, totaling 207. It is interesting to note that this journal, even as the most cited one, is not at all on the list of sources with the most published papers. This fact might suggest that the few articles published in this journal are highly relevant and have received numerous citations. This could be the case due to the tight connection between remote sensing and UHI management. Remote sensing not only makes it possible to identify and track SUHIs spatially, but it also offers additional environmental and spatial analysis, which makes comprehensive UHI management easier. Spatial analysis and data visualization are made possible by the use of GIS tools in the processing of satellite images. According to [31], the potential drawback of remote sensing could be its temporal resolution; however, its primary benefit lies in the more effortless and cost-effective acquisition of data, in comparison to the field measurements.

Chen L. and Zhang H. are deemed to be the most relevant authors, since they occupy the first two places as authors with the most citations (in that order) (Table 6) and they are also highly positioned in terms of their productivity. Moreover, Zhang H. is the most productive author (Figure 3).

6. Conclusions

This review paper provides an overview of the use of MCA methods and decision support systems when dealing with the UHI phenomenon, with special reference to the use of fuzzy theory. An extensive review of the literature, produced by research on UHI mitigation techniques, demonstrates that the methods listed above contribute to solving the problem and also prompted the writing of this paper. It was noted during that part of the study that MCA techniques and decision support systems have become more common in this field in recent years. In addition to confirming that the topic is up-to-date and that annual production is growing, the bibliometric analysis also revealed research trends in the area, as well as the most relevant authors and sources. However, it also revealed that the topic is not as well researched as it could be.

The contribution and innovation of this research is found in the analysis and detailed review of the literature on the use of MCA, DSSs, and fuzzy logic in UHI management, which has not been conducted in this way until now.

It is important to point out some limitations of this research. The research represents the static state of the literature and research at the time of writing the paper; but, as time goes on, there will certainly be some new knowledge and ways of using the discussed methods. Also, only records from the Scopus database were used in this bibliometric analysis. As a proposal for future research, records from several scientific databases should be integrated and analyzed.

This study demonstrated that the topic is current and evolving over time. Figure 4 shows that "urban planning" and "climate change adaptation" appear among the most frequent keywords, which shows that this problem is starting to be included in plans and strategies. The use of MCA methods and DSSs in UHI mitigation helps to take into account all factors, in order to achieve environmental sustainability goals. Only a few papers using fuzzy theory were found and the authors see this as an opportunity for improvement and for further research. Upon reviewing the literature, numerous works were discovered that address a specific measure or aspect of UHI mitigation, such as the application of green roofs and the selection of the most suitable one. A few studies have attempted to address this phenomenon by including more measures and combining them, as it is not an easy task. There were a few publications on fuzzy methodology and DSSs, but none on fuzzy DSS development. Given the complexity of the factors that influence the formation of UHIs, as well as the fact that there is no unified solution to this problem, other than the fact that mitigation techniques need to be combined, future research could go in the direction of forming a fuzzy DSS model and associated sub-models based on artificial intelligence and machine learning, in order to take all criteria into account and achieve improvement in UHI management. A city experiencing the UHI problem should be used to test such a model, and possible solutions could be compared to those used in other cities, similar as in [97].

Author Contributions: Conceptualization, M.Ć., K.R., J.K.P. and A.K.; methodology, M.Ć.; software, M.Ć.; validation, M.Ć.; formal analysis, M.Ć.; investigation, M.Ć.; resources, M.Ć.; data curation, M.Ć.; writing—original draft preparation, M.Ć.; writing—review and editing, M.Ć., K.R., J.K.P. and A.K.; visualization, M.Ć.; supervision, K.R., J.K.P. and A.K. All authors have read and agreed to the published version of the manuscript.

Funding: This research received no external funding.

Data Availability Statement: Not applicable.

Acknowledgments: This research is partially supported through the project KK.01.1.1.02.0027, a project co-financed by the Croatian Government and the European Union through the European. Regional Development Fund—the Competitiveness and Cohesion Operational Programme.

Conflicts of Interest: The authors declare no conflicts of interest.

Nomenclature

AHP	Analytical Hierarchy Process	MACBETH	Measuring Attractiveness by a Categorical-Based Evaluation Technique
AUHI	Atmospheric Urban Heat Island	MCA	Multi-criteria analysis
DSS	Decision support system	MCDM	Multi-criteria decision-making
EFDM	Enhanced Fuzzy Delphi method	SUHI	Surface Urban Heat Island
GIS	Geographic information system	TOPSIS	The Order of Preference by Similarity to Ideal Solution
GR	Green roof	UHI	Urban Heat Island
LCZ	Local Climate Zones	UHII	Urban Heat Island intensity
LST	Land Surface Temperature	WOS	Web of Science
LULC	Land use/Land cover	WSM	Weighted Scoring method

Appendix A

Table A1. Summary of the studies reviewed (full table).

Author(s)	Title	Year	Study Location	Methodology	Findings
Nuruzzaman, M. [20]	Urban heat island: causes, effects and mitigation measures-a review	2015	Not specified	Review of various measures to encounter UHI effect.	The most effective measures are green vegetation, high albedo materials, and pervious pavements.
Duplančić Leder, T. et al. [31]	Split Metropolitan area surface temperature assessment with remote sensing method	2016	Split, Croatia	Landsat thermal channels have been used to determine the LST.	Microclimate changes and severe changes in LST and UHI effects.
Amani-Beni, M. et al. [46]	Impact of urban park's tree, grass and waterbody on microclimate in hot summer days: A case study of Olympic Park in Beijing, China	2018	Beijing, China	Observation of the greenery impact on the park during summer days.	The park was 0.48–1.12 °C cooler during the day; increased air humidity was observed at 2.39–3.74%; a reduced human comfort index was used to generate a more comfortable thermal environment.
Nwakaire, C. M. et al. [61]	Urban Heat Island Studies with emphasis on urban pavements: A review	2020	Not specified	Literature review of UHIs, with emphasis on urban pavements.	One of the main findings included using creative designs that can provide cooling without compromising the structural integrity of the pavement, which is a key component of effective UHI mitigation techniques for highway pavements.
Kim, S. W. et al. [65]	Urban heat island (UHI) intensity and magnitude estimations: A systematic literature review	2021	Not specified	Literature review of 51 study dealing with UHI intensity and magnitude estimation.	The current UHI energy models for calculating UHIs must be updated to take into account the city's three-dimensional physical layout. The literature review demonstrates that UHI research requires the development of an optimal analysis method.
Almeida, C. R.d. et al. [66]	Study of the Urban Heat Island (UHI) Using Remote Sensing Data/Techniques: A Systematic Review	2021	Not specified	Literature review of publications in Scopus and Web of Science on UHI analysis using RS data/techniques and LST, from 2000 to 2020.	The Northern Hemisphere concentrates the majority of studied areas, particularly in Asia (69.94%), so Cfa climate areas are the most represented. Landsat products were most frequently used to estimate LST (68.39%) and LULC (55.96%); ArcGIS (30.74%) was the most frequently used software for data treatment; and correlation (38.69%) was the most frequently applied statistical technique.
Deilami, K. et al. [67]	Urban heat island effect: A systematic review of spatio-temporal factors, data, methods, and mitigation measures	2018	Not specified	Literature review of different spatial and temporal factors affecting the UHI effect.	Ordinary least square regression is the most widely used method (68%) to investigate the relationship between different spatio-temporal factors and the UHI effect, followed by comparative analysis (33%). The most common factors affecting the UHI effect, as reported in the reviewed studies, are vegetation cover (44%), season (33%), built-up area (28%), day/night (25%), population density (14%), and water body (12%), among others. In total, 54% of the studies used Landsat TM images for modeling the UHI effect, followed by Landsat ETM (34%) and MODIS (28%).

Table A1. *Cont.*

Author(s)	Title	Year	Study Location	Methodology	Findings
Nimac, I. et al. [68]	The contribution of urbanisation and climate conditions to increased urban heat load in Zagreb (Croatia) since the 1960s	2022	Zagreb, Croatia	Two land use/land cover (LULC) scenarios are examined, together with the appropriate climate conditions, using modeling techniques.	The findings show that, with an average increase in summer days of 35 days, climate change has a major impact on the change in total heat load (88%). Changes in LULC have less of an effect (12%), but they have a significant impact on the spatial variability of the heat load.
Chen, Y. et al. [60]	Numerical simulation of local climate zone cooling achieved through modification of trees, albedo and green roofs—a case study of Changsha	2020	Changsha, China	Through the integration of in situ measurements and ENVI-met numerical simulations, it constructed and modeled 39 scenarios and analyzed the cooling impacts of different cooling factor combinations.	The findings demonstrate that, in three LCZs, an increased albedo and more trees are more effective than green roofs at lowering summer potential temperatures at street level (2 m high); the effects of cooling factors differ depending on the LCZ class, with an increase of 60% in trees resulting in lower outdoor temperatures; the application of combined cooling methods can cause an increase in air temperature (up to 0.96 ○C).
Duplančić Leder, T. et al. [69]	Land Surface Temperature Determination in the Town of Mostar Area	2018	Mostar, Bosnia and Herce-govina	The atmospheric corrections and LST were calculated using accessible meteorological data and Landsat 5, 7, and 8 satellite images.	Mostar is a town where the maximum land surface temperatures can be expected, since it has LST values of more than 50 °C, which are documented in this study.
Duplančić Leder, T. and Bačić, S. [70]	The influence of local climate zones on the thermal characteristics of the city of Split	2021	Split, Croatia	Local climatic zoning (LCZ) and its occurrence with the zones of the highest urban temperatures are applied.	Water surfaces and greenery reduce the intensity of UHIs.
Estacio, I. et al. [71]	GIS-based mapping of local climate zones using fuzzy logic and cellular automata	2019	Quezon City, Philip-pines	Automated GIS-based methodology for determining LCZs and Landsat 8 were used. The membership percentage of 100 m cells to an LCZ type was determined using fuzzy logic. To extract the LCZ map from the fuzzy layers, cellular automata were used.	The findings indicate that five out of seven land cover LCZs and seven out of ten built-up LCZs were detected. Every LCZ type had temperatures that matched those reported in the literature, according to LST data obtained from Landsat 8.
Bokaie, M. et al. [72]	Hosseini, A. Assessment of urban heat island based on the relationship between land surface temperature and land use/land cover in Tehran	2016	Tehran, Iran	The relationship between LST and LULC was studied using Landsat TM satellite images. Vegetation and greenery in different areas were studied using the normalized vegetation index (NDVI), using remotely sensed data.	The findings demonstrated that the causal agent of the UHIs produced in Tehran is distinct. This discrepancy illustrates the strong correlation between land surface temperature and land cover and is mostly caused by the state of LULC in the area.

Table A1. *Cont.*

Author(s)	Title	Year	Study Location	Methodology	Findings
Jiménez-Muñoz, J. C. and Sobrino, J. A. [73]	A generalized single-channel method for retrieving land surface temperature from remote sensing data	2003	Not specified	A single-channel algorithm is developed that can be applied to different sensors onboard a satellite to estimate LST.	The thermal channels with effective wavelengths close to 11 µm yield the greatest findings; for AVHRR-4, ATSR2-11, and TM-6, root mean square deviation values of 1.6 K, 2 K, and 1.3 K have been found. For AVHRR-5 and ASTR2-12, thermal channels with an effective wavelength close to 12 µm yield an inferior performance, with root mean square deviation values greater than 2 K.
Feizizadeh, B. and Blaschke, T. [74]	Examining urban heat island relations to land use and air pollution: Multiple endmember spectral mixture analysis for thermal remote sensing	2013	Tabriz, Iran	Spectral Mixture Analysis and Endmember Remote Sensing Indices are combined to calculate LST, detect UHIs, and look into the connections between UHI, LULC, and air pollution.	The findings show that LULC has a significant impact on LST and that LST and LULC are intimately related to UHIs.
Zhu, W. et al. [75]	How to measure the urban park cooling island? A perspective of absolute and relative indicators using remote sensing and buffer analysis	2021	Jinan, China	The land cover of parks was determined using high-spatial-resolution GF-2 pictures, and the thermal environment was examined using buffer analysis on Landsat 8 TIR photos. To investigate the connections between the park cooling island and park attributes, linear statistical models were created.	The average park cooling area was roughly 120.68 ha and the average land surface temperature (LST) of urban parks was found to be around 3.6 °C lower than that of the study area. The biggest temperature differential, of 7.84 °C, occurred during summer daylight.
Firozjaei, M.K. et al. [76]	Land Surface Ecological Status Composition Index (LSESCI): A novel remote sensing-based technique for modeling land surface ecological status	2021	14 test sites	The Landsat multi-temporal imagery, National Land Cover Database (NLCD), and Imperviousness and High Resolution Layer Imperviousness (HRLI) datasets were used. Improved Ridd's conceptual Vegetation–Impervious–Soil triangle model was used. Combination of the Biophysical Composition Index (BCI) information and LST was applied.	Over the past 20 years, the mean values of the Remote Sensing-based Ecological Index (RSEI) and Land Surface Ecological Status Composition Index (LSESCI) have grown, which is indicative of the detrimental effects of Anthropogenic Destructive Activities (ADAs) on the ecosystem. Nevertheless, there was a considerable difference in the modeling findings of LSES derived from the RSEI and LSESCI. The LSESCI showed a stronger association with the moisture, dryness, heat, and greenness indices than with the RSEI.

Table A1. *Cont.*

Author(s)	Title	Year	Study Location	Methodology	Findings
Zhang, Z. et al. [77]	Evaluating Natural Ecological Land Change in Function-Oriented Planning Regions Using the National Land Use Survey Data from 2009 to 2018 in China	2021	China	Natural ecological land types were classified into forest, grassland, wetland, and bare land using land use data from the National Land Use Survey from 2009 to 2018. The changes in natural ecological land types in the major function-oriented zones between 2009 and 2018 were then discussed.	Between 2009 and 2018, there was a general downward tendency in the amount of natural ecological lands. However, this trend was reversed after 2015, when regulations for environmental conservation and ecological projects were put into place.
Zhang, T. et al. [78]	Assessing the Urban Eco-Environmental Quality by the Remote-Sensing Ecological Index: Application to Tianjin, North China	2021	Tianjin, China	Methodology for the new RSEI is proposed.	The case study's findings demonstrate that seasonal variability affects both the contributions of RSEI indicators to eco-environment quality and RSEI values. To account for this seasonal variability, differentiating the normalization of indicator measures and utilizing more representative remote-sensing images should be used.
Jiang, Y. and Lin, W. [79]	A Comparative Analysis of Retrieval Algorithms of Land Surface Temperature from Landsat-8 Data: A Case Study of Shanghai, China	2021	Shanghai, China	A variety of algorithms, including the Radiative Transfer Equation (RTE), Mono-Window Algorithm (MWA), Split-Window Algorithm (SWA), and Single-Channel Algorithm (SCA), have been developed for the purpose of extracting LST from satellite imagery.	The outcomes demonstrated that all four algorithms were capable of recovering LST with reasonable success and that the LST retrieval outcomes were largely constant throughout a given spatial scale. The SWA is better suited for recovering LST in Shanghai in the summer, when the city experiences extremely high humidity and temperatures.
Peng, T. et al. [80]	Temporal and Spatial Variation of Anthropogenic Heat in the Central Urban Area: A Case Study of Guangzhou, China	2021	Guangzhou, China	Using Landsat data and the surface energy balance equation, the urban anthropogenic heat flux (AHF) in the central Guangzhou urban area in 2004, 2009, 2014, and 2020 was retrieved. The temporal and spatial characteristics of various anthropogenic heat types were investigated by combining the transfer matrix and the migration of the gravity center.	The findings show that, while different types of anthropogenic heat had different characteristics in terms of area expansion and spatial changes, the overall change trend of anthropogenic heat in Guangzhou's central urban area was enhanced, with the degree of enhancement being related to the type of urban functional land.

Table A1. *Cont.*

Author(s)	Title	Year	Study Location	Methodology	Findings
You, M. et al. [81]	Quantitative analysis of a spatial distribution and driving factors of the urban heat island effect: a case study of Fuzhou central area, China	2021	Fuzhou, China	The application of Moran's I and hot-spot analysis helped to clarify the geographical pattern of UHI in the center area of Fuzhou, China.	According to the findings, the LST displayed a gradient layer structure with low temperatures in the northwest and high temperatures in the southeast that was significantly correlated with industrial zones. Moreover, soil moisture (impact = 0.792) > NDBI (influence = 0.732) > MNDWI (influence = 0.618) > NDVI (influence = 0.604) were the four parameters that had the biggest influence (q-Value) on LST.
Despini, F. et al. [82]	Urban surfaces analysis with remote sensing data for the evaluation of UHI mitigation scenarios	2021	Modena, Italy	The Worldview3 sensor (WV3) collected satellite photos, which were then processed to identify the various types of urban surfaces and to determine each surface's albedo value.	The five scenarios that comprised the mitigation interventions assumed the replacement or retrofitting of specific urban surfaces, such as parking lots, rooftops, and roadways, with materials that reflect solar radiation. From the standpoint of public administration, scenarios 4 and 5 were shown to be the most favorable, with advantages for the general welfare of the populace.
Santos, L. G. et al. [83]	Climate-informed decision-making for urban design: Assessing the impact of urban morphology on urban heat island	2021	Singapore	A novel framework for urban design that takes climate change into account is carried out. With the help of this framework, various options can be impartially examined, in order to assess various scenarios. It offers a foundation for doing so. The Data Processing Unit (DPU), the Climate Model, and the Analysis are the three primary components of the framework.	The outcome is a matrix of scores for each scenario that shows which design performs greatest on predetermined measures. The scenarios that include the tallest buildings (81 m) and either a medium (40%) or low (30%) density provide a good compromise between the external trade-offs associated with the environmental effect and the number of people assigned to each site area, as well as the energy costs associated with running the district.
Amani-Beni, M. et al. [84]	Impacts of urban green landscape patterns on land surface temperature: Evidence from the adjacent area of Olympic Forest Park of Beijing, China	2019	Beijing, China	This study investigates the connection between the surrounding areas' cooling effect and urban greening trends.	According to the findings, waterbodies and forests might decrease temperatures by 12.82% and 6.51%, respectively, below those of the impermeable surface.
Pritipadmaja, Garg, R. D. and Sharma, A. K. [85]	Assessing the cooling effect of blue-green spaces: implications for Urban Heat Island mitigation	2023	Bhubaneswar, India	Google Earth Engine (GEE) was used to interpret satellite photos and generate LST data for the blue–green spaces. The presence and features of these blue–green regions were measured using the Normalized Difference Vegetation Index (NDVI) and the Modified Normalized Difference Water Index (MNDWI).	Significant geographical variations in the LST were found, with lower temperatures in the blue–green spaces and higher temperatures in built-up and bare land areas. Furthermore, a correlation study demonstrated the built-up index's (NDBI) significant influence on the LST, highlighting the effect of urbanization on regional climate dynamics.

Table A1. *Cont.*

Author(s)	Title	Year	Study Location	Methodology	Findings
Dong, J. et al. [86]	Quantitative study on the cooling effect of green roofs in a high-density urban Area—A case study of Xiamen, China	2020	Xiamen Island, China	Using Landsat 8 remote sensing images from the summers of 2014 and 2017, the relative difference between the average land surface temperature (LST) of Xiamen Island and the green roofs was estimated in geographic information systems (GISs), to illustrate the cooling effect of the green roof project.	Results showed that the average LST difference between green roofs and Xiamen Island decreased by 0.91 °C, indicating that green roofs could effectively alleviate UHI effects in high-density urban areas; the cooling effect was significant up to 100 m from the green roof installation in Xiamen Island, known as the characteristic cooling buffer zone; regression analysis revealed that for every 1000 m2 increase in green roof area, the average LST of the roof and its characteristic cooling buffer zone decreased by 0.4 °C.
Imran, H. M. et al. [87]	Effectiveness of green and cool roofs in mitigating urban heat island effects during a heatwave event in the city of Melbourne in southeast Australia	2018	Melbourne, Australia	The non-hydrostatic regional climate models (RCMs) model employed in this study is called WRFv3.8.1 and it has been used extensively in studies on urban meteorology.	As a result of raising the green roof fractions from 30% to 90% and the cool roof albedo from 0.50 to 0.85, the maximum roof surface UHI is lowered by 1 °C to 3.8 °C and 2.2 °C to 5.2 °C during the day, according to the results. Cool roofs can reduce UHIs by up to 1.4 °C, making them more effective than green roofs, in this regard.
Sanchez, L. and Reames, T. G. [88]	Cooling Detroit: A socio-spatial analysis of equity in green roofs as an urban heat island mitigation strategy	2019	Detroit, USA	The most vulnerable places for the ecosystem services provided by green roofs, as well as the demographic makeup of the populations that make up these regions, were identified using spatial data on land surface temperature, income, and race.	The majority of low-income residents are within walking distance of cooling centers, but are not included in the Detroit Future City Urban Green Neighborhoods, according to an analysis of the study's spatial data; in contrast, green roofs were found in the wealthy, primarily white area of Detroit's urban core.
Gagliano, A. et al. [89]	A multi-criteria methodology for comparing the energy and environmental behavior of cool, green and traditional roofs	2015	Mediterranean	Three types of roofs are compared numerically in terms of their energy and environmental performance—standard roofs (SRs), cool roofs (CRs), and green roofs (GRs).	Consequently, it is discovered that cool and green roofs offer greater environmental and energy savings than typical, heavily insulated roofs. For instance, under the usual Mediterranean climate, green roofs with minimal insulation performed the best in terms of mitigating UHIs.
Gunawardena, K. R. et al. [90]	Utilising green and bluespace to mitigate urban heat island intensity	2017	London, UK	This research offers a meta-analysis of the main influences that green space and blueprint have on the temperatures of the urban canopy and boundary layer, as viewed from the angles of urban climatology, city planning, and climate science.	This research indicates that tree-dominated greenspace provides the greatest heat stress alleviation when it is most needed and that the evapotranspiration-based cooling influence of both green and blue space is primarily significant for urban canopy layer circumstances.

Table A1. *Cont.*

Author(s)	Title	Year	Study Location	Methodology	Findings
Guo, G. et al. [91]	Complex mechanisms linking land surface temperature to greenspace spatial patterns: Evidence from four southeastern Chinese cities	2019	Guangzhou, Foshan, Dong-guan, and Shenzhen, China	Greenspace data were taken from 0.5 m resolution photos and LST was estimated using Landsat 5/8 summer and winter images.	The findings showed that LST is systematically impacted by the spatial composition and layout of greenspace. The size and importance of these associations, however, differed greatly. Particularly during the summer, the combined contributions of the greenspace landscape measures were more important in determining LST than their individual contributions.
He, X. et al. [92]	Observational and modeling study of interactions between urban heat island and heatwave in Beijing	2020	Beijing, China	The Advanced Research version WRF (ARW) model is used in conjunction with a multilayer urban canopy model (Building Environment Parameterization, or BEP) and a sub-model for indoor–outdoor heat exchange (Building Energy Model, or BEM) to simulate the spatiotemporal variations of UHIs over the course of a heatwave period.	The findings indicated that higher surface evapotranspiration differences between urban and rural areas are the primary source of heatwave-related urban heat island augmentation during the day; whereas, increased anthropogenic heat and improved warm advection are the primary causes of this enhancement at night.
Semenzato, P. and Bortolini, L. [93]	Urban Heat Island Mitigation and Urban Green Spaces: Testing a Model in the City of Padova (Italy)	2023	Padova, Italy	At a height of two meters above the ground, temporal trends, variations in air temperature, and their spatial distribution were all simulated using the i-Tree Cool Air model. The model is a component of the USDA Forest Service's i-Tree Hydro+ software suite, which consists of process-based environmental models.	The findings indicate that there are temperature variations between green spaces shaded by trees and urban open places with impermeable cover (streets and squares) of up to nearly 10 °C. In metropolitan areas with sealed surfaces, the simulated night time air temperature is 4.4 °C higher than the reference station readings, although it is only marginally colder in areas with tree cover.
Zheng, T. et al. [94]	A Novel Urban Heat Island Mitigation Strategies-Engaged City Scale Building Energy Consumption Prediction Workflow: Case Study and Validation	2022	Osaka, Japan	The urban weather generating workflow, 3D urban model, data-driven modeling, urban energy consumption modeling, and simulation outcome comprise the five steps of this workflow.	According to the findings, the cool pavement approach is the best one, since it minimizes the rise in heating energy use (4.86%), maximizes the reduction in total urban operational energy use (0.29%), and is insensitive to the embodied energy and CO_2 emissions of buildings. It also maximizes the reduction in cooling energy use (2.57%). Therefore, increasing the pavement's albedo, or "cool pavement", is the best way to reduce urban heat island effects in Osaka city.
Sangkakool, T. et al. [95]	Prospects of green roofs in urban Thailand–a multi-criteria decision analysis	2018	Thailand	This paper deals with identifying and quantifying the key factors that influence green roof adoption in Thailand, which was achieved through a combination of SWOT analysis and AHP.	The key factors were quantified and it was concluded that builders, architects, and planners should be further educated and encouraged to utilize green roofs, since specific technical knowledge is not yet widespread.

Table A1. *Cont.*

Author(s)	Title	Year	Study Location	Methodology	Findings
Qi, J. et al. [96]	A decision-making framework to support urban heat mitigation by local governments	2022	Not specified	A combination of the best UHI mitigation strategies for the urban context is selected using ontology-based knowledge, sensitivity analysis, and genetic algorithm-based multi-objective optimization.	The paper presents a novel framework that enables automated decision-making for choosing optimal combination of UHI mitigation strategies, using AI.
Sangiorgio, V. et al. [97]	Comparative Analysis and Mitigation Strategy for the Urban Heat Island Intensity in Bari (Italy) and in Other Six European Cities	2022	Bari (Italy) and in another six European cities	Using the recently developed index-based approach, I_{uhii}, this paper assesses the absolute maximum UHI intensity in Bari and suggests various mitigation strategies. Secondly, comparative evaluation of seven European cities is given.	The Bari districts most vulnerable to high intensity UHI levels were identified. Good examples of reducing the phenomenon in other cities are found through comparative analyses. For a city in Puglia, practical mitigation scenarios are put forth for the first time.
Temizkan, S. and Kayili, M. T. [98]	Investigation of proper material selection for rainwater harvesting in squares having higher urban heat island effect potential: KBU Social Life Center example	2021	Turkey (Demir Çelik Campus)	Finding the best cover designs that encourage green spaces and reduce heat island effects was the aim of the project. The PROMETHEE method was utilized to identify a material that is significantly optimal for use in the cover.	This study suggested a top cover to mitigate the effects of the heat island that was observed in the KBU Social Life Center Square, which can be described as a large heat island on campus, and to collect rainwater over a large area of the square.
Qureshi, A. M. and Rachid, A. [99]	Comparative Analysis of Multi-Criteria Decision-Making Techniques for Outdoor Heat Stress Mitigation	2022	Not specified	Eight MCDM approaches were compared in order to determine which measurements would be best for mitigating urban heat under particular conditions. The models were used with weighting criteria that came from the direct weighting method and the AHP.	The outcomes demonstrate that for every normalization technique, WSM and PROMETHEE produced dependable and consistent results. The frequency of consistent ranking was enhanced by the combination of AHP and applied MCDMs, with the exception of ELECTRE-NS.
Teixeira, D. C. F. and Amorim, M. C. D. C. T. [100]	Multicriteria Spatial Modeling: Methodological Contribution to the Analysis of Atmospheric and Surface Heat Islands in Presidente Prudente, Brazil	2022	Presidente Prudente, Brazil	In order to analyze AUHIs, researchers combine spatial data from a multi-criteria model, based on multiple linear regression, with air temperature data, including relief and land use. The surface temperature (Landsat) is compared to the estimated and measured air temperatures.	The study demonstrates that vegetation lowers atmospheric temperatures, but urban surface materials are the primary energy sources influencing heat transfer. Precise mappings such as the one proposed is important for decision-making and planning measures.

Table A1. *Cont.*

Author(s)	Title	Year	Study Location	Methodology	Findings
Turhan, C. et al. [101]	An Integrated Decision-Making Framework for Mitigating the Impact of Urban Heat Islands on Energy Consumption and Thermal Comfort of Residential Buildings	2023	Vilayetler Evi Zone (VEZ) in Izmir/Turkey	Research proposes an integrated framework that combines hybrid microclimates and building energy performance simulations (in order to investigate four different strategies for UHI mitigation) with MCDM.	The findings demonstrated that, of all the mitigation strategies, the application of vegetation—such as green roofs and replacing existing trees with ones with a high leaf area density—ranks highest.
Tabatabaee, S. et al. [102]	An assessment model of benefits, opportunities, costs, and risks of green roof installation: A multi criteria decision making approach	2019	Malaysia	This paper proposed a framework for evaluating the key benefits, opportunities, costs, and risks of GR installation and their mutual dependence, using EFDM and the fuzzy-DEMATEL method.	Among the identified benefits, opportunities, costs, and risks, storm water management, contribution to mitigation of urban heat islands, additional structural support, and irregular maintenance were identified as being the most influential. It was also demonstrated that, in order to fully benefit from GR installation, the most influential benefits and opportunities should receive the majority of attention rather than the most important.
Sturiale, L. and Scuderi, A. [103]	The role of green infrastructures in urban planning for climate change adaptation	2019	Catanya, Italy	This framework integrates participatory planning with social multi-criteria evaluation framework for assessing how the public views urban green spaces from a social perspective.	This study demonstrates an intriguing possibility for the broader application of Multi-Critical Social Assessment in green space governance, due to its capacity to incorporate ecological, social, and economic values.
Rosasco, P. and Perini, K. [104]	Selection of (green) roof systems: A sustainability-based multi-criteria analysis	2019	Not specified	This paper uses a sustainability-based multi-criteria analysis to compare a traditional solution with a greening system, in order to investigate the factors that influence choice of the building roof systems.	When choosing between a green roof and a traditional roof, performance, thermal insulation qualities, roof protection, and system weight are the most important factors to consider.
Rosenzweig, C. et al. [106]	Mitigating New York City's Heat Island with Urban Forestry, Living Roofs, and Light Surfaces	2006	New York, USA	This study compares observed meteorological, satellite, and GIS data with a regional climate model (MM5) to assess how various mitigation strategies affect surface and near-surface air temperatures in New York.	The study's findings indicate that there is a significant amount of variation in the mitigation strategies' effects amongst scenarios, case study locations, and heatwave days and that the application of these strategies needs to be adapted to the local conditions.
Rabbani, G. et al. [107]	Multi-criteria modeling for land suitability evaluation of the urban greenbelts in Iran	2021	Iran	This study proposes multi-criteria spatial modeling for a land suitability evaluation of the urban greenbelt in 25 major cities of Iran.	The rise in the environmental change index values over time suggests that new, appropriate urban green belt plans with updated regulations and best practices are required to stop the degradation of urban land use.

Table A1. *Cont.*

Author(s)	Title	Year	Study Location	Methodology	Findings
Mushtaha, E. et al. [108]	A study of the impact of major Urban Heat Island factors in a hot climate courtyard: The case of the University of Sharjah, UAE	2021	University of Sharjah, UAE	The Analytical Hierarchy Process (AHP) was used to rank the UHI factors. ENVI-met (4.4.2.) simulation software was used to test and evaluate each factor.	Air movement is the most effective element in the environmental category, according to the data, with a value of 0.283, while urban greenery is the most effective factor in the urban category, with a recorded value of 0.317.
Moradi, B. et al. [109]	A scenario-based spatial multi-criteria decision-making system for urban environment quality assessment: case study of Tehran	2023	Tehran, Iran	The AHP method was used to determine the weight of the effective criteria. The approach known as ordered weighted averaging (OWA) was then applied.	The study's findings demonstrated that a sizable portion of the local populace lives under unacceptable UEQ settings, highlighting the need to improve the situation.
Meerow, S. and Newell, J. P. [110]	Spatial planning for multifunctional green infrastructure: Growing resilience in Detroit	2017	Detroit, USA	The Green Infrastructure Spatial Planning (GISP) model is presented, which is a multi-criteria, GIS-based method that includes the following benefits: air quality, storm water management, green space, urban heat island mitigation, and landscape connectivity.	The analysis offers preliminary evidence that green infrastructure is not being placed in storm water abatement high-priority locations, much less to mitigate the effects of urban heat islands, enhance habitat connectivity, or improve air quality. But, as the Detroit GISP model shows, it might be built in areas that reduce air pollution, urban heat islands, and storm water all at the same time.
Mahmoudzade, H. et al. [111]	Evaluating urban environmental quality using multi criteria decision making	2024	Tabriz, Iran	This study used a multi-criteria decision-making (MCDM) approach that used CRITIC to assess the quality of the urban environment using spatial analysis.	Air pollution, green space per capita, recreational space, and health care per capita do not seem to differ significantly, on average. In two urban areas, the creation of environmental quality maps highlights the significance of relevant neighborhood-level variables.
Lassandro, P. and Di Turi, S. [112]	Multi-criteria and multiscale assessment of building envelope response-ability to rising heat waves	2019	Bari, Italy	The selected approaches are examined in three distinct cities with rising summer temperatures, using an integrated, multilevel analysis with EnergyPlus and ENVI_met. Applying a multi-criteria analysis based on the discovered indicators, the final comparative analysis is conducted.	The results demonstrate the value of employing a multiple criterion analysis and a double-level approach when assessing how well-suited various building envelope retrofitting methods are to handle the escalating frequency of heat waves. Green solutions with high albedo values were the most responsive.

Table A1. *Cont.*

Author(s)	Title	Year	Study Location	Methodology	Findings
Kotharkar, R. et al. [113]	A systematic approach for urban heat island mitigation strategies in critical local climate zones of an Indian city	2020	Nagpur, India	Determination of the LCZ criticality using The Order of Preference by Similarity to Ideal Solution (TOPSIS) technique.	In the older, unplanned settlement with dense urban agglomeration (LCZ 3), the application of cool roof shows significant reductions in air temperature; however, increasing the green area ration is found to be a more effective strategy for the sparsely built (LCZ 9) and planned settlement with open spaces (LCZ 3F).
Putra, M. I. J. et al. [114]	Spatial Multi-Criteria Analysis for Urban Sustainable Built Up Area Based on Urban Heat Island in Serang City	2019	Serang, Indonesia	A simulation model was developed with a sustainable principle, carried out by performing equal weighting on each factor so that the obtained value and spatial distribution from the appropriate area was obtained and was suitable for the development of the built-up area in Serang City.	The region's suitability area of 3.313 Ha was determined using the results of SMCE modeling. This area was distributed at various locations in Serang City and was expanded linearly along the road network to cover 3.538 Ha. In the meantime, the majority of Serang City's central, north, and west regions—which together account for 19.553 Ha—are unsuitable for a built-up area.
Yan, Y. et al. [115]	A multi-criteria evaluation of the urban ecological environment in Shanghai based on remote sensing	2021	Shanghai, China	Development of an ecological environment evaluation method, based on remote sensing and a projection pursuit model.	In order to assess the urban ecological environment in a more convenient and objective manner, remote sensing-based detection has been used. Next, a multi-criteria assessment approach has been suggested for the analysis of the ecological environment, based on a projection pursuit model. Finally, a thorough assessment of Shanghai City's ecological environment changes over the last five years was conducted.
Teotónio, I. et al. [116]	Decision support system for green roofs investments in residential buildings	2020	Lisbon, Portugal	The proposed methodology is based on the MACBETH method and determines the green roof option with the best trade-off between costs and benefits, in agreement with the preferences of the users/investors.	With a score of 69.43 out of 100, the methodology application selects the intensive green roof as the optimal alternative. The results of the sensitivity and robustness analyses supported the best option conclusions. This strategy maximizes building retrofitting, while assisting in the decision-making process regarding green roofs, as well as enabling sound and well-informed urban planning decisions.
Sangiorgio, V. et al. [117]	Development of a holistic urban heat island evaluation methodology	2020	European cities	Development of a new index aimed at quantifying the hazard of the absolute maximum UHI intensity in urban districts during the summer season, by taking all the parameters influencing the phenomenon into account.	The results are obtained by utilizing three interrelated techniques, as follows: an optimization process, using a Jackknife resampling approach to calibrate the index by utilizing the effective UHI intensity measured in a total of 41 urban districts and 35 European cities; the Analytic Hierarchy Processes to analyze the parameters involved in the UHI phenomenon; and a state-of-the-art technique to acquire a large set of data.
Philipps, N. et al. [118]	Urban Heat Island Mapping Based on a Local Climate Zone Classification: a Case Study in Strasbourg City, France	2022	Strasbourg, France	Establishment of an LCZ classification for the city of Strasbourg by using a vector-based method that relies on a large vector database composed of land cover and cadastral parcels data.	The obtained final LCZ map demonstrates that the devised vector-based approach enables the acquisition of pertinent LCZ classification. The values of the LCZ parameters are then utilzsed to calculate a multiple linear regression (MLR), with the goal of obtaining an UHI intensity for every LCZ polygon. The great regional heterogeneity of the phenomena is accurately illustrated in the resulting UHI map of the Eurométropole de Strasbourg (EMS).

Table A1. *Cont.*

Author(s)	Title	Year	Study Location	Methodology	Findings
Mostafa, E. et al. [119]	Urbanization Trends Analysis Using Hybrid Modeling of Fuzzy Analytical Hierarchical Process-Cellular Automata-Markov Chain and Investigating Its Impact on Land Surface Temperature over Gharbia City, Egypt	2023	Gharbia, Egypt	The development of two comparable models for the simulation of spatiotemporal dynamics of land use in the study area—CA–Markov chain and FAHP–CA–Markov chain hybrid models.	The two comparable models were validated using the Jaccard coefficient, which confirmed that both models are valid and can be utilized for future predictions. In contrast to the hybrid FAHP–CA–Markov chain model, which can predict urban sprawl-prone sites in a methodical manner, while taking the dynamics driving urban growth into account, the results of the classic CA–Markov chain model were more haphazard.
Kazak, Jan K. [25]	The use of a decision support system for sustainable urbanization and thermal comfort in adaptation to climate change actions—The case of the Wrocław larger urban zone (Poland)	2018	Wrocław, Poland	The development of a decision support system that can be used for the assessment of areas, in relation to their potential exposure to the UHI effect.	The scenario that is least susceptible to UHI impacts is revealed by the computations. The study gives local government officials recommendations on where to concentrate their efforts to build more environmentally friendly urban structures and improve their ability to withstand extreme weather conditions and climate change.
Mostofi, N. et al. [120]	Developing an SDSS for optimal sustainable roof covering planning based on UHI variation at neighborhood scale	2021	Tehran, Iran	The development of a spatial decision support system (SDSS) to investigate the effect of parcels' roof covering type on surface heat island (SHI) values and their variation, at the neighborhood scale.	The two primary components of the present research's innovation, the SDSS, are determining the study area's UHI value and selecting the best set of parcels to replace their roof coverings with flagstone, high-albedo material, or three different types of vegetation. The findings show that, because flagstone and high-albedo materials have local impacts on reducing the UHI effects, it is important to inhibit UHI effects at the study area boundary with plant roof covering, in order to control UHI in the center of the region.
Bathaei, B. [121]	Decision Support System to Select the Most Effective Strategies for Mitigating the Urban Heat Island Effect Using Sustainability and Resilience Performance Measures	2021	Not specified	The development of a decision support system (DSS) to assist decision-makers in reducing the effects of UHIs, by allowing them to choose the most viable mitigation method/technique based on resiliency and sustainability concerns.	The study's contribution is the creation of a DSS that resembles a knowledge-sharing platform, to assist decision-makers, policymakers, urban planners, and architects in extracting UHIMSs. A more resilient and sustainable design is the anticipated outcome in a broad sense. The groundwork for developing a dynamic computer-based decision support system (DSS) to choose the most effective UHIMSs is laid by this study.
Tuczek, M. et al. [123]	Toward a decision support system for mitigating urban heat	2019	Not specified	The development of a DSS with an optimization model at its core, which optimizes the corresponding urban areas with respect to the highest possible revenue, while maintaining an optimal building/vegetation balance.	To address the identified research gap and to address the research question posed, the best solution would likely be an optimization model that provides a thorough discounted cash flow calculation in the future and takes into account a range of economic factors, including site-specific land prices, electricity costs for energy demand, and air conditioning, as well as a variety of potential alternatives for building and vegetation types.

Table A1. *Cont.*

Author(s)	Title	Year	Study Location	Methodology	Findings
Qureshi, A. M. and Rachid, A. [124]	Review and Comparative Study of Decision Support Tools for the Mitigation of Urban Heat Stress	2021	Not specified	Review of different decision support tools for mitigating UHI.	This review demonstrates how MCA can be applied to any research area and how criteria can be modified to fit the specific area. A comparative analysis leads to the conclusion that the DSS tool meets many requirements for mitigating UHIs.
Mahdiyar, A. et al. [125]	A prototype decision support system for green roof type selection: A cybernetic fuzzy ANP method	2019	Kuala Lumpur, Malaysia	The development of a decision support system (DSS) for selecting the optimum type of GR for residential buildings in Kuala Lumpur.	During the project's design phase, a number of interrelated selection criteria for GR types were taken into account. This study's unique contribution, from the perspective of MCDM, is the prototype DSS that was created by employing a CFANP technique to automate the complete GR type selection decision-making process.
Werbin, Z. et al. [62]	A tree-planting decision support tool for urban heat island mitigation	2020	Boston, USA	The development of a Boston-specific Heat Vulnerability Index (HVI).	Researchers from Boston University examined the City of Boston's strategy for expanding the urban canopy, because the city has encountered challenges in establishing a long-lasting growth. They determined what barriers there were to applying scientific information to tree-planting decisions and collaborated with the city to create a tool that would help with the process. The tool itself is replicable or adaptable to other cities and the process of development offers a model of a fruitful collaboration between academia and the public sector.
Acosta, M. P. et al. [63]	How to bring UHI to the urban planning table? A data-driven modeling approach	2021	Montreal, Canada	The development of a decision support tool for the modeling of UHIs at the street level.	The methodology for creating a decision assistance tool for street-level UHI modeling was described in this research study. Urban planners can utilize this simple-to-use tool to look at how their design decisions will affect street-level traffic. There are five levels of UHI potential, ranging from low to high, represented by the UHI evaluation matrix.
Qi, J. et al. [64]	Planning for cooler cities: A framework to support the selection of urban heat mitigation techniques	2020	Sydney, Australia	The development of a decision-making framework, related to UHI mitigation	One of the study's contributions is the creation of a method that can determine the best combinations of UHMTs and planning and design elements with the greatest potential for cooling in a particular urban setting. The framework can support high-performance production and sustainable development, in addition to giving decision-makers the best UHMTs for creating a workable policy for mitigating urban heat islands.

References

1. Yamamoto, Y. Measures to mitigate urban heat islands. *Sci. Technol. Trends Q. Rev.* **2006**, *18*, 6583.
2. Oke, T.R. The energetic basis of the urban heat island. *Q. J. R. Meteorol. Soc.* **1982**, *108*, 1–24. [CrossRef]
3. Quattrochi, D.A.; Luvall, J.C.; Rickman, D.L.; Estes, M.G.; Laymon, C.A.; Howell, B.F. A decision support information system for urban landscape management using thermal infrared data: Decision support systems. *Photogramm. Eng. Remote Sens.* **2000**, *66*, 1195–1207.
4. Sen, S.; Roesler, J.; Ruddell, B.; Middel, A. Cool Pavement Strategies for Urban Heat Island Mitigation in Suburban Phoenix, Arizona. *Sustainability* **2019**, *11*, 4452. [CrossRef]
5. Wijeyesekera, D.C.; Nazari, N.A.R.B.M.; Lim, S.M.; Masirin, M.I.M.; Zainorabidin, A.; Walsh, J. Investigation into the Urban Heat Island Effects from Asphalt Pavements. *OIDA Int. J. Sustain. Dev.* **2012**, *5*, 97–118.
6. Akbari, H.; Rose, L.S. *Characterising the Fabric of the Urban Environment: A Case Study of Metropolitan Chicago, Illinois*; Lawrence Berkeley National Laboratory: Berkeley, CA, USA, 2001.
7. Voogt, J.A. Urban Heat Island. In *Encyclopedia of Global Environmental Change*; Munn, T., Ed.; Wiley: Chichester, UK, 2002; Volume 3, pp. 660–666.
8. Anyanwu, E.C.; Kanu, I. The role of urban forest in the protection of human environmental health in geographically prone unpredictable hostile weather conditions. *Int. J. Environ. Sci. Technol* **2006**, *3*, 197–201. [CrossRef]
9. Li, H.; Harvey, J.T.; Holland, T.J.; Kayhanian, M. The use of reflective and permeable pavements as a potential practice for heat island mitigation and storm water management. *Environ. Res. Lett* **2013**, *8*, 015023. [CrossRef]
10. Emmanuel, M.R. *An Urban Approach to Climate-Sensitive Design: Strategies for the Tropics*; Spon Press: London, UK, 2005; p. 208.
11. Yu, C.; Hien, W.N. Thermal benefits of city parks. *Energy Build.* **2006**, *38*, 105–120. [CrossRef]
12. Salazar, A.; Baldi, G.; Hirota, M.; Syktus, J.; McAlpine, C. Land use and land cover change impacts on the regional climate of non-Amazonian South America: A review. *Glob. Planet. Chang.* **2015**, *128*, 103–119. [CrossRef]
13. Shiflett, S.A.; Liang, L.L.; Crum, S.M.; Feyisa, G.L.; Wang, J.; Jenerette, G.D. Variation in the urban vegetation, surface temperature, air temperature nexus. *Sci. Total Environ.* **2017**, *579*, 495–505. [CrossRef] [PubMed]
14. Vitanova, L.L.; Kusaka, H. Study on the urban heat island in Sofia City: Numerical simulations with potential natural vegetation and present land use data. *Sustain. Cities Soc.* **2018**, *40*, 110–125. [CrossRef]
15. Gartland, L.M. *Heat Islands: Understanding and Mitigating Heat in Urban Areas*, 1st ed.; Routledge: London, UK, 2012.
16. Santamouris, M.; Paraponiaris, K.; Mihalakakou, G. Estimating the ecological footprint of the heat island effect over Athens, Greece. *Clim. Chang.* **2007**, *80*, 265–276. [CrossRef]
17. Akbari, H.; Gartland, L.; Konopacki, S. *Measured Energy Savings of Light Colored Roofs: Results from Three California Demonstration Sites: Lawrence Berkeley National Lab*; Environmental Energy Technologies Div.: Berkeley, CA, USA, 1998.
18. Oke, T. *Boundary Layer Climates*, 2nd ed.; Methuen: London, UK, 1987; p. 289.
19. Chen, J.; Zhou, Z.; Wu, J. Field and laboratory measurement of albedo and heat transfer for pavement materials. *Constr. Build. Mater.* **2019**, *202*, 46–57. [CrossRef]
20. Nuruzzaman, M. Urban heat island: Causes, effects and mitigation measures—A review. *Int. J. Environ. Monit. Anal.* **2015**, *3*, 67–73. [CrossRef]
21. Masson, V. Urban surface modeling and the mesoscale impact of cities. *Theor. Appl. Climatol.* **2006**, *84*, 35–45. [CrossRef]
22. Giridharan, R.; Ganesan, S.; Lau, S.S.Y. Daytime urban heat island effect in high-rise and high-density residential developments in Hong Kong. *Energy Build.* **2004**, *36*, 525–534. [CrossRef]
23. Priyadarsini, R.; Hien, W.N.; David, C.K.W. Microclimatic modeling of the urban thermal environment of Singapore to mitigate urban heat island. *Sol. Energy* **2008**, *82*, 727–745. [CrossRef]
24. Tumanov, S.; Stan-Sion, A.; Lupu, A.; Soci, C.; Oprea, C. Influences of the city of Bucharest on weather and climate parameters. *Atmos. Environ.* **1999**, *33*, 4173–4183. [CrossRef]
25. Kazak, J.K. The use of a decision support system for sustainable urbanization and thermal comfort in adaptation to climate change actions—The case of the Wrocław larger urban zone (Poland). *Sustainability* **2018**, *10*, 1083. [CrossRef]
26. Bousse, Y.S. Mitigating the Urban Heat Island Effect with an Intensive Green Roof during Summer in Reading. Doctoral Dissertation, Reading University, Reading, UK, 2009.
27. Pongracz, R.; Bartholy, J.; Dezso, Z. Remotely sensed thermal information applied to urban climate analysis. *Adv. Space Res.* **2006**, *37*, 2191–2196. [CrossRef]
28. Oke, T.R.; Mills, G.; Christen, A.; Voogt, J.A. *Urban Climates*; Cambridge University Press: Cambridge, UK, 2017.
29. Fadhil, M.; Hamoodi, M.N.; Ziboon, A.R.T. Mitigating urban heat island effects in urban environments: Strategies and tools. In *IOP Conference Series: Earth and Environmental Science*; IOP Publishing: Bristol, UK, 2023; Volume 1129, p. 012025.
30. Stewart, I.D.; Oke, T.R. Local Climate Zones for Urban Temperature Studies. *Bull. Amer. Meteor. Soc.* **2012**, *93*, 1879–1900. [CrossRef]
31. Duplančić Leder, T.; Leder, N.; Hećimović, Ž. Split Metropolitan area surface temperature assessment with remote sensing method. *Građevinar* **2016**, *68*, 895–905.
32. Mendez-Astudillo, J.; Lau, L.; Lun, I.Y.F.; Tang, Y.T.; Moore, T. Urban Heat Island Monitoring with Global Navigation Satellite System (GNSS) Data. In *Urban Heat Island (UHI) Mitigation: Hot and Humid Regions*; Enteria, N., Santamouris, M., Eicker, U., Eds.; Springer: New York, NY, USA, 2021; pp. 43–59.

33. Rehan, R.M. Cool city as a sustainable example of heat island management case study of the coolest city in the world. *HBRC* **2016**, *12*, 191–204. [CrossRef]
34. Filho, W.L.; Icaza, L.E.; Emanche, V.O.; Al-Amin, A.Q. An Evidence-Based Review of Impacts, Strategies and Tools to Mitigate Urban Heat Islands. *Int. J. Environ. Res. Public Health* **2017**, *14*, 1600. [CrossRef]
35. Leal Filho, W.; Wolf, F.; Castro-Díaz, R.; Li, C.; Ojeh, V.N.; Gutiérrez, N.; Nagy, G.J.; Savić, S.; Natenzon, C.E.; Al-Amin, A.Q.; et a Addressing the urban heat islands effect: A cross-country assessment of the role of green infrastructure. *Sustainability* **2021**, *1* 753. [CrossRef]
36. Vujovic, S.; Haddad, B.; Karaky, H.; Sebaibi, N.; Boutouil, M. Urban heat island: Causes, consequences, and mitigation measure with emphasis on reflective and permeable pavements. *CivilEng* **2021**, *2*, 459–484. [CrossRef]
37. US Environmental Protection Agency. Urban Heat Island Basics. In *Reducing Urban Heat Islands: Compendium of Strategies*; U Environmental Protection Agency: Washington, DC, USA, 2008. Available online: https://19january2017snapshot.epa.gov/sites production/files/2014-06/documents/basicscompendium.pdf (accessed on 8 February 2024).
38. Yuan, C.; Adelia, A.S.; Mei, S.; He, W.; Li, X.X.; Norford, L. Mitigating intensity of urban heat island by better understanding o urban morphology and anthropogenic heat dispersion. *Build. Environ.* **2020**, *176*, 106876. [CrossRef]
39. Gagliano, A.; Nocera, F.; Aneli, S. Computational fluid dynamics analysis for evaluating the urban heat island effects. *Energ Procedia* **2017**, *134*, 508–517. [CrossRef]
40. Kouhirostami, M.; Abukhalaf, A.H.I.; Kouhirostamkolaei, M. Eliminating Air Pollution in Cities Through Sustainable Urba Planning. *Acad. Lett.* **2022**, 4588. [CrossRef]
41. Santamouris, M.; Ding, L.; Fiorito, F.; Oldfield, P.; Osmond, P.; Paolini, R.; Prasad, D.; Synnefa, A. Passive and active cooling fo the outdoor built environment e analysis and assessment of the cooling potential of mitigation technologies using performanc data from 220 large scale projects. *Sol. Energy* **2017**, *154*, 14–33. [CrossRef]
42. Wang, X.; Dallimer, M.; Scott, C.E.; Shi, W.; Gao, J. Tree species richness and diversity predicts the magnitude of urban heat islan mitigation effects of greenspaces. *Sci. Total Environ.* **2021**, *770*, 145–211. [CrossRef] [PubMed]
43. Kleerekoper, L.; van Esch, M.; Salcedo, T.B. How to make a city climate-proof addressing the urban heat island effect. *Resource Conserv. Recycl.* **2012**, *64*, 30–38. [CrossRef]
44. Zhang, L.; Fukuda, H.; Liu, Z. The value of cool roof as a strategy to mitigate urban heat island effect: A contingent valuatio approach. *J. Clean. Prod.* **2019**, *228*, 770–777. [CrossRef]
45. Maleki, A.; Mahdavi, A. Evaluation of Urban Heat Islands Mitigation Strategies Using 3dimentional Urban Micro-climate Mode ENVI-Met. *Asian J. Civ. Eng.* **2016**, *17*, 357–371.
46. Amani-Beni, M.; Zhang, B.; Xu, J. Impact of urban park's tree, grass and waterbody on microclimate in hot summer days: A cas study of Olympic Park in Beijing, China. *Urban For. Urban Green.* **2018**, *32*, 1–6. [CrossRef]
47. Wu, Z.; Zhang, Y. Water bodies' cooling effects on urban land daytime surface temperature: Ecosystem service reducing hea island effect. *Sustainability* **2019**, *11*, 787. [CrossRef]
48. Gregory, R.; Failing, L.; Harstone, M.; Long, G.; McDaniels, T.; Ohlson, D. *Structured Decision Making: A Practical Guide t Environmental Management Choices*; John Wiley & Sons: New York, NY, USA, 2012.
49. Liu, S.; Duffy, A.H.; Whitfield, R.I.; Boyle, I.M. Integration of decision support systems to improve decision support performanc *Knowl. Inf. Syst.* **2010**, *22*, 261–286. [CrossRef]
50. Jajac, N.; Marović, I.; Rogulj, K.; Kilić, J. Decision support concept to selection of wastewater treatment plant location—The cas study of town of Kutina, Croatia. *Water* **2019**, *11*, 717. [CrossRef]
51. Ivić, M.; Kilić, J.; Rogulj, K.; Jajac, N. Decision Support to Sustainable Parking Management—Investment Planning throug Parking Fines to Improve Pedestrian Flows. *Sustainability* **2020**, *12*, 9485. [CrossRef]
52. Huang, I.B.; Keisler, J.; Linkov, I. Multi-criteria decision analysis in environmental sciences: Ten years of applications and trend *Sci. Total Environ.* **2011**, *409*, 3578–3594. [CrossRef]
53. Taranath, N.L.; Prabhu, B.A.; Dani, R.; Tiwari, D.; Darshan, L.M. Non-knowledge Based Decision Support System. In Proceeding of the Third International Conference on Sustainable Expert Systems: ICSES 2022, Lalitpur, Nepal, 9–10 September 2022; Springe Nature Singapore: Singapore, 2023; pp. 399–409.
54. Kilić, J.; Rogulj, K.; Jajac, N. Fuzzy expert system for land valuation in land consolidation processes. *Croat. Oper. Res. Rev.* **2019** *10*, 89–103. [CrossRef]
55. Rogulj, K.; Kilić Pamuković, J.; Antucheviciene, J.; Zavadskas, E.K. Intuitionistic fuzzy decision support based on EDAS and gre relational degree for historic bridges reconstruction priority. *Soft Comput.* **2022**, *26*, 9419–9444. [CrossRef]
56. Zadeh, L.A. Fuzzy sets. *Inform. Control* **1965**, *8*, 338–353. [CrossRef]
57. Zadeh, L. Fuzzy sets as a basis for a theory of possibility. *Fuzzy Set. Syst.* **1978**, *1*, 3–28. [CrossRef]
58. Unwin, S.D. A fuzzy set theoretic foundation for vagueness in uncertainty analysis. *Risk Anal.* **1986**, *6*, 27–34. [CrossRef]
59. United Nations, Department of Economic and Social Affairs, Population Division. *World Urbanization Prospects: The 2018 Revisio (ST/ESA/SER.A/420)*; United Nations: New York, NY, USA, 2019.
60. Chen, Y.; Zheng, B.; Hu, Y. Numerical simulation of local climate zone cooling achieved through modification of trees, albedo an green roofs—A case study of Changsha, China. *Sustainability* **2020**, *12*, 2752. [CrossRef]
61. Nwakaire, C.M.; Onn, C.C.; Yap, S.P.; Yuen, C.W.; Onodagu, P.D. Urban Heat Island Studies with emphasis on urban pavement A review. *Sustain. Cities Soc.* **2020**, *63*, 102476. [CrossRef]

62. Werbin, Z.; Heidari, L.; Buckley, S.; Brochu, P.; Butler, L.; Connolly, C.; Bloemendaal, L.H.; McCabe, T.D.; Miller, T.; Hutyra, L.R. A tree-planting decision support tool for urban heat island mitigation. *bioRxiv* **2020**, *15*, 821785. [CrossRef]
63. Acosta, M.P.; Vahdatikhaki, F.; Santos, J.; Hammad, A.; Dorée, A.G. How to bring UHI to the urban planning table? A data-driven modeling approach. *Sustain. Cities Soc.* **2021**, *71*, 102948. [CrossRef]
64. Qi, J.; Ding, L.; Lim, S. Planning for cooler cities: A framework to support the selection of urban heat mitigation techniques. *J. Clean. Prod.* **2020**, *275*, 122903. [CrossRef]
65. Kim, S.W.; Brown, R.D. Urban heat island (UHI) intensity and magnitude estimations: A systematic literature review. *Sci. Total Environ.* **2021**, *779*, 146389. [CrossRef]
66. Almeida, C.R.d.; Teodoro, A.C.; Gonçalves, A. Study of the Urban Heat Island (UHI) Using Remote Sensing Data/Techniques: A Systematic Review. *Environments* **2021**, *8*, 105. [CrossRef]
67. Deilami, K.; Kamruzzaman, M.; Liu, Y. Urban heat island effect: A systematic review of spatio-temporal factors, data, methods, and mitigation measures. *Int. J. Appl. Earth Obs. Geoinf.* **2018**, *67*, 30–42. [CrossRef]
68. Nimac, I.; Herceg-Bulić, I.; Žuvela-Aloise, M. The contribution of urbanisation and climate conditions to increased urban heat load in Zagreb (Croatia) since the 1960s. *Urban Clim.* **2022**, *46*, 101343. [CrossRef]
69. Duplančić Leder, T.; Leder, N. Land Surface Temperature Determination in the Town of Mostar Area. *Teh. Vjesn.* **2018**, *25*, 1219–1226.
70. Duplančić Leder, T.; Bačić, S. Utjecaj lokalnih klimatskih zona na termalna obilježja područja grada Splita. In Proceedings of the 16th Symposium of Authorized Geodesy Engineers, Opatija, Croatia, 4–7 November 2021; pp. 73–80.
71. Estacio, I.; Babaan, J.; Pecson, N.J.; Blanco, A.C.; Escoto, J.E.; Alcantara, C.K. GIS-based mapping of local climate zones using fuzzy logic and cellular automata. *Int. Arch. Photogramm. Remote Sens. Spat. Inf. Sci.* **2019**, *42*, 199–206. [CrossRef]
72. Bokaie, M.; Zarkesh, M.K.; Arasteh, P.D.; Hosseini, A. Assessment of urban heat island based on the relationship between land surface temperature and land use/land cover in Tehran. *Sustain. Cities Soc.* **2016**, *23*, 94–104. [CrossRef]
73. Jiménez-Muñoz, J.C.; Sobrino, J.A. A generalized single-channel method for retrieving land surface temperature from remote sensing data. *J. Geophys. Res. Atmos.* **2003**, *108*, 4688. [CrossRef]
74. Feizizadeh, B.; Blaschke, T. Examining urban heat island relations to land use and air pollution: Multiple endmember spectral mixture analysis for thermal remote sensing. *IEEE J. Sel. Top. Appl. Earth Obs. Remote Sens.* **2013**, *6*, 1749–1756. [CrossRef]
75. Zhu, W.; Sun, J.; Yang, C.; Liu, M.; Xu, X.; Ji, C. How to measure the urban park cooling island? A perspective of absolute and relative indicators using remote sensing and buffer analysis. *Remote Sens.* **2021**, *13*, 3154. [CrossRef]
76. Firozjaei, M.K.; Fathololoumi, S.; Kiavarz, M.; Biswas, A.; Homaee, M.; Alavipanah, S.K. Land Surface Ecological Status Composition Index (LSESCI): A novel remote sensing-based technique for modeling land surface ecological status. *Ecol. Indic.* **2021**, *123*, 107375. [CrossRef]
77. Zhang, Z.; Zhang, Y.; Yu, X.; Lei, L.; Chen, Y.; Guo, X. Evaluating Natural Ecological Land Change in Function-Oriented Planning Regions Using the National Land Use Survey Data from 2009 to 2018 in China. *ISPRS Int. J. -Geo-Inf.* **2021**, *10*, 172. [CrossRef]
78. Zhang, T.; Yang, R.; Yang, Y.; Li, L.; Chen, L. Assessing the Urban Eco-Environmental Quality by the Remote-Sensing Ecological Index: Application to Tianjin, North China. *ISPRS Int. J. -Geo-Inf.* **2021**, *10*, 475. [CrossRef]
79. Jiang, Y.; Lin, W. A Comparative Analysis of Retrieval Algorithms of Land Surface Temperature from Landsat-8 Data: A Case Study of Shanghai, China. *Int. J. Environ. Res. Public Health* **2021**, *18*, 5659. [CrossRef] [PubMed]
80. Peng, T.; Sun, C.; Feng, S.; Zhang, Y.; Fan, F. Temporal and Spatial Variation of Anthropogenic Heat in the Central Urban Area: A Case Study of Guangzhou, China. *ISPRS Int. J. -Geo-Inf.* **2021**, *10*, 160. [CrossRef]
81. You, M.; Lai, R.; Lin, J.; Zhu, Z. Quantitative analysis of a spatial distribution and driving factors of the urban heat island effect: A case study of fuzhou central area, China. *Int. J. Environ. Res. Public Health* **2021**, *18*, 13088. [CrossRef] [PubMed]
82. Despini, F.; Ferrari, C.; Santunione, G.; Tommasone, S.; Muscio, A.; Teggi, S. Urban surfaces analysis with remote sensing data for the evaluation of UHI mitigation scenarios. *Urban Clim.* **2021**, *35*, 100761. [CrossRef]
83. Santos, L.G.; Nevat, I.; Pignatta, G.; Norford, L.K. Climate-informed decision-making for urban design: Assessing the impact of urban morphology on urban heat island. *Urban Clim.* **2021**, *36*, 100776. [CrossRef]
84. Amani-Beni, M.; Zhang, B.; Xie, G.D.; Shi, Y. Impacts of urban green landscape patterns on land surface temperature: Evidence from the adjacent area of Olympic Forest Park of Beijing, China. *Sustainability* **2019**, *11*, 513. [CrossRef]
85. Pritipadmaja, G.R.D.; Sharma, A.K. Assessing the cooling effect of blue-green spaces: Implications for Urban Heat Island mitigation. *Water* **2023**, *15*, 2983. [CrossRef]
86. Dong, J.; Lin, M.; Zuo, J.; Lin, T.; Liu, J.; Sun, C.; Luo, J. Quantitative study on the cooling effect of green roofs in a high-density urban Area—A case study of Xiamen, China. *J. Clean. Prod.* **2020**, *255*, 120152. [CrossRef]
87. Imran, H.M.; Kala, J.; Ng, A.W.M.; Muthukumaran, S. Effectiveness of green and cool roofs in mitigating urban heat island effects during a heatwave event in the city of Melbourne in southeast Australia. *J. Clean. Prod.* **2018**, *197*, 393–405. [CrossRef]
88. Sanchez, L.; Reames, T.G. Cooling Detroit: A socio-spatial analysis of equity in green roofs as an urban heat island mitigation strategy. *Urban For. Urban Green.* **2019**, *44*, 126331. [CrossRef]
89. Gagliano, A.; Detommaso, M.; Nocera, F.; Evola, G. A multi-criteria methodology for comparing the energy and environmental behavior of cool, green and traditional roofs. *Build. Environ.* **2015**, *90*, 71–81. [CrossRef]
90. Gunawardena, K.R.; Wells, M.J.; Kershaw, T. Utilising green and bluespace to mitigate urban heat island intensity. *Sci. Total Environ.* **2017**, *584*, 1040–1055. [CrossRef]

91. Guo, G.; Wu, Z.; Chen, Y. Complex mechanisms linking land surface temperature to greenspace spatial patterns: Evidence from four southeastern Chinese cities. *Sci. Total Environ.* **2019**, *674*, 77–87. [CrossRef]
92. He, X.; Wang, J.; Feng, J.; Yan, Z.; Miao, S.; Zhang, Y.; Xia, J. Observational and modeling study of interactions between urban heat island and heatwave in Beijing. *J. Clean. Prod.* **2020**, *247*, 119169. [CrossRef]
93. Semenzato, P.; Bortolini, L. Urban Heat Island Mitigation and Urban Green Spaces: Testing a Model in the City of Padova (Italy). *Land* **2023**, *12*, 476. [CrossRef]
94. Zheng, T.; Qu, K.; Wang, Y.; Darkwa, J.; Calautit, J.K. A Novel Urban Heat Island Mitigation Strategies-Engaged City Scale Building Energy Consumption Prediction Workflow: Case Study and Validation. SSRN 4159963. Available online: https://ssrn.com/abstract=4159963 (accessed on 15 February 2023).
95. Sangkakool, T.; Techato, K.; Zaman, R.; Brudermann, T. Prospects of green roofs in urban Thailand—A multi-criteria decision analysis. *J. Clean. Prod.* **2018**, *196*, 400–410. [CrossRef]
96. Qi, J.; Ding, L.; Lim, S. A decision-making framework to support urban heat mitigation by local governments. *Resour. Conserv. Recycl.* **2022**, *184*, 106420. [CrossRef]
97. Sangiorgio, V.; Bruno, S.; Fiorito, F. Comparative Analysis and Mitigation Strategy for the Urban Heat Island Intensity in Bari (Italy) and in Other Six European Cities. *Climate* **2022**, *10*, 177. [CrossRef]
98. Temizkan, S.; Kayili, M.T. Investigation of proper material selection for rainwater harvesting in squares having higher urban heat island effect potential: KBU Social Life Center example. *Int. Adv. Res. Eng. J.* **2021**, *5*, 454–463. [CrossRef]
99. Qureshi, A.M.; Rachid, A. Comparative Analysis of Multi-Criteria Decision-Making Techniques for Outdoor Heat Stress Mitigation. *Appl. Sci.* **2022**, *12*, 12308. [CrossRef]
100. Teixeira, D.C.F.; Amorim, M.C.D.C.T. Multicriteria Spatial Modeling: Methodological Contribution to the Analysis of Atmospheric and Surface Heat Islands in Presidente Prudente, Brazil. *Climate* **2022**, *10*, 56. [CrossRef]
101. Turhan, C.; Atalay, A.S.; Gokcen Akkurt, G. An Integrated Decision-Making Framework for Mitigating the Impact of Urban Heat Islands on Energy Consumption and Thermal Comfort of Residential Buildings. *Sustainability* **2023**, *15*, 9674. [CrossRef]
102. Tabatabaee, S.; Mahdiyar, A.; Durdyev, S.; Mohandes, S.R.; Ismail, S. An assessment model of benefits, opportunities, costs, and risks of green roof installation: A multi criteria decision making approach. *J. Clean. Prod.* **2019**, *238*, 117956. [CrossRef]
103. Sturiale, L.; Scuderi, A. The role of green infrastructures in urban planning for climate change adaptation. *Climate* **2019**, *7*, 119. [CrossRef]
104. Rosasco, P.; Perini, K. Selection of (green) roof systems: A sustainability-based multi-criteria analysis. *Buildings* **2019**, *9*, 134. [CrossRef]
105. Rowe, B. Chapter 3.5—Green Roofs for Pollutants' Reduction. In *Nature Based Strategies for Urban and Building Sustainability*; Pérez, G., Perini, K., Eds.; Butterworth-Heinemann: Oxford, UK, 2018; pp. 141–148.
106. Rosenzweig, C.; Solecki, W.D.; Slosberg, R.B. *Mitigating New York City's Heat Island with Urban Forestry, Living Roofs, and Light Surfaces*; New York City Regional Heat Island Initiative; New York State Energy Research and Development Authority (NYSERDA): New York, NY, USA, 2006.
107. Rabbani, G.; Madanian, S.; Mansouri Daneshvar, M.R. Multi-criteria modeling for land suitability evaluation of the urban greenbelts in Iran. *Model. Earth Syst. Environ.* **2021**, *7*, 1291–1307. [CrossRef]
108. Mushtaha, E.; Shareef, S.; Alsyouf, I.; Mori, T.; Kayed, A.; Abdelrahim, M.; Albannay, S. A study of the impact of major Urban Heat Island factors in a hot climate courtyard: The case of the University of Sharjah, UAE. *Sustain. Cities Soc.* **2021**, *69*, 102844. [CrossRef]
109. Moradi, B.; Akbari, R.; Taghavi, S.R.; Fardad, F.; Esmailzadeh, A.; Ahmadi, M.Z.; Attarroshan, S.; Nickravesh, F.; Arsanjani, J.J.; Amirkhani, M.; et al. A scenario-based spatial multi-criteria decision-making system for urban environment quality assessment: Case study of Tehran. *Land* **2023**, *12*, 1659. [CrossRef]
110. Meerow, S.; Newell, J.P. Spatial planning for multifunctional green infrastructure: Growing resilience in Detroit. *Landsc. Urban Plan.* **2017**, *159*, 62–75. [CrossRef]
111. Mahmoudzadeh, H.; Abedini, A.; Aram, F.; Mosavi, A. Evaluating urban environmental quality using multi criteria decision making. *Heliyon* **2024**, *10*. [CrossRef] [PubMed]
112. Lassandro, P.; Di Turi, S. Multi-criteria and multiscale assessment of building envelope response-ability to rising heat waves. *Sustain. Cities Soc.* **2019**, *51*, 101755. [CrossRef]
113. Kotharkar, R.; Bagade, A.; Singh, P.R. A systematic approach for urban heat island mitigation strategies in critical local climate zones of an Indian city. *Urban Clim.* **2020**, *34*, 100701. [CrossRef]
114. Putra, M.I.J.; Affandani, A.Y.; Widodo, T.; Wibowo, A. Spatial Multi-Criteria Analysis for Urban Sustainable Built Up Area Based on Urban Heat Island in Serang City. In *IOP Conference Series: Earth and Environmental Science*; IOP Publishing: Bristol, UK, 2019; Volume 338, p. 012025.
115. Yan, Y.; Yu, X.; Long, F.; Dong, Y. A multi-criteria evaluation of the urban ecological environment in Shanghai based on remote sensing. *ISPRS Int. J. Geo-Inf.* **2021**, *10*, 688. [CrossRef]
116. Teotónio, I.; Cabral, M.; Cruz, C.O.; Silva, C.M. Decision support system for green roofs investments in residential buildings. *J. Clean. Prod.* **2020**, *249*, 119365. [CrossRef]
117. Sangiorgio, V.; Fiorito, F.; Santamouris, M. Development of a holistic urban heat island evaluation methodology. *Sci. Rep.* **2020**, *10*, 17913. [CrossRef]

18. Philipps, N.; Landes, T.; Kastendeuch, P.; Najjar, G.; Gourguechon, C. Urban Heat Island Mapping Based on a Local Climate Zone Classification: A Case Study in Strasbourg City, France. *Int. J. Environ. Geoinform.* **2022**, *9*, 57–67. [CrossRef]
19. Mostafa, E.; Li, X.; Sadek, M. Urbanization Trends Analysis Using Hybrid Modeling of Fuzzy Analytical Hierarchical Process-Cellular Automata-Markov Chain and Investigating Its Impact on Land Surface Temperature over Gharbia City, Egypt. *Remote Sens.* **2023**, *15*, 843. [CrossRef]
20. Mostofi, N.; Aghamohammadi Zanjirabad, H.; Vafaeinejad, A.; Ramezani, M.; Hemmasi, A. Developing an SDSS for optimal sustainable roof covering planning based on UHI variation at neighborhood scale. *Environ. Monit. Assess.* **2021**, *193*, 372. [CrossRef] [PubMed]
21. Bathaei, B. Decision Support System to Select the Most Effective Strategies for Mitigating the Urban Heat Island Effect Using Sustainability and Resilience Performance Measures. Doctoral Thesis, The University of Texas Rio Grande Valley, Edinburg, TX, USA, 2021.
22. Metronimica. Available online: http://www.metronamica.nl/ (accessed on 12 November 2023).
23. Tuczek, M.; Degirmenci, K.; Desouza, K.C.; Watson, R.T.; Yigitcanlar, T.; Hansen, V.G.; Omrani, S.; Bamdad, K.; Breitner, M.H. *Toward a Decision Support System for Mitigating Urban Heat*; Association for Information Systems: Atlanta, GA, USA, 2019.
24. Qureshi, A.M.; Rachid, A. Review and Comparative Study of Decision Support Tools for the Mitigation of Urban Heat Stress. *Climate* **2021**, *9*, 102. [CrossRef]
25. Mahdiyar, A.; Tabatabaee, S.; Durdyev, S.; Ismail, S.; Abdullah, A.; Rani, W.N.M.W.M. A prototype decision support system for green roof type selection: A cybernetic fuzzy ANP method. *Sustain. Cities Soc.* **2019**, *48*, 101532. [CrossRef]
26. Zupic, I.; Cater, T. Bibliometric methods in management and organization. *Organ. Res. Methods* **2015**, *18*, 429–472. [CrossRef]
27. Aria, M.; Cuccurulo, C. bibliometrix: An R-tool for comprehensive science mapping analysis. *J. Informetr.* **2017**, *11*, 959–975. [CrossRef]
28. Scopus Fact Sheet. Available online: https://assets.ctfassets.net/o78em1y1w4i4/28v2L8eQgAGxOnnvZlqJWh/7947feb83982b078ec1d70c297055c34/ELSV_15617_Scopus_Fact_Sheet_Update_WEB.pdf (accessed on 2 November 2023).
29. Racetin, I.; Krtalic, A. Systematic Review of Anomaly Detection in Hyperspectral Remote Sensing Applications. *Appl. Sci.* **2021**, *11*, 4878. [CrossRef]
30. Tavra, M.; Lisec, A.; Galešić Divić, M.; Cetl, V. Unpacking the role of volunteered geographic information in disaster management: Focus on data quality. *Geomat. Nat. Hazards Risk* **2024**, *15*, 2300825. [CrossRef]
31. Lissner, T.K.; Holsten, A.; Walther, C.; Kropp, J.P. Towards sectoral and standardised vulnerability assessments: The example of heatwave impacts on human health. *Clim. Chang.* **2012**, *112*, 687–708. [CrossRef]
32. Borri, D.; Camarda, D.; Pluchinotta, I. Planning urban microclimate through multiagent modelling: A cognitive mapping approach. In Proceedings of the Cooperative Design, Visualization, and Engineering: 10th International Conference, CDVE, Alcudia, Mallorca, Spain, 22–25 September 2013; Springer: Berlin/Heidelberg, Germany, 2013; pp. 169–176.
33. Donthu, N.; Kumar, S.; Mukherjee, D.; Pandey, N.; Lim, W.M. How to conduct a bibliometric analysis: An overview and guidelines. *J. Bus. Res.* **2021**, *133*, 285–296. [CrossRef]
34. Alsharif, A.H.; Salleh, N.Z.; Baharun, R. Research trends of neuromarketing: A bibliometric analysis. *J. Theor. Appl. Inf. Technol.* **2020**, *98*, 2948–2962.
35. Broadus, R. Toward a definition of bibliometrics. *Scientometrics* **1987**, *12*, 373–379. [CrossRef]
36. Diodato, V. *Dictionary of Bibliometrics*, 1st ed.; Haworth Press: Binghamton, NY, USA, 1994.
37. Pritchard, A. Statistical bibliography or bibliometrics. *J. Doc.* **1969**, *25*, 348.
38. Bibliometrix. Available online: https://www.bibliometrix.org/home/ (accessed on 10 November 2023).
39. Biblioshiny. Available online: https://bibliometrix.org/biblioshiny/biblioshiny2.html (accessed on 10 November 2023).

energies

MDPI

Article

A Novel Trigonometric Entropy Measure Based on the Complex Proportional Assessment Technique for Pythagorean Fuzzy Sets

Sahil Kashyap [1], Bartosz Paradowski [2], Neeraj Gandotra [1], Namita Saini [1] and Wojciech Sałabun [2,3,*]

1 Yogananda School of AI, Computer and Data Sciences, Shoolini University, Solan 173229, HP, India; sahilkashyap@shooliniuniversity.com (S.K.); neerajgandotra@shooliniuniversity.com (N.G.); namita@shooliniuniversity.com (N.S.)
2 National Institute of Telecommunications, ul. Szachowa 1, 04-894 Warsaw, Poland; b.paradowski@il-pib.pl
3 Research Team on Intelligent Decision Support Systems, Department of Artificial Intelligence and Applied Mathematics, Faculty of Computer Science and Information Technology, West Pomeranian University of Technology in Szczecin, ul. Żołnierska 49, 71-210 Szczecin, Poland
* Correspondence: wojciech.salabun@zut.edu.pl; Tel.: +48-91-449-55-80

Abstract: The extension of intuitionistic fuzzy sets (IFS) to Pythagorean fuzzy sets (PFS) is a significant advancement, addressing the inherent limitations of IFS. This study introduces a novel entropy measure specifically designed for Pythagorean fuzzy sets, establishing its axiomatic definition and presenting key properties. Decision making guided by entropy is advantageous, as it effectively mitigates ambiguity with increasing entropy values. Furthermore, a numerical example is provided to facilitate a comparative assessment of our newly introduced entropy measure in contrast to existing PFS entropy measures. The validation of our findings is achieved through the application of the COPRAS method, which determines decision outcomes based on a multitude of influencing factors. Notably, the determination of weights in this method is underpinned by the utilization of our innovative entropy measure.

Keywords: intuitionistic fuzzy set; Pythagorean fuzzy sets; entropy measures; Pythagorean fuzzy entropy; multicriteria decision making; COPRAS technique

1. Introduction

In life, difficult and complex decision-making problems often arise, which in some cases are crucial and can significantly affect the subsequent course of events. In order to effectively deal with multicriteria decision-making problems, the field of multicriteria decision making (MCDM) is used. These techniques are often used in many areas of everyday life as well as in professional applications.

The application of these techniques has been demonstrated in a number of research studies that have considered problems in areas such as objective selection of personnel [1], supplier selection [2], selection of aircraft passage [3], innovation in the health sector regarding personnel selection [4] or evaluation in this sector [5], choice of factory location [6], evaluation of hydrogen energy storage methods [7], creation of a decision model for the development of offshore wind farms [8] or a sustainable approach to wastewater treatment technology selection [9].

There are many important problems, the solutions of which can significantly affect people's lives or the functioning of the state. One such area is energy, which, with the advancement of civilization and technology, is attracting increasing interest. The constant drive for development results in an increased demand for electricity, the storage of which is a process fraught with inevitable loss. That is why it is important to produce energy on an ongoing basis in a sustainable manner [10]. Multicriteria decision making is often applied in the selection of different sustainable energy sources [11,12]. One interesting type of power plant is the hydropower plant, which uses a natural source to generate energy. However, it is not only the type of power plant that deserves attention, but also the choice of where its site will be located. The appropriate location of the power plant is very important, as it can affect the environment and the public sentiment, as well as carry certain risks and increased operating costs.

Given the widespread use of multicriteria decision-making methods, it can be expected that as the complexity of the decision-making problems being solved increases, there is a need for new approaches that can more accurately represent the preferences of the decision maker [13], or solve the problem by approaching its evaluation objectively. Classical approaches tend to operate on crisp values that do not allow much freedom in regard to defining the decision variants that will be considered in the problem to be solved. However, when there is uncertainty in the decision problem under consideration, a solution by the classical approach is not always possible. To this end, fuzzy sets (FS) were introduced by Zadeh [14] so that decision makers can include uncertainty through the use of a membership function and express its degree of membership and non-membership. A number of examples using fuzzy approaches to solve multicriteria problems have been developed, such as the use of fuzzy technique for order of preference by similarity to ideal solution (TOPSIS) prioritization of patients on elective surgery waiting lists, presented by Rana et al. [15].

Due to their usefulness, fuzzy sets are widely used in multicriteria decision making [5,16]. In addition, many methods for multicriteria decision making have been extended for use in a fuzzy environment. Considering the solutions presented in the last few years, we can see the development of the method resistant to the rank reversal paradox, stable preference ordering towards ideal solution (SPOTIS) presented by Shekhovtsov et al. in 2022 [17] or a fuzzy decision by opinion method (FDOSM) extension to use Pythagorean fuzzy sets presented by Al-Samarraay et al., also in 2022 [18].

However, classical fuzzy sets are not the only possible approach to problems where uncertainty and fuzzy logic arise. Another such tool was presented by Turksen in 1986, namely the interval-valued fuzzy set (IVFS), which dealt with some of the limitations arising from the use of classical fuzzy sets [19]. These sets were then subject to many improvements, for example, by using bidirectional approximate inference, which was based precisely on IVFS and was presented by Chen et al. in 1997 [20], followed by the presentation of its application to a rule-based system by Chen, Hsiao and Jong [21] in 2000. Furthermore, in 2012, Chen et al. [22] proposed fuzzy rule interpolation for interval-valued Gaussian fuzzy sets of type 2.

Classical fuzzy sets have some limitations, which were explored by Atanassov in 1986, where he proposed intuitionistic fuzzy sets (IFS) [23]. These sets, like the earlier ones, have found wide application in solving multicriteria decision-making problems. In many cases, these sets can be a suitable alternative to classical fuzzy sets or linguistic values [24]. Because of their adoption in the decision-making environment, these sets have also been used to extend multicriteria approaches to decision making. A good example is the work of Stanujkić et al. [25], in which they presented an extension of the weighted aggregated sum product assessment (WASPAS) method for this particular fuzzy set and showed its application to the website evaluation problem. In addition, the sets themselves continue to be extended to represent as many cases as possible, and extensions such as circular intuitionistic fuzzy sets [26] and continuous intuitionistic fuzzy sets [27] were presented.

Another improvement of fuzzy sets is Pythagorean fuzzy sets (PFS), which represent values using a pair of numbers that are degrees of membership and non-membership. This type of fuzzy set has also found wide application in the field of decision making. They allow for a better representation of data in uncertain, ambiguous situations, which translates into more informed decisions that better represent the decision maker's preferences [28]. Their application in solving real-world problems has been demonstrated by Peng et al. for the evaluation of the 5G industry [29], or by Boyacı et al. for the selection of a pandemic hospital location based on PFS and a geographic information system [30]. Moreover, PFSs are constantly being studied, and new approaches are presented, such as the significance of the

TOPSIS approach to multiple attribute decision making (MADM) in calculating exponential divergence measures for Pythagorean fuzzy sets presented by Arora et al. [31], directional correlation coefficient measures for Pythagorean fuzzy sets presented by Lin et al. [32], or Pythagorean fuzzy Multi-Objective Optimization on the basis of a Ratio Analysis plus the full MULTIplicative form (MULTIMOORA) method based on distance measure and score function, presented by Huang et al. [33].

In cases where the problems under consideration contain a lot of data, measures that allow us to determine their characteristics are useful. One such measure is entropy, which informs us of the uncertainty in the values under consideration, so a higher entropy value informs us that the data carry more information. The first classical entropy is Shannon entropy, which allows us to determine the degree of uncertainty in a probability distribution [34]. According to Shannon entropy, a theoretical framework based on fundamental principles for fuzzy entropy measures was presented by De Luca et al. [35]. This enabled further work on entropy and its application to fuzzy sets, such as intuitionistic fuzzy sets presented by Hung and Yang [36], interval-valued fuzzy sets presented by Zeng and Li [37], and hesitant fuzzy sets presented by Hu et al. [38].

Entropy in Pythagorean fuzzy sets is also widely used. Yang and Hussain proposed a new Pythagorean fuzzy entropy (PFE) based on probabilistic type, distance, Pythagorean index, and min–max operator [39]. In 2020, Xu et al. introduced a new PFE, which was then used to calculate the criteria weights and establish the Pythagorean fuzzy multicriteria decision-making approach [40]. Rani et al. introduced another PFE and additionally, a score function to evaluate unknown criteria weights using the COPRAS technique [41]. Abhishek introduced a new Pythagorean fuzzy entropy of R-S norms whose application was shown in a problem of hydrogen plant site selection using the VIseKriterijumska Optimizacija I Kompromisno Resenje (VIKOR) and TOPSIS methods [42]. Biswas and Sarkar presented a new PFE measure for handling multicriteria group decision problems using TOPSIS-based methodology in a Pythagorean fuzzy environment [43]. Xue et al. proposed a PFE for decision making using a linear programming technique for a multidimensional analysis of preferences (LINMAP), which has been used in railway project investment evaluation [44]. Some researchers propose entropies for specific cases of PFS, such as the linguistic Pythagorean fuzzy-sets TOPSIS method based on correlation coefficient and entropy measure, presented by Lin et al. [45]. Over the years, many authors have continued to study entropy, which has translated into many published papers [46–50].

The research presented in this article proposes a new Pythagorean entropy of fuzzy sets, which has been compared with other entropies proposed by various authors. We prove that the proposed measure satisfies all conditions consistent with the axioms of valid entropy. In addition, we show the possibility of using the proposed entropy to calculate the weights of criteria in combination with a multicriteria decision-making method to solve decision-making problems, as demonstrated by the example of site selection for a hydropower plant.

The rest of the paper is structured as follows: Section 2 presents an introductory discussion that covers the basic concepts and axioms of intuitionistic fuzzy sets and Pythagorean fuzzy sets, the novel entropy of Pythagorean fuzzy sets, and the complex proportional assessment (COPRAS) approach that combines the proposed entropy with Pythagorean fuzzy data. In Section 3, an example Pythagorean fuzzy multicriteria decision problem is solved using COPRAS and the proposed entropy. Section 4 compares the proposed entropy with existing ones regarding the results obtained from their application. Additionally, Section 5 compares the used COPRAS method with two other MCDA methods, namely TOPSIS and VIKOR. Finally, Section 6 draws conclusions and discusses future directions.

2. Preliminaries

Definition 1. *Assume X is a given complete set; set S is said to be an Intuitionistic Fuzzy Set (IFS) if it can be expressed by the following formula [51]:*

$$S = \{\langle x_i, \mu_S(x_i), \vartheta_S(x_i)\rangle \mid x_i \in X\}, \tag{1}$$

for which the function $\mu_S : X \to [0,1]$ and $\vartheta_S : X \to [0,1]$ is the degree of membership and non-membership of x_i, and for every $x_i \epsilon X$, $0 \le \mu_S(x_i) + \vartheta_S(x_i) \le 1$. Also, $\pi_S(x_i) = 1 - \mu_S(x_i) - \vartheta_S(x_i)$ is the degree of uncertainty x_i.

Definition 2. *For every two IFS K and S of the set X, we define the following relations and operations [4]:*

i. $K \cup S = \{x, \max(\mu_K(x), \mu_S(x)), \min(\vartheta_K(x), \vartheta_S(x))\ \forall\, x \in X\}$
ii. $K \cap S = \{x, \min(\mu_K(x), \mu_S(x)), \max(\vartheta_K(x), \vartheta_S(x))\ \forall\, x \in X\}$
iii. $K \subset S\ if\ and\ only\ if\ \mu_K(x) \le \mu_S(x)\ and\ \vartheta_K(x) \ge \vartheta_S(x)\ \forall\, x \in X$
iv. $K \supset S\ if\ and\ only\ if\ S \subset K$
v. $K = S\ if\ and\ only\ if\ \mu_K(x) = \mu_S(x)\ and\ \vartheta_K(x) = \vartheta_S(x)\ \forall\, x \in X$
vi. $\bar{K} = \{x, \vartheta_K(x), \mu_S(x)\ \forall\, x \in X\}$
vii. $K + S = \{x, \mu_K(x) + \mu_S(x) - \mu_K(x) \cdot \mu_S(x), \vartheta_K(x) \cdot \vartheta_S(x)\ \forall\, x \in X\}$
viii. $K \cdot S = \{x, \mu_K(x) \cdot \mu_S(x), \vartheta_K(x) + \vartheta_S(x) - \vartheta_K(x) \cdot \vartheta_S(x)\ \forall\, x \in X\}$
ix. $K@S = \left\{x, \frac{\mu_K(x)+\mu_S(X)}{2}, \frac{\vartheta_K(x)+\vartheta_S(x)}{2}\ \forall\, x \in X\right\}$
x. $K\$S = \left\{x, \sqrt{\mu_K(x) \cdot \mu_S(x)}, \sqrt{\vartheta_K(x) \cdot \vartheta_S(x)}\ \forall\, x \in X\right\}$

Definition 3. *Let X be a given universal set; set S is said to be a Pythagorean fuzzy set (PFS) if it can be expressed by the following formula [28]:*

$$S = \{\langle x_i, \mu_S(x_i), \vartheta_S(x_i) \mid x_i \in X\rangle\}, \tag{2}$$

where the function μ_S: $X \to [0,1]$ and ϑ_S: $X \to [0,1]$ if the degrees of membership and non-membership of x_i, and $\forall x_i \epsilon X$, $0 \le \mu_S^2(x_i) + \vartheta_S^2(x_i) \le 1$.

Definition 4. *Consider three PFS: $S = (\mu_S(x), \vartheta_S(x))$, $S_1 = (\mu_{S_1}(x), \vartheta_{S_1}(x))$, and $S_2 = (\mu_{S_2}(x), \vartheta_{S_2}(x))$; then, we define the operations as presented below [28,52,53]:*

i. $S_1 \cup S_2 = \{x, \max(\mu_{S_1}(x), \mu_{S_2}(x)), \min(\vartheta_{S_1}(x), \vartheta_{S_2}(x)\ \forall\, x \in X\}$
ii. $S_1 \cap S_2 = \{x, \min(\mu_{S_1}(x), \mu_{S_2}(x)), \max(\vartheta_{S_1}(x), \vartheta_{S_2}(x)\ \forall\, x \in X\}$
iii. $\bar{S} = \{x, \vartheta_S(x), \mu_S(x)\ \forall\, x \in X\}$
iv. $S_1 \oplus S_2 = \left\{x, \sqrt{\mu_{S_1}^2(x) + \mu_{S_2}^2(x) - \mu_{S_1}^2(x)\mu_{S_2}^2(x)}, \vartheta_{S_1}\vartheta_{S_2}\ \forall\, x \in X\right\}$
v. $S_1 \otimes S_2 = \left\{x,\ \mu_{S_1}\mu_{S_2}, \sqrt{\vartheta_{S_1}^2(x) + \vartheta_{S_2}^2(x) - \vartheta_{S_1}^2(x)\vartheta_{S_2}^2(x)}\ \forall\, x \in X\right\}$
vi. $\lambda S = \left(\sqrt{1 - (1 - \mu_S^2(x))^\lambda}, \vartheta_S^\lambda(x)\right), \lambda > 0$
vii. $S^\lambda = \left(\mu_S^\lambda(x), \sqrt{1 - (1 - \vartheta_S^2(x))^\lambda}\right), \lambda > 0$
viii. $S_1 \ominus S_2 = \left(\sqrt{\frac{\mu_{S_1}^2(x)-\mu_{S_2}^2(x)}{1-\mu_{S_2}^2(x)}}, \frac{\vartheta_{S_1}(x)}{\vartheta_{S_2}(x)}\right),$
$if\ \mu_{S_1}(x) \ge \mu_{S_2}(x), \vartheta_{S_1}(x) \le \min\left\{\vartheta_{S_2}(x), \frac{\vartheta_{S_2}(x)\pi_{S_1}(x)}{\pi_{S_2}(x)}\right\}$
ix. $S_1 \oslash S_2 = \left(\frac{\mu_{S_1}(x)}{\mu_{S_2}(x)}\right), \sqrt{\frac{\vartheta_{S_1}^2(x)-\vartheta_{S_2}^2(x)}{1-\vartheta_{S_2}^2(x)}},$
$if\ \vartheta_{S_1}(x) \ge \vartheta_{S_2}(x), \mu_{S_1}(x) \le \min\left\{\mu_{S_2}(x), \frac{\mu_{S_2}(x)\pi_{S_1}(x)}{\pi_{S_2}(x)}\right\}$

Definition 5. *Given a PFS K over X, $K = \{x, \mu_K(x), \vartheta_K(x)\ \forall\ x \in X\}$, the score function is defined as [28]:*

$$\begin{gathered} S_K(x) = (\mu_K(x))^2 - (\vartheta_K(x))^2\ \forall\ x \in X \\ S_K(x) : X \rightarrow [-1, 1]. \end{gathered} \tag{3}$$

Definition 6. *Given a PFS K over X, $K = \{x, \mu_K(x), \vartheta_K(x)\ \forall\ x \in X\}$, the accuracy function is given as [52]:*

$$\begin{gathered} A_K(x) = (\mu_K(x))^2 + (\vartheta_K(x))^2\ \forall\ x \in X \\ A_K(x) : X \rightarrow [0, 1]. \end{gathered} \tag{4}$$

2.1. Novel Entropy for Pythagorean Fuzzy Set

Classical Shannon entropy, also known as information entropy, is a fundamental concept in information theory and probability theory. It is used to measure the information content or uncertainty of random variables, data, or events. The fuzzy set theory uses entropy to quantify uncertainty or vagueness within these sets, which incorporate both membership and non-membership degrees [35]. In this section, the new Pythagorean fuzzy entropy will be presented along with proof that it satisfies all the required axioms to consider the proposed measure as entropy.

Definition 7. *The function $E : PFS(X) \longrightarrow [0, 1]$ is said to be an entropy on $PSF(X)$ if E has the following properties:*

1. ***Minimality:*** *$E(S) = 0$ if S is a crisp set.*
2. ***Maximality:*** *$E(S) = 1$ if $\mu_{\tilde{S}} = \vartheta_{\tilde{S}} = \frac{1}{\sqrt{3}}$ for all $x \in X$*
3. ***Resolution:*** *$E(S) \leq E(K)$ if S is crisper than K, that is if $\mu_S \leq \mu_K$ for $\mu_K \leq \frac{1}{\sqrt{3}}$ and $\mu_S \geq \mu_K$ for $\mu_K \geq \frac{1}{\sqrt{3}}$*
4. ***Symmetry:*** *$E(S) = E(S^c)$ where S^c is the complement of S.*

In addition to the aforementioned Pythagorean measures of fuzzy entropy, we have developed the following Pythagorean measure of fuzzy entropy:

$$\begin{aligned} E(S) = \frac{1}{n}\sum_{i=1}^{n}\Bigg[\sin\Bigg[\frac{1}{\sqrt{e}-1}\Bigg(\Bigg(\frac{\mu_S^2(x_i) + 1 - \vartheta_S^2(x_i)}{2}\Bigg)e^{\frac{\left(\vartheta_S^2(x_i)+1-\mu_S^2(x_i)\right)}{2}} \\ + \Bigg(\frac{\vartheta_S(x_i)^2 + 1 - \mu_S^2(x_i)}{2}\Bigg)e^{\frac{\left(\mu_S(x_i)^2+1-\vartheta_S(x_i)^2\right)}{2}} - 1\Bigg)\frac{\pi}{2}\Bigg]\Bigg] \end{aligned} \tag{5}$$

where n is the number of alternatives.

Theorem 1. *The previously mentioned function E(S) is a valid entropy measure on PFS.*

Proof. To demonstrate the theorem's validity, it must satisfy the axioms, according to the following definitions [39].

1. **Minimality:** if S is a crisp set, i.e., $\mu_S(x_i) = 1$, $\vartheta_S(x_i) = 0$ or $\mu_S(x_i) = 0$, $\vartheta_S(x_i) = 1\ \forall x_i\ \in N$ such that

$$\begin{aligned} E(S) = \frac{1}{n}\sum_{i=1}^{n}\Bigg[\sin\Bigg[\frac{1}{\sqrt{e}-1}\Bigg(\Bigg(\frac{\mu_S^2(x_i) + 1 - \vartheta_S(x_i)^2}{2}\Bigg)e^{\frac{\left(\vartheta_S^2(x_i)+1-\mu_S^2(x_i)\right)}{2}} \\ + \Bigg(\frac{\vartheta_S^2(x_i) + 1 - \mu_S^2(x_i)}{2}\Bigg)e^{\frac{\left(\mu_S^2(x_i)+1-\vartheta_S^2(x_i)\right)}{2}} - 1\Bigg)\frac{\pi}{2}\Bigg]\Bigg] \end{aligned} \tag{6}$$

$$\therefore\ E(S) = 0. \tag{7}$$

2. **Maximality:** for all $x_i \in N$, if $\mu_S(x_i) = \vartheta_S(x_i) = \frac{1}{\sqrt{3}}$

$$\therefore E(S) = 1. \tag{8}$$

3. **Resolution:** to prove the third axiom, let us assume a function $f(x,y)$ such that:

$$f(x,y) = \sin\left[\frac{1}{\sqrt{e}-1}\left(\left(\frac{x^2+1-y^2}{2}\right)e^{\frac{(y^2+1-x^2)}{2}} + \left(\frac{y^2+1-x^2}{2}\right)e^{\frac{(x^2+1-y^2)}{2}} - 1\right)\frac{\pi}{2}\right] \tag{9}$$

where $x, y \in [0,1]$.
We can obtain the partial derivatives for x and y

$$\frac{\partial f}{\partial x} = \frac{x\pi}{2(\sqrt{e}-1)}\cos\left[\frac{1}{\sqrt{e}-1}\left[\left(\frac{x^2+1-y^2}{2}\right)e^{\frac{(y^2+1-x^2)}{2}} + \left(\frac{y^2+1-x^2}{2}\right)e^{\frac{(x^2+1-y^2)}{2}} - 1\right]\frac{\pi}{2}\right]\left[e^{\frac{(y^2+1-x^2)}{2}}\left(\frac{y^2+1-x^2}{2}\right) + e^{\frac{(x^2+1-y^2)}{2}}\left(\frac{y^2-1-x^2}{2}\right)\right] \tag{10}$$

$$\frac{\partial f}{\partial y} = \frac{y\pi}{2(\sqrt{e}-1)}\cos\left[\frac{1}{\sqrt{e}-1}\left[\left(\frac{x^2+1-y^2}{2}\right)e^{\frac{(y^2+1-x^2)}{2}} + \left(\frac{y^2+1-x^2}{2}\right)e^{\frac{(x^2+1-y^2)}{2}} - 1\right]\frac{\pi}{2}\right]\left[e^{\frac{(y^2+1-x^2)}{2}}\left(\frac{x^2-1-y^2}{2}\right) + e^{\frac{(x^2+1-y^2)}{2}}\left(\frac{x^2+1-y^2}{2}\right)\right]. \tag{11}$$

We obtained that $\frac{\partial f(x,y)}{\partial x} \geq 0$ when $x \leq y$ and $\frac{\partial f(x,y)}{\partial x} \leq 0$ when $x \geq y$, whereas $\frac{\partial f(x,y)}{\partial y} \leq 0$ when $x \leq y$ and $\frac{\partial f(x,y)}{\partial x} \geq 0$ when $x \geq y$, then when f is increasing with respect to x when $x \leq y$ and decreasing when $x \geq y$. Moreover, f is decreasing with respect to y for $x \leq y$ and increasing when $x \geq y$.
Based on the above function, we can say that $E(S) \leq E(\dot{S})$, if S is less fuzzy than $\dot{S}$, i.e., $\mu_S(x_i) \leq \mu_{\dot{S}}(x_i) \leq \frac{1}{\sqrt{3}}$ and $\vartheta_S(x_i) \leq \vartheta_{\dot{S}}(x_i) \leq \frac{1}{\sqrt{3}}$ for $\mu_{\dot{S}}(x_i) \leq \mu_S(x_i)$ or $\mu_S(x_i) \geq \mu_{\dot{S}}(x_i) \geq \frac{1}{\sqrt{3}}$ and $\vartheta_{\dot{S}}(x_i) \geq \vartheta_S(x_i) \geq \frac{1}{\sqrt{3}}$ for $\mu_{\dot{S}}(x_i) \geq \mu_S(x_i)$.

4. **Symmetry:**

$$E(S) = \frac{1}{n}\sum_{i=1}^{n}\left[\sin\left[\frac{1}{\sqrt{e}-1}\left(\left(\frac{\mu_S^2(x_i)+1-\vartheta_S^2(x_i)}{2}\right)e^{\frac{(\vartheta_S^2(x_i)+1-\mu_S^2(x_i))}{2}} + \left(\frac{\vartheta_S^2(x_i)+1-\mu_S^2(x_i)}{2}\right)e^{\frac{(\mu_S^2(x_i)+1-\vartheta_S^2(x_i))}{2}} - 1\right)\frac{\pi}{2}\right]\right] = E(S^c) \tag{12}$$

where S^c is the complement of S.
Hence, $E(S)$ is a valid entropy for the Pythagorean fuzzy set. □

Theorem 2. *In the universe discourse X, consider A and B to be two Pythagorean fuzzy sets.* $A = \{x_i, \langle \mu_A(x_i), \mu_A(x_i) \rangle \mid x_i \in X\}$ *and* $B = \{x_i, \langle \mu_B(x_i), \mu_B(x_i) \rangle \mid x_i \in X\}$, *such that for any* $x_i \in X$ *either* $A \subseteq B$ *or* $B \subseteq A$,

$$E(S) = \frac{1}{n}\sum_{i=1}^{n}\left[\sin\left[\frac{1}{\sqrt{e}-1}\left(\left(\frac{\mu_S^2(x_i)+1-\vartheta_S^2(x_i)}{2}\right)e^{\frac{\left(\vartheta_S^2(x_i)+1-\mu_S^2(x_i)\right)}{2}} + \left(\frac{\vartheta_S^2(x_i)+1-\mu_S^2(x_i)}{2}\right)e^{\frac{\left(\mu_S^2(x_i)+1-\vartheta_S^2(x_i)\right)}{2}} - 1\right)\frac{\pi}{2}\right]\right]. \tag{13}$$

$E_\gamma(A)$ *and* $E_\gamma(B)$ *are the entropy of the fuzzy set, then*

$$E_\gamma(A \cup B) + E_\gamma(A \cap B) = E_\gamma(A) + E_\gamma(B). \tag{14}$$

Proof. Let us divide X into two subsets as X_1 and X_2, where $X_1 = \{x_i \in X : \mu_A(x_i) \geq \mu_B(x_i)\}$ and $X_2 = \{x_i \in X : \mu_A(x_i) \leq \mu_B(x_i)\}$ For subset X_1: $\mu_A(x_i) \geq \mu_B(x_i), \vartheta_A(x_i) \leq \vartheta_B(x_i)$ for all $x_i \in X$

$$\begin{aligned}
E_\gamma(A \cup B) =& \frac{1}{n}\sum_{i=1}^{n}\left[\sin\left[\frac{1}{\sqrt{e}-1}\left(\left(\frac{\mu^2_{(A\cup B)}(x_i)+1-\vartheta^2_{(A\cap B)}(x_i)}{2}\right)e^{\frac{\left(\vartheta^2_{(A\cap B)}(x_i)+1-\mu^2_{(A\cup B)}(x_i)\right)}{2}}\right.\right.\right. \\
&\left.\left.\left. + \left(\frac{\left(\vartheta^2_{(A\cap B)}(x_i)+1-\mu^2_{(A\cup B)}(x_i)\right)}{2}\right)e^{\left(\frac{\mu^2_{(A\cup B)}(x_i)+1-\vartheta^2_{(A\cap B)}(x_i)}{2}\right)} - 1\right)\frac{\pi}{2}\right]\right] \\
=& \frac{1}{n}\sum_{i=1}^{n}\left[\sin\left[\frac{1}{\sqrt{e}-1}\left(\left(\frac{\mu^2_A(x_i)+1-\vartheta^2_A(x_i)}{2}\right)e^{\frac{\left(\vartheta^2_A(x_i)+1-\mu^2_A(x_i)\right)}{2}}\right.\right.\right. \\
&\left.\left.\left. + \left(\frac{\left(\vartheta^2_A(x_i)+1-\mu^2_A(x_i)\right)}{2}\right)e^{\left(\frac{\mu^2_A(x_i)+1-\vartheta^2_A(x_i)}{2}\right)} - 1\right)\frac{\pi}{2}\right]\right] \\
=& E_\gamma(A).
\end{aligned} \tag{15}$$

Similarly,

$$\begin{aligned}
E_\gamma(A \cap B) =& \frac{1}{n}\sum_{i=1}^{n}\left[\sin\left[\frac{1}{\sqrt{e}-1}\left(\left(\frac{\mu^2_{(A\cap B)}(x_i)+1-\vartheta^2_{(A\cup B)}(x_i)}{2}\right)e^{\frac{\left(\vartheta^2_{(A\cup B)}(x_i)+1-\mu^2_{(A\cap B)}(x_i)\right)}{2}}\right.\right.\right. \\
&\left.\left.\left. + \left(\frac{\left(\vartheta^2_{(A\cup B)}(x_i)+1-\mu^2_{(A\cap B)}(x_i)\right)}{2}\right)e^{\left(\frac{\mu^2_{(A\cap B)}(x_i)+1-\vartheta^2_{(A\cup B)}(x_i)}{2}\right)} - 1\right)\frac{\pi}{2}\right]\right] \\
=& \frac{1}{n}\sum_{i=1}^{n}\left[\sin\left[\frac{1}{\sqrt{e}-1}\left(\left(\frac{\mu^2_B(x_i)+1-\vartheta^2_B(x_i)}{2}\right)e^{\frac{\left(\vartheta^2_B(x_i)+1-\mu^2_B(x_i)\right)}{2}}\right.\right.\right. \\
&\left.\left.\left. + \left(\frac{\left(\vartheta^2_B(x_i)+1-\mu^2_B(x_i)\right)}{2}\right)e^{\left(\frac{\mu^2_B(x_i)+1-\vartheta^2_B(x_i)}{2}\right)} - 1\right)\frac{\pi}{2}\right]\right] \\
=& E_\gamma(B).
\end{aligned} \tag{16}$$

Adding Equations (15) and (16), we obtain

$$E_\gamma(A \cup B) + E_\gamma(A \cap B) = E_\gamma(A) + E_\gamma(B). \tag{17}$$

Similarly, this result is true for a subset of $X_2 : \mu_A(x_i) \leq \mu_B(x_i), \vartheta_A(x_i) \geq \vartheta_B(x_i)$ for all $x_i \in X$:

$$E_\gamma(A \cup B) + E_\gamma(A \cap B) = E_\gamma(A) + E_\gamma(B). \tag{18}$$

This proves the above theorem. □

2.2. Pythagorean Fuzzy Multicriteria Decision Making Based on COPRAS Approach

The complex proportional assessment (COPRAS) approach was first proposed by Zavadskas and Kaklauskas in 1994 [54]. COPRAS has many advantages over other approaches to solving decision-making problems, such as the fact that it considers the most and least favorable solution in terms of further evaluation while keeping the calculations concise and simple, which in turn makes it fast [55]. Moreover, it ranks and estimates alternatives step by step in terms of their importance and degree of utility.

This approach is widely used in decision-making situations under uncertainty [56]. As a popular method for multicriteria decision making, it has seen many developments. Vahdani and Mousavi developed a new COPRAS approach based on interval values to solve the robot selection problem [57]. Bekar et al. integrated the COPRAS technique with grey numbers theory to create a decision support system to improve the performance of maintenance activities by evaluating total productive maintenance (TPM) strategies [58]. An extension of the COPRAS approach, which can be used with hesitant fuzzy sets, was presented by Mishra et al., where they considered evaluating the quality of service [59]. In addition, Kumari and Mishra presented an application of this method of multicriteria decision making using intuitionistic fuzzy sets to select a green supplier [60].

Figure 1 presents a general flowchart for the COPRAS approach.

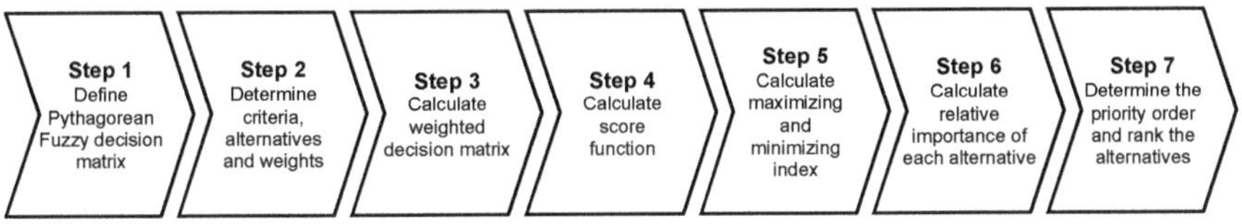

Figure 1. The COPRAS approach flowchart.

In this study, the COPRAS method is extended in such a way that it utilizes the proposed Pythagorean fuzzy entropy to calculate the weights for the problem under consideration. The steps presented in the flowchart are described in detail below.

Step 1: Establish a Pythagorean fuzzy decision matrix $R = (A_i, C_j)_{m\times n}$, where A_i denotes alternatives ($i = 1,2,3,\ldots m$) and C_j criteria ($j = 1,2,3,\ldots n$):

$$\begin{array}{c} \\ A_1 \\ A_2 \\ \vdots \\ A_m \end{array} \begin{array}{c} \begin{array}{cccc} C_1 & C_2 & \cdots & C_n \end{array} \\ \begin{bmatrix} P(\mu_{11},\vartheta_{11}) & P(\mu_{12},\vartheta_{12}) & \cdots & P(\mu_{1m},\vartheta_{1m}) \\ P(\mu_{21},\vartheta_{21}) & P(\mu_{22},\vartheta_{22}) & \cdots & P(\mu_{2m},\vartheta_{2m}) \\ \vdots & \vdots & \ddots & \vdots \\ P(\mu_{n1},\vartheta_{n1}) & P(\mu_{n2},\vartheta_{n2}) & \cdots & P(\mu_{11},\vartheta_{nm}) \end{bmatrix} \end{array}$$

Step 2: Calculate the entropy of Pythagorean fuzzy set e_j for each criterion C_j ($j = 1,2,3,\ldots n$) using Equation (5) and determine the criteria weight w_j of each criterion C_j ($j = 1,2,3,\ldots n$) by using the following formula:

$$w_j = \frac{1 - e_j}{\sum_{j=1}^{n}(1 - e_j)} \; (j = 1,2,\ldots n) \tag{19}$$

Step 3: Compute the weighted decision matrix $R = [r_{ij}]_{m\times n}$ using the following equation:

$$r_{ij} = w_{ij}\, d_{ij} = \left(\sqrt{1 - \left(1 - \mu_{ij}^2\right)^{w_j}}, \vartheta_{ij}^{w_j}\right) \tag{20}$$

Step 4: Determine the value of the score function $s(r_{ij})$ using Equation (3) $\forall i = 1,2,\ldots m$; $j = 1,2,\ldots n$

Step 5: Calculate maximizing $s(P_i)$ and minimizing $s(R_i)$ index for benefit and non-benefit criteria as follows:

$$s(P_i) = \frac{1}{|B|} \sum_{j \in B} s(r_{ij}) \tag{21}$$

$$s(R_i) = \frac{1}{|NB|} \sum_{j \in NB} s(r_{ij}) \tag{22}$$

where NB stands for the collection of all non-benefit criteria and B represents the set of benefit criteria, $\forall\ (i = 1,2\ldots m)$

Step 6: Determine the relative importance of each alternative Q_i for all $(i = 1,2,\ldots m)$ using following equation:

$$Q_i = s(P_i) + \frac{\sum_{i=1}^{n} e^{s(R_i)}}{e^{s(R_i)} \sum_{i=1}^{n} \frac{1}{e^{s(R_i)}}} \tag{23}$$

Step 7: Determine the priority order P_{ri} for all $(i = 1,2,\ldots m)$ using Equation (24) and rank the alternatives in the descending order, which means that the alternative with the highest value is considered the best.

$$P_{ri} = \frac{Q_i}{\max Q_i} \times 100 \tag{24}$$

2.3. TOPSIS

TOPSIS is one of the most widely used methods for multicriteria decision making, which dates back to 1994, when it was presented by Hwang and Yoon [61]. This method, through the use of positive ideal solution (PIS) and negative ideal solution (NIS), allows the assessment of individual alternatives in the context of ideal solution. Its application has been presented in a number of papers: Alao et al. presented solving the problem of waste to energy technology selection [62], Javad et al. proposed a solution for the green supplier selection for the steel industry [63] and Konstantinos et al. designed a decision support system methodology for selecting wind farm installation locations using TOPSIS [64]. The method has seen many extensions over the years, but the most relevant to this study is the extension presented by Zhang and Xu in 2014 [65], which offers the possibility of using this method to solve problems described on Pythagorean fuzzy sets.

2.4. VIKOR

Another prevalent approach is the VIKOR method. The main difference with the TOPSIS method is that this method offers three final rankings: a S ranking, a R ranking and a compromise Q ranking. This article uses the compromise ranking, obtained by setting the compromise value to 0.5, meaning that the S ranking has the same effect on the final result as the R ranking. This method has also been used to solve various problems, such as the balanced supplier selection presented by Abdel-Baset et al. [66], or the evaluation of the service level of bike-sharing companies presented by Liang et al. [67]. In addition, it has received many extensions, for example, to group decision making based on complex spherical fuzzy sets, presented by Akram et al. [68], or the intuitionistic-fuzzy extension for solving the personnel selection problem, presented by Krishankumar et al. [69]. However, again, the most relevant extension in the context of this study is the one that allows us to operate on Pythagorean fuzzy sets, and it was presented by Bakioglu and Atahan in 2021 [70].

2.5. Ranking Similarity Coefficients

Ranking similarity coefficients are helpful when analyzing solutions to multicriteria decision-making problems offered by different methods. They allow the degree of similarity between two rankings to be determined using a single value, making the comparison more transparent and accessible. The most commonly used ranking similarity coefficients are the weighted Spearman coefficient presented by Pinto da Costa in 2005 [71] and the weighted similarity coefficient (WS) presented by Sałabun in 2020 [72]. The WS coefficient is asymmetric, so when using it, it is crucial to determine which ranking is being compared to which ranking. In addition, it allows for more accurate modeling of the change in places of individual alternatives within the podium. Both coefficients are widely used, and their application has been demonstrated by, among others, Sałabun et al., who investigated whether multicriteria decision-making methods are benchmarkable [73]; Kizielewicz et al., who used these coefficients to compare solutions in the problem supplier selection [74]; or Shekhovtsov, who examined how strongly the rank similarity coefficients vary [75]. The weighted Spearman coefficient is presented as Equation (25), while the WS coefficient is given as Equation (26).

$$r_w = 1 - \frac{6\sum_{i=1}^{n}(R_i - Q_i)^2((n - R_i + 1) + (n - Q_i + 1))}{n^4 + n^3 - n^2 - n}, \tag{25}$$

where R_i—position in the reference ranking; Q_i—position in the second ranking; n—number of alternatives.

$$WS = 1 - \sum_{i=1}^{n}\left(2^{-R_i} \cdot \frac{|R_i - R_i|}{\max\{|1 - R_i|, |n - R_i|\}}\right), \tag{26}$$

where R_i—position of reference ranking; Q_i—position of second ranking; n—number of alternatives.

3. Numerical Example

This section will present a numerical example that is solved using the procedure described in Section 2.2, namely the COPRAS approach, which integrates the proposed entropy using the numerical space of Pythagorean fuzzy sets. The presented example solves the problem of selecting the site for a hydropower plant. The exact framework for the problem under consideration is presented in Figure 2.

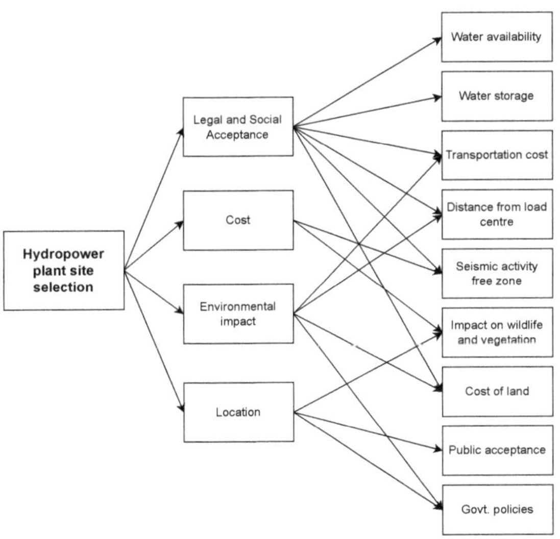

Figure 2. Framework of site selection for Hydropower Plant.

Next, let us consider a problem in which four sites $S = \{S_1, S_2, S_3, S_4\}$ and nine criteria $C = \{C_1, C_2, C_3, \ldots, C_9\}$ define our problem. The criteria are defined as availability (C_1), water storage (C_2), transportation cost (C_3), distance from load centre (C_4), seismic activity free zone (C_5), impact on wildlife and vegetation (C_6), cost of land (C_7), public acceptance (C_8) and government policies (C_9). In this study, we took C_1, C_2, $C_3 \ldots C_8$ as benefit criteria and C_9 as non-benefit criteria. The aforementioned alternatives and criteria form our decision matrix, which is shown in Table 1.

Table 1. Pythagorean Fuzzy matrix.

	S_1	S_2	S_3	S_4
C_1	(0.94000, 0.23000)	(0.93000, 0.08000)	(0.95000, 0.04500)	(0.95000, 0.23000)
C_2	(0.05800, 0.97500)	(0.90000, 0.03000)	(0.92000, 0.08000)	(0.23000, 0.98000)
C_3	(0.96000, 0.22000)	(0.95000, 0.05500)	(0.18000, 0.95000)	(0.97000, 0.05800)
C_4	(0.05500, 0.95000)	(0.45000, 0.95000)	(0.96000, 0.23000)	(0.98000, 0.18000)
C_5	(0.97500, 0.20000)	(0.04900, 0.89600)	(0.95000, 0.05500)	(0.08000, 0.97000)
C_6	(0.98000, 0.04500)	(0.92000, 0.02200)	(0.45000, 0.98000)	(0.93000, 0.08000)
C_7	(0.95000, 0.18000)	(0.89600, 0.04900)	(0.95000, 0.05500)	(0.05500, 0.95000)
C_8	(0.96000, 0.23000)	(0.05500, 0.95000)	(0.98000, 0.04200)	(0.98000, 0.05800)
C_9	(0.04900, 0.89600)	(0.02000, 0.97500)	(0.93000, 0.08000)	(0.95000, 0.18000)

Next, we calculate the entropy for each criterion according to Equation (5). The resulting values are $e_1 = 0.409201$, $e_2 = 0.360482$, $e_3 = 0.31632$, $e_4 = 0.412761$, $e_5 = 0.33419$, $e_6 = 0.40687$, $e_7 = 0.386817$, $e_8 = 0.241232$, $e_9 = 0.376839$.

We can then calculate the weight values for each criterion using Equation (19), from which we obtain $w_1 = 0.102653$, $w_2 = 0.111118$, $w_3 = 0.118792$, $w_4 = 0.102035$, $w_5 = 0.115687$, $w_6 = 0.103058$, $w_7 = 0.106543$, $w_8 = 0.131838$, $w_9 = 0.108276$. Next, we use the calculated weight values to create a weighted decision matrix according to Equation (20). The resulting weighted decision matrix is shown in Table 2.

Table 2. Weighted decision matrix.

	S_1	S_2	S_3	S_4
C_1	(0.44509, 0.85996)	(0.43098, 0.77161)	(0.46104, 0.72736)	(0.46104, 0.85996)
C_2	(0.01935, 0.99719)	(0.41050, 0.67730)	(0.43351, 0.75529)	(0.07760, 0.99776)
C_3	(0.51087, 0.83538)	(0.49152, 0.70854)	(0.06249, 0.99393)	(0.53421, 0.71303)
C_4	(0.01758, 0.99478)	(0.15107, 0.99478)	(0.47830, 0.86074)	(0.52980, 0.83948)
C_5	(0.54214, 0.83012)	(0.01668, 0.98738)	(0.48589, 0.71495)	(0.02725, 0.99648)
C_6	(0.53204, 0.72644)	(0.41902, 0.67480)	(0.15182, 0.99792)	(0.43175, 0.77082)
C_7	(0.46867, 0.83302)	(0.39856, 0.72519)	(0.46867, 0.73417)	(0.01796, 0.99455)
C_8	(0.53397, 0.82386)	(0.01998, 0.99326)	(0.58880, 0.65840)	(0.58880, 0.68702)
C_9	(0.01613, 0.98818)	(0.00658, 0.99726)	(0.44143, 0.76073)	(0.47202, 0.83055)

The next step requires us to calculate the value of the result function using Equation (3), and the results are shown in Table 3.

Table 3. Score function values.

	S_1	S_2	S_3	S_4
C_1	− 0.541429	−0.409636	−0.316490	−0.526976
C_2	−0.994015	−0.290222	−0.382531	−0.989499
C_3	−0.436880	−0.260439	−0.983983	−0.223026
C_4	−0.989278	−0.966764	−0.512107	−0.424042
C_5	−0.395175	−0.974634	−0.275064	−0.992235
C_6	−0.244659	−0.279776	−0.972795	−0.407760
C_7	−0.474264	−0.367047	−0.319345	−0.988807
C_8	−0.393611	−0.986167	−0.086808	−0.125318
C_9	−0.976240	−0.994489	−0.383849	−0.467007

The final steps to be performed are to calculate the maximizing and minimizing index using Equations (21) and (22), respectively, and then to calculate the relative importance of each alternative using Equation (23). The final importance values obtained should be ranked in descending order, that is, the alternative with the highest value should have the best position. The results are presented in Table 4. From these results, we can see that the best-ranked alternative was the second alternative, and the worst-ranked alternative was the fourth alternative.

Table 4. Values for benefit and non-benefit criteria, relative weight and resulting ranking.

S_i	$s(P_i)$	$s(R_i)$	Q_i	$\frac{Q_i}{MaxQ_i} \times 100$	Ranking
S_1	−0.55866	−0.97624	0.08904	95.95120	2
S_2	−0.56684	−0.99449	0.09279	100.00000	1
S_3	−0.48114	−0.38385	−0.12296	−132.51081	3
S_4	−0.58471	−0.46701	−0.19547	−210.65095	4

4. Comparison with Other Entropies

Since other researchers have already considered entropy creation for Pythagorean fuzzy sets, it is necessary to compare the newly obtained entropy with those already created. Such a comparison will allow us to make sure that the newly proposed approach will allow us to obtain results that do not deviate significantly from those expected, thus obtaining the accuracy and reliability of the proposed technique. The same numerical example was used to compare entropies, and the entropies considered in this comparison are as follows:

1. The entropy of a Pythagorean fuzzy set proposed by Thao in 2019 [76]:

$$E(S) = \frac{1}{n}\sum_{i=1}^{n}\left(1 - \left|\mu_s^2(x_i) - \frac{1}{3}\right| - \left|\vartheta_s^2(x_i) - \frac{1}{3}\right|\right) \tag{27}$$

2. The Pythagorean fuzzy set entropy measure proposed by Ye in 2010 [77]:

$$E(S_1) = \frac{1}{(\sqrt{2}-1)n}\sum_{i=1}^{n}\left(\sin\left(\frac{\pi(1+\mu_s^2(x_i)-\vartheta_s^2(x_i))}{4}\right) + \sin\left(\frac{\pi(1-\mu_s^2(x_i)+\vartheta_s^2(x_i))}{4}\right) - 1\right) \tag{28}$$

$$E(S_2) = \frac{1}{(\sqrt{2}-1)n}\sum_{i=1}^{n}\left(\cos\left(\frac{\pi(1+\mu_s^2(x_i)-\vartheta_s^2(x_i))}{4}\right) + \cos\left(\frac{\pi(1-\mu_s^2(x_i)+\vartheta_s^2(x_i))}{4}\right) - 1\right) \tag{29}$$

3. The Pythagorean fuzzy set entropy introduced by Neeraj et al. in 2021 [46]:

$$E(S) = \frac{1}{n}\sum_{i=1}^{n}\left[\sec\left(\frac{\pi}{3} - \frac{\left|\mu_s^2(x_i)-\vartheta_s^2(x_i)\right|}{3}\pi\right) - 1\right] \tag{30}$$

The entropy values for each criterion obtained using the above formulae are shown in Table 5. The standard deviation is worth paying attention to, as it helps to show what the distribution of the obtained values looks like. As entropy returns values between 0 and 1, thus a more detailed analysis of the values obtained is possible as the range is the same in the case of all entropies. A larger standard deviation allows us to distinguish more accurately between individual values. In this case, the proposed entropy is characterized by the highest standard deviation; hence, for the problem at hand, we can conclude that the distinction between the different values will be most apparent. It should be noted that a higher standard deviation may also affect the distribution of the weights of individual criteria. The entropy presented by Thao has the smallest standard deviation, while the standard deviation for the other entropies is around a similar value.

Table 5. Entropy values for each criterion calculated using different entropies.

S_i	Proposed Entropy	Neeraj et al. [46]	Ye [77]	Ye [77]	Thao [76]
C_1	0.409201	0.140181	0.250113	0.250113	0.011248
C_2	0.360482	0.124035	0.220961	0.220961	0.010190
C_3	0.316320	0.104922	0.189942	0.189942	0.006479
C_4	0.412761	0.150956	0.262013	0.262013	0.017351
C_5	0.334190	0.113746	0.203627	0.203627	0.008641
C_6	0.406870	0.144827	0.254262	0.254262	0.014553
C_7	0.386817	0.132634	0.236598	0.236598	0.010676
C_8	0.241232	0.079038	0.143950	0.143950	0.004262
C_9	0.376839	0.130190	0.231495	0.231495	0.011003
Std	0.052791	0.021144	0.035262	0.035262	0.003694

Table 6 presents the results of utilization of each of the entropies in the problem under consideration. The rankings obtained using the selected entropies are exactly the same and are shown in Table 6. Obtaining the same results demonstrates the stability of the proposed entropy and that the results offered are at least similar to pre-existing entropies. Furthermore, it reinforces our belief that the newly proposed entropy offers reliable results that can be used in multicriteria decision making. Of course, the high similarity to the results offered by other entropies relates directly to the ranking, which is based on ranked data, and four alternatives are presented in the problem under study, so the characteristics of the problem create a low probability of changes in ranking. Future comparisons would require examination of other cases, especially those with more alternatives.

Table 6. Comparative analysis of the results of presented entropy with other entropies.

S_i	Proposed Entropy	Neeraj et al. [46]	Ye [77]	Ye [77]	Thao [76]
S_1	2	2	2	2	2
S_2	1	1	1	1	1
S_3	3	3	3	3	3
S_4	4	4	4	4	4

5. Comparison with Other MCDA Methods

An additional comparison with other multicriteria decision-making methods allows for a more detailed analysis of the solutions offered. In this case, the COPRAS method has been compared with the TOPSIS and VIKOR methods, and the preference results obtained by using each method are presented in Table 7. In this comparison, weights for criteria were calculated only using the proposed entropy. Each method returns values of preferences in different ranges, so their direct comparison is not straightforward. It is worth noting that for the VIKOR method, the values for the fourth and first alternatives, as well as for the second and third alternatives, are similar. A similar situation occurs for the COPRAS method, where alternatives one and two obtained similar preference values. It should also be noted that prior to ranking, it is easiest to see the differences between alternatives' preference for the COPRAS method because the standard deviation is approximately 137.5880159. The standard deviation for the preference values obtained using the VIKOR method is 0.445496, while the standard deviation for the TOPSIS method is the smallest, at approximately 0.386221. It can be concluded from this that with the TOPSIS method, it will be most difficult for the decision-maker to notice the differences between the preference values for the different alternatives.

Table 7. Preference values for the assessed alternatives in the problem of site selection for hydropower plant.

S_i	VIKOR	TOPSIS	COPRAS
S_1	0.8471	0.0000	95.9512
S_2	0.0821	−0.6317	100.0000
S_3	0.0000	−0.4881	−132.5108
S_4	1.0000	−1.0826	−210.6510

The alternatives were then ranked, as shown in Figure 3. The order changes significantly depending on the method used. Only the ranking of the fourth alternative, which was ranked as the worst according to all methods, remained constant. For the other alternatives, the rankings change, which may be due to the large number of criteria and similar key values across the alternatives. This solution shows that a broader analysis in multicriteria decision-making problems is needed, but often introduces additional questions about which solution is better. In cases where the consensus between multiple methods is unclear, it is worth asking an expert to evaluate the individual alternatives. As the final choice rests with the decision maker, it is essential to bear in mind that the analysis is intended to identify the best options, where we could reject alternative four. It would be worthwhile to conduct similar research for a problem containing a larger number of alternatives.

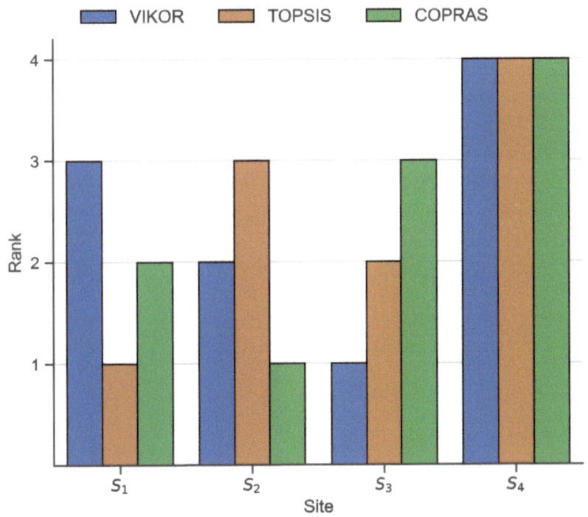

Figure 3. Ranking visualization for the problem of site selection for hydropower plant.

In addition, it is helpful to analyze the similarity of the rankings using coefficients. In this case, the weighted Spearman coefficient was used, the values of which were calculated using Equation (25), as well as the WS coefficient, for which Equation (26) was used, and the results are presented in Table 8. In this case, the weighted Spearman coefficient returned the same value for the comparison of rankings obtained using COPRAS and VIKOR as for the comparison of COPRAS and TOPSIS rankings. This is because the weighted Spearman coefficient does not reflect the precise distance between the order of alternatives. In this case, the WS rankings' similarity coefficient better reflects the rankings' discrepancies, as the orders obtained by the COPRAS method are more similar to the VIKOR method, where a change of one place from first to second can be observed for alternative two. Of course, it should be remembered that the WS coefficient is asymmetric, so it is crucial that the COPRAS ranking is compared with VIKOR and not vice versa, as otherwise, a change from first to third place for alternative three would be considered.

Table 8. Similarity of rankings of the proposed approach with other available MCDA methods.

Coefficient	VIKOR	TOPSIS
Weighted Spearman	0.280000	0.280000
WS coefficient	0.583333	0.47917

6. Conclusions and Future Directions

As the complexity of decision-making problems increases, the demand to find new and better approaches to produce more accurate results for a given problem arises. The use of fuzzy logic and sets allows us to include the uncertainties that are so often present in real-world problems, and consequently requires further research in this direction.

This paper presents a new entropy that can be applied to Pythagorean fuzzy sets. In addition, the integration of this entropy in a multicriteria decision-making method, such as COPRAS, is presented to obtain criteria weights in the problem of selecting hydropower plant sites. In addition, a preliminary comparison of the newly proposed entropy with existing ones is made, emphasizing that the results obtained by the new entropy are stable and reliable in terms of multicriteria decision making.

In future research, it would be worthwhile to demonstrate the use of the proposed entropy in real-world problems from other areas. In addition, it would be worth extending the comparative analysis of entropies to highlight the usefulness and effectiveness of the newly proposed entropy. Furthermore, simulation studies can be carried out to obtain a more detailed picture of the distribution of weights depending on the entropy used.

Author Contributions: Conceptualization, S.K., B.P., N.G., N.S. and W.S.; methodology, S.K., B.P., N.G., N.S. and W.S.; software, S.K., B.P., N.G., N.S. and W.S.; validation, S.K., B.P., N.G., N.S. and W.S.; formal analysis, S.K., B.P., N.G., N.S. and W.S.; investigation, S.K., B.P., N.G., N.S. and W.S.; resources, S.K., B.P., N.G., N.S. and W.S.; data curation, S.K., B.P., N.G., N.S. and W.S.; writing—original draft preparation, S.K., B.P., N.G., N.S. and W.S.; writing—review and editing, S.K., B.P., N.G., N.S. and W.S.; visualization, S.K., B.P., N.G., N.S. and W.S.; supervision, S.K., B.P., N.G., N.S. and W.S.; project administration, W.S.; funding acquisition, W.S. All authors have read and agreed to the published version of the manuscript.

Funding: This research was funded by National Science Center grant number 2021/41/B/HS4/01296.

Data Availability Statement: Data are contained within the article.

Conflicts of Interest: The authors declare no conflicts of interest.

Abbreviations

The following abbreviations are used in this manuscript:

MCDM	multicriteria decision making
MADM	multiple-attribute decision making
FS	fuzzy set(s)
IVFS	interval-valued fuzzy set(s)
IFS	intuitionistic fuzzy set(s)
PFS	Pythagorean fuzzy set(s)
PFE	Pythagorean fuzzy entropy
COPRAS	complex proportional assessment
SPOTIS	stable preference ordering towards ideal solution
LINMAP	linear programming technique for a multidimensional analysis of preferences
VIKOR	VIseKriterijumska Optimizacija I Kompromisno Resenje
TOPSIS	Technique for Order of Preference by Similarity to Ideal Solution
MULTIMOORA	Multi-Objective Optimization on the basis of a Ratio Analysis plus the full MULTIplicative form
FDOSM	fuzzy decision by opinion method

References

1. Liang, G.S.; Wang, M.J.J. Personnel selection using fuzzy MCDM algorithm. *Eur. J. Oper. Res.* **1994**, *78*, 22–33. [CrossRef]
2. Önüt, S.; Kara, S.S.; Işik, E. Long term supplier selection using a combined fuzzy MCDM approach: A case study for a telecommunication company. *Expert Syst. Appl.* **2009**, *36*, 3887–3895. [CrossRef]
3. Deveci, M.; Demirel, N.Ç.; Ahmetoğlu, E. Airline new route selection based on interval type-2 fuzzy MCDM: A case study of new route between Turkey-North American region destinations. *J. Air Transp. Manag.* **2017**, *59*, 83–99. [CrossRef]
4. Karacan, I.; Tozan, H.; Karatas, M. Multi criteria decision methods in health technology assessment: A brief literature review. *Eurasian J. Health Technol. Assess.* **2016**, *1*, 12–19.
5. Mardani, A.; Hooker, R.E.; Ozkul, S.; Yifan, S.; Nilashi, M.; Sabzi, H.Z.; Fei, G.C. Application of decision making and fuzzy sets theory to evaluate the healthcare and medical problems: A review of three decades of research with recent developments. *Expert Syst. Appl.* **2019**, *137*, 202–231. [CrossRef]
6. Deveci, M.; Akyurt, I.Z.; Yavuz, S. A GIS-based interval type-2 fuzzy set for public bread factory site selection. *J. Enterp. Inf. Manag.* **2018**, *31*, 820–847. [CrossRef]
7. Karatas, M. Hydrogen energy storage method selection using fuzzy axiomatic design and analytic hierarchy process. *Int. J. Hydrogen Energy* **2020**, *45*, 16227–16238. [CrossRef]
8. Deveci, M.; Cali, U.; Kucuksari, S.; Erdogan, N. Interval type-2 fuzzy sets based multi-criteria decision-making model for offshore wind farm development in Ireland. *Energy* **2020**, *198*, 117317. [CrossRef]
9. Priyanka; Kumar, S.; Kalia, S. MULTIMOORA-based MCDM model for sustainable ranking of wastewater treatment technologies under picture fuzzy environment. *Expert Syst.* **2023**, e13286. . [CrossRef]
10. Gunnarsdóttir, I.; Davidsdottir, B.; Worrell, E.; Sigurgeirsdóttir, S. Sustainable energy development: History of the concept and emerging themes. *Renew. Sustain. Energy Rev.* **2021**, *141*, 110770. [CrossRef]
11. Kumar, A.; Sah, B.; Singh, A.R.; Deng, Y.; He, X.; Kumar, P.; Bansal, R. A review of multi criteria decision making (MCDM) towards sustainable renewable energy development. *Renew. Sustain. Energy Rev.* **2017**, *69*, 596–609. [CrossRef]
12. Siksnelyte, I.; Zavadskas, E.K.; Streimikiene, D.; Sharma, D. An overview of multi-criteria decision-making methods in dealing with sustainable energy development issues. *Energies* **2018**, *11*, 2754. [CrossRef]
13. Sahoo, S.K.; Goswami, S.S. A comprehensive review of multiple criteria decision-making (MCDM) Methods: Advancements, applications, and future directions. *Decis. Mak. Adv.* **2023**, *1*, 25–48. [CrossRef]
14. Zadeh, L.A. Fuzzy sets as a basis for a theory of possibility. *Fuzzy Sets Syst.* **1978**, *1*, 3–28. [CrossRef]
15. Rana, H.; Umer, M.; Hassan, U.; Asgher, U.; Silva-Aravena, F.; Ehsan, N. Application of fuzzy TOPSIS for prioritization of patients on elective surgeries waiting list-A novel multi-criteria decision-making approach. *Decis. Mak. Appl. Manag. Eng.* **2023**, *6*, 603–630. [CrossRef]
16. Kaya, I.; Colak, M.; Terzi, F. A comprehensive review of fuzzy multi criteria decision making methodologies for energy policy making. *Energy Strategy Rev.* **2019**, *24*, 207–228. [CrossRef]
17. Shekhovtsov, A.; Paradowski, B.; Więckowski, J.; Kizielewicz, B.; Sałabun, W. Extension of the SPOTIS method for the rank reversal free decision-making under fuzzy environment. In Proceedings of the 2022 IEEE 61st Conference on Decision and Control (CDC), Cancun, Mexico, 6–9 December 2022; IEEE: Piscataway, NJ, USA, 2022; pp. 5595–5600.
18. Al-Samarraay, M.S.; Salih, M.M.; Ahmed, M.A.; Zaidan, A.; Albahri, O.S.; Pamucar, D.; AlSattar, H.; Alamoodi, A.H.; Zaidan, B.; Dawood, K.; et al. A new extension of FDOSM based on Pythagorean fuzzy environment for evaluating and benchmarking sign language recognition systems. *Neural Comput. Appl.* **2022**, *34*, 4937–4955. [CrossRef]
19. Turksen, I.B. Interval valued fuzzy sets based on normal forms. *Fuzzy Sets Syst.* **1986**, *20*, 191–210. [CrossRef]
20. Chen, S.M.; Hsiao, W.H.; Jong, W.T. Bidirectional approximate reasoning based on interval-valued fuzzy sets. *Fuzzy Sets Syst.* **1997**, *91*, 339–353. [CrossRef]
21. Chen, S.M.; Hsiao, W.H. Bidirectional approximate reasoning for rule-based systems using interval-valued fuzzy sets. *Fuzzy Sets Syst.* **2000**, *113*, 185–203. [CrossRef]
22. Chen, S.M.; Chang, Y.C.; Pan, J.S. Fuzzy rules interpolation for sparse fuzzy rule-based systems based on interval type-2 Gaussian fuzzy sets and genetic algorithms. *IEEE Trans. Fuzzy Syst.* **2012**, *21*, 412–425. [CrossRef]
23. Atanassov, K.T.; Stoeva, S. Intuitionistic fuzzy sets. *Fuzzy Sets Syst.* **1986**, *20*, 87–96. [CrossRef]
24. Liu, M.; Ren, H. A new intuitionistic fuzzy entropy and application in multi-attribute decision making. *Information* **2014**, *5*, 587–601. [CrossRef]
25. Stanujkić, D.; Karabašević, D. An extension of the WASPAS method for decision-making problems with intuitionistic fuzzy numbers: A case of website evaluation. *Oper. Res. Eng. Sci. Theory Appl.* **2018**, *1*, 29–39. [CrossRef]
26. Atanassov, K.T. Circular intuitionistic fuzzy sets. *J. Intell. Fuzzy Syst.* **2020**, *39*, 5981–5986. [CrossRef]
27. Alkan, N.; Kahraman, C. Continuous intuitionistic fuzzy sets (CINFUS) and their AHP&TOPSIS extension: Research proposals evaluation for grant funding. *Appl. Soft Comput.* **2023**, *145*, 110579.
28. Yager, R.R.; Abbasov, A.M. Pythagorean membership grades, complex numbers, and decision making. *Int. J. Intell. Syst.* **2013**, *28*, 436–452. [CrossRef]
29. Peng, X.; Zhang, X.; Luo, Z. Pythagorean fuzzy MCDM method based on CoCoSo and CRITIC with score function for 5G industry evaluation. *Artif. Intell. Rev.* **2020**, *53*, 3813–3847. [CrossRef]

30. Boyacı, A.Ç.; Şişman, A. Pandemic hospital site selection: A GIS-based MCDM approach employing Pythagorean fuzzy set *Environ. Sci. Pollut. Res.* **2022**, *29*, 1985–1997. [CrossRef]
31. Arora, H.; Naithani, A. Significance of TOPSIS approach to MADM in computing exponential divergence measures fo pythagorean fuzzy sets. *Decis. Mak. Appl. Manag. Eng.* **2022**, *5*, 246–263. [CrossRef]
32. Lin, M.; Huang, C.; Chen, R.; Fujita, H.; Wang, X. Directional correlation coefficient measures for Pythagorean fuzzy sets: The applications to medical diagnosis and cluster analysis. *Complex Intell. Syst.* **2021**, *7*, 1025–1043. [CrossRef]
33. Huang, C.; Lin, M.; Xu, Z. Pythagorean fuzzy MULTIMOORA method based on distance measure and score function: It application in multicriteria decision making process. *Knowl. Inf. Syst.* **2020**, *62*, 4373–4406. [CrossRef]
34. Shannon, C.E. A mathematical theory of communication. *Bell Syst. Tech. J.* **1948**, *27*, 379–423. [CrossRef]
35. De Luca, A.; Termini, S. A definition of a nonprobabilistic entropy in the setting of fuzzy sets theory. In *Readings in Fuzzy Sets fo Intelligent Systems*; Elsevier: Amsterdam, The Netherlands, 1993; pp. 197–202.
36. Hung, W.L.; Yang, M.S. Fuzzy entropy on intuitionistic fuzzy sets. *Int. J. Intell. Syst.* **2006**, *21*, 443–451. [CrossRef]
37. Zeng, W.; Li, H. Relationship between similarity measure and entropy of interval valued fuzzy sets. *Fuzzy Sets Syst.* **2006** *157*, 1477–1484. [CrossRef]
38. Hu, J.; Yang, Y.; Zhang, X.; Chen, X. Similarity and entropy measures for hesitant fuzzy sets. *Int. Trans. Oper. Res.* **2018** *25*, 857–886. [CrossRef]
39. Yang, M.S.; Hussain, Z. Fuzzy entropy for pythagorean fuzzy sets with application to multicriterion decision making. *Complexity* **2018**, *2018*, 2832839. [CrossRef]
40. Xu, T.T.; Zhang, H.; Li, B.Q. Pythagorean fuzzy entropy and its application in multiple-criteria decision-making. *Int. J. Fuzzy Sys* **2020**, *22*, 1552–1564. [CrossRef]
41. Rani, P.; Mishra, A.R.; Mardani, A. An extended Pythagorean fuzzy complex proportional assessment approach with new entrop and score function: Application in pharmacological therapy selection for type 2 diabetes. *Appl. Soft Comput.* **2020**, *94*, 106441 [CrossRef]
42. Guleria, A.; Bajaj, R.K. A robust decision making approach for hydrogen power plant site selection utilizing (R, S)-Norm Pythagorean Fuzzy information measures based on VIKOR and TOPSIS method. *Int. J. Hydrogen Energy* **2020**, *45*, 18802–18816 [CrossRef]
43. Biswas, A.; Sarkar, B. Pythagorean fuzzy TOPSIS for multicriteria group decision-making with unknown weight information through entropy measure. *Int. J. Intell. Syst.* **2019**, *34*, 1108–1128. [CrossRef]
44. Xue, W.; Xu, Z.; Zhang, X.; Tian, X. Pythagorean fuzzy LINMAP method based on the entropy theory for railway projec investment decision making. *Int. J. Intell. Syst.* **2018**, *33*, 93–125. [CrossRef]
45. Lin, M.; Huang, C.; Xu, Z. TOPSIS method based on correlation coefficient and entropy measure for linguistic Pythagorean fuzzy sets and its application to multiple attribute decision making. *Complexity* **2019**, *2019*, 6967390. [CrossRef]
46. Gandotra, N.; Kizielewicz, B.; Anand, A.; Bączkiewicz, A.; Shekhovtsov, A.; Wątróbski, J.; Rezaei, A.; Sałabun, W. New pythagorean entropy measure with application in multi-criteria decision analysis. *Entropy* **2021**, *23*, 1600. [CrossRef]
47. Thakur, P.; Kizielewicz, B.; Gandotra, N.; Shekhovtsov, A.; Saini, N.; Sałabun, W. The Group Decision-Making Using Pythagorean Fuzzy Entropy and the Complex Proportional Assessment. *Sensors* **2022**, *22*, 4879. [CrossRef] [PubMed]
48. Thakur, P.; Kaczyńska, A.; Gandotra, N.; Saini, N.; Sałabun, W. The Application of the New Pythagorean Fuzzy Entropy to Decision-Making using Linguistic Terms. *Procedia Comput. Sci.* **2022**, *207*, 4525–4534. [CrossRef]
49. Kumar, R.; Gandotra, N. Novel Pythagorean Fuzzy based Information Measure using TOPSIS Technique for Application in Multi-Criteria Decision Making. In Proceedings of the 2023 10th International Conference on Computing for Sustainable Global Development (INDIACom), New Delhi, India, 15–17 March 2023; IEEE: Piscataway, NJ, USA, 2023; pp. 1271–1276.
50. Kumar, R.; Saini, N.; Gandotra, N. Novel Pythagorean fuzzy entropy and its application based on MCDM for ranking the academic institutions. *AIP Conf. Proc.* **2022**, *2357*, 110005.
51. Atanassov, K.T. *Intuitionistic Fuzzy Sets*; Springer: Berlin/Heidelberg, Germany, 1999.
52. Peng, X.; Yang, Y.; Song, J.; Jiang, Y. Pythagorean fuzzy soft set and its application. *Comput. Eng.* **2015**, *41*, 224–229.
53. Peng, X.; Yang, Y.; Zhu, Y. Similarity measure and its application based on multiparametric intuitionistic fuzzy sets. *Comput. Eng Appl.* **2015**, *51*, 122–125.
54. Zavadskas, E.K.; Kaklauskas, A.; Šarka, V. The new method of multicriteria complex proportional assessment of projects *Technol. Econ. Dev. Econ.* **1994**, *1*, 131–139.
55. Chaurasiya, R.; Jain, D. Pythagorean fuzzy entropy measure-based complex proportional assessment technique for solving multi-criteria healthcare waste treatment problem. *Granul. Comput.* **2022**, *7*, 917–930. [CrossRef]
56. Keshavarz Ghorabaee, M.; Amiri, M.; Salehi Sadaghiani, J.; Hassani Goodarzi, G. Multiple criteria group decision-making for supplier selection based on COPRAS method with interval type-2 fuzzy sets. *Int. J. Adv. Manuf. Technol.* **2014**, *75*, 1115–1130 [CrossRef]
57. Vahdani, B.; Mousavi, S.M.; Tavakkoli-Moghaddam, R.; Ghodratnama, A.; Mohammadi, M. Robot selection by a multiple criteria complex proportional assessment method under an interval-valued fuzzy environment. *Int. J. Adv. Manuf. Technol.* **2014** *73*, 687–697. [CrossRef]
58. Turanoglu Bekar, E.; Cakmakci, M.; Kahraman, C. Fuzzy COPRAS method for performance measurement in total productive maintenance: A comparative analysis. *J. Bus. Econ. Manag.* **2016**, *17*, 663–684. [CrossRef]

59. Mishra, A.R.; Rani, P.; Pardasani, K.R. Multiple-criteria decision-making for service quality selection based on Shapley COPRAS method under hesitant fuzzy sets. *Granul. Comput.* **2019**, *4*, 435–449. [CrossRef]
60. Kumari, R.; Mishra, A.R. Multi-criteria COPRAS method based on parametric measures for intuitionistic fuzzy sets: Application of green supplier selection. *Iran. J. Sci. Technol. Trans. Electr. Eng.* **2020**, *44*, 1645–1662. [CrossRef]
61. Lai, Y.J.; Liu, T.Y.; Hwang, C.L. Topsis for MODM. *Eur. J. Oper. Res.* **1994**, *76*, 486–500. [CrossRef]
62. Alao, M.A.; Ayodele, T.R.; Ogunjuyigbe, A.; Popoola, O. Multi-criteria decision based waste to energy technology selection using entropy-weighted TOPSIS technique: The case study of Lagos, Nigeria. *Energy* **2020**, *201*, 117675. [CrossRef]
63. Javad, M.O.M.; Darvishi, M.; Javad, A.O.M. Green supplier selection for the steel industry using BWM and fuzzy TOPSIS: A case study of Khouzestan steel company. *Sustain. Futures* **2020**, *2*, 100012. [CrossRef]
64. Konstantinos, I.; Georgios, T.; Garyfalos, A. A Decision Support System methodology for selecting wind farm installation locations using AHP and TOPSIS: Case study in Eastern Macedonia and Thrace region, Greece. *Energy Policy* **2019**, *132*, 232–246. [CrossRef]
65. Zhang, X.; Xu, Z. Extension of TOPSIS to multiple criteria decision making with Pythagorean fuzzy sets. *Int. J. Intell. Syst.* **2014**, *29*, 1061–1078. [CrossRef]
66. Abdel-Baset, M.; Chang, V.; Gamal, A.; Smarandache, F. An integrated neutrosophic ANP and VIKOR method for achieving sustainable supplier selection: A case study in importing field. *Comput. Ind.* **2019**, *106*, 94–110. [CrossRef]
67. Liang, X.; Chen, T.; Ye, M.; Lin, H.; Li, Z. A hybrid fuzzy BWM-VIKOR MCDM to evaluate the service level of bike-sharing companies: A case study from Chengdu, China. *J. Clean. Prod.* **2021**, *298*, 126759. [CrossRef]
68. Akram, M.; Kahraman, C.; Zahid, K. Group decision-making based on complex spherical fuzzy VIKOR approach. *Knowl.-Based Syst.* **2021**, *216*, 106793. [CrossRef]
69. Krishankumar, R.; Premaladha, J.; Ravichandran, K.; Sekar, K.; Manikandan, R.; Gao, X. A novel extension to VIKOR method under intuitionistic fuzzy context for solving personnel selection problem. *Soft Comput.* **2020**, *24*, 1063–1081. [CrossRef]
70. Bakioglu, G.; Atahan, A.O. AHP integrated TOPSIS and VIKOR methods with Pythagorean fuzzy sets to prioritize risks in self-driving vehicles. *Appl. Soft Comput.* **2021**, *99*, 106948. [CrossRef]
71. Pinto da Costa, J.; Soares, C. A weighted rank measure of correlation. *Aust. N. Z. J. Stat.* **2005**, *47*, 515–529. [CrossRef]
72. Sałabun, W.; Urbaniak, K. A new coefficient of rankings similarity in decision-making problems. In *Computational Science—ICCS 2020, Proceedings of the 20th International Conference, Amsterdam, The Netherlands, 3–5 June 2020*; Part II 20; Springer: Cham, Switzerland, 2020; pp. 632–645.
73. Sałabun, W.; Wątróbski, J.; Shekhovtsov, A. Are MCDA methods benchmarkable? A comparative study of TOPSIS, VIKOR, COPRAS, and PROMETHEE II methods. *Symmetry* **2020**, *12*, 1549. [CrossRef]
74. Kizielewicz, B.; Więckowski, J.; Shekhovtsov, A.; Wątróbski, J.; Depczyński, R.; Sałabun, W. Study towards the time-based mcda ranking analysis—A supplier selection case study. *Facta Univ. Ser. Mech. Eng.* **2021**, *19*, 381–399. [CrossRef]
75. Shekhovtsov, A. How strongly do rank similarity coefficients differ used in decision making problems? *Procedia Comput. Sci.* **2021**, *192*, 4570–4577. [CrossRef]
76. Thao, N.X.; Smarandache, F. A new fuzzy entropy on Pythagorean fuzzy sets. *J. Intell. Fuzzy Syst.* **2019**, *37*, 1065–1074. [CrossRef]
77. Ye, J. Two effective measures of intuitionistic fuzzy entropy. *Computing* **2010**, *87*, 55–62. [CrossRef]

energies

MDPI

Article

Empowering Sustainable Energy Solutions through Real-Time Data, Visualization, and Fuzzy Logic

Adam Stecyk [1] and Ireneusz Miciuła [2,*]

[1] Institute of Spatial Management and Socio-Economic Geography, University of Szczecin, 70-453 Szczecin, Poland; adam.stecyk@usz.edu.pl
[2] Institute of Economics and Finance, University of Szczecin, 70-453 Szczecin, Poland
* Correspondence: ireneusz.miciula@usz.edu.pl

Abstract: This article shows the evaluation of the Integrated Real-time Energy Management Framework (IREMF), a cutting-edge system designed to develop energy management practices. The framework leverages real-time data collection, advanced visualization techniques, and fuzzy logic to optimize energy consumption patterns. To assess the performance and importance of each layer and main factor within IREMF, we employ a multi-step methodology. First, the Fuzzy Delphi Method is utilized to harness expert insights and collective intelligence, providing a holistic understanding of the framework's functionality. Researchers used a fuzzy analytic hierarchy process (AHP) to determine the relative importance of each component of the energy system (first stage). This careful evaluation process helps ensure that resources are allocated effectively and that strategic decisions are made based on sound data. The findings of the study not only improve our understanding of the capabilities of the IREMF platform but also pave the way for future developments in energy system management. The study highlights the critical role of real-time data, visualization, fuzzy logic, and advanced decision-making methods in shaping a sustainable energy future.

Keywords: energy; real-time data; fuzzy logic; IREMF; DELPHI; AHP

1. Introduction

The world's growing population, cities, and factories are using more and more energy. This is putting a strain on our limited fossil fuel resources and increasing carbon dioxide emissions, which are causing climate change [1]. To address these challenges, one is turning to renewable energy sources such as solar, wind, hydro, and geothermal power, which are cleaner and more sustainable [2]. One is also working to improve energy efficiency in all sectors of the economy, which means reducing the amount of energy one uses to receive the same results [3]. By using energy-efficient technologies, adopting energy management systems, and changing behaviors, one can achieve sustainable energy consumption patterns [4].

Energy stands as an essential linchpin of contemporary civilization, underpinning economic expansion, societal progress, and driving technological breakthroughs [5]. Its ubiquitous influence spans a gamut of applications, from industrial processes to residential power consumption, affirming its pivotal role across diverse sectors [6]. However, the world's growing demand for energy and the urgent need to fight climate change and environmental damage are driving the search for sustainable energy solutions [7]. This compelling mandate has spurred the exploration of alternative energy reservoirs, the refinement of energy-efficient practices, and the innovation of dynamic energy management strategies, all geared towards forging a resilient future for humanity [8].

The quest for sustainable energy solutions has led to the exploration of advanced technologies, particularly real-time data collection and visualization tools, as well as fuzzy logic. These innovative approaches are transforming energy systems by enabling intelligent decision-making and sophisticated energy management, thereby offering a dynamic method to optimize energy consumption [9]. By analyzing large datasets, identifying consumption patterns, and creating accurate predictive models, these methodologies empower key stakeholders, including energy policymakers, grid operators, and consumers, to make informed decisions. This holistic approach not only enhances the efficiency of energy systems but also contributes to their sustainability [10–12].

The objective of this paper is to delve into the synergies between real-time data collection and visualization tools, as well as fuzzy logic, in the realm of energy management. This exploration underscores the transformative potential of these technologies in reshaping the landscape of energy generation, distribution, and utilization. This manuscript delineates a variety of theoretical constructs and pragmatic implementations, wherein the power of real-time data acquisition and visualization instruments can be leveraged to address the extant energy conundrums. This, in turn, paves the way for substantial contributions towards the realization of a more ecologically responsible and sustainable future.

2. The Real-Time Data Collection and Visualization in Energy Systems

The evolution of real-time data collection in energy systems marks a pivotal milestone in the quest for efficient and sustainable energy management. By integrating advanced sensor technologies and networked monitoring systems, organizations can now capture and process a wealth of dynamic energy data in real time. This influx of information offers unprecedented insights into energy consumption patterns, grid operations, and demand fluctuations [13]. Moreover, with the infusion of fuzzy logic, this data can be interpreted and analyzed with a nuanced understanding of uncertainty and imprecision. Fuzzy logic, a mathematical framework that accommodates degrees of truth and allows for flexible decision-making, lends a crucial layer of intelligence to the data processing pipeline, enabling more refined and context-aware insights [14].

The integration of real-time data collection in energy systems has profound implications for grid resilience and stability. With the ability to capture granular information about energy supply and demand in real time, grid operators can respond swiftly to fluctuating conditions [15]. Fuzzy logic further fortifies this capability by enabling intelligent decision-making in the face of uncertain or ambiguous data [16]. By employing fuzzy sets and membership functions, the system can adapt to varying degrees of truth, ensuring that responses are judiciously tailored to the prevailing conditions. This combination of real-time data collection, fuzzy logic, and rapid response mechanisms represents a formidable toolset in fortifying energy grids against disruptions and optimizing resource allocation [17].

Data visualization emerges as a critical companion to real-time data collection, translating raw streams of data into actionable insights. Advanced visualization techniques, such as interactive dashboards and 3D representations, empower stakeholders to intuitively grasp complex energy trends. When coupled with fuzzy logic, these visualizations can convey not only precise information but also the degree of uncertainty associated with it [18]. This nuanced representation is invaluable in scenarios where imprecise data points are encountered, providing decision-makers with a comprehensive understanding of the underlying complexities. Consequently, the fusion of real-time data collection, data visualization, and fuzzy logic equips energy professionals with a powerful toolkit for optimizing operations and resource allocation [19].

At the heart of this paper is the amalgamation of real-time data collection, state-of-the-art visualization tools, and the sophisticated logic of fuzzy systems, all unified by the transformative power of artificial intelligence (AI). This integrated approach represents a paradigm shift in energy system management, fundamentally altering how we perceive, analyze, and act upon energy-related data. With AI acting as the catalyst, the system gains the ability to adapt dynamically to changing conditions, discern subtle patterns within complex datasets, and make nuanced decisions in the face of uncertainty [20]. Real-time data collection ensures that information is continuously harvested, whereas advanced visualization tools provide an intuitive means of comprehending intricate energy trends [21]. The incorporation of fuzzy logic enables the system to grapple with imprecise or uncertain data, a common occurrence in the dynamic context of energy systems. Altogether, this fusion of technologies empowers organizations to optimize energy utilization, enhance efficiency, and reduce environmental impact with unprecedented precision and agility [22–25].

3. Integrated Real-Time Energy Management Framework (IREMF)

IREMF stands at the forefront of modern energy management paradigms, offering a cohesive and dynamic solution that addresses the pressing need for efficiency, sustainability, and resilience in energy utilization. In this framework, real-time data collection serves as the bedrock, ensuring that a continuous stream of information is captured to inform decision-making. There are six main layers in IREMF model:

Layer 1: Real-time Data Collection and Preprocessing (RTDCP)

- L1A—Sensor Network Deployment: Placement of sensors with AI-enhanced predictive maintenance capabilities to ensure optimal performance.
- L1B—Data Transmission and Aggregation: Utilizing AI algorithms for efficient data compression and transmission, reducing bandwidth requirements.
- L1C—Data Preprocessing: Employing AI-powered anomaly detection techniques to identify and rectify erroneous data points.

Layer 2: Fuzzy Logic-based Data Interpretation (FLDI)

- L2A—Fuzzy Membership Functions: Incorporating techniques to dynamically adjust membership functions based on real-time data characteristics.
- L2B—Rule Base Creation: Leveraging machine learning algorithms to autonomously refine and expand the rule base over time.
- L2C—Inference Engine: Enhancing the inference engine with reinforcement learning capabilities for adaptive decision-making.

Layer 3: Data Visualization and Human–computer Interaction (DVHCI)

- L3A—Interactive Dashboards: Integrating various algorithms to tailor dashboards to individual user preferences and roles.
- L3B—Graphical Representations: Applying AI-powered anomaly detection to visually highlight abnormal trends or patterns in the data.
- L3C—Alerting and Notification Systems: Utilizing natural language processing for sentiment analysis in alert notifications.

Layer 4: Decision Support and Optimization (DSO)

- L4A—Decision Support Algorithms: Implementing tools for dynamic decision-making, utilizing reinforcement learning to refine recommendations.
- L4B—Optimization Models: Integrating AI-based predictive modeling for more accurate load forecasting and energy supply demand matching.
- L4C—Scenario Analysis and Predictive Modeling: Employing deep learning models for more accurate and granular predictions in scenario analysis.

Layer 5: Feedback Loop and Adaptive Control (FLAC)

- L5A—Learning and Adaptation Mechanisms: Incorporating deep reinforcement learning techniques to enable the system to learn from its own actions and adapt in real time.
- L5B—Closed-Loop Control Systems: Employing AI-based control algorithms with predictive capabilities to anticipate system behavior and proactively make adjustments.
- L5C—Performance Monitoring and Evaluation: Utilizing AI-powered anomaly detection to automatically identify performance deviations and trigger corrective actions.

Layer 6: Regulatory and Policy Compliance (RPC)

- L6A—Compliance Assessment: Applying compliance monitoring tools to automatically flag potential regulatory violations and ensure adherence.
- L6B—Reporting and Documentation: Using natural language processing and AI-driven summarization techniques to automate the generation of compliance reports.

The IREMF model integrates real-time data collection, fuzzy logic-based interpretation, advanced visualization, decision support, and adaptive control with AI-powered solutions. This comprehensive framework leverages AI's capabilities to enhance the efficiency, adaptability, and intelligence of energy systems management, aiding in the creation of a more enduring and adaptable energy future. Here are main advantages of adopting IREMF:

- Real-time Optimization: IREMF enables organizations to make instantaneous adjustments to energy consumption, production, and distribution.
- Enhanced Efficiency: By harnessing the power of AI-driven decision support and optimization algorithms, IREMF maximizes energy efficiency, reducing waste and operational costs.
- Adaptability to Uncertainty: The incorporation of fuzzy logic allows IREMF to effectively handle imprecise or uncertain data, ensuring accurate decision-making even in dynamic and uncertain energy environments.
- Predictive Capabilities: Through the integration of AI-powered predictive modeling, IREMF can anticipate future energy demands, enabling proactive measures to be taken to meet evolving needs.
- Resilient Grid Operations: IREMF's real-time data collection and adaptive control mechanisms fortify energy grids, enabling them to respond swiftly to fluctuations in demand, ensuring stability and reliability.
- Compliance and Regulatory Adherence: The model's ability to monitor and report on energy-related metrics ensures organizations remain in compliance with local, regional, and international energy regulations.
- Sustainable Practices: IREMF promotes supportable energy management by minimizing environmental impact, contributing to a more sustainable future.

Although the IREMF presents numerous advantages, it is crucial to also weigh potential drawbacks. Below are some considerations regarding its potential disadvantages:

- Implementation Costs: The initial investment required to deploy IREMF, including the integration of sensors, AI systems, and visualization tools, may be substantial and could pose a barrier for some organizations.
- Complexity of Integration: Integrating diverse technologies and ensuring seamless interoperability can be a complex undertaking, requiring specialized expertise and careful planning.
- Data Security and Privacy Concerns: As IREMF relies heavily on real-time data collection, organizations must implement robust cybersecurity measures to safeguard sensitive information from potential threats or breaches.
- Dependence on Technology Infrastructure: Reliance on a sophisticated technological infrastructure may leave organizations vulnerable to disruptions in the event of system failures or cyber-attacks.
- Learning Curve for Stakeholders: Training and familiarizing stakeholders with the intricacies of IREMF, particularly in interpreting data and utilizing advanced visualization tools, may pose challenges.
- Regulatory Compliance Complexity: Adhering to evolving energy regulations and policies may require ongoing adjustments and enhancements to the IREMF model, potentially incurring additional costs.
- Scalability Challenges: Scaling IREMF to meet the needs of larger, more complex energy systems may require significant adjustments and expansions, potentially leading to logistical challenges.

The Integrated Real-time Energy Management Framework (IREMF) brings forth a host of benefits in energy system management. It enables real-time optimization, enhancing efficiency and resilience in energy utilization. Through the incorporation of fuzzy logic and AI technology, IREMF adapts dynamically to uncertain data, predicts future demands, and ensures compliance with energy regulations. However, implementing IREMF may incur high initial costs and require a complex integration process. Data security concerns and the need for a robust technological infrastructure also pose potential challenges. Additionally, training stakeholders and addressing scalability for larger energy systems may necessitate additional investments and resources.

4. Research Design and Methodology

The research adopts a comprehensive approach to evaluate the Integrated Real-time Energy Management Framework (IREMF) by employing advanced fuzzy decision-making techniques. The assessment process involves two pivotal methodologies: the Fuzzy Delphi Method [26,27] and Fuzzy Analytic Hierarchy Process (FAHP) [28,29]. Initially, the Fuzzy Delphi Method will be applied to harness expert opinions and collective intelligence for the evaluation of every layer and main factor within IREMF. This inclusive assessment aims to elicit and aggregate diverse perspectives, ensuring a comprehensive understanding of the framework's performance. Subsequently, the Fuzzy method will be employed to ascertain the relative importance and weights assigned to each layer and factor. These weightings are pivotal for prioritizing and allocating resources effectively, thus influencing the future development and successful implementation of IREMF. The research underscores the critical role these weightings play in steering the trajectory of future projects, ensuring their alignment with the overarching objectives of IREMF for efficient and sustainable energy management.

The research process begins with a comprehensive review of existing literature on the subject. This is followed by an assessment of the IREMF model using the Fuzzy Delphi method [30]. Next, the Fuzzy AHP method [31] is employed to determine the weights for the layers and main factors. The final steps involve interpreting the results and formulating development recommendations. The research model encompasses four pivotal steps in its evaluation approach (Figure 1).

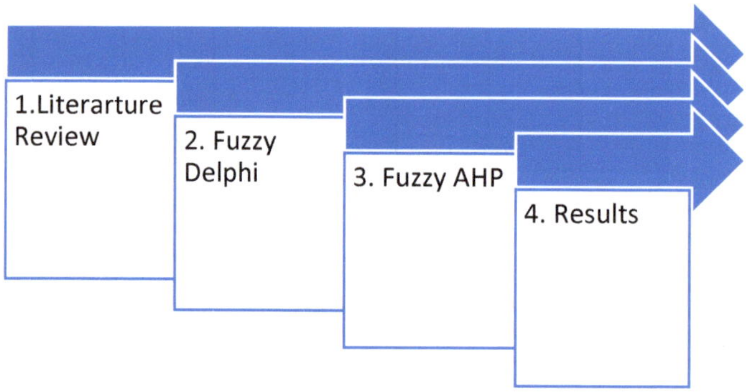

Figure 1. Research design and methodology. Source: own elaboration.

The initial phase involves the utilization of the Fuzzy Delphi method to validate the layers and factors proposed in the IREMF model. In academic discourse, the Delphi method is characterized as a technique to structure group communication, aiming to enhance the problem-solving efficiency of a collective of independent individuals. The Delphi technique is categorized among creative thinking research methods and defined as an iterative evaluation procedure based on selection analysis of empirical data gathered. Given that the conventional Delphi method has certain constraints, including lengthy procedure time and associated high research costs, its modification, the Fuzzy Delphi method, is often employed in scientific research [32,33].

For the purposes of this investigation, an expert panel was assembled, proposing 6 layers and 17 associated factors. The panel comprised six experts in the field of energy management and three experts specializing in modern technologies and real-time data collection. The expert panel's process was divided into several stages.

The first stage involved the evaluation of the proposed layers. This was followed by the assessment of the primary factors for each layer. Next, the values obtained were fuzzified using triangular fuzzy numbers. The fourth stage entailed data aggregation, after which the aggregated data were defuzzified. An acceptance threshold was then established, culminating in the acceptance of layers and factors. This systematic approach ensured a comprehensive and rigorous analysis of the proposed layers and factors.

Upon the determination of the triangular fuzzy spectrum, the linguistic expressions (opinions) of the experts were gathered and subsequently fuzzified, as depicted in Table 1. In the ensuing step, the opinions of the experts were amalgamated in accordance with Formula (1). The lower fuzzy number l (min) signifies the smallest conceivable value for the layer (or factor) as perceived by the experts, whereas the upper fuzzy number u (max) denotes the largest conceivable value for the layer (or factor) as perceived by the experts. The geometric mean (middle fuzzy number m) represents the most likely value of each layer and factor.

$$F_{agr} = \left(min\{l\}, \left(\prod_{i=1}^{n} \{m\}\right)^{\frac{1}{n}}, \max\{u\} \right) \quad (1)$$

Table 1. Triangular fuzzy number of seven-point Likert scale.

Extremely Unimportant	Very Unimportant	Unimportant	Merely Important	Important	Very Important	Extremely Important
(0; 0; 0.1)	(0; 0.1; 0.3)	(0.1; 0.3; 0.5)	(0.3; 0.5; 0.75)	(0.5; 0.75; 0.9)	(0.75; 0.9; 1)	(0.9; 1; 1)

Source: own elaboration.

To determine the acceptance threshold for the layer and factor, the aggregated values were subjected to defuzzification using the Centre of Area method, as per Formula (2):

$$COA = \frac{(l + m + u)}{3} \quad (2)$$

The final step in this phase involved setting the acceptance threshold at S = 0.6. This threshold was used to filter and select the suitable layers and factors. As a result, 5 out of the 6 proposed layers were accepted (as shown in Table 2), and 15 out of the 17 proposed factors met the acceptance criteria.

Table 2. Fuzzification and data aggregation for 6 layers of IREMF model.

Layer	Expert 1	...	Expert 9	l	m	u	CoA	Result
RTDCP	0.9; 1; 1	...	0.9; 1; 1	0.75	0.94	1.00	0.90	Accepted
FLDI	0.9; 1; 1	...	0.9; 1; 1	0.50	0.90	1.00	0.80	Accepted
DVHCI	0.75; 0.9; 1	...	0.9; 1; 1	0.75	0.82	1.00	0.81	Accepted
DSO	0.75; 0.9; 1	...	0.9; 1; 1	0.50	0.92	1.00	0.81	Accepted
FLAC	0.5; 0.75; 0.9	...	0.75; 0.9; 1	0.50	0.82	1.00	0.77	Accepted
RPC	0.1; 0.3; 0.5	...	0.3; 0.5; 0.75	0.20	0.72	0.68	0.57	Not accepted

Source: own elaboration.

A graphical representation of the IREMF model is shown in Figure 2, along with all 15 main factors responsible for the proper operation of the energy management system.

Figure 2. Five layers of IREMF model with main factors. Source: own elaboration.

The next stage of this investigation seeks to determine the weights for the identified layers and factors using the Fuzzy Analytic Hierarchy Process (FAHP) [34]. The Analytic Hierarchy Process (AHP) is a renowned multi-criteria decision-making method, designed to tackle complex problems across various fields. The fundamental principle of the AHP method is its ability to break down the decision problem into a hierarchical structure and then choose the best solution based on the defined criteria and sub-criteria (layers and factors). However, a significant limitation of the AHP method is its inability to handle uncertainties or inaccuracies inherent in group decision-making. To overcome these limitations, a combination of AHP and fuzzy theory, known as FAHP, has been proposed [16]. An essential step in the FAHP process is the creation of a pairwise comparison matrix. In this step, crisp numerical values are transformed into fuzzy numbers using a specific membership function, often using the triangular membership function described in Formula (3). This transformation follows Saaty's fundamental scale, as explained in Table 3, which outlines the scale of relative importance.

$$\tilde{A} = (l, m, u) \tag{3}$$

The primary objective of pairwise comparisons is to ascertain the extent to which one element supersedes another in terms of their relative significance. If element A is exceedingly preferred over B, the fuzzy number is denoted as $\tilde{A} = (6, 7, 8)$, and the fuzzy reciprocal value is represented as $\tilde{A}^{-1} = \left(\frac{1}{8}, \frac{1}{7}, \frac{1}{6}\right)$, in accordance with Formula (4).

$$\tilde{A}^{-1} = (u, m, l)^{-1} \tag{4}$$

In the subsequent stage of the research, the Consistency Ratio ($C.R.$) is scrutinized. It is posited that for matrices of dimensions 3×3 and 4×4, the $C.R.$ value should be confined within 5% and 8%, respectively. For larger matrices, the $C.R.$ should not surpass 10% ($C.R. \leq 10\%$). If the consistency ratio $C.R.$ adheres to these stipulated thresholds, the pairwise comparisons executed are considered consistent. On the contrary, if the $C.R.$ exceeds 10%, it necessitates a reassessment of criteria to rectify the inconsistency in pairwise comparisons. During this phase, the FAHP method entails computing a defuzzied, normalized matrix for selected criteria and pinpointing the largest eigenvalue (λ_{max}) of the matrix. The method's progenitor demonstrated that pairwise comparisons tend to exhibit greater consistency when the λ_{max} value closely approximates the number of matrix elements (n). Consequently, the Consistency Index (*C.I.*) is computed in accordance with Formula (5).

$$C.I. = \frac{\lambda_{max} - n}{n - 1} \quad (5)$$

and *C.R.* to Formula (6),

$$C.R. = \frac{100\% \times C.I.}{R.I.} \quad (6)$$

where *R.I.* represents a random consistency index, which is derived from several thousand matrices and presented by the author in the form of Table 4.

Table 3. The fundamental scale for pairwise comparisons [28].

Intensity of Importance	Explanation	AHP	FAHP (l, m, u)
Equal importance	Element a and b contribute equally to the objective	1	(1, 1, 1)
Moderate importance of one over another	Slightly favor element A over B	3	(2, 3, 4)
Essential importance	Strongly favor element A over B	5	(4, 5, 6)
Demonstrated importance	Element A is favored very strongly over B	7	(6, 7, 8)
Absolute importance	The evidence favoring element A over B is of the highest possible order of importance	9	(9, 9, 9)
Intermediate values between the two adjacent judgments	When compromise is needed. For example, 4 can be used for the intermediate value between 3 and 5	2, 4, 6, 8	(1, 2, 3) (3, 4, 5) (5, 6, 7) (7, 8, 9)

Source: [31].

Table 4. Consistency indices for a randomly generated matrix.

n	1	2	3	4	5	6	7	8	9	10	11	12	13	14	15
R.I.	0	0	0.52	0.89	1.11	1.25	1.35	1.40	1.45	1.49	1.52	1.54	1.56	1.58	1.59

Source: [31].

Once the consistency of the experts' opinions has been confirmed, the fuzzy geometric mean $\tilde{r}_i$ (as per Formula (7)) and the fuzzy weights $\tilde{w}_i$ for all the criteria were computed (in accordance with Formula (8)).

$$\tilde{r}_i = \left(\left(\prod_{i=1}^{n}\{l\}\right)^{\frac{1}{n}}, \left(\prod_{i=1}^{n}\{m\}\right)^{\frac{1}{n}}, \left(\prod_{i=1}^{n}\{u\}\right)^{\frac{1}{n}} \right) \quad (7)$$

$$\tilde{w}_i = \tilde{r}_i \otimes (\tilde{r}_1 \oplus \tilde{r}_2 \oplus \ldots \oplus \tilde{r}_n)^{-1} \quad (8)$$

Subsequently, the fuzzy weights were defuzzified into crisp values w_i using the Centre of Area method (as per Formula (9)) and then normalized to yield $w_{\_(i\text{-}norm)}$ values, in accordance with Formula (10).

$$w_i = \frac{(l_i + m_i + u_i)}{3} \quad (9)$$

$$w_{i-norm} = \frac{w_i}{\sum_{i=1}^{n} w_i} \quad (10)$$

In the concluding phase, the aggregation of results from nine experts was executed utilizing the geometric mean. This procedure yielded the ultimate weights for the six specified layers (refer to Tables 5–7).

Table 5. Pairwise comparison of five layers and weight calculations by Expert 1–part 1.

	RTDCP			FLDI			DVHCI			DSO			FLAC		
RTDCP	1.00	1.00	1.00	1.00	1.00	1.00	0.33	0.50	1.00	0.33	0.50	1.00	0.33	0.50	1.00
FLDI	1.00	1.00	1.00	1.00	1.00	1.00	0.33	0.50	1.00	0.33	0.50	1.00	0.33	0.50	1.00
DVHCI	1.00	2.00	3.03	1.00	2.00	3.00	1.00	1.00	1.00	1.00	2.00	3.00	1.00	1.00	1.00
DSO	1.00	2.00	3.03	1.00	2.00	3.03	0.33	0.50	1.00	1.00	1.00	1.00	1.00	1.00	1.00
FLAC	1.00	2.00	3.03	1.00	2.00	3.03	1.00	1.00	1.00	1.00	1.00	1.00	1.00	1.00	1.00

Table 6. Pairwise comparison of five layers and weight calculations by Expert 1–part 2.

	Geometric Mean			Fuzzy Weight			Center of Area	Weight
	l	m	u	l	m	u		
RTDCP	0.51	0.66	1.00	0.07	0.12	0.26	0.15	13.54%
FLDI	0.52	0.66	1.00	0.07	0.12	0.26	0.15	13.55%
DVHCI	1.00	1.52	1.94	0.14	0.29	0.51	0.31	27.57%
DSO	0.80	1.15	1.56	0.11	0.22	0.41	0.25	21.78%
FLAC	1.00	1.32	1.56	0.14	0.25	0.41	0.27	23.56%
Sum	3.83	5.30	7.05			Sum	1.10	100.00%
Reciprocal	0.14	0.19	0.26					

Source: own elaboration.

Table 7. List of all 15 factors and their weights.

Layer Weight	Local Factor Weight	Global Weight
13.54%	33.07%	4.48%
13.54%	28.80%	3.90%
13.54%	38.13%	5.16%
13.55%	47.80%	6.48%
13.55%	27.40%	3.71%
13.55%	24.80%	3.36%
27.57%	46.00%	12.68%
27.57%	26.60%	7.33%
27.57%	27.40%	7.56%
21.78%	38.50%	8.39%
21.78%	22.50%	4.90%
21.78%	39.00%	8.49%
23.56%	36.00%	8.48%
23.56%	33.00%	7.77%
23.56%	31.00%	7.30%
	Sum	100.00%

Following this, the subsequent phase in the Fuzzy Analytic Hierarchy Process (FAHP) entailed the application of the identical analytical methodology (as delineated in Formulas 3–10) to all factors within each layer.

Within the research framework presented here, this analytical process encompassed six layers, entailing the comparison of all factors within each respective group. This extensive analysis was conducted by a panel of nine experts, resulting in the generation of a total of 36 tables. Given the intricacy of the empirical data, this article provides only select excerpts of this calculation.

Following the acceptance (FAHP consistency test, CR < 10%) and combination (geometric mean) of the assessments from the 9 experts for all pairwise comparisons (layers and factors), the results yielded: weights for the 5 layers, local weights for the 15 factors and global weights for the 15 factors, which were calculated as the product of the layer weight and local factor weight.

5. Discussion

The Integrated Real-time Energy Management Framework (IREMF) stands at the forefront of modern energy management paradigms, offering a cohesive and dynamic solution for optimizing energy utilization and enhancing grid stability. As the quest for effective and supportable energy answers intensifies, the adaptability of IREMF becomes increasingly evident. Recognizing the diverse landscapes in which energy management operates, we propose four distinct variants of IREMF, each tailored to specific scenarios. These variants reflect the paramount importance of adapting IREMF to address the unique challenges and opportunities presented by different domains. Here, we delve into the significance of these variations and their pivotal roles in shaping the future of energy management.

Here are four variants of the Integrated Real-time Energy Management Framework (IREMF) for future analysis and development, each with distinct configurations in terms of layers and main factors:

Variant 1: IREMF with Enhanced Data Analytics:

1. Real-time Data Collection and Preprocessing
2. Advanced Data Analytics and Machine Learning
3. Data Visualization and Human–Computer Interaction
4. Decision Support and Optimization
5. Feedback Loop and Adaptive Control

Enhanced Data Analytics: This variant places a strong emphasis on leveraging advanced data analytics techniques, including machine learning, for in-depth analysis of real-time energy data. This layer is equipped with predictive modeling and anomaly detection capabilities.

Variant 2: IREMF with IoT Integration:

1. IoT-enabled Real-time Data Collection
2. Fuzzy Logic-based Data Interpretation
3. Visualization and User Interface Design
4. AI-driven Decision Support
5. Adaptive Control and IoT Feedback Loop

IoT Integration: This variant incorporates a dedicated layer for IoT-enabled data collection, allowing for a more extensive network of sensors and devices to provide real-time data. This layer enhances the granularity and scope of data collection.

Variant 3: IREMF with Demand Response Emphasis:

1. Real-time Data Collection and Preprocessing
2. Fuzzy Logic-based Data Interpretation
3. Visualization and Human–computer Interaction
4. Demand Response Optimization
5. Feedback Loop and Adaptive Control

Demand Response Optimization: This variant places a significant focus on optimizing demand response mechanisms, enabling the system to dynamically adapt energy consumption patterns to align with grid conditions and cost-effectiveness goals.

Variant 4: IREMF for Microgrid Management:

1. Microgrid Data Aggregation and Preprocessing
2. Fuzzy Logic-based Data Interpretation for Microgrid
3. Visualization and Human–computer Interaction for Microgrid
4. Optimization for Microgrid Operations
5. Feedback Loop and Adaptive Control for Microgrid

Microgrid Focus: This variant is tailored specifically for managing microgrids, with layers and factors designed to address the unique challenges and requirements of decentralized energy systems.

The diverse scenarios addressed by our four variants exemplify the adaptability and versatility of IREMF. Through these tailored solutions, we seek to empower industries, microgrid operators, and other stakeholders with the precise tools necessary to maximize efficiency, optimize demand response, and ensure regulatory compliance. By honing in on the unique features of each context, these variants promise to revolutionize energy management practices, resulting in not only improved operational efficiency but also reduced environmental impact.

In practical application, these tailored solutions are poised to bring about transformative changes. For industries, the specialized variant offers a set of precise tools meticulously designed to optimize energy consumption within complex industrial processes. This means that manufacturers and industrial operators can now harness the power of IREMF to streamline their operations, reduce energy wastage, and ultimately enhance their bottom line. This innovation contributes to the body of theoretical knowledge by demonstrating how a nuanced understanding of industry-specific processes can be translated into an effective energy management strategy.

Similarly, for microgrid operators, the dedicated variant represents a monumental leap forward in the management of decentralized energy systems. By providing a framework that is finely tuned to the unique challenges and requirements of microgrids, IREMF empowers operators to make more informed decisions in real-time. This, in turn, leads to greater stability and reliability in energy supply, fostering a more resilient and sustainable energy ecosystem. This practical application advances theory by showcasing how a tailored approach can significantly enhance the efficiency and reliability of microgrid operations, thus contributing to the broader discourse on decentralized energy management.

6. Conclusions

The research delves into the Integrated Real-time Energy Management Framework (IREMF), an innovative model designed to revolutionize energy management practices. Initially, a comprehensive evaluation process was employed, involving the identification of five distinct layers and fifteen main factors within the IREMF framework. These layers and factors were meticulously selected based on a consensus reached by an expert panel, facilitated by the rigorous application of the Fuzzy Delphi method. This initial phase established a robust foundation for the subsequent analytical stages, ensuring that the chosen criteria were both pertinent and reflective of the framework's multifaceted nature.

Following this, the research aimed to figure out the relative importance of the identified layers and factors, and, for this purpose, it used the first two main stages of Fuzzy Analytic Hierarchy Process (AHP). This analytical method was used to calculate exact weights for each of the five layers and their corresponding main factors. The goal of using the Fuzzy AHP method was to assess in a quantitative manner the hierarchical relationships and contributions of each component. The calculations of the weights are extremely important because they play a key role in guiding the future development and successful implementation of IREMF. They help in making decisions about resource allocation and strategy, ensuring that the framework is optimized to meet the changing needs of the energy management landscape.

Author Contributions: This paper was inspired by the assistance of artificial intelligence tools such as Chat GPT, BARD, BING AI, and DEEPL GOOGLE. The authors of this paper utilized the capabilities of the AI tools to generate ideas and assist in formulating the main concepts discussed herein. However, it is important to note that the literature review, research, methodology, and conclusions presented in this paper were conducted entirely by the authors. While the AI tools provided valuable assistance in generating ideas and content, the authors took full responsibility for the research process, including the selection of the topic, the development of the methodology, the data collection, and the interpretation of the results. The authors used their expertise in the field of new technologies, real-time data collection, visualization, AI, and energy systems to conduct the research and ensure the accuracy and reliability of the information presented. All authors have read and agreed to the published version of the manuscript.

Funding: This research was funded from the programme of the Minister of Science and Higher Education "Regional Excellence Initiative" in 2019–2023; project number 001/RID/2018/19; the amount of financing: PLN 10,684,000.00. Research results are a part of research project financed by the National Science Centre Poland (NCN) Miniatura 6 2022/06/X/HS4/01426.

Data Availability Statement: Data are contained within the article.

Conflicts of Interest: The authors declare no conflict of interest.

References

1. Ye, Y.; Koch, S.F.; Zhang, J. Modelling Required Energy Consumption with Equivalence Scales. *Energy J.* **2022**, *43*, 123–145. [CrossRef]
2. Gaitan, N.C.; Ungurean, I.; Corotinschi, G.; Roman, C. An Intelligent Energy Management System Solution for Multiple Renewable Energy Sources. *Sustainability* **2023**, *15*, 2531. [CrossRef]
3. Liu, R.E.; Ravikumar, A.P.; Bi, X.T.; Zhang, S.; Nie, Y.; Brandt, A.; Bergerson, J.A. Greenhouse Gas Emissions of Western Canadian Natural Gas: Proposed Emissions Tracking for Life Cycle Modeling. *Environ. Sci. Technol.* **2021**, *55*, 9711–9720. [CrossRef]
4. Streimikiene, D.; Kyriakopoulos, G.L.; Lekavicius, V.; Pazeraite, A. How to support sustainable energy consumption in households? *Acta Montan. Slovaca* **2022**, *27*, 479–490. [CrossRef]
5. Su, T.; Meng, L.; Wang, K.; Wu, J. The role of green credit in carbon neutrality: Evidence from the breakthrough technological innovation of renewable energy firms. *Environ. Impact Assess. Rev.* **2023**, *101*, 107135. [CrossRef]
6. Sun, L.; Wang, Z.; Yang, L. Efficiency and Influencing Factors of Energy Conservation and Emission Reduction in High-Energy-Consuming Industries Driven by Technological Innovation. *Pol. J. Environ. Stud.* **2023**, *32*, 3769–3785. [CrossRef] [PubMed]
7. Oladapo, B.I.; Bowoto, O.K.; Adebiyi, V.A.; Ikumapayi, O.M. Energy harvesting analysis of hip implantin achieving sustainable development goals. *Structures* **2023**, *55*, 28–38. [CrossRef]
8. Wang, X.; Huang, Y.; Guo, F.; Zhao, W. Energy Management Strategy based on Dynamic Programming Considering Engine Dynamic Operating Conditions Optimization. In Proceedings of the 39th Chinese Control Conference, Shenyang, China, 27–29 July 2020; Fu, J., Sun, J., Eds.; IEEE: New York, NY, USA, 2020; pp. 5485–5492. Available online: https://www.webofscience.com/wos/woscc/full-record/WOS:000629243505107 (accessed on 1 October 2023).
9. Li, V.O.K.; Lam, J.C.K.; Han, Y.; Chow, K. A Big Data and Artificial Intelligence Framework for Smart and Personalized Air Pollution Monitoring and Health Management in Hong Kong. *Environ. Sci. Policy* **2021**, *124*, 441–450. [CrossRef]
10. Breitbach, M.; Edinger, J.; Kaupmees, S.; Trotsch, H.; Krupitzer, C.; Becker, C. Voltaire: Precise Energy-Aware Code Offloading Decisions with Machine Learning. In Proceedings of the 2021 IEEE International Conference on Pervasive Computing and Communications (Percom), Kassel, Germany, 22–26 March 2021; IEEE: New York, NY, USA, 2021. [CrossRef]
11. da Silva, E.T.; Martins, M.A.F.; Ferreira, A.M.S.; Rodriguez, J.L.M. A Fuzzy Approach to Assess the Perception of a Rural Community Concerning the Impact of Distributed Power Generation on Local Sustainability. *Braz. Arch. Biol. Technol.* **2021**, *64*, e21200486. [CrossRef]
12. Abdallah, A.; Chaker, A.; Allaoui, T. An adaptive RST fuzzy logic and an adaptive PI fuzzy logic controllers of a DFIG in Wind Energy Conversion. *Prz. Elektrotechniczny* **2021**, *97*, 11–20. [CrossRef]
13. Kwon, I.; Shin, D.; Oh, J.; Kim, C.-H.; Kim, H. Preprocessing Energy Intervals on Spectrum for Real-Time Radionuclide Identification. *IEEE Trans. Nucl. Sci.* **2021**, *68*, 2202–2209. [CrossRef]
14. Harb, H.; Nader, D.A.; Sabeh, K.; Makhoul, A. Real-time Approach for Decision Making in IoT-based Applications. In Proceedings of the 11th International Conference on Sensor Networks (Sensornets), Online, 7–8 February 2021; Prasad, R.V., Pesch, D., Ansari, N., BenaventePeces, C., Eds.; Scitepress: Setubal, Portugal, 2021; pp. 223–230. [CrossRef]
15. Smith, O.; Cattell, O.; Farcot, E.; O'Dea, R.D.; Hopcraft, K. The effect of renewable energy incorporation on power grid stability and resilience. *Sci. Adv.* **2022**, *8*, eabj6734. [CrossRef] [PubMed]

16. Boutkhoum, O.; Hanine, M.; Agouti, T.; Tikniouine, A. A decision-making approach based on fuzzy AHP-TOPSIS methodolog for selecting the appropriate cloud solution to manage big data projects. *Int. J. Syst. Assur. Eng. Manag.* **2017**, *8* (Suppl. S2 1237–1253. [CrossRef]
17. Zulfiqar, M.; Kamran, M.; Rasheed, M.B. A blockchain-enabled trust aware energy trading framework using games theory an multi-agent system in smat grid. *Energy* **2022**, *255*, 124450. [CrossRef]
18. Zehra, S.S.; Wood, M.J.; Grimaccia, F.; Mussetta, M. A Cost-Effective Fuzzy-based Demand-Response Energy Management fo Batteries and Photovoltaics. In Proceedings of the 2023 11th International Conference on Smart Grid, Icsmartgrid, Paris, France 4–7 June 2023; IEEE: New York, NY, USA, 2023. [CrossRef]
19. Singh, V.K.; Govindarasu, M. A Novel Architecture for Attack-Resilient Wide-Area Protection and Control System in Smart Gric In *2020 Resilience Week (RWS)*; IEEE: New York, NY, USA, 2020; pp. 41–47. [CrossRef]
20. Aljohani, T.M.; Ebrahim, A.; Mohammed, O. Real-Time metadata-driven routing optimization for electric vehicle energy consumption minimization using deep reinforcement learning and Markov chain model. *Electr. Power Syst. Res.* **2021**, *192*, 10696 [CrossRef]
21. Matthieu, M.; Toufik, A.; Mehdi, M.; Chaibet, A. Real-time and multi-layered energy management strategies for fuel cell electri vehicle overview. In Proceedings of the 2022 IEEE 95th Vehicular Technology Conference: VTC2022-Spring, Helsinki, Finland 19–22 June 2022; IEEE: New York, NY, USA, 2022. [CrossRef]
22. Mdluli, N.; Sharma, G.; Akindeji, K.; Narayanan, K.; Sharma, S. Development of short term solar radiation forecasting using A techniques. In Proceedings of the 30th Southern African Universities Power Engineering Conference (Saupec 2022), Durban South Africa, 25–27 January 2022; IEEE: New York, NY, USA, 2022. [CrossRef]
23. Strezoski, L. Distributed energy resource management systems-DERMS: State of the art and how to move forward. *Wile Interdiscip. Rev. Energy Environ.* **2023**, *12*, e460. [CrossRef]
24. Akkaoui, R.; Stefanov, A.; Palensky, P.; Epema, D.H.J. A Taxonomy and Lessons Learned from Blockchain Adoption within th Internet of Energy Paradigm. *IEEE Access* **2022**, *10*, 106708–106739. [CrossRef]
25. Bokkisam, H.R.; Singh, S.; Acharya, R.M.; Selvan, M.P. Blockchain-based Peer-to-Peer Transactive Energy System for Communit Microgrid with Demand Response Management. *CSEE J. Power Energy Syst.* **2022**, *8*, 198–211. [CrossRef]
26. Ribeiro, A.S.; DeCastro, M.; Costoya, X.; Rusu, L.; Dias, J.M.; Gomez-Gesteira, M. A Delphi method to classify wave energ resource for the 21st century: Application to the NW Iberian Peninsula. *Energy* **2021**, *235*, 121396. [CrossRef]
27. Shah, S.A.A.; Cheng, L. Evaluating renewable and sustainable energy impeding factors using an integrated fuzzy-grey decisior approach. *Sustain. Energy Technol. Assess.* **2022**, *51*, 101905. [CrossRef]
28. Dey, B.; Roy, B.; Datta, S. Identification and prioritisation of barriers and drivers for achieving ethanol blending target in India using Delphi-PESTEL-Fuzzy-AHP method. *Environ. Dev. Sustain.* **2022**, *I*, 143–156. [CrossRef]
29. Saraswat, S.K.; Digalwar, A.K.; Yadav, S.S. Sustainability Assessment of Renewable and Conventional Energy Sources in India Using Fuzzy Integrated AHP-WASPAS Approach. *J. Mult. Valued Log. Soft Comput.* **2021**, *37*, 335–362.
30. Noor, N.M.; Rasli, A.; Rashid, M.A.A.; Mubarak, M.F.; Abas, I.H. Ranking of Corporate Governance Dimensions: A Delphi Stud *Adm. Sci.* **2022**, *12*, 173. [CrossRef]
31. Saaty, T.L. *Fundamentals of Decision Making and Priority Theory with the Analytic Hierarchy Process*; RWS Publications: New York NY, USA, 2012.
32. Li, S.; Gu, X. A Risk Framework for Human-centered Artificial Intelligence in Education: Based on Literature Review and Delphi-AHP Method. *Educ. Technol. Soc.* **2023**, *26*, 187–202. [CrossRef]
33. Ullah, S.; Jianjun, Z.; Hayat, K.; Palmucci, D.N.; Durana, P. Exploring the factors for open innovation in post-COVID-19 conditions by fuzzy Delphi-ISM-MICMAC approach. *Eur. J. Innov. Manag.* 2021, *ahead of print*. [CrossRef]
34. Turk, A.; Ozkok, M. Shipyard location selection based on fuzzy AHP and TOPSIS. *J. Intell. Fuzzy Syst.* **2020**, *39*, 4557–4576 [CrossRef]

energies

Article

Fuzzy Decision-Making Model for Solar Photovoltaic Panel Evaluation

Paweł Ziemba * and Marta Szaja

Institute of Management, University of Szczecin, Aleja Papieża Jana Pawła II 22A, 70-453 Szczecin, Poland; marta.szaja@usz.edu.pl
* Correspondence: pawel.ziemba@usz.edu.pl

Abstract: The use of solar photovoltaic (PV) panels is one of the most promising ways to generate electricity. However, the complex technical parameters associated with them make the choice between different PV panels a complicated task. The aim of the article is the analysis and multi-criteria evaluation of PV panels available on the Polish market and to indicate the optimal solar PV panels according to the adopted technical criteria. The practical goal was achieved using a fuzzy approach, taking into account the uncertainty of operational parameters. Based on the applied approach and multi-criteria NEAT F-PROMETHEE method, a fuzzy decision model was built for the evaluation of PV panels. The results of this model were compared with the results of an analogous model that did not take into account the uncertainty of the data. As a result of the research, it was found that the results of the fuzzy model should be considered more reliable, because fuzzy numbers allow for capturing more data than real numbers, which translates into greater reliability of the results of the fuzzy model.

Keywords: solar energy; photovoltaic panels; multi-criteria decision-making; fuzzy sets; fuzzy decision model; NEAT F-PROMETHEE; imprecision; uncertainty

1. Introduction

Energy is of great importance for the economic development of every country in the world. Its sources include both fossil fuels: coal, gas, and crude oil; and renewable energy: sun, wind, water, biomass, hydrogen, and geothermal energy [1,2]. Fossil fuel deposits are limited. They have a negative impact on the environment and climate change. All this makes it very necessary to increase the degree of use of renewable energy sources (RES) [3]. More than 75% of the source of greenhouse gases emitted in the European Union (EU) is the production and use of energy. Reducing or completely excluding CO_2 production from the EU energy system is important for achieving the climate goals for 2030. To reduce greenhouse gas emissions by at least 55% by 2030, the share of renewable energy should be increased and energy efficiency improved. It is also extremely important in the longer term, as a stage on the path leading to climate neutrality by 2050 [4].

Existing technological innovations enable the replacement of fossil fuels with low-emission solutions. This leads to an energy balance characterized by an adequacy between the generation and use of energy. The operation of a sustainable energy system is within the limits of environmental tolerance, which means that it has little or no negative impact on the environment. Moreover, it enables conducting normal economic and social activity in the country [5].

The use of RESs is currently enjoying great interest. However, the complex issues involved make the choice between different proposals for the use of RESs a complicated task. There are institutional, legal, political, technical, socio-economic, and environmental barriers to be overcome [3]. One of the more promising ways of supplying and generating electricity is the use of solar energy [6].

Solar energy can be converted into heat or electricity. Depending on the type of energy obtained, solar panels and photovoltaic (PV) panels are distinguishable. Solar panels are primarily used to heat water [7–9]. On the other hand, PV panels directly transform the sun rays falling on their surface into electricity [10–12]. The electricity generated in this way can be used to power all electrical equipment, including, for example, a heat pump. In this respect, PV panels can be considered more universal, which is why in this article we focused primarily on PV panels. However, since in the literature PV panels are most often referred to as solar PV panels, in the further part of the article we also often use this name.

Currently, several types of solar PV panel manufacturing technologies are available. They differ in the elements that are used to produce the cells that make up the panel. The elements used determine the color, structure, and efficiency of the cell. The following basic types of cells are distinguished [6,10,13–18]:

1. Monocrystalline silicon—are made of melted silica sand with the addition of boron; cells produced on their basis are characterized by the highest efficiency, but also the highest price;
2. Polycrystalline silicon—they are made of ground silicon, which is melted and cast in the form of a block composed of non-homogenous crystals with a diameter of several millimeters to several centimeters; the distances between the crystals weaken the efficiency of the cell compared to monocrystalline cells;
3. Cadmium telluride—they are created in the process of applying a thin layer of cadmium telluride to glass or other substrate; the entire photovoltaic module is usually made of one cell;
4. Copper indium gallium selenide—they can absorb more solar radiation than other cells, which is why they work well in poorer insolation;
5. Amorphous silicon—they are created in the process of applying a thin layer of allotropic silicon to glass or another substrate; due to the small amount of semiconductor used and low energy consumption in the production process, their production is quick and cheap, but their efficiency is worse than other types of cells.

Monocrystalline and polycrystalline cells belong to the group of crystalline silicon cells, while amorphous silicon, cadmium telluride, and copper indium gallium selenide cells belong to the thin-film group, while amorphous cells are thin film Si, and the others belong to thin film non-Si. Thin-film cells have much worse efficiency than crystalline silicon cells. In terms of market share, there is a huge advantage for crystalline silicon cells, which have an approx. 98% share in the global market of PV panels [19].

One of the basic decision problems in the field of solar energy is the selection of the appropriate solar PV panel. In order to find the best solar PV panel, the properties of each panel should be examined, taking into account carefully selected criteria [18]. It should be noted that many of the criteria for evaluating solar PV panels are uncertain and imprecise. One of the main causes of uncertainty is the testing of PV panels under benchmark conditions. As a result of such tests, the technical characteristics of solar PV panels describe their performance in standard test conditions. Meanwhile, in the real working environment, solar PV panels obtain diametrically different values of the generated power and current–voltage characteristics. Unfortunately, articles on the selection of solar PV panels do not usually take into account the uncertainty and imprecision of PV panel operating parameters. Therefore, a research gap is visible, consisting of the need to include uncertain criteria describing the parameters of the operation of solar PV panels.

Consideration of a decision problem from the perspective of many uncertain and often contradictory criteria is possible with the use of fuzzy multi-criteria decision-making (MCDM) methods. They give the opportunity to take into account the multidimensionality of the problem under consideration and enable a comparative analysis of the assessed solar PV panels according to the considered criteria. The MCDM approach supports rational decision-making that takes into account the decision-maker's priorities, resulting in a pareto-optimal solution combining all the decision-maker's goals [20,21]. In other words, the MCDM methods are suitable for evaluating the available alternatives, taking into account many attributes and selecting the most advantageous of them. A relatively new method of this kind is new easy approach to fuzzy preference ranking organization method for enrichment evaluation (NEAT F-PROMETHEE). This method eliminates the basic disadvantages of other fuzzy variants of the PROMETHEE method [22], and its applicability in decision problems related to RES has been confirmed in previous studies [22–26].

The aim of the article and its practical contribution is to analyze and evaluate the PV panels available on the Polish market and to indicate the optimal solar PV panels according to the adopted technical criteria. In turn, the scientific contribution involves the use of a fuzzy approach that takes into account the uncertainty of operational parameters and the construction of a fuzzy decision model for the assessment of solar PV panels. Since some parameters of solar PV panels are precise, this model must combine uncertain and imprecise data with certain and precise data.

The rest of the article is prepared in the following order. Section 2 provides an overview of contemporary work on the application of MCDM methods to solar energy research. In Section 3, we discussed the research procedure and methodology. The results obtained using the developed methodology are presented in Section 4. Section 5 contains a discussion of the results, and in Section 6 we include a conclusion along with an indication of research limitations and further research directions.

2. Review of the Literature

In the contemporary literature, there are many studies on the use of renewable energy sources, including solar energy. MCDM methods have been used by the authors of scientific publications, among others, to assess PV technology as a potential alternative for future energy generation and consumption of fossil fuels [27–29]. In each of the cited studies, the authors used the analytic hierarchy process (AHP) method. The study by Garni et al. [28] presents a case study of Saudi Arabia. The obtained results show that PV panels are the most advantageous technologies. Next came the concentrated solar power. Ahmad and Tahar [29] set out to review the potential of various RESs for electricity generation in Malaysia. They characterized the power system as a social, technical, and institutional complex. They used an AHP method to rank renewable sources. The ranking was to serve the decision-makers in developing a strategy for the development of a sustainable electricity generation system. Also in this ranking, solar energy was indicated as the most promising RES. In turn, Seddiki and Bennadji [27] used the integrated Delphi–fuzzy AHP–fuzzy preference ranking organization method for enrichment evaluation (PROMETHEE) methodology. The authors studied the selection of the best available RES alternatives for generating electricity in a residential building. To this end, the researchers used the Delphi method, which was also used to define an initial set of criteria (environmental, social, economic, etc.). A questionnaire was used to examine the preferences of the building's residents regarding the potential use of alternative renewable energy sources. The fuzzy AHP method was used to obtain the weights of the criteria, taking into account the uncertainty in the expert assessments. Finally, using the FPROMETHEE method, a ranking of alternative renewable energy solutions was developed, taking into account the uncertainties associated with the assessments of the alternatives. As in the previously cited studies, here various variants of PV technology also turned out to be dominant over other solutions.

The MCDM methods were also used in scientific research to indicate effective criteria for the location of solar power plants and their construction technology [30–36]. Chen et al. [34] examined the interdependence and influence of weights between the selection criteria for the location of solar PV farms. They used a hybrid MCDM model using decision-making trial and evaluation laboratory (DEMATEL) and DEMATEL-based analytic network process (DANP) methods based on a geographic information system (GIS). Watson and Hudson [33] used the GIS–MCDM approach in their work to assess the impact of wind and solar PV farms on the development of the region and compared the results with the existing degree of development in the study area. They used the AHP method to weigh the variables and validated them through consultation with experts who were professionals in the field of renewable energy localization. Kereush and Perovych [32] also used the AHP method in their work. They proposed a way of defining and classifying individual criteria taken into account when choosing the location of a solar PV farm. The credibility of the criteria helping decision-makers in planning new investments in solar PV power plants has been tested and proven in the pilot area (the Zastavna district within the Chernivtsi region). In turn, in the study by Vafaeipour et al. [36], a hybrid MCDM approach was applied and priorities were set for 25 dispersed cities across the country where future investments in solar PV power plants should be implemented. Stepwise weight assessment ratio analysis (SWARA) was performed to rank the identified criteria, and the weighted aggregates sum product assessment (WASPAS) method was then used for evaluation and prioritization. In the work of Sánchez-Lozano et al. [35], GIS and a combination of fuzzy AHP and fuzzy technique for order of preference by similarity to ideal solution (TOPSIS) methods were used. The fuzzy AHP method was used to weight the criteria, while the fuzzy TOPSIS method was used to rank alternative locations. In order to compare the results obtained with fuzzy TOPSIS, the elimination and choice translating reality (ELECTRE-TRI) method was additionally used. GIS was also used in the study by Kengpol et al. [30]. The aim of the study was to develop a decision support system that served for the optimal selection of a place for a solar power plant in Thailand. The study sought a location that would meet all the expectations of the decision-makers, i.e., avoiding the effects of flooding, reducing costs, time, and reducing environmental impact. Qualitative and quantitative variables based on the fuzzy AHP and TOPSIS models were integrated in the work. Fuzzy AHP was used to model linguistic ambiguity, vagueness, and incomplete knowledge. The TOPSIS method was used to rank locations based on overall performance. In a study by Mokarram et al. [31], an innovative solution was proposed to select locations for the construction of PV farms in the Fars province in Iran. In the first stage of the research, a fuzzy system was used to homogenize data from various inputs. Then, the fuzzy output data was fed into the AHP and Dempster–Shafer (DS) systems. Finally, maps were generated using fuzzy AHP (no confidence level) and fuzzy DS (at 95%, 99%, and 99.5% confidence levels), and the capabilities of both methods were compared and evaluated.

In an article by Ponce et al. [37], the problem of selection of optimal suppliers of solar PV panels for three production companies was considered, using the fuzzy TOPSIS method for this purpose. In articles by van de Kaa et al. [17], Balo and Şağbanşua [38], Kozlov and Sałabun [39], Mehr et al. [18], and Bączkiewicz et al. [40], the selection of the best PV technology or panel was considered. In each of these studies, after taking into account the adopted criteria, the most useful type of solar PV panel from a specific set of alternative solutions was indicated. In the aforementioned studies, the assessment was carried out using following MCDM methods: logarithmic fuzzy preference programming (LFPP) [17], AHP [17,38], COMET [39,40], TOPSIS [39], best–worst method (BWM) [18], MULTIMOOSRAL [18], and SPOTIS [40]. All cited studies are included in the overview presented in Table 1.

Table 1. Applications of MCDM methods in solar PV panels study.

Aim of the Study	Subject of the Study	Location	MCDM Methods	No of Criteria/Sub-criteria	Ref.
Evaluation of five renewable power generation sources and choose the most favorable technology	Renewable energy sources	Saudi Arabia	AHP	4/14	[28]
Identification of the best renewable resource for electricity generation	Renewable resources for electricity generation	Malaysia	AHP	4/12	[29]

Table 1. *Cont.*

Aim of the Study	Subject of the Study	Location	MCDM Methods	No of Criteria/Sub-criteria	Ref.
Selection of the best alternative renewable energy sources for electricity production	Residential building	Oran, Algeria	Delphi, fuzzy AHP, fuzzy PROMETHEE	7/15	[27]
Establishing a decision model for improving the performance of solar PV farms	Solar PV plants sites	China	DEMATEL, DANP	10	[34]
Development of the wind farm and solar PV farm	Wind farm and solar PV farm	South Central England	GIS, AHP	3/5	[33]
Defining and classifying particular criteria considered for solar PV farm siting	Solar PV power plant	Zastavna district, Ukraine	AHP	13	[32]
Evaluation of the region's priority for the installation of solar PV projects	Solar PV plants sites	Iran	SWARA, WASPAS	4/14	[36]
Determination of the best location for a solar thermoelectric power plant	Location of solar thermoelectric power plants	Region of Murcia, Spain	Fuzzy AHP, Fuzzy TOPSIS	4/10	[35]
Proposing a decision support system to avoid flooding when choosing a location for a solar power plant	Sites for a solar power plant	Thailand	Fuzzy AHP, TOPSIS	5/19	[30]
Identification of optimal locations for solar PV farms	Areas for the construction of solar PV farms	Fars province, Iran	Fuzzy AHP, fuzzy DS	11	[31]
Choosing a solar PV panel supplier from a variety of options that best suits the needs of manufacturing companies	Solar PV energy systems in manufacturing companies	Mexico	Fuzzy TOPSIS	4/37	[37]
Selection of the PV technology	Five PV technologies	-	LFPP, AHP	4/13	[17]
Selection of the best solar PV panel for the photovoltaic system design	Solar PV panels up to 200W	-	AHP	5/26	[38]
Finding the most rational solar PV panel from a given set of alternatives	Public available solar PV panels	-	COMET, TOPSIS	6	[39]
Selection of the best technology for solar PV panels	First, second, and third generations of solar PV panels	Iran	MULTIMOOSRAL, BWM	5/20	[18]
Proposing a decision support system for the assessment of solar PV panels used in photovoltaic installations	Solar PV panels	-	COMET, SPOTIS	6	[40]

Abbreviations: AHP—analytic hierarchy process, PROMETHEE—preference ranking organization method for enrichment of evaluation, DEMATEL—decision-making trial and evaluation laboratory, DANP—DEMATEL-based analytic network process, GIS—geographic information system, SWARA—stepwise weight assessment ratio analysis, WASPAS—weighted aggregates sum product assessment, TOPSIS—technique for order of preference by similarity to ideal solution, DS—Dumpster–Schafer method, LFPP—logarithmic fuzzy preference programming, COMET—characteristic objects method, MULTIMOOSRAL—integrates following methods: multi-objective optimization on the basis of simple ratio analysis (MOOSRA), multi-objective optimization method by ratio analysis (MOORA), and multi-objective optimization by ratio analysis plus the full multiplicative form (MULTIMOORA), BWM—best–worst method, SPOTIS—stable preference ordering towards ideal solution.

Among the discussed studies, the most important in the context of the purpose of this article are the works of Balo and Şağbanşua [38], Kozlov and Sałabun [39], Mehr et al. [18], and Bączkiewicz et al. [40], in which many criteria describing the technical parameters of PV panels are considered. Based on the analysis of these publications, the most important characteristics that act as criteria for the assessment of solar PV panels can be identified. These criteria are presented in Table 2.

Table 2. Basic criteria for assessing solar PV panels.

Criterion	Reference
Maximum power (Pmax) [Wp]/PTC power rating [W]/STC power per unit of area [W/m^2]/peak power [W]/peak power per m^2 [W/m^2]	[18,38–40]
Panel efficiency [%]/peak efficiency [%]/module efficiency [%]	[18,38–40]
Open-circuit voltage (VOC) (STC) [V]	[18,38–40]
Short-circuit current (ISC) (STC) [A]	[18,38–40]
Panel cost [USD]/cost per watt [USD]/price [USD]/cost [USD]/cost per m^2 [USD/m^2]	[18,38–40]
Weight [kg]/weight per m^2 [kg/m^2]	[18,38,40]
L × W × H [cm^3]/length × width × depth [mm]/area [m^2]	[18,38,39]
Product warranty [years]/service support	[18,38]

It should be noted that the maximum power, open-circuit voltage, and short-circuit current values vary over time, as they are highly dependent on atmospheric conditions (ambient temperature, cell temperature, irradiance, etc.). In the case of maximum power, it should also be pointed out that modern solar PV panels have a positive power tolerance, so the maximum power value may actually be slightly higher than the results from the technical specification of the PV panel. The panel efficiency value also changes over time and is dependent on the age of the PV panel. In the case of each of the given criteria, there is uncertainty and imprecision regarding the numerical value of this criterion. Meanwhile, in each of the articles cited in Table 2, the assessment criteria had crisp, precise, and certain values. These criteria reflect the operating parameters of PV panels only in the standard test conditions. Moreover, in the article by Bączkiewicz et al. [40], the open-circuit voltage criterion was ill-defined because the direction of preference of this criterion was incorrectly indicated as the minimum. The indicated errors and research limitations mean that the assessment of solar PV panels in the given articles can be largely undermined. Therefore, in this study, a fuzzy approach was used to define uncertain and imprecise values of parameters describing solar PV panels. Thanks to this, the study did not use only the values obtained by PV panels in the standard test conditions, but a wider range of values of the basic characteristics of solar PV panels was captured, making their assessments more realistic.

3. Materials and Methods

3.1. Preliminaries

One of the most popular techniques for capturing the uncertainty and imprecision of data is the fuzzy set theory, developed by Zadeh [41]. Of particular importance in this context is the trapezoidal membership function $\mu_{\tilde{a}}(x) \in [0,1]$, defining trapezoidal fuzzy number (TFN) $\widetilde{a} = (a_1, a_2, a_3, a_4)$. The trapezoidal membership function is described by the Formula (1) [42]:

$$\mu_{\widetilde{a}}(x) = \begin{cases} 0 & if\ x < a_1 \\ \frac{x-a_1}{a_2-a_1} & if\ a_1 \leq x < a_2 \\ 1 & if\ a_2 \leq x \leq a_3 \\ \frac{a_4-x}{a_4-a_3} & if\ a_3 < x \leq a_4 \\ 0 & if\ x > a_4 \end{cases} \quad (1)$$
where $a_1 \leq a_2 \leq a_3 \leq a_4$

The trapezoidal membership function is a generalization of simpler membership functions: triangular, interval, or singleton. In the literature, it is recognized that the advantage of the trapezoidal membership function over more complex representations of fuzzy sets is the ease of interpretation and ease of use [43]. Moreover, it was found that trapezoidal membership functions are a reasonable compromise between the tendency to lose too much information and the tendency to introduce forms of approximation too sophisticated from the computational point of view [44]. Therefore, using the trapezoidal membership functions, a relatively high universality is obtained, in principle without increasing the difficulty of use and interpretation. The choice of TFNs still allows the use of simpler representations, i.e., triangular fuzzy numbers (TrFNs), interval numbers (INs) and real numbers—singletons (RNs) [23,42]. Fuzzy arithmetic defines the basic operations performed on TFNs, which are the addition, subtraction, multiplication, and division of two TFNs. These algebraic operations are described by Formulas (2)–(5):

$$\widetilde{a} \oplus \widetilde{b} = (a_1, a_2, a_3, a_4) \oplus (b_1, b_2, b_3, b_4) = (a_1 + b_1, a_2 + b_2, a_3 + b_3, a_4 + b_4) \quad (2)$$

$$\widetilde{a} \ominus \widetilde{b} = (a_1, a_2, a_3, a_4) \ominus (b_1, b_2, b_3, b_4) = (a_1 - b_4, a_2 - b_3, a_3 - b_2, a_4 - b_1) \quad (3)$$

$$\widetilde{a} \otimes \widetilde{b} = (a_1, a_2, a_3, a_4) \otimes (b_1, b_2, b_3, b_4) = (a_1 \times b_1, a_2 \times b_2, a_3 \times b_3, a_4 \times b_4) \quad (4)$$

$$\widetilde{a} \oslash \widetilde{b} = (a_1, a_2, a_3, a_4) \oslash (b_1, b_2, b_3, b_4) = (a_1/b_4, a_2/b_3, a_3/b_2, a_4/b_1) \quad (5)$$

Operations on simpler fuzzy representations are carried out in the same way, assuming that for RN $a_1 = a_2 = a_3 = a_4$, dla IN $a_1 = a_2$ and $a_3 = a_4$, a dla TrFN $a_2 = a_3$.

The NEAT F-PROMETHEE fuzzy method used in the study is based on TFNs, and, at the same time, allows the use of TrFNs, Ins, and RNs. Calculation details of the method are presented, among others, in Ziemba's paper [22]. In the NEAT F-PROMETHEE method, a set $\widetilde{A}$ of m fuzzy alternatives defined by n criteria belonging to the set C is considered. The most important steps of this method are deviation mapping of alternatives, calculation of preference indices, calculation of outranking flows, and ranking of alternatives. The mapping is performed using the selected preference function f (6):

$$P_j(\widetilde{a}, \widetilde{b}) = f\left[c_j(\widetilde{a}) \ominus c_j(\widetilde{b})\right], \forall \widetilde{a}, \widetilde{b} \in \widetilde{A}, \forall c_j \in C \quad (6)$$

Preference indices are calculated based on the Formula (7):

$$\widetilde{\pi}(\widetilde{a}, \widetilde{b}) = \sum_{j=1}^{n} P_j(\widetilde{a}, \widetilde{b}) \otimes w_j \quad (7)$$

where w_j is the weight of the j-th criterion. Positive, negative, and net outranking flows are determined using Formulas (8)–(10), respectively:

$$\widetilde{\phi}^+\left(\widetilde{a}\right) = \frac{\sum_{i=1}^{m} \widetilde{\pi}(\widetilde{a}, \widetilde{b}_i)}{m-1} \quad (8)$$

$$\tilde{\phi}^-(\tilde{a}) = \frac{\sum_{i=1}^{m} \tilde{\pi}(\tilde{b_i}, \tilde{a})}{m-1} \tag{9}$$

$$\tilde{\phi}_{net}\left(\tilde{a}\right) = \tilde{\phi}^+(\tilde{a}) \ominus \tilde{\phi}^-(\tilde{a}) \tag{10}$$

Then the outranking flows are defuzzified and RNs are obtained: $\phi^+(a)$, $\phi^-(a)$, and $\phi_{net}(a)$. A partial order is constructed from the positive and negative outranking flow, and the net outranking flow is used to construct a total order of the alternatives.

3.2. Uncertain Criteria and a Fuzzy Model for Assessing PV Panels

At the beginning of the development of the decision model, information about the considered set of decision alternatives was collected. The study included popular models of PV panels with a power of approx. 400 W in Poland. Their parameters are presented in Table 3.

On the basis of the assessment criteria used in the literature presented in Table 2 and using the information on the technical parameters of PV panels given in Table 3, a fuzzy model for the assessment of solar PV panels was developed. The criteria presented in Table 4 were used in the model.

Criterion C1 was defined as TFN $\tilde{a} = (a_1, a_2, a_3, a_4)$ based on the characteristics: power—NOCT (P_{NOCT}), power—STC (P_{max}), positive power tolerance (PT), and temperature coefficient of Pmax (TCP) according to Formula (11):

$$c_1\left(\tilde{a}\right) = (a_1, a_2, a_3, a_4) = (P_{NOCT},\ P_{max} + P_{max} * TCP * 60, P_{max},\ P_{max} + PT) \tag{11}$$

Criterion C2 took the form TrFN $\tilde{a} = (a_1, a_2, a_4)$ using the characteristics: module efficiency (ME), guaranteed power performance after 1 year (PP1), and guaranteed power performance after 25 years (PP25) (12):

$$c_2\left(\tilde{a}\right) = (a_1, a_2, a_4) = (PP25 * ME,\ PP1 * ME, ME) \tag{12}$$

Criteria C3 and C4 are also expressed as TrFN $\tilde{a} = (a_1, a_2, a_4)$ using the characteristics, respectively: open-circuit voltage—NOCT (VOC_{NOCT}), open-circuit voltage—STC (VOC_{STC}), and temperature coefficient of VOC_{STC} (TCV) for C3 (13), and short-circuit current—NOCT (ISC_{NOCT}), short-circuit current—STC (ISC_{STC}), and temperature coefficient of ISC_{STC} (TCI) for C4 (14):

$$c_3\left(\tilde{a}\right) = (a_1, a_2, a_4) = (VOC_{STC} + VOC_{STC} * TCV * 60,\ VOC_{NOCT}, VOC_{STC}) \tag{13}$$

$$c_4\left(\tilde{a}\right) = (a_1, a_2, a_4) = (ISC_{NOCT}, ISC_{STC}, ISC_{STC} + ISC_{STC} * TCI * 60) \tag{14}$$

In the case of criteria C1, C3, and C4, as one of the values of the trapezoidal membership function, the values of power, open-circuit voltage, and short- circuit current were used, respectively, determined for standard test conditions (STC), but with the cell temperature increased by 60 °C (from 25 °C to 85 °C). It should be noted that the cell temperature of 85 °C is the maximum allowable operating temperature for all tested PV panels, so this is how the operation of the cells in peak conditions (but with high irradiance of 1000 W/m^2) was included.

Table 3. Technical parameters of the analyzed solar PV panels.

Manufacturer	Astronergy	JA Solar	Jinko Solar	Kensol	Meyer Burger	Phono Solar	REC	Risen	Selfa	Trina Solar
Country of Manufacture	China	China	China	Poland/China	Germany	China	Norway/Singapore	Poland/China	Poland	China
Model	**CHSM54M-HC (182)**	**JAM60S20 390/MR**	**JKM430N-54HL4**	**KS395M-SH**	**White**	**PS420M4-22/WH**	**REC380AA**	**RSM40-8-410M**	**SV108M.3-410**	**TSM-DE09.08 405W**
Power—NOCT (P_{NOCT}) [W]	306.4	295	323	297	302	310	289	310.7	309.6	306
Power—STC (P_{max}) [W]	410	390	430	395	400	420	380	410	410	405
Positive power tolerance (PT) [W]	5	5	12.9	5	5	5	5	12.3	5	5
Temperature coefficient of P_{max} (TCP) [%/°C]	−0.350%	−0.350%	−0.300%	−0.340%	−0.259%	−0.380%	−0.260%	−0.340%	−0.360%	−0.340%
Open-circuit voltage—NOCT (VOC_{NOCT}) [V]	35.34	39.63	36.56	47.1	42.3	41.8	41.7	38.97	35.2	38.9
Open-circuit voltage—STC (VOC_{STC}) [V]	37.4	41.94	38.49	49.4	44.6	45.69	44.3	41.9	37.45	41.4
Temperature coefficient of VOC_{STC} (TCV) [%/°C]	−0.270%	−0.272%	−0.250%	−0.270%	−0.234%	−0.300%	−0.240%	0.250%	−0.300%	−0.250%
Short-circuit current—NOCT (ISC_{NOCT}) [A]	11.26	9.4	11.49	8.11	8.7	9.25	8.57	10.22	11.16	9.95
Short-circuit current—STC (ISC_{STC}) [A]	13.88	11.58	14.23	10.07	10.9	11.45	10.61	12.47	13.88	12.34

Table 3. *Cont.*

Manufacturer	Astronergy	JA Solar	Jinko Solar	Kensol	Meyer Burger	Phono Solar	REC	Risen	Selfa	Trina Solar
Country of Manufacture	**China**	**China**	**China**	**Poland/China**	**Germany**	**China**	**Norway/Singapore**	**Poland/China**	**Poland**	**China**
Model	**CHSM54M-HC (182)**	**JAM60S20 390/MR**	**JKM430N-54HL4**	**KS395M-SH**	**White**	**PS420M4-22/WH**	**REC380AA**	**RSM40-8-410M**	**SV108M.3-410**	**TSM-DE09.08 405W**
Temperature coefficient of ISC_{STC} (TCI) [%/°C]	0.045%	0.044%	0.046%	0.040%	0.033%	0.050%	0.040%	0.040%	0.060%	0.040%
Module efficiency (ME) [%]	21.00%	20.90%	22.02%	21.10%	21.70%	20.98%	21.70%	21.30%	21.00%	21.10%
Guaranteed power performance after 1 year (PP1) [%]	98.0%	98.0%	99.0%	98.0%	98.0%	98.0%	98.0%	98.0%	97.0%	98.0%
Guaranteed power performance after 25 years (PP25) [%]	84.8%	83.0%	89.4%	84.8%	92.0%	84.8%	92.0%	84.8%	83.0%	84.8%
Product warranty (PrW) [years]	12	12	12	25	25	15	20	12	20	15
Performance warranty (PfW) [years]	25	25	30	25	25	25	25	25	30	25
Dimensions—length (DL) [mm]	1722	1776	1722	1646	1767	1925	1721	1754	1724	1754
Dimensions—width (DW) [mm]	1134	1052	1134	1140	1041	1040	1016	1096	1134	1096
Dimensions—height (DH) [mm]	30	35	30	30	35	35	30	30	30	30
Weight (We) [kg]	21.6	20.7	22	19	19.7	23	19.5	21.5	22.1	21
Price per W (PW) [PLN/W]	1.52	1.57	1.59	1.76	3.77	1.6	2.93	1.76	1.99	1.6

Abbreviations: NOCT—nominal operating cell temperature (irradiance: 800 W/m^2; ambient temperature: 20 °C; wind speed: 1 m/s; air mass: 1.5 G); STC—standard test conditions (irradiance: 1000 W/m^2; cell temperature: 25 °C; air mass: 1.5 G).

Table 4. Evaluation criteria for PV panels used in the study.

No.	Name	Unit of Measure	Preference Direction	Membership Function Type
C1	Power	[W]	max	TFN
C2	Module efficiency	[%]	max	TrFN
C3	Open-circuit voltage	[V]	max	TrFN
C4	Short-circuit current	[A]	max	TrFN
C5	Price per watt	[PLN/W]	min	RN
C6	Weight	[kg]	min	RN
C7	Area	[m^2]	min	RN
C8	Warranty	[years]	max	IN

Abbreviations: TFN—trapezoidal fuzzy number, TrFN—triangular fuzzy number, IN—interval number, RN—real number.

Criteria C5—price per watt (PW) and C6—weight (We) were taken directly from Table 3, and their values were RNs: $c_5\left(\tilde{a}\right) = PW$, $c_6\left(\tilde{a}\right) = We$. Similarly, criterion C7 was expressed as RN, but its value was determined as the product of length (DL) and width (DW) dimensions and normalized to m^2 (15):

$$c_7\left(\tilde{a}\right) = DL * DW/1000000 \tag{15}$$

The last criterion, C8, took the form of a IN $\tilde{a} = (a_1, a_4)$, built using the following values: product warranty (PrW) and performance warranty (PfW) (16):

$$c_8\left(\tilde{a}\right) = (a_1, a_4) = (PrW,\ PfW) \tag{16}$$

Table 5 presents alternative values for the following criteria, prepared in accordance with the formulas given above. The fuzzy decision model was supplemented with a preference model defining the preference functions, thresholds, and criteria weights. The preference model is presented in Table 6. The preference model uses a V-shaped preference function whose value increases linearly in the range [0, 1]. A value of 0 means that the compared alternatives have the same numerical value of a given criterion (indifference relation), and 1 means that the first of the compared alternatives outranks the second by at least the value of the preference threshold (strict preference relation). Intermediate values in the range (0, 1) indicate a weak preference relation. The preference thresholds were determined as twice the sample standard deviation, and all values of a given criterion included in the TFN were taken into account when determining it. The criteria were assigned weights in the form of linguistic values used in the NEAT F-PROMETHEE method. The most important criteria were power and price per watt. Slightly less important are module efficiency, warranty, open-circuit voltage and short-circuit current. Area and weight were considered the least important criteria. The correctness of the assigned weights was confirmed by comparing the defined importance of the criteria with the importance ranks of the criteria in the article by Mehr et al. [18]. Although in the compared article the weights are expressed numerically, the ordering of the criteria by weights is very similar to this article.

Table 5. Fuzzy decision matrix containing alternative values on individual criteria.

	A1—Astronergy CHSM54M-HC (182)	A2—JA Solar JAM60S20 390/MR	A3—Jinko Solar JKM430N-54HL4	A4—Kensol KS395M-SH	A5—Meyer Burger White	A6—Phono Solar PS420M4-22/WH	A7—REC 380AA	A8—Risen RSM40-8-410M	A9—Selfa SV108M.3-410	A10—Trina Solar TSM-DE09.08 405W
C1	(306.40, 323.90, 410.00, 415.00)	(295.00, 308.10, 390.00, 395.00)	(323.00, 352.60, 430.00, 442.90)	(297.00, 314.42, 395.00, 400.00)	(302.00, 337.84, 400.00, 405.00)	(310.00, 324.24, 420.00, 425.00)	(289.00, 320.72, 380.00, 385.00)	(310.70, 326.36, 410.00, 422.30)	(309.60, 321.44, 410.00, 415.00)	(306.00, 322.38, 405.00, 410.00)
C2	(17.81, 20.58, 21.00)	(17.35, 20.48, 20.90)	(19.69, 21.80, 22.02)	(17.89, 20.68, 21.10)	(19.96, 21.27, 21.70)	(17.79, 20.56, 20.98)	(19.96, 21.27, 21.70)	(18.06, 20.87, 21.30)	(17.43, 20.37, 21.00)	(17.89, 20.68, 21.10)
C3	(31.34, 35.34, 37.40)	(35.10, 39.63, 41.94)	(32.72, 36.56, 38.49)	(41.40, 47.10, 49.40)	(38.34, 42.30, 44.60)	(37.47, 41.80, 45.69)	(37.92, 41.70, 44.30)	(35.62, 38.97, 41.90)	(30.71, 35.20, 37.45)	(35.19, 38.90, 41.40)
C4	(11.26, 13.88, 14.25)	(9.40, 11.58, 11.89)	(11.49, 14.23, 14.62)	(8.11, 10.07, 10.31)	(8.70, 10.90, 11.12)	(9.25, 11.45, 11.79)	(8.57, 10.61, 10.86)	(10.22, 12.47, 12.77)	(11.16, 13.88, 14.38)	(9.95, 12.34, 12.64)
C5	1.52	1.57	1.59	1.76	3.77	1.60	2.93	1.76	1.99	1.60
C6	21.6	20.7	22.0	19.0	19.7	23.0	19.5	21.5	22.1	21.0
C7	1.95	1.87	1.95	1.88	1.84	2.00	1.75	1.92	1.96	1.92
C8	(12, 25)	(12, 25)	(12, 30)	(25, 25)	(25, 25)	(15, 25)	(20, 25)	(12, 25)	(20, 30)	(15, 25)

Table 6. Model of criteria preferences.

No.	Name	Weight	Preference Function	Preference Threshold
C1	Power	VH	V-shaped	99.098
C2	Module efficiency	H	V-shaped	0.026
C3	Open-circuit voltage	M	V-shaped	8.505
C4	Short-circuit current	M	V-shaped	3.491
C5	Price per watt	VH	V-shaped	1.434
C6	Weight	VL	V-shaped	2.468
C7	Area	L	V-shaped	0.138
C8	Warranty	MH	V-shaped	12.126

Abbreviations: VH—very high, H—high, M—medium, L—low, VL—very low.

4. Results

Preference models together with a fuzzy decision model allowed us to generate rankings of the tested PV panels. In accordance with the NEAT F-PROMETHEE calculation procedure, rankings based on positive and negative outranking flows are obtained, allowing for the construction of a partial order of alternatives, and a ranking based on net outranking flow, which is also a total order of alternatives. These rankings, together with fuzzy and defuzzified outranking flows, are presented in Table 7 and Figure 1. On the other hand, Figure 2 shows a partial order constructed on the basis of positive and negative outranking flows.

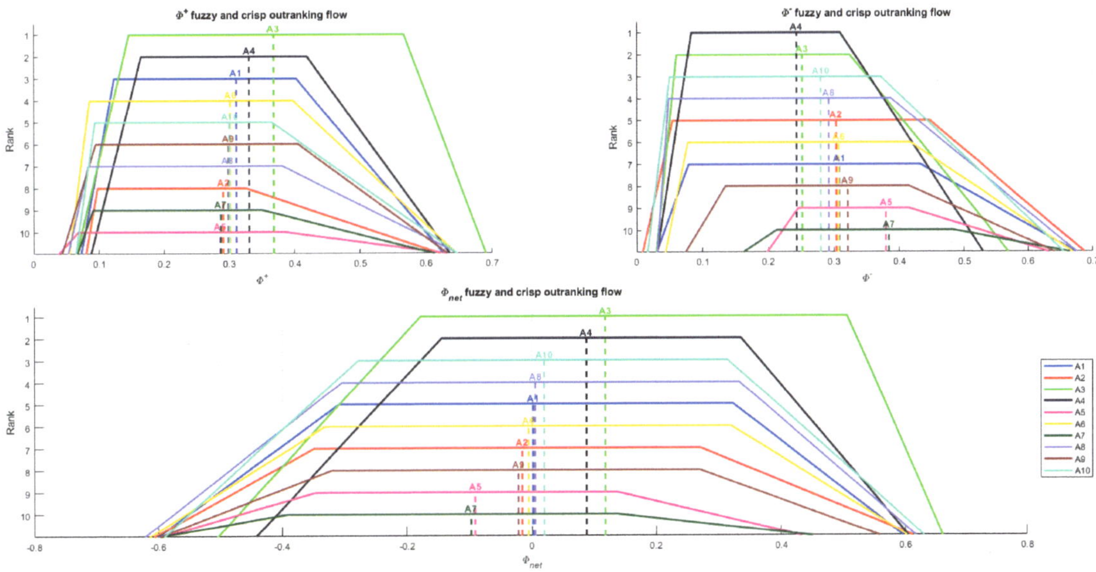

Figure 1. Outranking flows and alternative rankings.

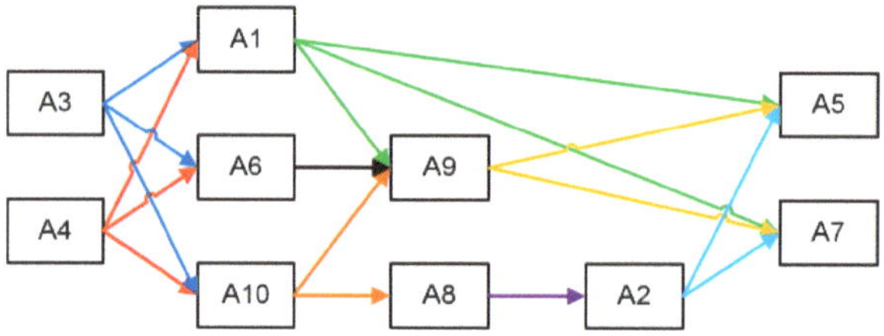

Figure 2. Partial order of alternatives.

Table 7. Values of outranking flows and rankings of alternatives.

	A1	A2	A3	A4	A5	A6	A7	A8	A9	A10
$\tilde{\phi}^{+}(\tilde{a})$	(0.0727, 0.1233, 0.4023, 0.6264)	(0.0800, 0.0977, 0.3256, 0.6215)	(0.0658, 0.1460, 0.5665, 0.6907)	(0.0878, 0.1648, 0.4192, 0.6357)	(0.0376, 0.0681, 0.3838, 0.6322)	(0.0544, 0.0852, 0.3976, 0.6465)	(0.0667, 0.0910, 0.3504, 0.6128)	(0.0527, 0.0835, 0.3814, 0.6482)	(0.0433, 0.0949, 0.4052, 0.6325)	(0.0646, 0.0939, 0.3652, 0.6473)
$\phi^{+}(a)$	0.3110	0.2906	0.3680	0.3311	0.2860	0.3016	0.2873	0.2980	0.2985	0.3004
Rank ϕ^{+}	3	8	1	2	10	4	9	7	6	5
$\tilde{\phi}^{-}(\tilde{a})$	(0.0302, 0.0791, 0.4316, 0.6734)	(0.0090, 0.0547, 0.4465, 0.6866)	(0.0297, 0.0607, 0.3236, 0.5694)	(0.0311, 0.0835, 0.3092, 0.5291)	(0.1982, 0.2459, 0.4145, 0.6322)	(0.0436, 0.0777, 0.4164, 0.6687)	(0.1620, 0.2125, 0.4828, 0.6639)	(0.0310, 0.0487, 0.3868, 0.6745)	(0.0742, 0.1351, 0.4147, 0.6411)	(0.0166, 0.0505, 0.3710, 0.6549)
$\phi^{-}(a)$	0.3083	0.3036	0.2520	0.2435	0.3789	0.3070	0.3836	0.2923	0.3210	0.2802
Rank ϕ^{-}	7	5	2	1	9	6	10	4	8	3
$\tilde{\phi}_{net}(\tilde{a})$	(−0.6007, −0.3084, 0.3232, 0.5963)	(−0.6066, −0.3488, 0.2709, 0.6124)	(−0.5037, −0.1776, 0.5059, 0.6611)	(−0.4413, −0.1444, 0.3357, 0.6046)	(−0.5946, −0.3464, 0.1379, 0.4340)	(−0.6142, −0.3312, 0.3198, 0.6029)	(−0.5972, −0.3918, 0.1379, 0.4508)	(−0.6219, −0.3033, 0.3327, 0.6172)	(−0.5978, −0.3198, 0.2700, 0.5583)	(−0.590 −0.2771 0.3147, 0.6307)
$\phi_{net}(a)$	0.0021	−0.0158	0.1177	0.0878	−0.0908	−0.0057	−0.0971	0.0053	−0.0220	0.0196
Rank ϕ_{net}	5	7	1	2	9	6	10	4	8	3

According to the ranking based on the value of ϕ_{net} (total order), the best PV panel among those considered is A3—Jinko Solar JKM430N-54HL4. However, taking into account the values of ϕ^{+}, ϕ^{-}, and partial order created on their basis, the A3 panel is matched by A4—Kensol KS395M-SH. These two alternatives definitely outrank the next group of alternatives, which include A1—Astronergy CHSM54M-HC (182), A2—JA Solar JAM60S20 390/MR, A6—Phono Solar PS420M4-22/WH, A8—Risen RSM40-8-410M, A9—Selfa SV108M.3-410, and A10—Trina Solar TSM-DE09.08 405W. At the forefront of this group are the alternatives A10, A1, and A6, which, according to partial order, are second only to the A3 and A4 panels. However, in total order, the alternatives A1 and A6 are outranked by the alternative A8. According to both orders, at the end of this group there are A2 and A9 panels, which are outranked by the other alternatives. Both according to partial order as well as according to total order, the worst panels are A5—Meyer Burger White, and A7—REC 380AA, which form the last group of alternatives and are strongly outranked by all other alternatives.

When analysing the characteristics of PV panels occupying the highest places in the rankings, it should be noted that A3 is characterized by the highest values of the criteria C1—power, C2—module efficiency C4—short-circuit current. In turn, the A4 dominates the other alternatives in terms of the criteria C3—open-circuit voltage, and C6—weight. Alternative A4 also has the longest product warranty period, which makes it better than the other alternatives in terms of criterion C8—warranty. As for the alternatives A5 and A7, which occupy the last positions in the rankings, their position is mainly influenced by the very high price per watt (C5), because the other considered characteristics of these panels are relatively good.

5. Discussion

As indicated in Section 2, in previous studies on multi-criteria assessment of solar PV panels, the parameters of panels obtained in standard test conditions were usually used, and the numerical data were treated as reliable and precise. Therefore, it is interesting to compare the results of the developed fuzzy model with the results of the corresponding model without uncertainty, based on the parameters of solar PV panels obtained in standard test conditions. The comparison model used the same criteria as the fuzzy model, but the values were in the form of RNs. The values of the criteria were taken from Table 3. For C1, C3, and C4, these were current–voltage parameters obtained in standard test conditions (power—STC, open-circuit voltage—STC, short-circuit current—STC). The initial value of module efficiency was used as C2, and the average duration of the product warranty and performance warranty was indicated as C8. A comparative model using precise numerical values is presented in Table 8. The evaluation results obtained using the model based on precise values are presented in Table 9 and Figures 3 and 4.

Table 8. Decision matrix containing precise values of alternatives.

	A1	A2	A3	A4	A5	A6	A7	A8	A9	A10
C1	410.00	390.00	430.00	395.00	400.00	420.00	380.00	410.00	410.00	405.00
C2	21.00	20.90	22.02	21.10	21.70	20.98	21.70	21.30	21.00	21.10
C3	37.40	41.94	38.49	49.40	44.60	45.69	44.30	41.90	37.45	41.40
C4	13.88	11.58	14.23	10.07	10.90	11.45	10.61	12.47	13.88	12.34
C5	1.52	1.57	1.59	1.76	3.77	1.60	2.93	1.76	1.99	1.60
C6	21.6	20.7	22.0	19.0	19.7	23.0	19.5	21.5	22.1	21.0
C7	1.95	1.87	1.95	1.88	1.84	2.00	1.75	1.92	1.96	1.92
C8	18.5	18.5	21	25	25	20	22.5	18.5	25	20

Table 9. Outranking flows and alternative rankings according to the precise model.

	A1	A2	A3	A4	A5	A6	A7	A8	A9	A10
$\phi^{+}(a)$	0.2026	0.1235	0.4862	0.2933	0.3285	0.2582	0.2833	0.2149	0.2706	0.1838
Rank ϕ^{+}	8	10	1	3	2	6	4	7	5	9
$\phi^{-}(a)$	0.2629	0.3528	0.1249	0.2421	0.3355	0.2266	0.4282	0.2166	0.2311	0.2242
Rank ϕ^{-}	7	9	1	6	8	4	10	2	5	3
$\phi_{net}(a)$	0.2629	0.3528	0.1249	0.2421	0.3355	0.2266	0.4282	0.2166	0.2311	0.2242
Rank ϕ_{net}	8	10	1	2	6	4	9	5	3	7

Comparison of the results of the fuzzy evaluation model with the results of the precise model shows that in the case of the total order and the precise model (Figures 1 and 3), the advantage of A3 over the other alternatives, in particular over A4, increase significantly. Substantial changes also take place in subsequent positions in this ranking. Alternative A2 significantly weakens and is no longer superior to alternatives A9, A5, and A7, but is worse than them. Similarly, the ranks of alternatives A10 and A1 deteriorate, while the ranks of other alternatives improve or do not change significantly. Also, when comparing partial orders (Figures 2 and 4), it can be seen that in the case of the precise model, the positions of alternatives A4, A1, A10, and A2 deteriorate, and the positions of alternatives A5 and A9 improve significantly.

The observed differences between the results of the fuzzy model and the precise model show how important it is to properly build the decision model and to take into account the uncertainty and imprecision of the data. It should be emphasized that both models differ only in the numbers describing the criteria C1–C4 and C8. However, for criteria C5–C7, criteria weights and preference functions are the same, and the values of preference thresholds are defined in the same way (as twice the sample standard deviation). However, the indicated differences cause significant discrepancies between the rankings obtained based on the fuzzy decision model and the precise model.

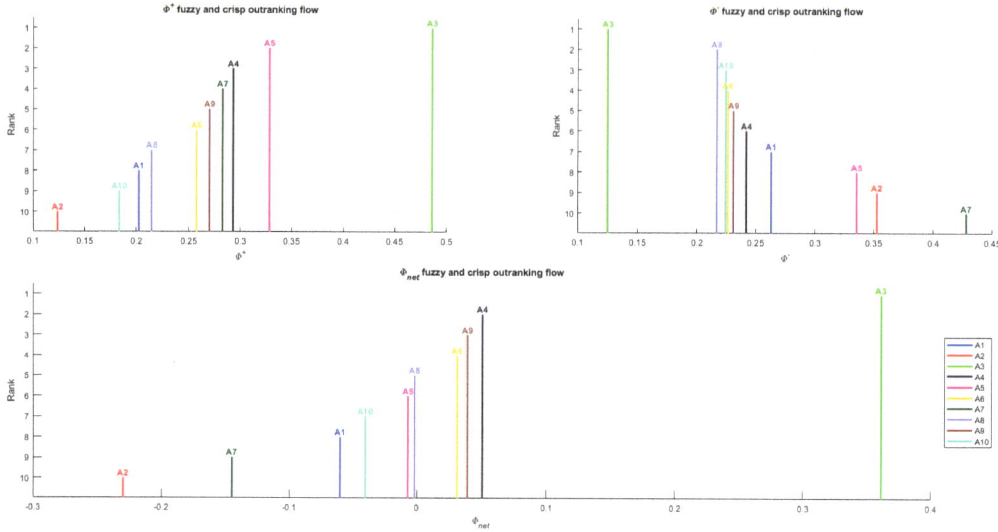

Figure 3. Outranking flows and alternative rankings according to the precise model.

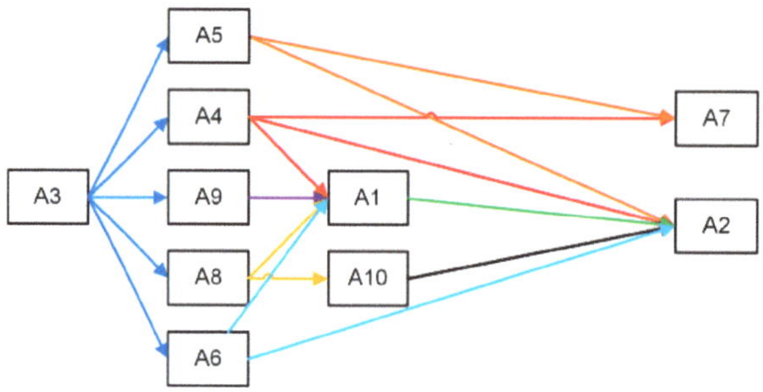

Figure 4. Partial order of alternatives according to the precise model.

The indicated differences in the rankings are related to the fact that the amount of data included in TFNs, TrFNs, and Ins is greater than in RNs (singletons). A fuzzy number contains information about two, three or four values of a given alternative, while RN is a carrier of only one value. Generally speaking, fuzzy numbers carry information about the entire range of possible values of a given criterion, thus, taking into account the uncertainty of data and the imprecision of measurements. As a result, the ranking obtained based on fuzzy numbers is more "conservative" than the ranking obtained on the basis of RNs, which are assumed to be certain and precise. The fuzzy ranking takes into account a certain margin of uncertainty as to the mutual advantages between the alternatives, is more "soft", less categorical, and less definitively determines the order of the alternatives.

6. Conclusions

The practical purpose of the article was to evaluate the PV panels available on the Polish energy market and to select solar PV panels with the best technical parameters, taking into account many criteria. Based on the conducted research, Jinko Solar JKM430N-54HL4 and Kensol KS395M-SH panels are indicated as optimal. The scientific contribution of the article include capturing the uncertainty and imprecision of technical parameters using a fuzzy approach. The conducted research partly fills the identified research gap, consisting of the need to take into account uncertain criteria describing the operating parameters of solar PV panels in study. During the research, a fuzzy PV panel assessment model was developed, based on TFNs and the NEAT F-PROMETHEE multi-criteria method. The calculation results obtained using this model were compared with the results of the model based on precise RNs. As a result of the conducted investigations, it is found that the precise model can give completely different results than the fuzzy model. However, the results of the fuzzy model should be considered more reliable, because fuzzy numbers allow for the capturing of more data than RNs, which translates into greater reliability of the obtained results.

The presented study, both in practical and scientific terms, had some limitations. Referring to the practical goal, the limited number of PV panels considered in the study should be indicated as the basic limitation. Collecting reliable data on solar PV panels requires finding and carefully analysing their specification sheets. Data collection takes a long time, which automatically limits the number of solar PV panels that can be analyzed in one study. The basic limitation related to the scientific aspect is also related to data collection. Namely, collecting more data would improve the accuracy of mapping reliability by fuzzy numbers, and this would further increase the credibility of the obtained results. Other membership functions and alternative ways of constructing fuzzy numbers describing individual technical parameters of PV panels can also be considered. Further research should lead to the elimination of the indicated limitations and include works leading to increasing the accuracy of the assessment by using fuzzy numbers describing the given alternatives in more detail.

Author Contributions: Conceptualization, P.Z.; methodology, P.Z.; software, P.Z.; validation, M.S.; formal analysis, M.S.; data curation, P.Z. and M.S.; writing—original draft preparation, P.Z. and M.S.; writing—review and editing, P.Z. and M.S.; supervision, P.Z. All authors have read and agreed to the published version of the manuscript.

Funding: This research was funded by the National Science Centre, Poland, grant number 2019/35/D/HS4/02466.

Data Availability Statement: Data are contained within the article.

Conflicts of Interest: The authors declare no conflict of interest.

References

1. Li, K.; Liu, C.; Jiang, S.; Chen, Y. Review on Hybrid Geothermal and Solar Power Systems. *J. Clean. Prod.* **2020**, *250*, 119481. [CrossRef]
2. Tian, M.-W.; Yan, S.-R.; Han, S.-Z.; Nojavan, S.; Jermsittiparsert, K.; Razmjooy, N. New Optimal Design for a Hybrid Solar Chimney, Solid Oxide Electrolysis and Fuel Cell Based on Improved Deer Hunting Optimization Algorithm. *J. Clean. Prod.* **2020**, *249*, 119414. [CrossRef]
3. Strantzali, E.; Aravossis, K. Decision Making in Renewable Energy Investments: A Review. *Renew. Sustain. Energy Rev.* **2016**, *55*, 885–898. [CrossRef]
4. *Decarbonising Our Energy System to Meet Our Climate Goals*; European Union: Brussels, Belgium, 2021.
5. Wang, J.-J.; Jing, Y.-Y.; Zhang, C.-F.; Zhao, J.-H. Review on Multi-Criteria Decision Analysis Aid in Sustainable Energy Decision-Making. *Renew. Sustain. Energy Rev.* **2009**, *13*, 2263–2278. [CrossRef]
6. Ju, X.; Xu, C.; Hu, Y.; Han, X.; Wei, G.; Du, X. A Review on the Development of Photovoltaic/Concentrated Solar Power (PV-CSP) Hybrid Systems. *Sol. Energy Mater. Sol. Cells* **2017**, *161*, 305–327. [CrossRef]
7. Guyer, J.P. *Introduction to Solar Collectors for Heating and Cooling of Buildings and Domestic Hot Water Heating*; Continuing Education and Development, Inc.: Stony Point, NY, USA, 2012.
8. Kalogirou, S.A. Solar Thermal Collectors and Applications. *Prog. Energy Combust. Sci.* **2004**, *30*, 231–295. [CrossRef]
9. Wojcik, W.; Amirgaliyev, Y.; Kunelbayev, M.; Kalizhanova, A.; Kozbakova, A.; Sundetov, T.; Yedilkhan, D. Developing the System of Collecting, Storing and Processing Information from Solar Collectors. *Int. J. Electron. Telecommun.* **2021**, *67*, 65–70. [CrossRef]
10. Chacko, J.; Thomas, K. Analysis of Different Solar Panel Arrangements Using PVSYST. *Int. J. Eng. Res. Technol.* **2015**, *4*, 510–513. [CrossRef]
11. Budea, S.; Safta, C.A. Review on Modern Photovoltaic Panels—Technologies and Performances. *IOP Conf. Ser.: Earth Environ. Sci.* **2021**, *664*, 012032. [CrossRef]
12. Zeman, M. Introduction to Photovoltaic Solar Energy. *Solar Cells*. Available online: https://www.aerostudents.com/courses/solar-cells/solarCellsTheoryFullVersion.pdf (accessed on 27 June 2023).

13. Joël Tchognia Nkuissi, H.; Kouadio Konan, F.; Hartiti, B.; Ndjaka, J.-M. Toxic Materials Used in Thin Film Photovoltaics and Thei Impacts on Environment. In *Reliability and Ecological Aspects of Photovoltaic Modules*; Gok, A., Ed.; IntechOpen: London, UK, 202(ISBN 978-1-78984-822-9.
14. Kushiya, K. CIS-Based Thin-Film PV Technology in Solar Frontier K.K. *Sol. Energy Mater. Sol. Cells* **2014**, *122*, 309–313. [CrossRef]
15. Nowak, W. Kolektory Słoneczne I Panele Fotowoltaiczne Jako Źródło Energii W Małych Instalacjach Cieplnych I Elektroenergety cznych. *Autom. Elektr. Zakłócenia* **2011**, *2*, 55–64.
16. Tan, D.; Kian Seng, A. *Handbook for Solar Photovoltaic (PV) Systems*; Energy Market Authority, Building and Construction Authority Singapore, 2009; ISBN 978-981-08-4462-2.
17. van de Kaa, G.; Rezaei, J.; Kamp, L.; de Winter, A. Photovoltaic Technology Selection: A Fuzzy MCDM Approach. *Renew. Sustain Energy Rev.* **2014**, *32*, 662–670. [CrossRef]
18. Shayani Mehr, P.; Hafezalkotob, A.; Fardi, K.; Seiti, H.; Movahedi Sobhani, F.; Hafezalkotob, A. A Comprehensive Framework for Solar Panel Technology Selection: A BWM- MULTIMOOSRAL Approach. *Energy Sci. Eng.* **2022**, *10*, 4595–4625. [CrossRef]
19. Schmela, M.; Rossi, R.; Lits, C.; Chunduri, S.K.; Shah, A.; Muthyal, R.; Moghe, P.; Kalam, S.; Jamkhedkar, A.; Goel, S.; et a Advancements in Solar Technology, Markets, and Investments—A Summary of the 2022 ISA World Solar Reports. *Sol. Compas* **2023**, *6*, 100045. [CrossRef]
20. Nesticò, A.; Elia, C.; Naddeo, V. Sustainability of Urban Regeneration Projects: Novel Selection Model Based on Analytic Network Process and Zero-One Goal Programming. *Land Use Policy* **2020**, *99*, 104831. [CrossRef]
21. Nesticò, A.; Somma, P. Comparative Analysis of Multi-Criteria Methods for the Enhancement of Historical Buildings. *Sustainability* **2019**, *11*, 4526. [CrossRef]
22. Ziemba, P. NEAT F-PROMETHEE—A New Fuzzy Multiple Criteria Decision Making Method Based on the Adjustment o Mapping Trapezoidal Fuzzy Numbers. *Expert Syst. Appl.* **2018**, *110*, 363–380. [CrossRef]
23. Ziemba, P. Multi-Criteria Approach to Stochastic and Fuzzy Uncertainty in the Selection of Electric Vehicles with High Socia Acceptance. *Expert Syst. Appl.* **2021**, *173*, 114686. [CrossRef]
24. Ziemba, P. Uncertain Multi-Criteria Analysis of Offshore Wind Farms Projects Investments—Case Study of the Polish Economi Zone of the Baltic Sea. *Appl. Energy* **2022**, *309*, 118232. [CrossRef]
25. Ziemba, P. Selection of Electric Vehicles for the Needs of Sustainable Transport under Conditions of Uncertainty—A Comparative Study on Fuzzy MCDA Methods. *Energies* **2021**, *14*, 7786. [CrossRef]
26. Ziemba, P. Energy Security Assessment Based on a New Dynamic Multi-Criteria Decision-Making Framework. *Energies* **2022**, *15* 9356. [CrossRef]
27. Seddiki, M.; Bennadji, A. Multi-Criteria Evaluation of Renewable Energy Alternatives for Electricity Generation in a Residentia Building. *Renew. Sustain. Energy Rev.* **2019**, *110*, 101–117. [CrossRef]
28. Al Garni, H.; Kassem, A.; Awasthi, A.; Komljenovic, D.; Al-Haddad, K. A Multicriteria Decision Making Approach for Evaluating Renewable Power Generation Sources in Saudi Arabia. *Sustain. Energy Technol. Assess.* **2016**, *16*, 137–150. [CrossRef]
29. Ahmad, S.; Tahar, R.M. Selection of Renewable Energy Sources for Sustainable Development of Electricity Generation System Using Analytic Hierarchy Process: A Case of Malaysia. *Renew. Energy* **2014**, *63*, 458–466. [CrossRef]
30. Kengpol, A.; Rontlaong, P.; Tuominen, M. A Decision Support System for Selection of Solar Power Plant Locations by Applying Fuzzy AHP and TOPSIS: An Empirical Study. *J. Softw. Eng. Appl.* **2013**, *6*, 470–481. [CrossRef]
31. Mokarram, M.; Mokarram, M.J.; Khosravi, M.R.; Saber, A.; Rahideh, A. Determination of the Optimal Location for Constructing Solar Photovoltaic Farms Based on Multi-Criteria Decision System and Dempster–Shafer Theory. *Sci. Rep.* **2020**, *10*, 820([CrossRef]
32. Kereush, D.; Perovych, I. Determining Criteria for Optimal Site Selection for Solar Power Plants. *GLL* **2017**, 39–54. [CrossRef]
33. Watson, J.J.W.; Hudson, M.D. Regional Scale Wind Farm and Solar Farm Suitability Assessment Using GIS-Assisted Multi-Criteria Evaluation. *Landsc. Urban Plan.* **2015**, *138*, 20–31. [CrossRef]
34. Chen, C.-R.; Huang, C.-C.; Tsuei, H.-J. A Hybrid MCDM Model for Improving GIS-Based Solar Farms Site Selection. *Int. J Photoenergy* **2014**, *2014*, e925370. [CrossRef]
35. Sánchez-Lozano, J.M.; García-Cascales, M.S.; Lamata, M.T. Evaluation of Suitable Locations for the Installation of Solar Thermo electric Power Plants. *Comput. Ind. Eng.* **2015**, *87*, 343–355. [CrossRef]
36. Vafaeipour, M.; Hashemkhani Zolfani, S.; Morshed Varzandeh, M.H.; Derakhti, A.; Keshavarz Eshkalag, M. Assessment o Regions Priority for Implementation of Solar Projects in Iran: New Application of a Hybrid Multi-Criteria Decision Making Approach. *Energy Convers. Manag.* **2014**, *86*, 653–663. [CrossRef]
37. Ponce, P.; Pérez, C.; Fayek, A.R.; Molina, A. Solar Energy Implementation in Manufacturing Industry Using Multi-Criteria Decision-Making Fuzzy TOPSIS and S4 Framework. *Energies* **2022**, *15*, 8838. [CrossRef]
38. Balo, F.; Şağbanşua, L. The Selection of the Best Solar Panel for the Photovoltaic System Design by Using AHP. *Energy Procedia* **2016**, *100*, 50–53. [CrossRef]
39. Kozlov, V.; Sałabun, W. Challenges in Reliable Solar Panel Selection Using MCDA Methods. *Procedia Comput. Sci.* **2021**, *192* 4913–4923. [CrossRef]
40. Bączkiewicz, A.; Kizielewicz, B.; Shekhovtsov, A.; Yelmikheiev, M.; Kozlov, V.; Sałabun, W. Comparative Analysis of Solar Panels with Determination of Local Significance Levels of Criteria Using the MCDM Methods Resistant to the Rank Reversal Phenomenon. *Energies* **2021**, *14*, 5727. [CrossRef]

41. Zadeh, L.A. Fuzzy Sets. *Inf. Control* **1965**, *8*, 338–353. [CrossRef]
42. Liu, G.; Wang, X. A Trapezoidal Fuzzy Number-Based VIKOR Method with Completely Unknown Weight Information. *Symmetry* **2023**, *15*, 559. [CrossRef]
43. Buckley, J.J. Portfolio Analysis Using Possibility Distributions. In *Approximate Reasoning in Intelligent Systems, Decision and Control*; Sanchez, E., Zadeh, L.A., Eds.; Pergamon: Amsterdam, The Netherlands, 1987; pp. 69–76. ISBN 978-0-08-034335-8.
44. Brândaş, A. Approximation of Fuzzy Numbers by Trapezoidal Fuzzy Numbers Preserving the Core and the Expected Value. *Stud. Univ. Babes-Bolyai Math.* **2011**, *56*, 247–259.

energies

MDPI

Article

Fuzzy Multi-Criteria Decision for Geoinformation System-Based Offshore Wind Farm Positioning in Croatia

Ivana Racetin [1,*], Nives Ostojić Škomrlj [1], Marina Peko [2] and Mladen Zrinjski [3]

1 Faculty of Civil Engineering, Architecture and Geodesy, University of Split, Matice Hrvatske 15, 21000 Split, Croatia
2 Independent Researcher, 21000 Split, Croatia
3 Faculty of Geodesy, University of Zagreb, Kačićeva 26, 10000 Zagreb, Croatia
* Correspondence: ivana.racetin@gradst.hr

Abstract: Renewable energy is one of the main components of a sustainable world and its future. The consumption of electricity from renewable sources in Croatia has an impressive rate of 53.5%, but offshore wind turbines (OWT) have not yet been installed in the Adriatic Sea. The aim of this study is to determine the possibilities for offshore wind farm (OWF) positioning in the Croatian part of the Adriatic Sea using marine spatial planning (MSP). Initial research to determine the points of interest was conducted based on wind speed. The authors established ten possible points for further research. Subsequently, different parameters were used as inputs for exclusion. The Fuzzy Analytic Hierarchy Process (AHP) method was used to calculate the weighting coefficients for a suitable set of criteria, exactly six of them. Using a combination of geoinformation system (GIS) analysis and weighting coefficients established through Fuzzy AHP, four points were established as suitable for OWF installation in Croatia. Finally, the Technique for Order of Preference by Similarity to Ideal Solution (TOPSIS) method was used to select the best order for OWF positioning in the eastern part of the Adriatic Sea. To conclude, there are not many options for OWF positioning in Croatia. Furthermore, it is clear that they exist and should be explored further.

Keywords: fuzzy AHP; GIS; marine spatial planning; offshore wind farm; renewable wind energy; TOPSIS

1. Introduction

Renewable energy is one of the main components of sustainable development in the contemporary world. New energy sources are the precondition to the existence of the world "as we know it", and renewable energy is a precondition to the survival of mankind. The European Union (EU) is one of the leaders in sustainable world development. In addition, EU leadership strongly strives towards clean energy development. The goal is to become the first climate-neutral continent by 2050 [1]. Electricity consumption from renewable sources is highest in Austria and Sweden, followed by Denmark, Portugal and Croatia, which is in fifth place in the EU, with 53.5% of consumption coming from renewable sources [2].

In EU countries, Marine Spatial Planning (MSP) has been established as a concept with clear goals and timing for its implementation in practice. The problem with the majority of non-EU countries, not including developed countries such as the United States of America (USA) or Australia, but in the case of less developed ones, is the lack of a systematic and global approach to the topic. They are less focused on MSP due to implementation problems, for instance, lack of regulations, governmental interest, etc. In general, MSP deals with human activities in the marine domain, primarily taking their ecological and economic segments into account, as well as social ones. Today, but also in the future, it will not be possible to even think about energy without considering the ecological and sustainable concepts in which it will be developed. One of the activities of the EU, considering their environmental and ecological concepts, is finding new and sustainable ways of energy production. Wind energy production through the strong establishment and development of wind farms in the EU is one of the possibilities. Wind farms could be established both on land and at sea. The authors of this paper considered offshore wind farms (OWF) in the MSP context.

1.1. Research Focus

Many papers have been published on OWF [3], as described in the next subchapter. Most of this research focuses on micro-locations and finding the best positions for OWF installations in certain coastal countries. To the best of the authors' knowledge, several papers have been written about the Croatian part of the Adriatic Sea in the context of energy production and energy usage at sea. On the other hand, they were mostly focused on technical and economic aspects, but none focused on OWF in the MSP context and its other aspects such as environment, ecology, and social aspects.

In addition, MSP is focused on a participatory approach that requires the inclusion of all relevant stakeholders in the decision-making process, such as the best OWF positioning at sea). Involving all of the relevant stakeholders in the planning process is an important step forward in order to achieve broader acceptance and support for its implementation.

Secondly, Croatia is not a sufficiently marine-oriented country in the ecological energy production segment. It still does not have a full legal framework for setting up an MSP, and there is no unified spatial plan for the entire Croatian maritime area. As shown further in this paper, some steps were taken, in the right direction, considering OWF in terms of the legislative framework. However, as of the writing of this paper, no OWF has been installed in the Croatian part of the sea.

Contemporary studies worldwide are taking into consideration not only technical or economic frameworks for OWF positioning but also ecological and social components. The research goals of this study were as follows:

1. Analyze the trends in EU and non-EU countries in OWF positioning methodology;
2. The question of whether it is possible to position OWF in the Croatian part of the Adriatic Sea (considering Croatian legislation, waterways and some MSP and other parameters);
3. Find the best positions for OWFs installing in Croatia based on different parameters.

1.2. Literary Review

Wind farms positioned on and offshore are very valuable sources of energy production that are focused on electricity production. According to Chen and Su [3], the OWF scientific field is rapidly expanding, and it was stated that the growth in paper publishing has been significant in the last decade. Moreover, a lot of papers deal with OWFs and their technical, technological [4–13] and economic [14–19] aspects. Some of them analyze the wind–wave combined energy [20–22] and the concept of Smart OWF and 5G technology [23]. Some other aspects of OWF positioning and a different approach are explained further in this chapter. A literary review was established for EU and non-EU countries with a focus on the methodology used by different authors, so the decision could be made on the best possible methodology to be used in this research. The other focus will be on what has been written so far in Croatia on the topic of OWF positioning.

1.2.1. EU Countries

The European Parliament and Council of the European Union adopted Directive 2014/89/EU [24] in 2014, which established a framework for MSP in the EU. The EU has 22 member states with access to the sea, and one of them is Croatia.

The current positions and number of all offshore wind turbines (OWTs) in Europe can be found in [25]. This shows that the United Kingdom has the most OWT in Europe (2679). It is followed by Germany (1539), Denmark (631), Netherlands (496) and Belgium (399). The only state bordering Croatia that has OWTs is Italy, with 10 OWT.

Croatia and Its Part of the Adriatic Sea

The Adriatic Sea is not a large sea (138.595 km^2 [26]) compared to others, such as the Mediterranean or Black Sea. The Croatian part of the sea occupies an area of 31,479 km^2 [27], while the coastline is 6278 km long. The coast consists of 1880 km on the mainland and 4398 km on the islands. Also, there are 1244 islands, islets, rocks and reefs. A total of 47 islands are permanently inhabited [28]. Croatia borders Italy, Slovenia and Montenegro at sea. Several papers were written on OWF and other kinds of renewable energy equipment in Croatia and the Adriatic Sea. For instance, Klarin [29] deals with energy islands, which include floating OWFs and fish farms. The turbine production for OWF is possible in Croatian shipyards, and the author finds it economically viable. Moreover, Hadžić et al. [30] analyzed wind speed in the Croatian Adriatic Sea and came to the conclusion that energy production is more efficient at sea than on land due to the highest average wind speed and its constancy at sea. Furthermore, they are dealing with OWT design, its mechanical structure and energetic possibilities. The authors of the paper [22] were more focused on the wave/wind energy potential in Croatia, analyzing wind speed for this purpose. They singled out seven different locations in the Adriatic Sea that could be used for energy extraction. All things considered, from the perspective of this paper, the most interesting is the research by Liščić et al. [31]. In this research, the authors suggested three potential locations for OWT installation. Those are in the open sea near the town of Pula and the island of Mali Lošinj, the area near the harbour of the town of Šibenik and the outer side of the island of Mljet. The authors suggested that the best option is the open sea near the town of Pula. Since they did not conduct their research in the MSP context, as explained below, their results and the results of this paper's research are different.

Some EU States and Their Methodology Usage Experience

Vagiona and Kamilakis [32] analyzed the best possible OWF positioning in the South Aegean Sea using the Analytic Hierarchy Process (AHP) and Technique for Order of Preference by Similarity to Ideal Solution (TOPSIS) methods in combination with Geographic Information Systems (GIS). Moreover, Vagiona and Karanikolas [33] dealt with OWF and their positioning using AHP and GIS methodology. Baltic state (Estonia, Latvia and Lithuania) OWF installation was also analyzed using the AHP method [34]. Poland has plans to install OWF, and the best positions were analyzed using modified fuzzy TOPSIS [35]. Similarly, Cradden et al. [36] used GIS methodology to analyze the combination of wave, wind and tidal current power, mostly in western and north-western Europe.

1.2.2. Some Non-EU Countries and Their Methodology Usage Experience

China is more focused on the decision-making framework for offshore wind power station (OWP) positioning. Wu et al. [37] analyzed eight possible multi-criteria decision-making (MCDM) methods and their advantages and disadvantages. The authors finally decided to use the Preference Ranking Organization Method for Enrichment Evaluations (PROMETHEE) method. On the African continent, a significant contribution is given in the papers from Nigeria [38], Morocco [39] and Egypt [40]. In Nigeria's case, authors used AHP and Fuzzy TOPSIS methods [38]. Morocco has no OWF installed yet, and researchers used Fuzzy AHP and GIS [39] for selecting possible OWF locations, the same as in Brazil's case [41]. Another study was conducted in Egypt, combining MCDM and GIS [40] methodology.

It is necessary to highlight the paper that deals with different methods of comparison and analyzing their impact on decision-making in the field of renewable energy sources [42]. This implies that the top five methods used in the area are AHP, Analytic Network Process (ANP), ELimination Et Choix Traduisant la REalité (ELECTRE), TOPSIS and Preference Ranking Organization Method for Enrichment Evaluations (PROMETHEE). It also explains the increased usage of Fuzzy AHP in this research area, as does Tasri and Susilawati's study [43].

A large number of existing studies in the broader literature have been examined, and it can be pointed out that there is no optimal method for decision-support analysis and that there is no unique methodology that should be used for OWF positioning. Nevertheless, the following conclusions can be drawn. The most commonly used methods were GIS and some of the MCDM methods, specifically AHP and TOPSIS. Recently, it has been observed that the fuzzy method is used more often as a tool for OWF position selection. The author's decision regarding the methodology used in this paper is explained in Section 2.

2. Materials and Methods

As a result of an analysis of the available literature, the authors of this paper decided to use geoinformation system (GIS) analysis and multi-criteria decision-making methods to determine the best possible OWF positions in the Croatian part of the Adriatic Sea. Based on the literature review and the opinion of a team of Croatian experts on MCDM methodologies, the authors decided to apply a combination of fuzzy AHP and TOPSIS methods for the purpose of this study.

2.1. Research Inputs and Their Description

First of all, available inputs for the Croatian part of the Adriatic Sea were studied:

1. Wind speed;
2. Water depths;
3. Seabed sediment;
4. Sea borders and legislation frame;
5. Exclusion areas (Natura 2000; cables and pipelines; navigation corridors, tourism, explosive ordnance);
6. Vessel's density;
7. Electric grid, airports and ports.

The authors would like to emphasize that there was a possibility to analyze some additional parameters, such as different environmental impacts besides Natura 2000 exclusion or cost–benefit analysis, construction costs, etc. Due to the complexity of the economic field, the authors decided to explore it in the future in a separate research paper. Considering the increasing impact on the environment, the Ministry of Economy and Sustainable Development of the Republic of Croatia started an Action Program of Marine Environment and Coastal Areas Management Strategy in 2021. [44]. Therefore, more significant information about environmental protection should be produced, along with some new observations and measurements established at the Croatian part of Adriatic Sea.

2.1.1. Wind Speed

Wind speed is one of the most important (if not the most important) factors in OWF positioning. According to Liščić et al. [31], constant wind speed between 5 and 25 m/s is the best possible option for energy extraction. In several studies [32,45,46], the lowest suggested wind speed was 6 m/s, whereas in [47,48], the authors proposed an even lower speed limit of 4 m/s. Data for the mean annual wind speed (m/s) in the period from 1992 to 2001 in the Croatian part of the Adriatic Sea can be found in the Wind Atlas [49], along with the mean annual power density (W/m^2). The wind data are presented for heights of 10 and 80 m above sea level. It is notable that the strongest wind speed zones are between Pula and the island of Mali Lošinj, in front of town Senj, at the open sea in front of town Šibenik, south of the islands of Hvar and Mljet and town of Dubrovnik. For example, the wind speed increases to 6.6 m/s in front of Šibenik and Mljet and up to 6.2 m/s in front of Pula. Likewise, Hvar has a slightly lower wind speed. The other source used for this research is the Global Wind Atlas (GWA) 3.0 [50]. GWA has the possibility of showing mean wind speeds at 10, 50, 100, 150 and 200 m above sea level. Because the height of OWT is 80–100 m, the GWA data for 100 m above sea level were further analyzed (Figure 1).

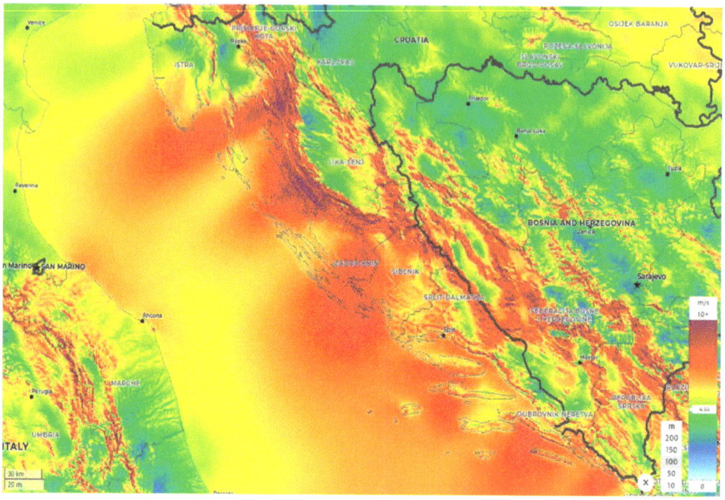

Figure 1. Mean Wind Speed (m/s) at 100 m above the sea level (Source: GWA [50]).

GWA shows a higher mean wind speed than [49], more than 10 m/s in the northern coastal areas and up to 8.5 m/s in the open sea zone. The mean annual power density reaches approximately 800 W/m^2 in the northern coastal belt (Figure 2).

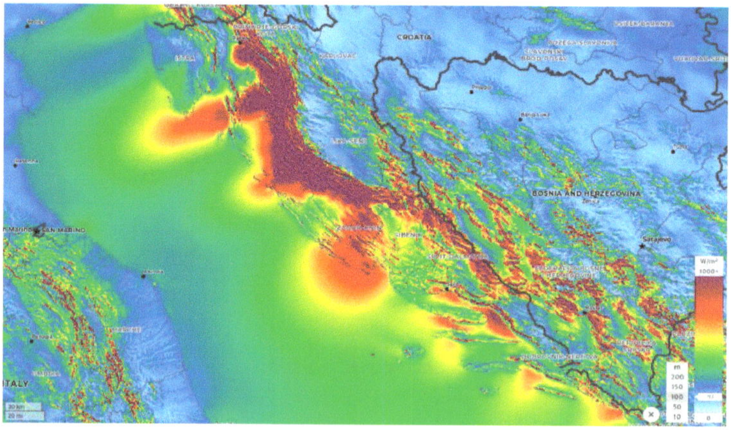

Figure 2. Mean Power Density (W/m^2) at 100 m above the sea level (Source: GWA [50]).

2.1.2. Water Depths

The Adriatic Sea is not very deep (Figure 3). The average depth is 173 m, and the deepest recorded point is 1233 m [26].

For instance, the maximum depths of the Mediterranean Sea, Tironian Sea and Ionian Sea are 5267 m, 3785 m, and 5267 m, respectively. The Adriatic Sea is 783 km long, with an average width of 248.3 km, and it covers 138.600 km^2. In its east, the Croatian region has approximately 1300 islands and islets [26]. The northern part of the Adriatic Sea is very shallow, with depths up to 100 m due to the influence of the river Po. The middle part has depths of up to 500 m. The deepest part, with a maximum depth of 1233 m, is located in the Otranto Passage.

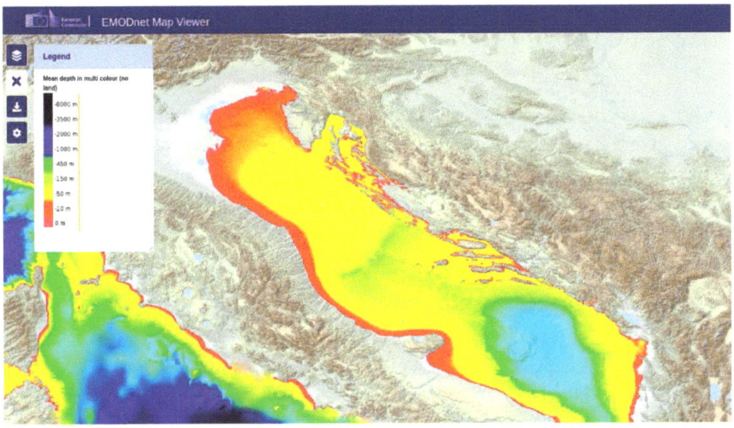

Figure 3. Adriatic Sea depth shown in hypsometric scale of colours (Source: EMODnet [51]).

2.1.3. Seabed Sediment and Its Thickness

Marine sediments differ with respect to the depth of the Adriatic Sea. Consequently, at water depths higher than 100 m, the sediment is muddy, and in other parts, it is mostly sandy (Figure 4), [52].

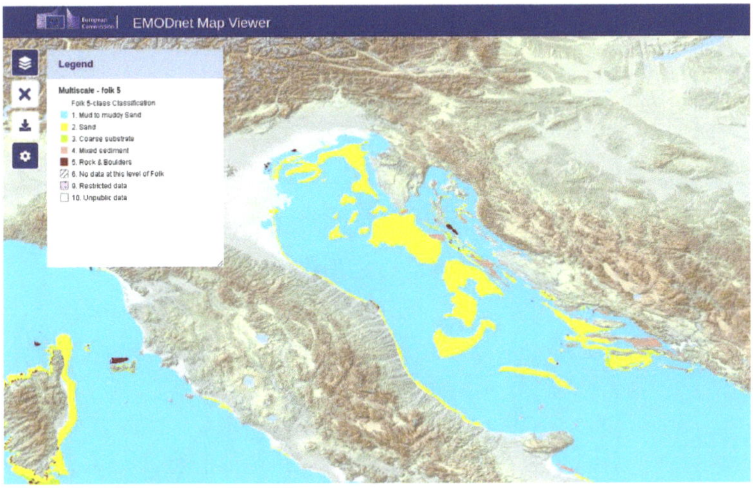

Figure 4. Seabed substrate in the Adriatic Sea (Source: EMODnet [51]).

Both types of sediments are favourable for OWF installation. According to Straume et al. [53], the sediment thickness in the Adriatic Sea is approximately 3–4 km which makes it suitable for OWF installation.

2.1.4. Sea Borders and Legislation Frame

The Croatian part of the Adriatic Sea consists of inland waters, territorial sea and continental shelf. An act from 2021, with the name "Decision on the declaration of the Exclusive Economic Zone of the Republic of Croatia in the Adriatic Sea" [54], contains two new rights, the construction of artificial islands and the usage of the power of the sea, wind and currents in continental shelf.

The backbone for legislation of spatial planning in Croatia is the "Spatial Planning Act" [55]. Its Amendments [56] from the year 2017 enabled the full transfer of the MSP

Directive into the legislative of the Republic of Croatia. Based on the act, drafting of the State Spatial Planning Plan for the entire land and sea area (up to the outer border of the territorial waters) of the Republic of Croatia has begun. Spatial plans for the protected terrestrial and marine areas have also been drawn up [57]. Amendments [56] defined Croatia's cooperation with other EU member states in the area of MSP in the Adriatic Sea, cooperation with non-EU countries and the definition of competent authorities for SMEs. Important document for Croatian marine environment protection is "Regulation on the establishment of a framework for the activities of the Republic of Croatia in the protection of the marine environment" [58]. Based on the "Decision on the adoption of the Action Program of the Strategy for the Management of the Marine Environment and the Coastal Area: Monitoring and Observation System for the Constant Assessment of the State of the Adriatic Sea (2021–2026)" [44], the document "Action Program of Marine Environment and Coastal Area Management Strategy" [59] was established.

Looking at the technical aspect of OWFs placement possibilities, it was important to consult "Croatian Maritime law" [60] and its sub-act "Rulebook on the system of marking waterways and navigation safety facilities" [61], which refers to OWF markings for the purpose of safety of navigation at sea. It can be concluded, as determined from variety of sources, that Croatian legislation recognizes the possibility of OWF installation in the Croatian part of Adriatic Sea.

2.1.5. Exclusion Areas

Several sea areas were excluded from the research due to submarine cables and pipelines being positioned. The rule of a restriction belt spreading 500 m on both sides of the cable or pipeline was followed to avoid possible damage. In the northern part of the Adriatic Sea, there are some navigation corridors that had to be avoided. Tourism is one of the main economic activities on the Croatian coast and islands; therefore, the rule of an OWF distance of at least 10 km from the islands and the coast had to be followed. The authors also considered the official data from the charts of the Hydrographic Institute of the Republic of Croatia regarding residual danger from explosive ordnance on the seabed. The Natura 2020 [62] network area (Figure 5) was respected and excluded, since MSP context needed to be followed, and the authors wished to avoid jeopardizing the environment.

Figure 5. Natura 2020 network area (in different shades of green) in the Adriatic Sea (Source: EMODnet [51]).

The Natura 2020 network covers EU countries at sea and on land, defining protected areas for different species. The aim is to ensure the survival of some of the most valuable species. It consists of special protection areas and conservation interests.

2.1.6. Vessel's Density

The vessel density was also taken into consideration, as shown in Table 1. Because of GNSS (Global Navigation Satellite System) technology, each vessel's route can be traced. Blue colour shows fewer vessels, whereas green, yellow and red show more vessel density (Figure 6).

Table 1. Suitability scores of selected criteria.

Criterion/Score	0	1	2	3	4	5
C1 Water depth (m)	>1000	500–1000	200–500	100–200	50–100	0–50
C2 Wind speed (m/s)	<4	4–5	5–6	6–7	7–8	>8
C3 Distance from ports (km)	10–20	20–30	30–40	40–50	50–60	>60
C4 Distance to airports (km)	10–15	15–20	20–25	25–30	30–35	>35
C5 Distance from power grid (km)	-	>60	40–60	30–40	20–30	<20
C6 Traffic density	-	VHD	HD	MD	LD	VLD

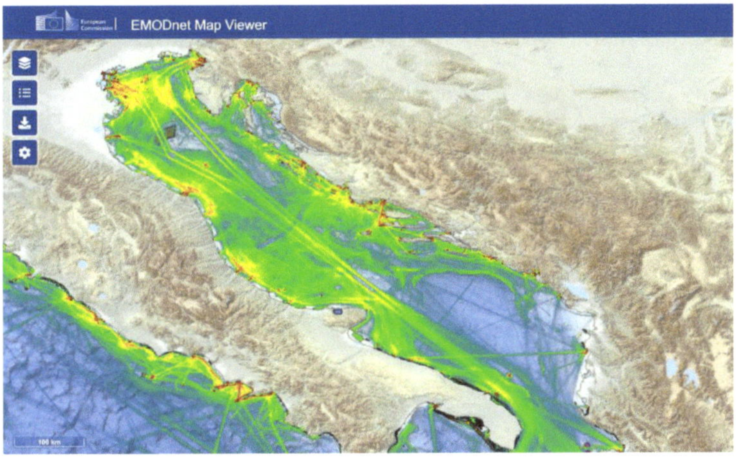

Figure 6. Average vessel density (2017–2021) in the Adriatic Sea (Source: EMODnet [51]).

2.1.7. Electric Grid, Airports, Ports

The electric grid is an important factor in OWF positioning. The closer the network is, the cheaper the electricity production. In this study, the grid of 110 kV or higher was considered, as was its closeness to the points of interest. There are three main lines of 110 kV cables on the coast. The first one is laid along the coast and main towns on the coast, and the second one is set down connecting islands of Krk, Cres, Mali Lošinj and also Krk with Rab and Pag. The third one is laid along the islands of Brač, Hvar, Korčula and Pelješac and further towards Dubrovnik.

Moreover, the OWF should not be installed close to airports (symbol of the plane in Figure 7) or ports (symbol of the circle in Figure 7), thereby creating additional restriction zones (Table 1).

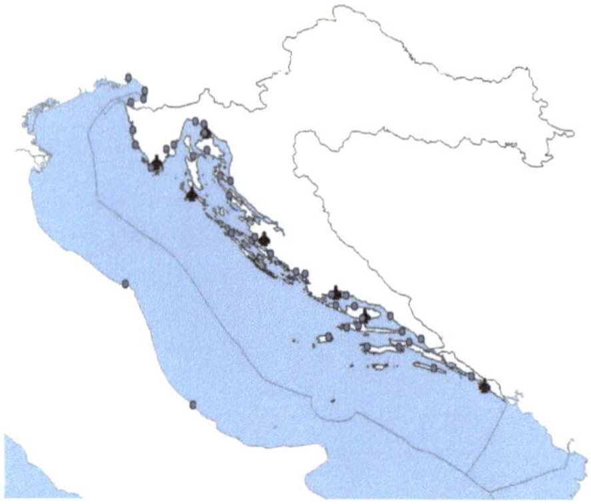

Figure 7. Ports and airports (Source: Open Street Map [63]).

2.2. GIS, Fuzzy AHP and TOPSIS Analysis

The procedure for selecting the most favourable offshore wind farms (OWF) locations is shown in Figure 8. Firstly, the analysis of possible OWF positions was performed based only on the wind speed on the east coast of the Adriatic Sea. Ten possible points were selected based on the mean wind speed input (Figure 9). The authors analyzed the mean wind speed, as shown in Figure 1, because it is the main issue to consider in OWF positioning. Ten points initially chosen had the strongest mean wind speed, according to [50]. Based on a literature review and features of the Croatian part of the Adriatic Sea, the exclusion and selection criteria were defined, and the fuzzy AHP methodology was used to define weights for each of the selected criteria. Several experts were consulted for the input parameters for the Fuzzy AHP analysis. GIS analysis was performed based on the exclusion criteria in the QGIS software (Version 3.30.1), and six initially proposed OWF positions were excluded. The TOPSIS analysis was used for the four remaining OWF position points in order to find the best positioning solution.

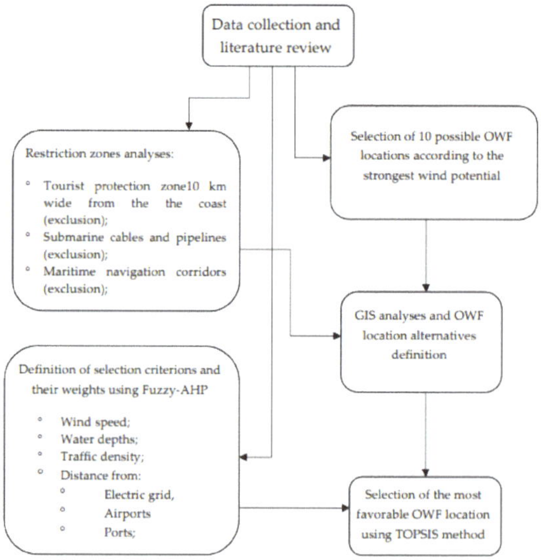

Figure 8. Methodological diagram.

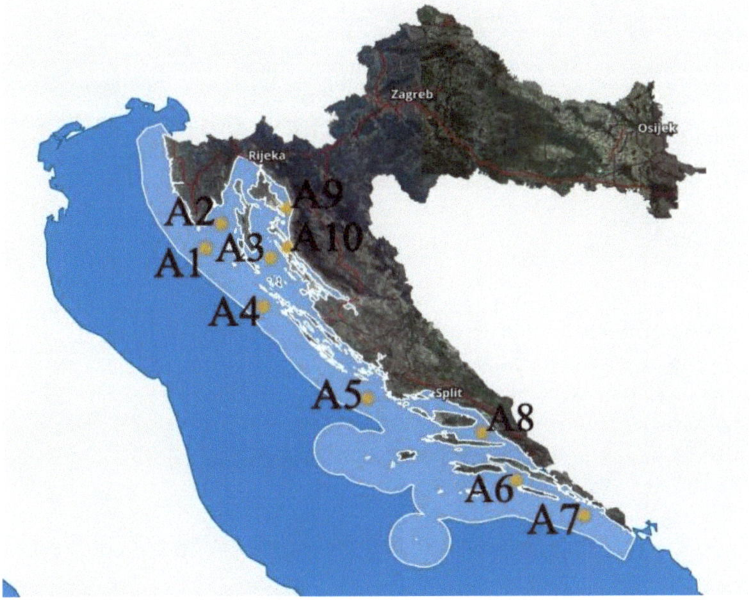

Figure 9. Ten points initially chosen based on the wind speed.

The first group of criteria includes the following elimination criteria:

- Maritime navigation corridors;
- Submarine cables and pipelines;
- Sea borders;
- Natura 2000 *;
- Tourist protection zone.

* denotes a network of core breeding and resting sites for rare and threatened species.

In the areas covered by the above criteria, it is not possible to position OWF.

Other criteria by which it is necessary to determine weight values include the following:

- Water depth (C1);
- Wind speed (C2);
- Distance from ports (C3);
- Distance to airports (C4);
- Distance from power grid (C5);
- Traffic density (C6).

When all restrictions were considered, four major areas of possible OWF locations remained (A1, A4, A5 and A7 alternatives).

Subsequently, the weights for all six criteria were determined using the Fuzzy AHP method, and in the last stage of the calculation, the most favourable location of the potential OWF was calculated using the TOPSIS method.

The criteria and suitability scores for the selected criteria are listed in Table 1.

A pairwise comparison matrix was created to determine the weights of the individual criteria using the Fuzzy AHP method (Table 2).

Table 2. Pairwise comparison matrix.

Criteria	C1	C2	C3	C4	C5	C6
C1 Water depth (m)	1	1/3	7	9	5	7
C2 Wind speed (m/s)	3	1	9	7	5	7
C3 Distance from ports (km)	1/7	1/9	1	3	1/7	1/5
C4 Distance to airports (km)	1/9	1/7	1/3	1	1/5	3
C5 Distance from power grid (km)	1/5	1/5	7	5	1	7
C6 Traffic density	1/7	1/5	5	1/3	1/7	1

To determine the criteria weights, the decision maker for each pair of criteria (C_i, C_j) must estimate their relative and decide on one of the following statements:

(a) Both criteria are equally important;
(b) Criterion C_i is more important than C_j;
(c) Criterion C_j is more important than C_i.

Choosing any of these statements entails the corresponding quantification of criteria weights ratio w_i/w_j as follows:

$$a_{ij} = \frac{w_i}{w_j} = 1, \text{ both criteria are equally important;}$$

$$a_{ij} = \frac{w_i}{w_j} > 1, \text{ criterion } X_i \text{ is more important than } C_j;$$

$$a_{ij} = \frac{w_i}{w_j} < 1, \text{ criterion } X_j \text{ is more important than } C_i.$$

The comparison matrix above is then converted into triangular fuzzy numbers, and each grade is expanded with a lower and upper value, as shown in Table 3.

Table 3. Pairwise comparison matrix, triangular fuzzy numbers.

Criterion	C1	C2	C3	C4	C5	C6
C1	1,1,1	1/4,1/3,1/2	6,7,8	6,7,8	4,5,6	6,7,8
C2	2,3,4	1,1,1	6,7,8	6,7,8	3,4,5	6,7,8
C3	1/8,1/7,1/6	1/8,1/7,1/6	1,1,1	1,1,1	1/5,1/4,1/3	1/3,1/2,1
C4	1/8,1/7,1/6	1/8,1/7,1/6	1,1,1	1,1,1	1/4,1/3,1/2	1,2,3
C5	1/6,1/5,1/4	1/5,1/4,1/3	3,4,5	2,3,4	1,1,1	4,5,6
C6	1/8,1/7,1/6	1/8,1/7,1/6	1,2,3	1/3,1/2,1	1/6,1/5,1/4	1,1,1

For each criterion, it is necessary to create a separate matrix and then calculate the geometric mean for each row of the matrix (each criterion) according to Formula (1):

$$r_i = \left(\prod_{j=1}^{n} d_{ij}\right)^{1/n}, i = 1, 2, \cdots, n \tag{1}$$

For example,

$$r_{11} = (1 \times 0.25 \times 6 \times 6 \times 4 \times 6)^{1/6} = 2.449489743$$

$$r_{12} = (1 \times 0.3333 \times 7 \times 7 \times 5 \times 7)^{1/6} = 2.880871$$

In addition, weights were calculated (as triangular fuzzy numbers—3 values) according to Formula (2), and the fuzzy weights of each criterion (Table 4) were defined by incorporating the next three sub-steps.

Table 4. Weights as triangular fuzzy numbers.

$r_1^{\sim}$	2.449489743	2.880871	3.396762659
$r_2^{\sim}$	3.301927249	4.00324861	4.659972203
$r_3^{\sim}$	0.31838661	0.3696457	0.458243212
$r_4^{\sim}$	0.396850263	0.48859848	0.588795922
$r_5^{\sim}$	0.963492484	1.20093696	1.467799268
$r_6^{\sim}$	0.308857335	0.39976581	0.524557532
SUM	7.739003684	9.34306655	11.0961308
INVERSE	0.129215599	0.10703124	0.090121504
incr. order	0.090121504	0.10703124	0.129215599

i. Define the vector summation of each r_i;
ii. Find the (−1) power of the summation vector. Replace the fuzzy triangular number to make it in increasing order;
iii. Find the fuzzy weight of criterion i (w_i), and multiply each r_i with this reverse vector.

$$w_i = r_i \cdot (r_1^{\sim} + r_2^{\sim} + \cdots + r_6^{\sim})^{-1} = (lw_i, mw_i, uw_i) \tag{2}$$

$$M_i = \frac{lw_i + mw_i + uw_i}{3}, \; i = 1, \ldots, 6 \tag{3}$$

$$N_i = \frac{M_i}{\sum\limits_{i=1}^{n} M_i}, \; i = 1, \ldots, n \tag{4}$$

Because w_i are still fuzzy triangular numbers, they need to be de-fuzzed; thus, the following matrix of weights (three values) is obtained, and the average value M_i—relation (3) is calculated from them; M_i is a non-fuzzy number; therefore, these values are normalized by following Equation (4). Table 5 shows the values of N_i, which represent the final weights of the criterion obtained by Fuzzy AHP.

$$lw_1 = 2.449489743 \times 0.090121504 = 0.220751701$$

$$mw_1 = 2.880871 \times 0.10703124 = 0.3083432$$

$$uw_1 = 3.396762659 \times 0.129215599 = 0.43891472$$

$$M_1 = \frac{lw_1 + mw_1 + uw_1}{3} = \frac{0.220751701 + 0.3083432 + 0.43891472}{3} = 0.322669873$$

$$N_1 = \frac{M_1}{\sum_{i=1}^{n} M_i} = \frac{0.322669873}{1.043747949} = 0.309145396$$

In the final part of the study, the most favourable location for the OWF was calculated using the TOPSIS method. Moreover, this procedure involves several steps to obtain the most favourable alternative. The criterion values for each of the four potential locations/alternatives are listed in Table 6.

Table 5. Final criterion weights obtained by Fuzzy AHP.

		w_i~		M_i	N_i
C1	0.220751701	0.3083432	0.43891472	0.322669873	0.309145396
C2	0.297574651	0.42847266	0.6021411	0.442729472	0.424172783
C3	0.02869348	0.03956364	0.05921217	0.042489763	0.040708835
C4	0.035764743	0.0522953	0.07608162	0.054713887	0.052420594
C5	0.086831392	0.12853777	0.18966256	0.135010575	0.129351704
C6	0.027834688	0.04278743	0.06778102	0.046134378	0.044200689
			SUM	1.043747949	1

Table 6. Criterion value/alternative.

	C1	C2	C3	C4	C5	C6
	min	max	max	max	min	max
A1	50	7.1	35.2	30.2	28.5	2
A4	6.4	6.58	26.3	55	41	3
A5	170	7.26	34	43	19	1
A7	174	6.73	21	17.5	18	4

Furthermore, it is necessary to calculate the normalized matrix (Table 7) and weighted normalized matrix (Table 8).

Table 7. Normalization decision matrix.

	C1	C2	C3	C4	C5	C6
	min	max	max	max	min	max
A1	10.063238	3.640808	20.86112	11.68486	14.40773	0.730297
A4	0.16487609	3.127036	11.64565	38.75566	29.81767	1.643168
A5	116.331032	3.80675	19.46302	23.68899	6.403437	0.182574
A7	121.869838	3.271231	7.424905	3.92361	5.747129	2.921187

Table 8. Weighted normalized matrix (V).

	C1	C2	C3	C4	C5	C6
	min	max	max	max	min	max
A1	3.11100371	1.544332	0.849232	0.612527	1.863665	0.03228
A4	0.05097068	1.326404	0.474081	2.031595	3.856966	0.072629
A5	35.9632029	1.61472	0.792317	1.241791	0.828296	0.00807
A7	37.6754993	1.387567	0.302259	0.205678	0.743401	0.129118
w_j	0.3091454	0.424173	0.040709	0.052421	0.129352	0.044201

The normalization is conducted based on the following Formula (5),

$$R = r_{ij} = \frac{x_{ij}}{\sqrt{\sum_{i=1}^{n} x_{ij2}}} \tag{5}$$

where X_{ij} represents the value of the i-th alternative according to the j-th criterion, and n is the number of criteria.

The weighted normalized matrix (V) is calculated from relation (6).

$$V_{ij} = x_{ij} \times w_j \quad (6)$$

The TOPSIS process is based on the fact that the solution to the problem is the alternative that is closest to the ideal one and furthest from the anti-ideal alternative (Table 9). The ideal alternative S^+ contains the best values for each attribute, and the anti-ideal alternative S^- contains the worst values for each attribute. The two created alternatives indicate the most preferable alternative (ideal solution) and the least preferable alternative (negative-ideal solution). It is also obvious that these alternatives do not exist in the offered set of alternatives. Namely, if S^+ exists, the problem is solved, i.e., the perfect solution exists.

Table 9. Ideal best and anti-ideal value based on TOPSIS calculation.

	C1	C2	C3	C4	C5	C6	S_i^+	S_i^-
	min	max	max	max	min	max		
A1	3.111004	1.544332	0.849232	0.612527	1.863665	0.03228	3.556245	34.62933
A4	0.050971	1.326404	0.474081	2.031595	3.856966	0.072629	3.149817	37.66926
A5	35.9632	1.61472	0.792317	1.241791	0.828296	0.00807	35.92127	3.674455
A7	37.6755	1.387567	0.302259	0.205678	0.743401	0.129118	37.67346	3.116518
ideal best	0.050971	1.61472	0.849232	2.031595	0.743401	0.129118		
anti-ideal	37.6755	1.326404	0.302259	0.205678	3.856966	0.00807		

The calculation of the Euclidian distance from the best/anti-ideal value is shown in Formulas (7) and (8).

$$S_i^+ = \left(\sum_{i=1}^{n} (Vij - V_j^+)^2 \right)^{0.5} \quad (7)$$

$$S_i^- \left(\sum_{i=1}^{n} (Vij - V_j^-)^2 \right)^{0.5} \quad (8)$$

$V_j{}^+$ and $V_j{}^-$ represent the best ideal end anti-ideal value.

The relative closeness to the ideal solution is then calculated from the Formula (9). Obviously, $RC_i = 1$ if $S_i = S^+$ and $RC_i = 0$ if $S_i = S^-$. An alternative is closer to the ideal solution and, therefore, better as RC_i approaches 1.

$$RC_i = \frac{S_i^-}{S_i^+ + S_i^-} \quad (9)$$

The final ranking of the alternatives is presented in Table 10.

Table 10. Alternatives ranking.

	S_i^+	S_i^-	RC_i	Ranking
A1	3.556245	34.62933	0.906869414	2
A4	3.149817	37.66926	0.922834686	1
A5	35.92127	3.674455	0.092799293	3
A7	37.67346	3.116518	0.076403998	4

It can be seen that point A4 is the best possible option, followed by A1, A5 and A7.

3. Discussion and Conclusions

Three main questions were addressed in this paper. The first one was about the appropriate methodology for establishing OWF positioning. The scientific literature on trends in EU and non-EU countries in OWF positioning methodology was consulted for this purpose. Based on the research conducted, it was concluded that there is no single solution and no single answer to that question. The unique method does not exist, and there is no unique answer to the OWF position-establishing question. Good examples of GIS and MCMD methods combined in many EU and non-EU countries provided an answer to the question of what are the most used methods in OWF position establishment. Based on their experience and the experience of Croatian experts that were consulted, the methodology was established to answer the second question of the paper, that of the possibility of positioning an OWF in the Croatian part of the Adriatic Sea. The authors further consulted the available literature and established that no OWF was installed in the Adriatic Sea. The strong point of the research for OWF installation in Croatia was the cognition that there is legislation that supports this possibility. The legislation should be further developed, however, and its starting point is good and promising. The third question that required an answer was what would be the best possible location for installing an OWF in Croatia. For that purpose, a combination of GIS and fuzzy AHP methods was used. The suitability scores of the available selected criteria are listed in Table 1. The scores were based on the experience of the available literature and other countries' practices. Ten points of interest were initially considered (A1–A10), chosen on a mean wind speed basis and measured during a ten-year period. Based on the exclusion parameters defined in subchapter 2.1.5, six points of interest were excluded. The coast of Croatia is well developed and has more than 1000 islands and strong tourist activity for at least half a year. This creates a potential problem in OWF positioning if the tourism criterion of following the rule of distancing OWF positioning at least 10 km from the coast and islands is respected. Four points of interest (A1, A4, A5 and A7) were left for consideration. The best possible point (A4) was determined using the TOPSIS methodology.

The findings of this study should be considered as a starting point for further and more detailed analysis of OWF installation. They should also raise the topic of OWFs' stronger consideration in Croatia in the MSP context, as defined within EU regulations. Further research should address the economic value and technical aspects of OWF in the Adriatic Sea. A combination of wind and wave energy usage at sea should be considered together with the possibility of required construction built in Croatian shipyards, as mentioned in the paper by Klarin [29]. The authors of this paper emphasize that experts in different technical fields should, in their future research, consider ecological segments that are equally important for OWF and similar topics. However, this was not the case in Croatia. Future studies could consider more inputs than those chosen in Table 1 and methods other than those used in this paper, but the MSP context should always be included. The authors believe that there is a good perspective for raising sustainable energy usage in Croatia and that the positive trends established on Croatian land will extend themselves to the Croatian part of the Adriatic Sea as well.

Author Contributions: Conceptualization, I.R. and N.O.Š.; methodology, I.R.; software, M.P. and N.O.Š.; validation, I.R., M.Z. and N.O.Š.; formal analysis, I.R. and M.P.; investigation, I.R., M.P. and N.O.Š.; resources, I.R., M.P. and N.O.Š.; data curation, M.Z.; writing—original draft preparation, I.R., M.P. and N.O.Š.; writing—review and editing, I.R., M.P., N.O.Š. and M.Z.; visualization, M.P.; supervision, I.R., N.O.Š. and M.Z. All authors have read and agreed to the published version of the manuscript.

Funding: This research received no external funding.

Acknowledgments: This research is partially supported through project KK.01.1.1.02.0027, a project co-financed by the Croatian Government and the European Union through the European Regional Development Fund—the Competitiveness and Cohesion Operational Programme.

Conflicts of Interest: The authors declare no conflict of interest.

References

1. EUROSTAT. Share of Renewable Energy More than Doubled between 2004 and 2021. Available online: https://ec.europa.eu/eurostat/statistics-explained/index.php?title=Renewable_energy_statistics#Share_of_renewable_energy_more_than_doubled_between_2004_and_2021 (accessed on 1 March 2023).
2. EUROSTAT. Wind and Water Provide Most Renewable Electricity; Solar Is the Fastest-Growing Energy Source. Available online: https://ec.europa.eu/eurostat/statistics-explained/index.php?title=Renewable_energy_statistics#Wind_and_water_provide_most_renewable_electricity.3B_solar_is_the_fastest-growing_energy_source (accessed on 1 March 2023).
3. Chen, C.-H.; Su, N.-J. Global Trends and Characteristics of Offshore Wind Farm Research over the Past Three Decades: A Bibliometric Analysis. *J. Mar. Sci. Eng.* **2022**, *10*, 1339. [CrossRef]
4. Ramsay, W.; Goupee, A.; Allen, C.; Viselli, A.; Kimball, R. Optimization of a Lightweight Floating Offshore Wind Turbine with Water Ballast Motion Mitigation Technology. *Wind* **2022**, *2*, 535–570. [CrossRef]
5. Xu, S.; Xue, Y.; Zhao, W.; Wan, D. A Review of High-Fidelity Computational Fluid Dynamics for Floating Offshore Wind Turbines. *J. Mar. Sci. Eng.* **2022**, *10*, 1357. [CrossRef]
6. Altuzarra, J.; Herrera, A.; Matías, O.; Urbano, J.; Romero, C.; Wang, S.; Guedes Soares, C. Mooring System Transport and Installation Logistics for a Floating Offshore Wind Farm in Lannion, France. *J. Mar. Sci. Eng.* **2022**, *10*, 1354. [CrossRef]
7. Belvasi, N.; Judge, F.; Murphy, J.; Desmond, C. Analysis of Floating Offshore Wind Platform Hydrodynamics Using Underwater SPIV: A Review. *Energies* **2022**, *15*, 4641. [CrossRef]
8. Fan, Q.; Wang, X.; Yuan, J.; Liu, X.; Hu, H.; Lin, P. A Review of the Development of Key Technologies for Offshore Wind Power in China. *J. Mar. Sci. Eng.* **2022**, *10*, 929. [CrossRef]
9. Guo, X.; Zhang, Y.; Yan, J.; Zhou, Y.; Yan, S.; Shi, W.; Li, X. Integrated Dynamics Response Analysis for IEA 10-MW Spar Floating Offshore Wind Turbine. *J. Mar. Sci. Eng.* **2022**, *10*, 542. [CrossRef]
10. Alsubal, S.; Liew, M.S.; Shawn, L.E. Preliminary Design and Dynamic Response of Multi-Purpose Floating Offshore Wind Turbine Platform: Part 1. *J. Mar. Sci. Eng.* **2022**, *10*, 336. [CrossRef]
11. Amiri, N.; Shaterabadi, M.; Reza Kashyzadeh, K.; Chizari, M. A Comprehensive Review on Design, Monitoring, and Failure in Fixed Offshore Platforms. *J. Mar. Sci. Eng.* **2021**, *9*, 1349. [CrossRef]
12. Gao, S.; Zhang, L.; Shi, W.; Wang, B.; Li, X. Dynamic Responses for WindFloat Floating Offshore Wind Turbine at Intermediate Water Depth Based on Local Conditions in China. *J. Mar. Sci. Eng.* **2021**, *9*, 1093. [CrossRef]
13. Basbas, H.; Liu, Y.-C.; Laghrouche, S.; Hilairet, M.; Plestan, F. Review on Floating Offshore Wind Turbine Models for Nonlinear Control Design. *Energies* **2022**, *15*, 5477. [CrossRef]
14. Ghigo, A.; Cottura, L.; Caradonna, R.; Bracco, G.; Mattiazzo, G. Platform Optimization and Cost Analysis in a Floating Offshore Wind Farm. *J. Mar. Sci. Eng.* **2020**, *8*, 835. [CrossRef]
15. Díaz, H.; Serna, J.; Nieto, J.; Guedes Soares, C. Market Needs, Opportunities and Barriers for the Floating Wind Industry. *J. Mar. Sci. Eng.* **2022**, *10*, 934. [CrossRef]
16. Cordal-Iglesias, D.; Filgueira-Vizoso, A.; Baita-Saavedra, E.; Graña-López, M.Á.; Castro-Santos, L. Framework for Development of an Economic Analysis Tool for Floating Concrete Offshore Wind Platforms. *J. Mar. Sci. Eng.* **2020**, *8*, 958. [CrossRef]
17. Filgueira-Vizoso, A.; Castro-Santos, L.; Iglesias, D.C.; Puime-Guillén, F.; Lamas-Galdo, I.; García-Diez, A.I.; Uzunoglu, E.; Díaz, H.; Guedes Soares, C. The Technical and Economic Feasibility of the CENTEC Floating Offshore Wind Platform. *J. Mar. Sci. Eng.* **2022**, *10*, 1344. [CrossRef]
18. Li, H.; Guedes Soares, C. Assessment of failure rates and reliability of floating offshore wind turbines. *Reliab. Eng. Syst. Saf.* **2022**, *228*, 108777. [CrossRef]
19. Myhr, A.; Bjerkseter, C.; Ågotnes, A.; Nygaard, T.A. Levelised cost of energy for offshore floating wind turbines in a life cycle perspective. *Renew. Energy* **2014**, *66*, 714–728. [CrossRef]
20. Li, J.; Shi, W.; Zhang, L.; Michailides, C.; Li, X. Wind–Wave Coupling Effect on the Dynamic Response of a Combined Wind–Wave Energy Converter. *J. Mar. Sci. Eng.* **2021**, *9*, 1101. [CrossRef]
21. Fenu, B.; Attanasio, V.; Casalone, P.; Novo, R.; Cervelli, G.; Bonfanti, M.; Sirigu, S.A.; Bracco, G.; Mattiazzo, G. Analysis of a Gyroscopic-Stabilized Floating Offshore Hybrid Wind-Wave Platform. *J. Mar. Sci. Eng.* **2020**, *8*, 439. [CrossRef]
22. Farkas, A.; Degiuli, N.; Martić, I. Assessment of Offshore Wave Energy Potential in the Croatian Part of the Adriatic Sea and Comparison with Wind Energy Potential. *Energies* **2019**, *12*, 2357. [CrossRef]
23. Wang, Z.; Guo, Y.; Wang, H. Review on Monitoring and Operation-Maintenance Technology of Far-Reaching Sea Smart Wind Farms. *J. Mar. Sci. Eng.* **2022**, *10*, 820. [CrossRef]
24. European Parliament. Available online: https://www.eea.europa.eu/policy-documents/directive-2014-89-eu-maritime (accessed on 27 February 2023).
25. WindEurope. Available online: https://windeurope.org/intelligence-platform/product/european-offshore-wind-farms-map-public/ (accessed on 16 January 2023).
26. Croatian Encyclopedia, Leksikografski Zavod Miroslav Krleža. Adriatic Sea. Available online: https://www.enciklopedija.hr/Natuknica.aspx?ID=28478 (accessed on 23 November 2022).
27. Frančula, N.; Lapaine, M. Površina hrvatskoga mora. *Hrvat. Rev.* **2001**, *51*, 107–111.
28. The European Maritime Spatial Planning Platform. Available online: https://maritime-spatial-planning.ec.europa.eu/countries/croatia (accessed on 27 October 2022).

29. Klarin, B. Energetski otoci—Hibridni pučinski objekti. *Pomor. Zb.* **2016**, *Special edition*, 187–200. [CrossRef]
30. Hadžić, N.; Čatipović, I.; Tomić, M.; Vladimir, N.; Kozmar, H. Offshore Wind Turbines—Research and Development. *Pomor. Zb* **2018**, *Special edition*, 59–70. [CrossRef]
31. Liščić, B.; Senjanović, I.; Čorić, V.; Kozmar, H.; Tomić, M.; Hadžić, N. Offshore Wind Power Plant in the Adriatic Sea: An Opportunity for the Croatian Economy. *Trans. Marit. Sci.* **2014**, *3*, 103–110. [CrossRef]
32. Vagiona, D.G.; Kamilakis, M. Sustainable Site Selection for Offshore Wind Farms in the South Aegean—Greece. *Sustainability* **2018**, *10*, 749. [CrossRef]
33. Vagiona, D.G.; Karanikolas, N.M. A multicriteria approach to evaluate offshore wind farms siting in Greece. *Glob. NEST J.* **2012** *14*, 235–243.
34. Chaouachib, A.; Covriga, C.F.; Ardeleana, M. Multi-criteria selection of offshore wind farms: Case study for the Baltic States *Energy Policy* **2017**, *103*, 179–192. [CrossRef]
35. Ziemba, P. Multi-Criteria Fuzzy Evaluation of the Planned Offshore Wind Farm Investments in Poland. *Energies* **2021**, *14*, 978 [CrossRef]
36. Cradden, L.; Kalogeri, C.; Martinez Barrios, I.; Galanis, G.; Ingram, D.; Kallos, G. Multi-criteria site selection for offshore renewable energy platforms. *Renew. Energy* **2016**, *87*, 791–806. [CrossRef]
37. Wu, Y.; Tao, Y.; Zhang, B.; Wang, S.; Xu, C.; Zhou, J. A decision framework of offshore wind power station site selection using a PROMETHEE method under intuitionistic fuzzy environment: A case in China. *Ocean. Coast. Manag.* **2020**, *184*, 105016 [CrossRef]
38. Mayaki, E.A.; Adedipe, O.; Lawal, S.A. Multi-Criteria Evaluation of the Appropriate Offshore Wind Farm Location in Nigeria *IOP Conf. Ser. Mater. Sci. Eng.* **2018**, *413*, 012041. [CrossRef]
39. Taoufik, M.; Fekri, A. GIS-based multi-criteria analysis of offshore wind farm development in Morocco. *Energy Convers. Manag. X* **2021**, *11*, 100103. [CrossRef]
40. Mahdy, M.; Bahaj, A.S. Multi criteria decision analysis for offshore wind energy potential in Egypt. *Renew. Energy* **2018**, *118*, 278–289 [CrossRef]
41. Pereira de Azevedo, S.S.; Pereira Junior, A.O.; Fidelis da Silva, N.; Barbosa de Araújo, R.S.; Carlos Júnior, A.A. Assessment of Offshore Wind Power Potential along the Brazilian Coast. *Energies* **2020**, *13*, 2557. [CrossRef]
42. Ilbahara, E.; Cebia, S.; Kahramanb, C. A state-of-the-art review on multi-attribute renewable energy decision making. *Energy Strategy Rev.* **2019**, *25*, 18–33. [CrossRef]
43. Tasri, A.; Susilawati, A. Selection among renewable energy alternatives based on a fuzzy analytic hierarchy process in Indonesia *Sustain. Energy Technol. Assess.* **2014**, *7*, 34–44. [CrossRef]
44. Ministry of Economy and Sustainable Development of the Republic of Croatia. Action Program of Marine Environment and Coastal Area Management Strategy. Available online: https://mingor.gov.hr/UserDocsImages/Uprava_vodnoga_gospodarstva_i_zast_mora/Strategija_upravljanja_morem/Akcijski%20program%20Sustav%20pra%C4%87enja%202021_2026.pdf (accessed on 20 January 2023).
45. Sourianos, E.; Kyriakou, K.; Hatiris, G.A. GIS-based spatial decision support system for the optimum siting of offshore windfarms *Eur. Water* **2017**, *58*, 337–343.
46. Schallenberg-Rodríguez, J.; García Montesdeoca, N. Spatial planning to estimate the offshore wind energy potential in coastal regions and islands. Practical case: The Canary Islands. *Energy* **2018**, *143*, 91–103. [CrossRef]
47. Gavériaux, L.; Laverrière, G.; Wang, T.; Maslov, N.; Claramunt, C. GIS-based multicriteria analysis for offshore wind turbine deployment in Hong Kong. *Ann. GIS* **2019**, *25*, 207–218. [CrossRef]
48. Díaz, H.; Fonseca, R.B.; Guedes Soares, C. Site selection process for floating offshore wind farms in Madeira Islands. In *Advances in Renewable Energies Offshore*; Taylor & Francis Group: London, UK, 2019; pp. 729–737.
49. Croatian Meteorological and Hydrological Service. Wind Atlas. Available online: https://meteo.hr/klima_e.php?section=klima_hrvatska&param=k1_8 (accessed on 2 November 2022).
50. Global Wind Atlas (GWA). Available online: https://globalwindatlas.info/en (accessed on 3 November 2022).
51. EMODnet. Available online: https://emodnet.ec.europa.eu/en (accessed on 11 December 2022).
52. Schwartz, M.L. (Ed.) *Encyclopedia of Coastal Science*; Encyclopedia of Earth Sciences; Springer: Amsterdam, The Netherlands, 2005 Volume 24.
53. Straume, E.O.; Gaina, C.; Medvedev, S.; Hochmuth, K.; Gohl, K.; Whittaker, J.M.; Abdul Fattah, R.; Doornenbal, J.C.; Hopper, J.R GlobSed: Updated total sediment thickness in the world's oceans. *Geochem. Geophys. Geosyst.* **2019**, *20*, 1756–1772. [CrossRef]
54. Official Gazette 10/21. Available online: https://narodne-novine.nn.hr/clanci/sluzbeni/2021_02_10_192.html (accessed on 7 January 2023)
55. Official Gazette 153/13. Available online: https://narodne-novine.nn.hr/clanci/sluzbeni/2013_12_153_3220.html (accessed on 17 January 2023)
56. Official Gazette 65/17. Available online: https://narodne-novine.nn.hr/clanci/sluzbeni/2017_07_65_1494.html (accessed on 17 January 2023)
57. Kilić Pamuković, J.; Rogulj, K.; Racetin, I.; Vrdoljak, L. Prostorno planiranje na moru. In Proceedings of the 15th Symposium of Chartered Geodetic Engineers, Opatija, Croatia, 12–15 October 2022; Racetin, I., Zrinjski, M., Župan, R., Eds.; Croatian Chamber of Chartered Geodetic Engineers: Zagreb, Croatia, 2022; pp. 161–166.
58. Official Gazette 136/11. Available online: https://narodne-novine.nn.hr/clanci/sluzbeni/2011_11_136_2724.html (accessed on 19 January 2023)
59. Official Gazette 28/21. Available online: https://narodne-novine.nn.hr/clanci/sluzbeni/full/2021_03_28_602.html (accessed on 21 January 2023)
60. Official Gazette 17/94. Available online: https://narodne-novine.nn.hr/clanci/sluzbeni/1994_03_17_313.html (accessed on 20 December 2022)
61. Official Gazette 39/20. Available online: https://narodne-novine.nn.hr/clanci/sluzbeni/2020_04_39_830.html (accessed on 20 December 2022)

2. Natura 2020. Available online: https://ec.europa.eu/environment/nature/natura2000/index_en.htm (accessed on 2 March 2023).
3. Open Street Map. Available online: https://www.openstreetmap.org/ (accessed on 9 January 2023).

energies

MDPI

Article

Site Selection of Solar Power Plants Using Hybrid MCDM Models: A Case Study in Indonesia

Chia-Nan Wang [1], Yu-Chi Chung [1], Fajar Dwi Wibowo [1,*], Thanh-Tuan Dang [2,*] and Ngoc-Ai-Thy Nguyen [3]

[1] Department of Industrial Engineering and Management, National Kaohsiung University of Science and Technology, Kaohsiung 80778, Taiwan; cn.wang@nkust.edu.tw (C.-N.W.); ycchung@nkust.edu.tw (Y.-C.C.)
[2] Department of Logistics and Supply Chain Management, Hong Bang International University, Ho Chi Minh 72320, Vietnam
[3] Faculty of Business, FPT University, Ho Chi Minh 70000, Vietnam; thynna@fe.edu.vn
* Correspondence: i110143105@nkust.edu.tw (F.D.W.); tuandt@hiu.vn (T.-T.D.)

Abstract: Among developing countries in Asia, Indonesia has realized the importance of transitioning from fossil fuels to renewable energy sources such as solar power. Careful consideration must be given to the strategic placement of solar power installations to fully leverage the benefits of solar energy. This study proposes a methodology to optimize the site selection of solar power plants in Indonesia by integrating Data Envelopment Analysis (DEA), Fuzzy Analytic Hierarchy Process (F-AHP), and Fuzzy Measurement of Alternatives and Ranking according to Compromise Solution (F-MARCOS) models. The proposed methodology considers quantitative and qualitative criteria to evaluate potential locations for solar power plants. In the first stage, DEA is used to identify the most efficient locations based on quantitative measures such as solar radiation, land availability, and grid connectivity. In the second stage, qualitative factors such as technological, economic, environmental, and socio-political aspects are evaluated using F-AHP to prioritize the most important criteria for site selection. Finally, F-MARCOS ranks potential locations based on the selected criteria. The methodology was tested using data from Indonesia as a case study. The results show that the proposed hybrid model optimizes Indonesia's solar power plant site selection. The optimal locations can contribute to a cost-effective long-term renewable energy supply nationwide. The findings from this study are relevant to policymakers, industry stakeholders, and researchers interested in renewable energy development and site selection. However, to promote sustainable solar energy development, governments and local authorities must also enact supportive policies and mechanisms that encourage the adoption and growth of renewable energy technologies in Indonesia.

Keywords: Indonesia; renewable energy; solar power; site selection; data envelopment analysis; multi-criteria decision making

1. Introduction

The availability of energy significantly impacts global economic and industrial progress. More than 80% of the world's energy is produced through coal, oil, and natural gas [1]. With 270 million people, Indonesia has the fastest-growing power demand in Asia-Pacific, highlighting the urgent need for a secure, affordable, and long-term energy transition in Southeast Asia [2]. Power demand has been growing at a rate of 6.1% per year, and infrastructure is under pressure to capitalize on the growth potential of the growing economy [3]. Solar photovoltaic projects of utility, commercial, and industrial scale have a tremendous chance to rapidly establish economies of scale to meet the 23% renewable energy goal by 2025 [4]. By 2030, projections anticipate a potential installed capacity of 47 GW, a significant increase compared to just over 9 GW estimated in the Reference Case. In light of this, plans are underway to utilize solar photovoltaic (PV) technology to power approximately 1.1 million off-grid households. Rooftop and utility-scale solar PV systems can be expanded significantly in Indonesia, particularly in Java-Bali (which accounts for 70% of power demand in Indonesia) due to the ample area, robust infrastructure, and growing need for electricity in the region [5]. In addition, these types of resources are numerous and excellent for local development and utilization. Unlike the possible depletion of fossil fuels, renewable energy can be naturally replenished. Multiple countries have enacted legislation for renewable energy development, and various applications for renewable energy have evolved. It is projected that renewable energy sources will play a significant part in the global energy supply in the future [6,7]. Solar energy development in Indonesia is promising, but progress is slow despite the country's significant potential. Various factors contribute to this slow growth, such as limited financial and human resources, institutional challenges, market-controlled processes, unclear policies, and inconsistent norms, despite the availability of modern technology. The public and government agencies know the country's situation and resources. The three primary challenges for utility-scale solar PV are inadequate transmission grid capacity, complex administrative procedures, and insufficient engagement with local communities. According to the available research, solar site selection in Indonesia has yet to be thoroughly investigated regarding sustainable development [8,9].

A reliable, systematic, and effective decision-making framework is required to aid policymakers in selecting optimal locations for solar power facilities [10]. Sites that could be better can save time and money, cause trouble for local citizens and harm the environment. This study was undertaken to determine the best places in Indonesia to build solar PV systems for long-term sustainability. In-depth literature reviews and interviews with industry professionals help identify potential sites for solar installations and other parameters that will affect the deployment of these systems [11,12]. Due to the numerous factors that must be considered, experts have turned to multi-criteria decision-making (MCDM) approaches [13]. These methods use the strengths of techniques such as the Data Envelopment Analysis (DEA), Fuzzy Analytic Hierarchy Process (F-AHP), and Fuzzy Measurement Alternatives and Ranking according to the Compromise Solution (F-MARCOS) to determine the most suitable locations for solar energy generation prioritization. Among the many firsts of this study is its in-depth examination of a topic that has yet to be previously discussed in the literature: solar site selection in Indonesia. The evaluation criteria are broad and thorough, covering quantifiable and qualitative aspects of identifying priority areas for sustainable development. In addition, this is the first time that DEA, F-AHP, and F-MARCOS have been combined to form a single appropriate and successful methodology for site selection. The developed model aims to provide decision-makers with a comprehensive aid tool for selecting the best site for solar power plants.

The structure of this paper is organized as follows: Section 2 presents a review of relevant research on solar power plant site selection techniques. Section 3 discusses the Data Envelopment Analysis (DEA), Fuzzy Analytic Hierarchy Process (F-AHP), and Fuzzy Multi-Attribute Rating Comparison System (F-MARCOS) methodologies. Section 4 discusses the Indonesian case study, which demonstrates the practical application of the proposed hybrid approach. Finally, Section 5 provides conclusions and highlights potential directions for future research in this area.

2. Literature Review

The growth of solar energy production in many countries has drawn the attention of universities, governments, and organizations worldwide [14]. However, one of the significant challenges in deploying large-scale solar systems is determining the priorities of different regions on a national level. Establishing new solar farms requires substantial real estate, capital, and labor. Thus, identifying technological, technical, economic, environmental, societal, risk-aspect, and political factors is crucial to avoid delays in central and government approval procedures and establishing new solar farms [15]. Prioritizing appropriate areas before investing in costly solar farms can result in optimal production, lower socioeconomic costs, reduced negative environmental impacts, and progress in concerned regions. In order to make informed decisions, criteria are derived from a review of relevant literature and consensus among experts on environmental, technological, financial, and societal factors, as outlined in Table 1.

Table 1. Considered primary criteria and parameters that determine the suitability for solar PV implementation.

Main Criteria	Criteria	References
Climatic	Air temperature	[16–21]
	Wind speed	[17,22,23]
	Relative humidity	[17,18,21,22,24]
	Precipitation	[17,24]
	Air Pressure	
	Sunshine hour	[16–18,24,25]
	Irradiation	[16–21,24,26–28]
	Elevation	[18,20,24]
Technical	Assistance and guidance with technical matters	[16]
	Geology	[17,22,27]
	Availability of skilled workers	[16]
Economic	Consumption of electricity	[17,26,28]
	Costs	[16,17,20,25,28,29]
	Terms of network accessibility	[16,17,27]
	Proximity to public transportation	[16–19,21,22,24]
	Proximity to residential areas	[16,17,19,22,24]
Social	Residents attitude	[16,29]
	Rules and regulations of the government	[16,17,28,29]
	Land acquisition	[16,21,28,29]
	Facilitating factors	[16,17,25,28,29]
Environmental	Impact of Wildlife and endangered species	[16,17,27]
	Noxious pollutant emission	[16,20]
	Benefits of conserving energy	[25,26]

The planning of renewable energy sources (RES) often involves the use of multi-criteria decision-making (MCDM) techniques, which assist decision-makers in selecting the best option from competing alternatives in site selection challenges [30]. Although numerous MCDM techniques are available, few have been applied when combining DEA with MCDM [9]. The fuzzy set theory incorporates uncertainty and ambiguity into the evaluation process. Uyan [31] used GIS and the AHP technique to identify promising areas for solar farms in the Karapinar region of Konya, Turkey. Sindhu et al. [16] investigated solar site selection in India using a combination of AHP and fuzzy TOPSIS analysis. Lee et al. [32] also used AHP and fuzzy TOPSIS analysis for solar site selection in India. Al Garni & Awasthi [33] used a GIS-AHP-based approach to select solar PV power plant sites in Saudi Arabia; their study contributes to SDG 7 (Affordable and Clean Energy) and SDG 13 (Climate Action). Seyed Alavi et al. [34] employed multi-criteria decision-making methods to identify optimal locations for wind power plants in eastern Iran. Wu et al. [35] also improved site selection for solar power installations in China by employing an MCDM framework based on fuzzy Preference Ranking Organization Methods for Enrichment Evaluations (PROMETHEE) II. Table 2 summarizes how MCDM methods have been applied to solar site selection research. These studies demonstrate the importance of integrating MCDM techniques with DEA for RES planning and provide valuable insights into selecting optimal solar sites.

Table 2. The literature review on MCDM techniques.

Reference	Location	Res	MCDM Technique
[35]	US	Wind-Solar PV	ANP
[25]	China	Solar thermal power plant	Linguistic Choquet operator/fuzzy measure
[36]	Southeast Spain	Solar PV	AHP and TOPSIS
[37]	Spain	Solar Thermal powerplant	AHP/ANP
[26]	China	Wind-Solar PV	ELECTRE
[28]	Iran	Solar PV	ELECTRE-II
[22]	UK	Wind-Solar PV	AHP
[38]	Murcia, Spain	CSP	SWARA and WASPAS
[24]	Iran	Solar Power Plant	AHP/fuzzy logic/WLC
[32]	Taiwan	Solar PV	AHP, Fuzzy TOPSIS, and ELECTRE
[39]	Iran	Solar PV	Fuzzy ANP and VIKOR
[40]	Afghanistan	Wind-Solar PV/CSP	MCDA
[16]	Haryana, India	Solar PV	Fuzzy AHP
[41]	Turkey	SPP	AHP/ELECTRE/TOPSIS/VIKOR
[20]	Northwest China	Solar PV	AHP and Fuzzy TOPSIS
[42]	Fars, Iran	Wind-Solar PV	Grey Cumulative Prospect Theory
[33]	Saudi Arabia	Solar PV	GIS-AHP
[27]	Turkey	Solar PV	Fuzzy TOPSIS
[43]	China	Solar PV	AHP and Fuzzy VIKOR
[8]	Indonesia	Solar PV	AHP-GIS
[17]	Taiwan	Solar PV	PROMETHEE
[44]	Western Libya	Solar PV	SWARA and DEMATEL
[45]	Iran	Solar PV	SWARA
[46]	Morocco	Solar PV	AHP-GIS
[9]	Vietnam	Solar PV	DEA/AHP/TOPSIS

After conducting a comprehensive review of the literature across multiple fields and methodologies, it has become clear that there is a lack of studies focused on selecting optimal solar locations in Indonesia. This research fills this gap by combining DEA, F-AHP, and F-MARCOS methodologies to identify the most suitable locations for solar PV installations. DEA is a powerful tool for comparing energy industry options based on measurable criteria, as it enables comparisons of locations in terms of their efficiency in converting inputs to outputs. F-AHP and F-MARCOS are flexible techniques incorporating human evaluations of immeasurable variables. Stankovi'c et al. [47] created the fuzzy MARCOS in 2019 to provide a strong sorting of alternatives in the fuzzy environment irrespective of the scale, which generates a basic, comprehensive decision-making information scheme using the ratio method and the reference point method. The fuzzy MARCOS approach is an effective tool for maximizing a number of objectives. By proposing an algorithm for examining the link between alternatives and reference points, fuzzy MARCOS revitalizes the MCDM domain. In order to make a strong decision, the fuzzy MARCOS method integrates the following elements: defining reference points (fuzzy ideal and fuzzy anti-ideal values), figuring out how alternatives relate to these values, and defining the utility level of alternatives concerning fuzzy ideal and fuzzy anti-ideal solutions. Because the results of the ratio approach and reference point sorting approach were combined, the results obtained by the fuzzy MARCOS method are more logical. In the research of Stević et al. [48] on sustainable supplier selection, it was proven that the robustness and stability of MARCOS outperformed TOPSIS in assessing the decision-making units. By combining DEA, F-AHP, and F-MARCOS, this study aims to provide a comprehensive approach to identifying optimal solar locations in Indonesia.

3. Methods

This section outlines the photovoltaic (PV) power plant site selection methodology, as illustrated in Figure 1. The proposed approach combines Data Envelopment Analysis (DEA), Analytic Hierarchy Process (AHP), and Fuzzy Measurement Alternatives and

Ranking according to the Compromise Solution (MARCOS) to develop a comprehensive decision-making framework for selecting optimal sites for PV power plants in Indonesia.

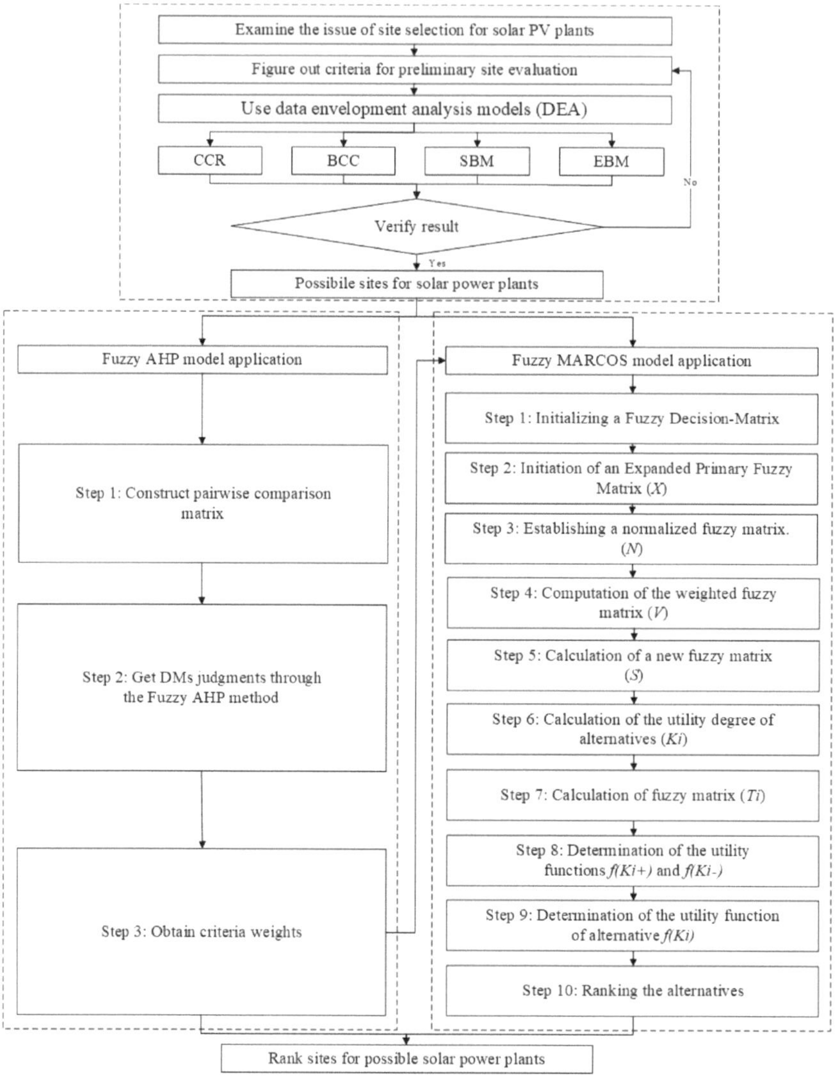

Figure 1. The process of the research.

3.1. Data Envelopment Analysis (DEA)

Data Envelopment Analysis (DEA) is a commonly used mathematical approach to measure the efficiency of Decision Making Units (DMUs) based on multiple inputs and outputs. This study uses DEA to screen and select the most efficient locations to host solar installations. The CCR, BCC, SBM, and EBM models are examples of DEA models that can assess DMU efficiency. These models differ in terms of the assumptions they make about inputs and outputs, as well as the type of efficiency measured [49].

3.1.1. Charnes, Cooper, Rhodes Model (CCR)

The CCR model is a DEA model commonly used to evaluate the efficiency of Decision-Making Units (DMUs) based on multiple inputs and outputs. This model measures the technical effectiveness of a DMU, assuming that each DMU can be represented by a set of inputs and outputs specified in the model (1).

$$\begin{gathered}\theta^* = \min_{\theta,\lambda,s^-} \theta \\ \text{subject to} \\ \theta x_0 = X\lambda - s^- \\ y_0 \leq Y\lambda, \\ \lambda \geq 0, s^- \geq 0\end{gathered} \tag{1}$$

The CCR model measures the technical efficiency of a DMU by comparing its input-output ratio with those of other DMUs in the dataset. A DMU is considered efficient if its efficiency score θ^* equals 1, indicating that the DMU is operating on the efficient frontier. Conversely, a DMU is considered inefficient if its efficiency score is less than 1, implying that the DMU is operating below the efficient frontier and could potentially improve its efficiency by adjusting its input-output ratio.

3.1.2. Banker, Charnes, and Cooper Model (BCC)

The Banker, Charnes, and Cooper (BCC) model, developed by Banker et al. [50], extends the DEA model to account for variable returns to scale (VRS). This model introduces a non-Archimedean element (ε), and s_i^- and s_r^+ represent the input and output slack variables, respectively.

$$\begin{gathered}min\varnothing - \varepsilon\left(\sum_{i=1}^{m} s_i^- + \sum_{r=1}^{s} s_r^+\right) \\ \text{subject to} \\ \sum_{j=1}^{n} \lambda_j x_{ij} + s_i^- = \varnothing x_{i0}(i = 1, .., p) \\ \sum_{j=1}^{n} \lambda_j y_{rj} - s_r^+ = y_{ro}(r = 1, .., q) \\ \sum_{k=1}^{n} \lambda_k = 1 \\ \lambda_k \geq 0, k = 1, 2, \ldots, n \\ s_i^- \geq 0, i = 1, 2, \ldots, p \\ s_j^+ \geq 0, j = 1, 2, \ldots, q\end{gathered} \tag{2}$$

The BCC model evaluates DMUs based on their technical efficiency at various operational scales. This allows for the differentiation between technical inefficiency and scale inefficiency. The model recognizes growth, decline, constant return scales, and other scale types. The BCC model's efficiency metric is sometimes called "pure technical efficiency" to highlight its focus on technical performance independent of scale effects.

3.1.3. Slacks-Based Measure Model (SBM)

The effectiveness of a DMU is determined by a ratio known as the "slacks-based measure" (SBM) score. This value is determined by dividing the DMU's actual output by the minimal number of inputs required to achieve that output, depending on the inputs and outputs of the other DMUs included in the analysis. A DMU with an SBM score of 1 is technically efficient, while a DMU with an SBM score of less than 1 is inefficient.

$$\tau^* = \min 1 - \frac{1}{m}\sum_{i=1}^{m}\frac{s_i^-}{x_{i0}}$$

subject to

$$x_{i0} = \sum_{j=1}^{n} x_{ij}\lambda_j + s_i^- (i = 1, \ldots, m)$$

$$y_{i0} \leq \sum_{j=1}^{n} y_{ij}\lambda_j (i = 1, \ldots, s) \tag{3}$$

$$\lambda_j \geq 0(\forall j), s_i^- \geq 0(\forall i)$$

In this model, τ^* represents the SBM score, and λ_j is the weight assigned to each DMU. The input and output variables are represented by x_{i0} and y_{i0}, respectively. The input slack variables, s_i^-, represent the excess inputs that can be reduced without affecting the output. The objective of the SBM model is to minimize the sum of the input slacks relative to the input levels, thus maximizing the efficiency of the DMU. This model provides a more accurate efficiency measure, directly incorporating input and output slack variables into the efficiency evaluation.

3.1.4. Epsilon-Based Measure Model (EBM)

The Epsilon-Based Measure (EBM) [51] model is a variant of Data Envelopment Analysis (DEA) that accounts for the diversity or dispersion of the observed data set by calculating a scalar epsilon. This model aims to address the limitations of the CCR and SBM models by combining the radial and non-radial approaches, which emphasize proportional changes in inputs and outputs and incorporate slack, respectively. The input-oriented EBM model with a constant return to scale is formulated as follows:

$$\delta^* = \underset{\theta,\lambda,s^-}{Min}\, \theta - \varepsilon_x \textstyle\sum_{i=1}^{m} \frac{w_i^- s_i^-}{x_{io}}$$

subject to

$$\sum_{j=1}^{n} x_{ij}\lambda_j = \theta x_{io} - s_i^- (i = 1, \ldots, m)$$

$$\sum_{j=1}^{n} y_{rj}\lambda_j \geq y_{ro} (r = 1, \ldots, s) \tag{4}$$

$$\lambda_j \geq 0, j = 1, 2, \ldots, n$$

$$s_i^- \geq 0, i = 1, 2, \ldots, m$$

In this model, δ^* represents the EBM score, λ_j is the weight assigned to each DMU, and the subscript "o" represents the DMU under evaluation. The input slack variables, s_i^-, indicate the excess inputs that can be reduced without affecting the output, and w_i^- denotes the weight assigned to the i-th input. The parameter ε_x specifies the radial qualities and is determined by the degree of input dispersion.

3.2. F-AHP

Table 3 shows that the fuzzy triangular numbers are the linguistic terms for the pairwise comparison scale and the fuzzy scale assigned. The relative importance of the two criteria is ranked on a scale from 1 to 9 based on the linguistic variables provided. A tilde sign () is placed above the parameter symbol to indicate uncertainty. Thus, the following are the details of the F-AHP process [16].

Table 3. Explanation of the F-AHP scale.

Fuzzy Set	Definition	Fuzzy Scale
$\tilde{1}$	Equal importance	(1, 1, 1)
$\tilde{2}$	Weak importance	(1, 2, 3)
$\tilde{3}$	Not bad	(2, 3, 4)
$\tilde{4}$	Preferable	(3, 4, 5)
$\tilde{5}$	Importance	(4, 5, 6)
$\tilde{6}$	Fairly importance	(5, 6, 7)
$\tilde{7}$	Very important	(6, 7, 8)
$\tilde{8}$	Absolute	(7, 8, 9)
$\tilde{9}$	Perfect	(8, 9, 10)

Step 1: To produce the integrated fuzzy pairwise comparison matrix used in the FAHP calculation, we apply the geometrical integration seen in Equation (5). $\tilde{l}_{ij}$ denotes the importance of the ith criterion over the jth criterion.

$$\tilde{M} = \begin{pmatrix} 1 & \tilde{l}_{12} & \cdots & \tilde{l}_{1n} \\ \tilde{l}_{21} & 1 & \cdots & \tilde{l}_{2n} \\ \cdots & \cdots & \cdots & \cdots \\ \tilde{l}_{n1} & \tilde{l}_{n2} & \cdots & 1 \end{pmatrix} = \begin{pmatrix} 1 & \tilde{l}_{12} & \cdots & \tilde{l}_{1n} \\ 1/\tilde{l}_{12} & 1 & \cdots & \tilde{l}_{2n} \\ \cdots & \cdots & \cdots & \cdots \\ 1/\tilde{l}_{1n} & 1/\tilde{l}_{2n} & \cdots & 1 \end{pmatrix} \tag{5}$$

$$\tilde{l}_{ij} = \begin{cases} \tilde{9}^{-1}, \tilde{8}^{-1}, \tilde{7}^{-1}, \tilde{6}^{-1}, \tilde{5}^{-1}, \tilde{4}^{-1}, \tilde{3}^{-1}, \tilde{2}^{-1}, \tilde{1}^{-1}, \tilde{1}, \tilde{2}, \tilde{3}, \tilde{4}, \tilde{5}, \tilde{6}, \tilde{7}, \tilde{8}, \tilde{9} & such\ that\ i \neq j \\ 1 & such\ that\ i = j \end{cases}$$

Step 2: Equation to determine the fuzzy geometric mean of each criterion (6).

$$\tilde{r}_i = \left(\prod\nolimits_{j=1}^{n} \tilde{l}_{ij}\right)^{1/n} such\ that\ i = 1, 2, \ldots, n \tag{6}$$

where $\tilde{r}_i$ approximated by the fuzzy geometric mean, and $\tilde{l}_{ij}$ is a fuzzy comparison value generated by a panel of decision–makers based on the ith criterion over the jth criterion.

Step 3: The fuzzy preference weight for each criterion is determined using the following Equation (7).

$$\tilde{w}_i = \tilde{r}_i \otimes \left(\tilde{r}_1 \oplus \tilde{r}_2 \oplus \ldots \oplus \tilde{r}_n\right)^{-1} \tag{7}$$

where $\tilde{w}_i$ is the fuzzy weight of the ith criterion.

Step 4: To obtain a clear result, we need to defuzzify the preference weights using the average weight criterion G_i, as shown in Equation (8).

$$G_i = \frac{lw_i + mw_i + uw_i}{3} \tag{8}$$

where $\tilde{w}_i$ is the fuzzy weight of the ith criterion, which can be presented as $\tilde{w}_i = (lw_i, mw_i, uw_i)$, such that lw_i, mw_i, uw_i are the lower-bound, middle-bound, and upper-bound of $\tilde{w}_i$, respectively.

Step 5: The relative importance of each criterion, as determined by the normalized preference weight H_i, as seen by Equation (9).

$$H_i = \frac{G_i}{\sum_{i=1}^{n} G_i} \tag{9}$$

3.3. F-MARCOS

For multi-criteria decision-making (MCDM) situations with a set of criteria and potential solutions, fuzzy measurement of alternatives and ranking based on compromise solutions (F-MARCOS) can help reduce the uncertainty. Decision-makers can improve the stability of MCDM in fuzzy situations by using this strategy, which has three pillars: reference points, relationships between choices, and alternative utility levels [47]. The process of F-MARCOS is as below.

Step 1: Defining an initial fuzzy decision-making matrix including n criteria (i.e., criteria) and m alternatives.

Step 2: Defining an extended initial fuzzy decision-making matrix by introducing the fuzzy ideal $\widetilde{A}(ID)$ and anti-ideal $\widetilde{A}(AI)$ solutions

$$\widetilde{X} = \begin{array}{c} \widetilde{A}(AI) \\ \widetilde{A}_1 \\ \widetilde{A}_2 \\ \cdots \\ \widetilde{A}_m \\ \widetilde{A}(ID) \end{array} \overset{\begin{array}{cccc} \widetilde{C}_1 & \widetilde{C}_2 & \cdots & \widetilde{C}_n \end{array}}{\overbrace{\begin{bmatrix} \widetilde{x}_{ai1} & \widetilde{x}_{ai2} & \cdots & \widetilde{x}_{ain} \\ \widetilde{x}_{11} & \widetilde{x}_{12} & \cdots & \widetilde{x}_{1n} \\ \widetilde{x}_{21} & \widetilde{x}_{22} & \cdots & \widetilde{x}_{2n} \\ \cdots & \cdots & \cdots & \cdots \\ \widetilde{x}_{m1} & \widetilde{x}_{m2} & \cdots & \widetilde{x}_{mn} \\ \widetilde{x}_{id1} & \widetilde{x}_{id2} & \cdots & \widetilde{x}_{idn} \end{bmatrix}}} \tag{10}$$

The fuzzy $\widetilde{A}(ID)$ is an alternative with the best performance, while the fuzzy $\widetilde{A}(AI)$ is the worst alternative. Depending on the type of the criteria, $\widetilde{A}(ID)$ and $\widetilde{A}(AI)$ are defined by applying Equations (11) and (12):

$$\widetilde{A}(ID) = \underset{i}{max}\widetilde{x}_{ij} if j \in B \ and \ \underset{i}{\min}\widetilde{x}_{ij} if j \in C \tag{11}$$

$$\widetilde{A}(AI) = \underset{i}{\min}\widetilde{x}_{ij} if j \in B \ and \ \underset{i}{max}\widetilde{x}_{ij} if j \in C \tag{12}$$

where B and C are a set of benefit and cost criteria, respectively.

Step 3: Determining the normalization of the extended initial fuzzy decision-making matrix, which is $\widetilde{N} = \left[\widetilde{n}_{ij}\right]_{m\times n}$ using Equations (13) and (14):

$$\widetilde{n}_{ij} = \left(n_{ij}^{l}, n_{ij}^{m}, n_{ij}^{u}\right) = \left(\frac{x_{ij}^{l}}{x_{id}^{u}}, \frac{x_{ij}^{m}}{x_{id}^{u}}, \frac{x_{ij}^{u}}{x_{id}^{u}}\right), j \in B \tag{13}$$

$$\widetilde{n}_{ij} = \left(n_{ij}^{l}, n_{ij}^{m}, n_{ij}^{u}\right) = \left(\frac{x_{id}^{l}}{x_{ij}^{u}}, \frac{x_{id}^{l}}{x_{ij}^{m}}, \frac{x_{id}^{l}}{x_{ij}^{l}}\right), j \in C \tag{14}$$

where elements $x_{ij}^{l}, x_{ij}^{m}, x_{ij}^{u}$, and $x_{id}^{l}, x_{id}^{m}, x_{id}^{u}$ represent the elements of the matrix $\widetilde{X}$.

Step 4: Determining the weighted fuzzy matrix $\widetilde{V} = \left[\widetilde{v}_{ij}\right]_{m\times n}$, calculated by multiplying matrix $\widetilde{N}$ with the fuzzy weight coefficients of the criteria $\widetilde{w}_j$ as follows.

$$\widetilde{v}_{ij} = \left(v_{ij}^{l}, v_{ij}^{m}, v_{ij}^{u}\right) = \widetilde{n}_{ij} \otimes \widetilde{w}_j = \left(n_{ij}^{l} \times w_j^{l}, n_{ij}^{m} \times w_j^{m}, n_{ij}^{u} \times w_j^{u}\right) \tag{15}$$

where $\widetilde{w}_j = \left(w_j^{l}, w_j^{m}, w_j^{u}\right)$ represents the elements of the fuzzy weight of the criteria.

Step 5: Calculating the fuzzy matrix $\tilde{S}_i$ using Equation (16) below.

$$\tilde{S}_i = \sum_{i=1}^{n} \tilde{v}_{ij} \tag{16}$$

where $\tilde{S}_i = \left(s_i^l, s_i^m, s_i^u\right)$ is the sum of the elements of the weighted fuzzy matrix $\tilde{V}$.

Step 6: Calculating the utility degree of alternative $\tilde{K}_i$ using Equations (17) and (18):

$$\tilde{K}_i^- = \frac{\tilde{S}_i}{\tilde{S}_{ai}} = \left(\frac{s_i^l}{s_{ai}^u}, \frac{s_i^m}{s_{ai}^m}, \frac{s_i^u}{s_{ai}^l}\right) \tag{17}$$

$$\tilde{K}_i^+ = \frac{\tilde{S}_i}{\tilde{S}_{id}} = \left(\frac{s_i^l}{s_{id}^u}, \frac{s_i^m}{s_{id}^m}, \frac{s_i^u}{s_{id}^l}\right) \tag{18}$$

Step 7: To determine the fuzzy matrix $\tilde{T}_i$, we use Equation (19):

$$\tilde{T}_i = \tilde{t}_i = \left(t_i^l, t_i^m, t_i^u\right) = \tilde{K}_i^- \oplus \tilde{K}_i^+ = \left(k_i^{-l} + k_i^{+l}, k_i^{-m} + k_i^{+m}, k_i^{-u} + k_i^{+u}\right) \tag{19}$$

Then, a new fuzzy number $\tilde{D}$ is determined by Equation (20):

$$\tilde{D} = \left(d^l, d^m, d^u\right) = \max_i \tilde{t}_{ij} \tag{20}$$

Following that, it is necessary to defuzzify the number $\tilde{D}$ using the expression $df_{crisp} = \frac{l+4m+u}{6}$ obtaining the number df_{crisp}.

Step 8: Determining the utility function to the ideal $f\left(\tilde{K}_i^+\right)$ and anti-ideal $f\left(\tilde{K}_i^-\right)$ solutions using Equations (21) and (22):

$$f\left(\tilde{K}_i^+\right) = \frac{\tilde{K}_i^-}{df_{crisp}} = \left(\frac{k_i^{-l}}{df_{crisp}}, \frac{k_i^{-m}}{df_{crisp}}, \frac{k_i^{-u}}{df_{crisp}}\right) \tag{21}$$

$$f\left(\tilde{K}_i^-\right) = \frac{\tilde{K}_i^+}{df_{crisp}} = \left(\frac{k_i^{+l}}{df_{crisp}}, \frac{k_i^{+m}}{df_{crisp}}, \frac{k_i^{+u}}{df_{crisp}}\right) \tag{22}$$

Finally, calculating the defuzzification of $\tilde{K}_i^-$, $\tilde{K}_i^+$, $f\left(\tilde{K}_i^-\right)$, and $f\left(\tilde{K}_i^+\right)$ values using the same defuzzification formula.

Step 9: Alternative utility functions $f(K_i)$ can be calculated with Equation (23):

$$f(K_i) = \frac{K_i^+ + K_i^-}{1 + \frac{1-f(K_i^+)}{f(K_i^+)} + \frac{1-f(K_i^-)}{f(K_i^-)}} \tag{23}$$

Step 10: The order of the alternatives is determined by the final values of the utility degree function. Favored is the alternative with the superior utility function value.

As shown in Table 4, a new linguistic scale has been established for assessing alternatives in addition to the F-MARCOS method. There are nine words in total, and each assigned its fuzzy triangular number.

Table 4. The linguistic equivalent of a rating system for alternatives.

Symbol	Definition	Scale of Triangular Fuzzy Number
EP	Extremely poor	(1, 1, 1)
VP	Very poor	(1, 1, 3)
P	Poor	(1, 3, 3)
MP	Medium poor	(3, 3, 5)
M	Medium	(3, 5, 5)
MG	Medium good	(5, 5, 7)
G	Good	(5, 7, 7)
VG	Very good	(7, 7, 9)
EG	Extremely good	(7, 9, 9)

4. A Case Study in Indonesia

In this subsection, we put into action the aggregated technique proposed for determining which of Indonesia's 32 provinces would best host solar power installations (Figure 2). The evaluation's criterion system and examined alternatives were created by consultation with experts and subsequent interactive conversations, in addition to reviewing the relevant literature.

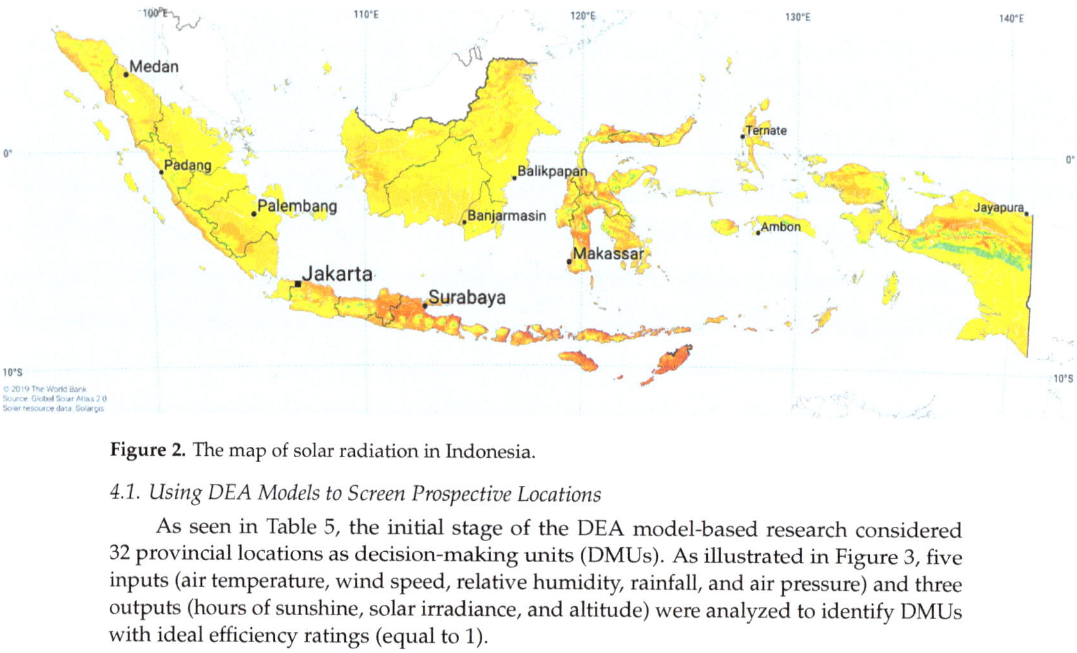

Figure 2. The map of solar radiation in Indonesia.

4.1. Using DEA Models to Screen Prospective Locations

As seen in Table 5, the initial stage of the DEA model-based research considered 32 provincial locations as decision-making units (DMUs). As illustrated in Figure 3, five inputs (air temperature, wind speed, relative humidity, rainfall, and air pressure) and three outputs (hours of sunshine, solar irradiance, and altitude) were analyzed to identify DMUs with ideal efficiency ratings (equal to 1).

Table 5. List of Indonesian locations (DMUs).

No.	Location	DMU	Irradiation (kWh/m^2/Year)
1	Aceh	DMU-01	1686.30
2	Bali	DMU-02	1799.45
3	Bangka Belitung	DMU-03	1653.45
4	Banten	DMU-04	1679.00
5	Bengkulu	DMU-05	1708.20
6	Gorontalo	DMU-06	1803.10
7	Jakarta	DMU-07	1726.45
8	Jambi	DMU-08	1627.90
9	Jawa Barat	DMU-09	1737.40

Table 5. Cont.

No.	Location	DMU	Irradiation (kWh/m^2/Year)
10	Jawa Tengah	DMU-10	1806.75
11	Jawa Timur	DMU-11	1879.75
12	Kalimantan Barat	DMU-12	1682.65
13	Kalimantan Selatan	DMU-13	1657.10
14	Kalimantan Tengah	DMU-14	1679.00
15	Kalimantan Timur	DMU-15	1668.05
16	Lampung	DMU-16	1708.20
17	Maluku	DMU-17	1679.00
18	Maluku Utara	DMU-18	1737.40
19	Nusa Tenggara Barat	DMU-19	1941.80
20	Nusa Tenggara Timur	DMU-20	2014.80
21	Papua	DMU-21	1631.55
22	Papua Barat	DMU-22	1679.00
23	Riau	DMU-23	1649.80
24	Sulawesi Barat	DMU-24	1708.20
25	Sulawesi Selatan	DMU-25	1777.55
26	Sulawesi Tengah	DMU-26	1700.90
27	Sulawesi Tenggara	DMU-27	1755.65
28	Sulawesi Utara	DMU-28	1755.65
29	Sumatera Barat	DMU-29	1646.15
30	Sumatera Selatan	DMU-30	1689.95
31	Sumatera Utara	DMU-31	1671.70
32	Yogyakarta	DMU-32	1861.50

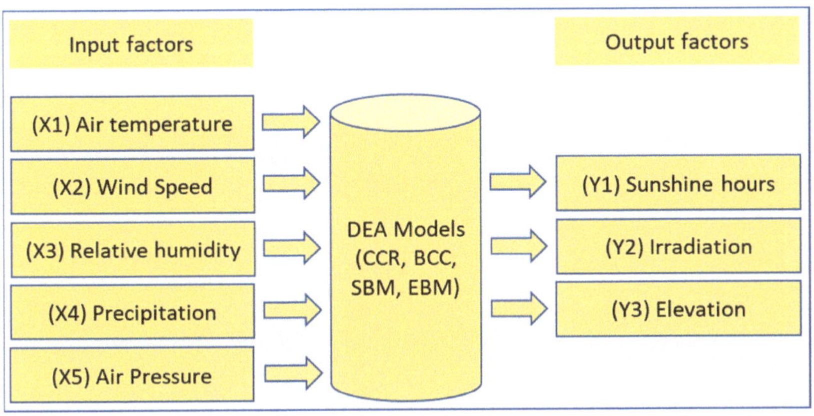

Figure 3. The input and output factors used in DEA models.

Input factors:

(X1) Air temperature (°C): Solar panel performance is affected by the panels' temperatures, which are affected by the surrounding temperature and the amount of sunlight they are exposed to. Simply put, solar panels produce more electricity when the temperature is lower. When the panel's operating temperature rises, the voltage it produces drops, and its efficiency drops.

(X2) Wind speed (m/s): The ability to withstand wind uplift and loads is essential for solar installations. Damage to machinery and increased wear and tear on operating components have been linked to the wind. Having more dust settles on the solar modules' surfaces due to increased wind speeds is another factor that can reduce production.

(X3) Relative humidity (%): Due to the absorption of short-wave solar radiation by atmospheric water vapor, locations with high humidity have limited potential for solar energy harvesting. In addition to diminishing power production, excessive humidity can cause dew to collect on the surfaces of solar panels, making it easier for airborne dust to settle on the modules.

(X4) Precipitation (mm/year): Precipitation, whether rain, snow, sleet, or hail. When clouds block out the sun, solar power plants are less efficient in producing electricity.

(X5) Air Pressure (Hpa): Air pressure is the force that air's weight exerts on the earth's surface. Air pressure decreases with increasing height. The ambient temperature decreases as altitude increases, allowing the solar system to function more efficiently. Due to fewer air layers that scatter, absorb, and reflect sunlight, there is more direct sunlight.

Output factors:

(Y1) Sunshine hour (hour/year): The sunshine hour of irradiation describes the duration of sunlight in a given area over a given period (year). Solar radiation of at least 120 W/m^2 is considered sunlight.

(Y2) Irradiation (kWh//m^2/year): The quantity of energy produced by the sun during a given period (in kWh) and surface area (in m^2) (year).

(Y3) Elevation (m): Solar potential characteristics are modified by a region's elevation above sea level. Specifically, solar panels can capture more energy from the sun at higher altitudes due to the thinner atmosphere's reduced absorption of solar radiation.

Statistical analysis of input and output factors is presented in Table 6.

Table 6. Factor statistical analysis.

Factors	Maximum	Minimum	Average	Standard Deviation
Air temperature	28.40	19.72	26.44	1.98
Wind speed	3.10	0.35	1.61	0.58
Relative humidity	90.59	77.18	84.36	3.14
Precipitation	4878.50	1770.40	2947.29	791.14
Air Pressure	1014.90	924.10	1009.18	15.32
Sunshine hours	2687.60	1203.80	1841.80	330.61
Irradiation	2014.80	1627.90	1731.35	89.41
Elevation	1653.00	2.00	137.16	343.14

The data collection on input and output factors of 32 locations are collected, as can be seen in Table A1 (Appendix A). According to the results presented in Table 7 of the journal, the DEA analysis shows that a total of 11 DMUs have attained perfect efficiency scores of 1. This suggests that these DMUs are operating at the highest level of efficiency possible given the inputs and outputs used in the analysis, which are Jawa Barat (DMU-09), Jawa Timur (DMU-11), Lampung (DMU-16), Maluku (DMU-17), Maluku Utara (DMU-18), Nusa Tenggara Barat (DMU-19), Nusa Tenggara Timur (DMU-20), Papua (DMU-21), Riau (DMU-23), Sulawesi Selatan (DMU-25), and Sulawesi Utara (DMU-28). In the second step, 11 DMUs are chosen for analysis because they are deemed the most promising locations for solar projects.

Table 7. The DEA score for efficiency.

No.	Location	DMU	CCR-I	BCC-I	SBM-I-C	EBM-I-C
1	Aceh	DMU-01	0.8847	0.9352	0.8303	0.8831
2	Bali	DMU-02	0.9918	0.9997	0.8715	0.9476
3	Bangka Belitung	DMU-03	0.8708	0.9552	0.8210	0.8648
4	Banten	DMU-04	0.9120	0.9908	0.8828	0.9042
5	Bengkulu	DMU-05	0.8812	0.9746	0.7863	0.8480
6	Gorontalo	DMU-06	1.0000	1.0000	1.0000	0.9948
7	Jakarta	DMU-07	0.9946	1.0000	0.9512	0.9798
8	Jambi	DMU-08	0.9394	0.9742	0.9011	0.9387
9	Jawa Barat	DMU-09	1.0000	1.0000	1.0000	1.0000
10	Jawa Tengah	DMU-10	0.9648	0.9932	0.9250	0.9554
11	Jawa Timur	DMU-11	1.0000	1.0000	1.0000	1.0000
12	Kalimantan Barat	DMU-12	0.9167	0.9527	0.8824	0.9153
13	Kalimantan Selatan	DMU-13	0.8973	0.9576	0.8452	0.8934
14	Kalimantan Tengah	DMU-14	0.9024	0.9499	0.8466	0.8941
15	Kalimantan Timur	DMU-15	0.8731	0.9662	0.8194	0.8656
16	Lampung	DMU-16	1.0000	1.0000	1.0000	1.0000
17	Maluku	DMU-17	1.0000	1.0000	1.0000	1.0000
18	Maluku Utara	DMU-18	1.0000	1.0000	1.0000	1.0000
19	Nusa Tenggara Barat	DMU-19	1.0000	1.0000	1.0000	1.0000
20	Nusa Tenggara Timur	DMU-20	1.0000	1.0000	1.0000	1.0000
21	Papua	DMU-21	1.0000	1.0000	1.0000	1.0000
22	Papua Barat	DMU-22	0.8862	0.9705	0.8350	0.8795
23	Riau	DMU-23	1.0000	1.0000	1.0000	1.0000
24	Sulawesi Barat	DMU-24	0.9482	0.9938	0.9237	0.9450
25	Sulawesi Selatan	DMU-25	1.0000	1.0000	1.0000	1.0000
26	Sulawesi Tengah	DMU-26	0.9952	0.9963	0.9815	0.9910
27	Sulawesi Tenggara	DMU-27	0.9778	0.9924	0.9487	0.9694
28	Sulawesi Utara	DMU-28	1.0000	1.0000	1.0000	1.0000
29	Sumatera Barat	DMU-29	0.8653	0.9603	0.7847	0.8447
30	Sumatera Selatan	DMU-30	0.8871	0.9835	0.8602	0.8816
31	Sumatera Utara	DMU-31	0.9004	0.9768	0.8610	0.8928
32	Yogyakarta	DMU-32	0.9762	0.9811	0.9520	0.9718

4.2. Rank the Remaining Locations Using F-AHP and F-MARCOS Values

In the second part of the study, F-AHP and F-MARCOS models are used to conduct additional analysis and rank the locations that were given efficiency scores of 1. F-AHP is utilized to assign relative importance to criteria, and F-MARCOS is then used to order the rank of potential sites. The criteria and their performance grade are assessed based on expert judgment.

4.2.1. Weighting the Criteria with F-AHP

In the process of using F-AHP, relative preference weights for each criterion are calculated. This involves dividing the criteria into categories, such as technical, economic, social, and environmental, and evaluating the relative importance of each criterion within each category. In order to calculate the consistency ratio and relative weights (eigenvectors) of the main factors, the assessment criteria are usually written down in depth in a table, such as Table 8. This table can help illustrate the steps involved in calculating the consistency ratio and relative weight of each factor. Overall, using F-AHP can help decision-makers consider various factors in the site selection process and make more informed decisions regarding the location of solar power plants or other developments. It makes evaluating the relative importance of different criteria and can help to ensure that decisions are made consistently and transparently.

The integrated fuzzy comparison matrix of F-AHP is shown in Table A3 (Appendix A). Table 9 and Figure 4 present the results of the F-AHP analysis. Based on the information provided, it can be seen that the top three impact criteria identified through the F-AHP analysis are "Facilitating factors," "Benefits of conserving energy," and "Terms of network accessibility." These criteria are particularly important in certain decisions, such as site selection for solar power plants or the development of energy conservation programs. It is important to note that the specific criteria and their relative importance depend on the specific context of the decision or project and may vary depending on the decision maker's goals and objectives. F-AHP helps decision-makers to consider multiple factors in the decision-making process and make more informed decisions based on a comprehensive evaluation of the relative importance of various criteria.

Table 8. The criteria and their respective definitions.

Main Criteria	Criteria	Definition
C1. Technical	C11. Assistance and guidance with technical matters	Assistance from local or worldwide experts to obtain reliable and available data if solar facilities are to be developed.
	C12. Geology	Processes that shape and alter the earth's surface, including its structure and composition
	C13. Availability of skilled workers	Installers, technicians, and other personnel with sufficient training and experience in the field of solar energy
C2. Economic	C21. Consumption of electricity	A regional breakdown of the amount of energy used in each area
	C22. Costs	Operating and maintenance expenses
	C23. Terms of network accessibility	Proximity to existing power transmission lines
	C24. Proximity to public transportation	Measuring the distance from a nearby road to various potential locations
	C25. Proximity to residential areas	Distance between the population centers (cities or towns) and the many potential sites
C3. Social	C31. Local residents attitude	The perceptions of local residents toward solar power projects
	C32. Rules and regulations of the government	Affectation of legislation and regulations on solar energy system development
	C33. Land acquisition	Maximum land available for solar installations is subject to government approval and discussion with property owners
	C34. Facilitating factors	Depending on local conventions, a political or local commitment to encouraging solar installations, such as feed-in tariffs, attractive financing, tax savings, or other subsidies
C4. Environmental	C41. Impact of wildlife and endangered species	The effects of solar power facilities on animal habitats and critical species
	C42. Noxious pollutant emission	During the production and collection of photovoltaic (PV) panels, there is a negative impact on metropolitan areas from the use of hazardous chemicals
	C43. Benefits of conserving energy	The indicator of energy-saving advantages refers to the beneficial environmental consequences that result from the operation of the project

Table 9. The relative significant fuzzy weights of F-AHP.

Criteria	Fuzzy Geometric Mean			Triangular Fuzzy Weights			Significant Level
C11. Assistance and guidance with technical matters	0.5597	0.6841	0.8652	0.0268	0.0445	0.0768	0.0436
C12. Geology	0.5907	0.7758	1.0326	0.0282	0.0505	0.0916	0.0502
C13. Availability of skilled workers	0.4982	0.6889	0.9640	0.0238	0.0448	0.0855	0.0454
C21. Consumption of electricity	0.5767	0.8094	1.1322	0.0276	0.0527	0.1005	0.0532
C22. Costs	0.7305	1.0048	1.3692	0.0349	0.0654	0.1215	0.0653
C23. Terms of network accessibility	0.9881	1.3157	1.7447	0.0472	0.0856	0.1548	0.0847
C24. Proximity to public transportation	0.7772	1.0612	1.4230	0.0372	0.0691	0.1263	0.0685
C25. Proximity to residential areas	0.7053	0.9772	1.2930	0.0337	0.0636	0.1147	0.0625
C31. Local residents attitude	0.7819	1.0884	1.4797	0.0374	0.0708	0.1313	0.0706
C32. Rules and regulations of the government	0.9143	1.2398	1.6709	0.0437	0.0807	0.1482	0.0803
C33. Land acquisition	0.6522	0.8775	1.2273	0.0312	0.0571	0.1089	0.0581
C34. Facilitating factors	0.9923	1.3911	1.8910	0.0474	0.0905	0.1678	0.0901
C41. Impact of wildlife and endangered species	0.7644	1.0565	1.4792	0.0365	0.0688	0.1312	0.0697
C42. Noxious pollutant emission	0.7754	1.0670	1.5009	0.0371	0.0694	0.1332	0.0706
C43. Benefits of conserving energy	0.9641	1.3276	1.8434	0.0461	0.0864	0.1635	0.0872

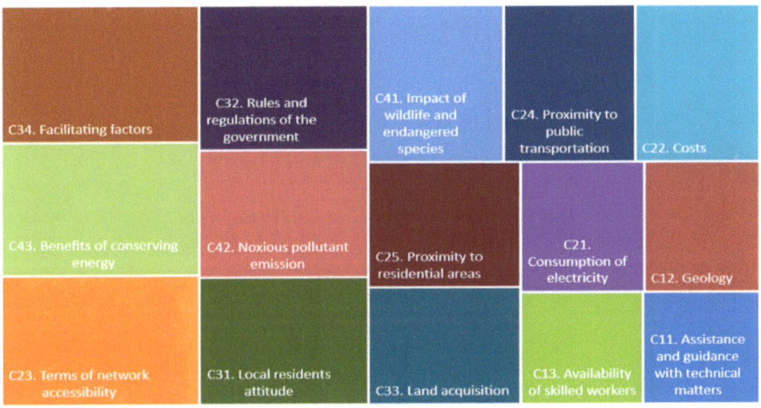

Figure 4. The significant level of criteria of F-AHP.

4.2.2. Ranking the Locations with F-MARCOS

The integrated normalized fuzzy decision matrix of F-MARCOS is shown in Table A3 (Appendix A). The F-MARCOS model has been used to evaluate the efficiency ranking of 11 different locations in Indonesia: Jawa Barat (DMU-09), Jawa Timur (DMU-11), Lampung (DMU-16), Maluku (DMU-17), Maluku Utara (DMU-18), Nusa Tenggara Barat (DMU-19), Nusa Tenggara Timur (DMU-20), Papua (DMU-21), Riau (DMU-23), Sulawesi Selatan (DMU-25), and Sulawesi Utara (DMU-28). The decision hierarchy tree for selecting solar power plant locations is depicted in Figure 5. The integrated matrix and linguistic matrix calculations of the experts' assessments can be seen in Table 10. The utility function and the final ranking of locations are shown in Table 11. Based on these results, the top three ranked locations are {DMU-09, DMU-20, DMU-23}, which occupy the first, second, and third positions with utility function values of 0.8272, 0.8211, and 0.8201, respectively. These locations are considered suitable for solar power generation based on the factors evaluated by the MARCOS fuzzy model. Figure 6 displays the final location ranking from the MARCOS fuzzy model. It is important to note that the ranking and utility function scores will depend on the attributes and criteria considered in the F-MARCOS analysis and the relative importance given to each attribute. F-MARCOS helps decision makers to consider various factors in the site selection process and make more informed decisions based on a comprehensive evaluation of the relative suitability of various sites.

In order to validate the location ranking, four different fuzzy MCDM models are considered, which are the fuzzy multi-attributive border approximation area comparison (fuzzy MABAC) [52], the fuzzy weighted aggregated sum product assessment (fuzzy WASPAS) [53], the fuzzy combined compromise solution (fuzzy CoCoSo) [54], and the fuzzy simple additive weighting (fuzzy SAW) [55]. During the comparative analysis, the same weight of criteria is used, and the results are provided in Table 12 and Figure 7. The findings show that there is no significant difference in the top three rankings of the solar location (Jawa Barat, Nusa Tenggara Timur, Riau). Hence, the proposed model is validated and applicable.

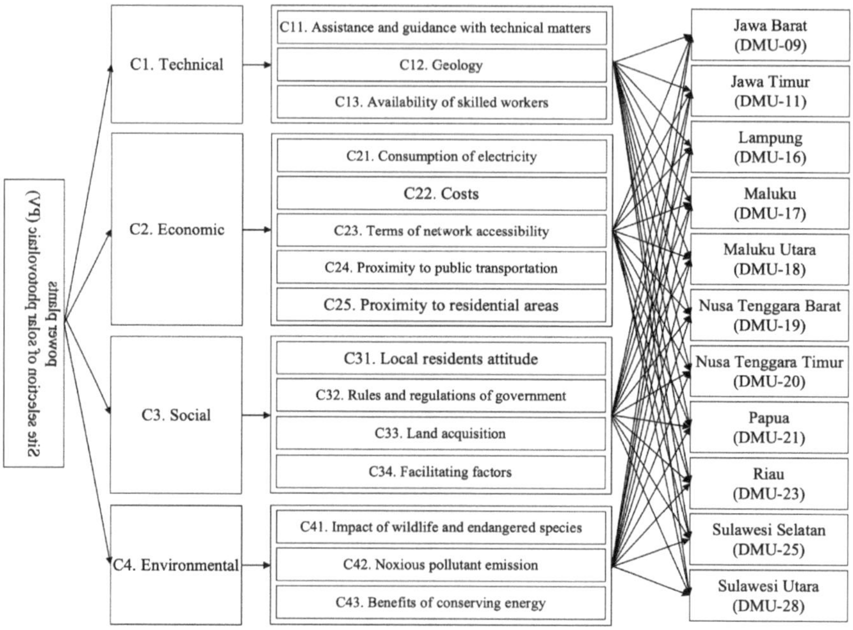

Figure 5. The hierarchy tree for selecting solar PV power plants.

Table 10. Utility degree and fuzzy matrix of $\tilde{T}_i$.

Location	Fuzzy $\tilde{S}_i$			Fuzzy $\tilde{K}_i^-$			Fuzzy $\tilde{K}_i^+$			Fuzzy $\tilde{T}_i$		
	l	m	u	l	m	u	l	m	u	l	m	u
A (AI)	0.1355	0.2521	0.4699									
Jawa Barat	0.2750	0.6254	1.3822	0.5852	2.4804	10.2012	0.1482	0.6254	2.5650	0.7334	3.1058	12.7662
Jawa Timur	0.2046	0.5501	1.3959	0.4354	2.1816	10.3025	0.1103	0.5501	2.5904	0.5457	2.7317	12.8929
Lampung	0.2227	0.5099	1.3167	0.4739	2.0224	9.7180	0.1200	0.5099	2.4435	0.5939	2.5324	12.1615
Maluku	0.2138	0.5683	1.3116	0.4549	2.2538	9.6805	0.1152	0.5683	2.4341	0.5701	2.8220	12.1146
Maluku Utara	0.2510	0.5878	1.3421	0.5341	2.3313	9.9051	0.1353	0.5878	2.4905	0.6693	2.9191	12.3956
Nusa Tenggara Barat	0.2084	0.5742	1.4113	0.4435	2.2773	10.4162	0.1123	0.5742	2.6190	0.5558	2.8515	13.0352
Nusa Tenggara Timur	0.2591	0.6169	1.3956	0.5513	2.4466	10.2999	0.1396	0.6169	2.5898	0.6909	3.0634	12.8897
Papua	0.2194	0.5227	1.4009	0.4668	2.0731	10.3394	0.1182	0.5227	2.5997	0.5850	2.5958	12.9391
Riau	0.2584	0.6034	1.4232	0.5499	2.3931	10.5042	0.1393	0.6034	2.6412	0.6892	2.9965	13.1454
Sulawesi Selatan	0.2113	0.5828	1.3383	0.4496	2.3113	9.8774	0.1139	0.5828	2.4836	0.5635	2.8941	12.3609
Sulawesi Utara	0.2785	0.6266	1.3467	0.5925	2.4851	9.9393	0.1501	0.6266	2.4991	0.7426	3.1117	12.4384
A (ID)	0.5389	1.0000	1.8558							$df_{crisp} = 4.3204$		

Table 11. Utility functions and final ranking of locations.

Location	Fuzzy $f\left(\tilde{K}_i^-\right)$			Fuzzy $f\left(\tilde{K}_i^+\right)$			K_i^-	K_i^+	$f(K_i^-)$	$f(K_i^+)$	$f(K_i)$	Rank
	l	m	u	l	m	u						
Jawa Barat	0.0343	0.1448	0.5937	0.1354	0.5741	2.3612	3.4513	0.8691	0.2012	0.7988	0.8272	1
Jawa Timur	0.0255	0.1273	0.5996	0.1008	0.5050	2.3846	3.2441	0.8168	0.1891	0.7509	0.7225	8
Lampung	0.0278	0.1180	0.5656	0.1097	0.4681	2.2493	3.0469	0.7672	0.1776	0.7052	0.6305	11
Maluku	0.0267	0.1315	0.5634	0.1053	0.5216	2.2406	3.1917	0.8037	0.1860	0.7388	0.6974	9
Maluku Utara	0.0313	0.1361	0.5765	0.1236	0.5396	2.2926	3.2940	0.8295	0.1920	0.7624	0.7470	6
Nusa Tenggara Barat	0.0260	0.1329	0.6062	0.1027	0.5271	2.4109	3.3281	0.8380	0.1940	0.7703	0.7639	5
Nusa Tenggara Timur	0.0323	0.1428	0.5994	0.1276	0.5663	2.3840	3.4396	0.8662	0.2005	0.7961	0.8211	2
Papua	0.0274	0.1210	0.6017	0.1080	0.4798	2.3931	3.1831	0.8015	0.1855	0.7368	0.6932	10
Riau	0.0322	0.1397	0.6113	0.1273	0.5539	2.4313	3.4377	0.8657	0.2004	0.7957	0.8201	3
Sulawesi Selatan	0.0264	0.1349	0.5748	0.1041	0.5350	2.2862	3.2620	0.8214	0.1901	0.7550	0.7313	7
Sulawesi Utara	0.0347	0.1450	0.5784	0.1371	0.5752	2.3005	3.4120	0.8593	0.1989	0.7897	0.8068	4

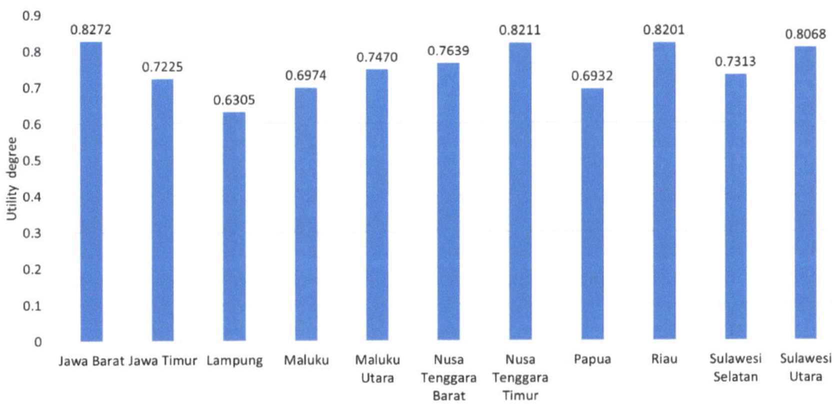

Figure 6. The final location ranking.

Table 12. Comparative analysis of MCDM methods.

Location	Fuzzy AHP and Fuzzy MARCOS		Fuzzy AHP and Fuzzy MABAC		Fuzzy AHP and Fuzzy WASPAS		Fuzzy AHP and Fuzzy CoCoSo		Fuzzy AHP and Fuzzy SAW	
	Value	Rank	Value	Rank	Value	Rank	Value	Rank	Value	Rank
Jawa Barat	0.8272	1	0.0848	2	0.5217	1	2.9004	3	0.6426	1
Jawa Timur	0.7225	8	−0.0279	8	0.4570	8	2.6586	8	0.5508	9
Lampung	0.6305	11	0.0401	6	0.4719	7	2.8513	4	0.5535	8
Maluku	0.6974	9	−0.0426	9	0.4491	10	2.6022	9	0.5355	11
Maluku Utara	0.7470	6	0.0631	4	0.5039	5	2.9111	2	0.6042	5
Nusa Tenggara Barat	0.7639	5	−0.0501	10	0.4550	9	2.5418	10	0.5570	7
Nusa Tenggara Timur	0.8211	2	0.1164	1	0.5199	2	3.0370	1	0.6239	4
Papua	0.6932	10	0.0230	7	0.4732	6	2.8024	6	0.5599	6
Riau	0.8201	3	0.0667	3	0.5069	4	2.8346	5	0.6256	3
Sulawesi Selatan	0.7313	7	−0.0584	11	0.4299	11	2.3403	11	0.5418	10
Sulawesi Utara	0.8068	4	0.0442	5	0.5071	3	2.7714	7	0.6390	2

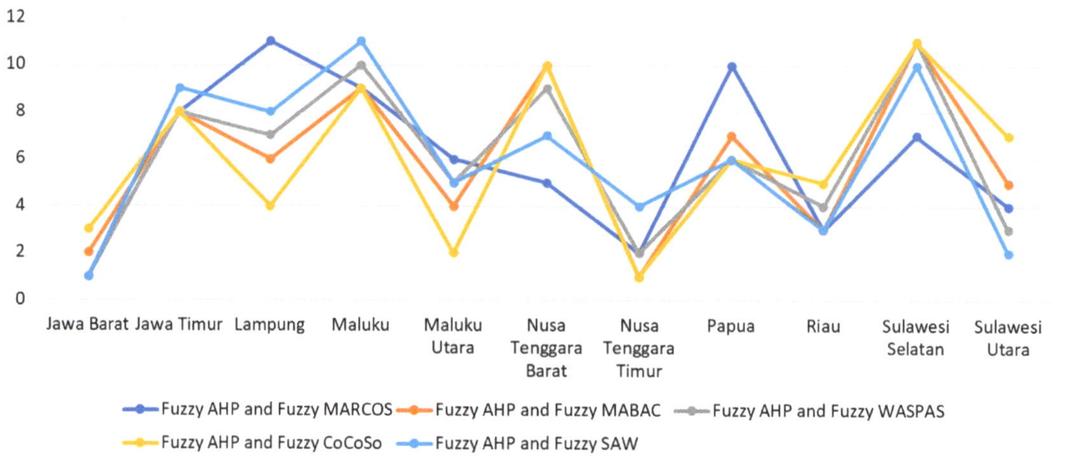

Figure 7. Comparison of proposed model with other MCDM methods.

5. Conclusions

This study identifies the most suitable locations for solar power plants in Indonesia. This study uses data envelopment analysis (DEA) to identify areas of high efficiency based on measured inputs and outputs. These areas were further evaluated using F-AHP to weigh the evaluation criteria and F-MARCOS to rank the provinces. Based on the analysis, this study identified 32 provinces in Indonesia that are excellent for solar power generation. These provinces have favorable conditions for solar power generation, such as high levels of solar radiation, availability of suitable land, and adequate infrastructure. DEA, F-AHP, and F-MARCOS allow for a comprehensive evaluation of the relative suitability of various locations for solar power generation based on several criteria. The most significant findings and achievements of this research are as follows:

- The potential for solar deployment in Indonesia was evaluated based on 23 criteria, and suitable locations were identified using a novel combination of DEA, F-AHP, and F-MARCOS techniques.
- According to F-AHP, the three most important elements were "Facilitating factors," "Benefits of conserving energy," and "Terms of network accessibility." Figure 4 displays the results of applying this technique to calculate the weights.
- Based on the final F-MARCOS ranking, the three best provinces in Indonesia to install solar power plants are Jawa Barat, Nusa Tenggara Timur, and Riau.

Future researchers are recommended to continue exploring the potential of renewable energy sources in Indonesia and other countries. Renewable energy sources such as solar, wind, and hydropower have the potential to play an important role in meeting the growing demand for energy while reducing the environmental impact of energy production. In addition to these established renewable energy sources, researchers are encouraged to explore the potential of newer technologies such as wave, geothermal, tidal, and hybrid systems (e.g., solar-wind and solar-biomass PV) in Indonesia and other countries. These technologies have the potential to provide additional sources of clean, renewable energy and can help diversify the energy mix. Assessing the ability to generate diverse renewable energy sources is also an important issue in the energy market, as decision-makers need to weigh the relative costs and benefits of different technologies to determine the best energy source. By continuing to research and develop new renewable energy technologies, researchers are improving the sustainability of energy systems and supporting the transition to a more renewable energy future.

Author Contributions: Conceptualization, T.-T.D.; data curation, F.D.W.; formal analysis, F.D.W.; funding acquisition, F.D.W.; investigation, N.-A.-T.N.; methodology, F.D.W.; project administration, C.-N.W.; software, T.-T.D.; validation, Y.-C.C.; writing—original draft, F.D.W.; writing—review and editing, N.-A.-T.N. and Y.-C.C. All authors have read and agreed to the published version of the manuscript.

Funding: This research received no external funding.

Institutional Review Board Statement: Not applicable.

Informed Consent Statement: Not applicable.

Data Availability Statement: Not applicable.

Acknowledgments: The authors appreciate the support from the National Kaohsiung University of Science and Technology, Taiwan; Hong Bang International University, Vietnam; and FPT University, Vietnam.

Conflicts of Interest: The authors declare no conflict of interest.

Appendix A

Table A1. Data of input and output of the DEA model.

No.	Location	DMU	X1	X2	X3	X4	X5	Y1	Y2	Y3
1	Aceh	DMU-01	26.81	1.50	89.28	3648.40	1010.70	1670.70	1686.30	3
2	Bali	DMU-02	27.31	3.10	81.68	2992.80	1011.30	2658.00	1799.45	4
3	Bangka Belitung	DMU-03	26.45	1.75	89.32	3012.90	1011.40	1646.50	1653.45	6
4	Banten	DMU-04	27.80	1.77	81.49	2290.50	1010.60	1710.50	1679.00	14
5	Bengkulu	DMU-05	27.01	2.52	83.59	3691.80	1011.00	2327.40	1708.20	12
6	Gorontalo	DMU-06	27.24	1.53	85.50	2285.50	1011.00	1931.40	1803.10	33
7	Jakarta	DMU-07	28.40	1.48	77.18	2394.60	1011.00	1532.00	1726.45	4
8	Jambi	DMU-08	27.01	0.72	86.23	3218.40	1011.40	1574.20	1627.90	24
9	Jawa Barat	DMU-09	26.06	1.09	84.16	3786.60	924.10	1862.40	1737.40	207
10	Jawa Tengah	DMU-10	28.12	1.99	81.06	2476.80	1011.90	2274.90	1806.75	6
11	Jawa Timur	DMU-11	24.10	1.93	79.53	2447.80	1011.80	2060.70	1879.75	590
12	Kalimantan Barat	DMU-12	26.80	1.26	87.70	3281.20	1011.80	1788.30	1682.65	15
13	Kalimantan Selatan	DMU-13	27.07	1.42	87.08	2996.20	1013.10	1418.70	1657.10	2
14	Kalimantan Tengah	DMU-14	26.96	1.29	87.02	4132.20	1013.90	1799.40	1679.00	10
15	Kalimantan Timur	DMU-15	27.60	1.89	83.52	2902.00	1012.90	1203.80	1668.05	3
16	Lampung	DMU-16	26.84	1.12	84.18	2063.50	1012.10	1810.60	1708.20	71
17	Maluku	DMU-17	26.58	0.97	89.08	2695.90	1012.40	1960.20	1679.00	10
18	Maluku Utara	DMU-18	26.35	0.67	90.59	3928.20	1013.00	1724.20	1737.40	130
19	Nusa Tenggara Barat	DMU-19	27.26	2.58	80.25	1770.40	1014.20	2687.60	1941.80	10
20	Nusa Tenggara Timur	DMU-20	19.92	2.02	87.55	4493.40	1011.00	2062.10	2014.80	1070
21	Papua	DMU-21	19.72	2.38	83.30	1933.50	1011.10	1751.60	1631.55	1653
22	Papua Barat	DMU-22	27.52	1.81	82.66	2891.60	1011.50	1433.00	1679.00	3
23	Riau	DMU-23	26.75	0.35	83.44	3072.20	1010.50	1502.90	1649.80	15
24	Sulawesi Barat	DMU-24	27.59	1.72	81.79	2268.10	1012.50	2122.00	1708.20	29
25	Sulawesi Selatan	DMU-25	26.98	1.16	84.00	4448.20	1013.10	2178.60	1777.55	14
26	Sulawesi Tengah	DMU-26	27.25	0.97	85.56	2372.80	1011.90	1653.00	1700.90	10
27	Sulawesi Tenggara	DMU-27	28.04	1.51	80.61	2420.80	1012.80	1831.30	1755.65	14
28	Sulawesi Utara	DMU-28	23.15	1.24	87.69	2220.40	1012.30	1518.50	1755.65	204
29	Sumatera Barat	DMU-29	26.70	1.83	85.02	4878.50	1010.90	2007.20	1646.15	6
30	Sumatera Selatan	DMU-30	27.21	2.13	82.76	2297.90	1011.00	1716.60	1689.95	10
31	Sumatera Utara	DMU-31	27.25	1.72	84.22	2543.40	1010.60	1623.20	1671.70	25
32	Yogyakarta	DMU-32	26.37	2.04	82.40	2456.70	1014.90	1896.20	1861.50	182

Table A2. The integrated fuzzy comparison matrix of F-AHP.

Criteria	C11			C12			C13			C21		
C11	1.0000	1.0000	1.0000	0.8920	1.1107	1.4241	0.4663	0.5776	0.7496	0.2245	0.2716	0.3425
C12	0.7022	0.9003	1.1211	1.0000	1.0000	1.0000	0.6507	0.8116	1.0532	0.6507	0.8116	1.0532
C13	1.3341	1.7313	2.1446	0.9494	1.2321	1.5368	1.0000	1.0000	1.0000	0.6711	1.0371	1.4902
C21	2.9196	3.6814	4.4541	0.9494	1.2321	1.5368	0.6711	0.9642	1.4902	1.0000	1.0000	1.0000
C22	0.9349	1.2099	1.5029	0.9494	1.2321	1.5368	0.9883	1.4788	2.2442	0.7017	1.0000	1.5368
C23	0.7242	0.9338	1.1722	0.6654	0.8610	1.0770	0.7708	1.1534	1.7826	0.8060	1.1962	1.8384
C24	0.7242	0.9338	1.1722	0.6654	0.8610	1.0770	0.7708	1.1534	1.7826	0.8060	1.1962	1.8384
C25	0.9494	1.2321	1.5368	0.9349	1.2099	1.5029	1.8206	2.7629	3.8043	2.9612	4.0774	5.1412
C31	2.8552	3.6149	4.3860	1.4963	2.0180	2.6586	1.0481	1.4368	1.9871	1.0334	1.5337	2.3144
C32	0.9521	1.2372	1.5468	2.3868	3.1469	4.2117	1.2671	1.8421	2.6531	1.0334	1.5337	2.3144
C33	2.0009	2.5262	3.0737	0.5296	0.6935	1.0118	1.0184	1.3797	1.8541	1.0334	1.5337	2.3144
C34	0.9669	1.2599	1.5817	1.3580	2.1161	3.0837	1.8206	2.7629	3.8043	1.8206	2.7629	3.8043
C41	0.9669	1.2599	1.5817	1.3580	2.1161	3.0837	1.8206	2.7629	3.8043	0.9330	1.3636	1.9537
C42	0.9669	1.2599	1.5817	0.7490	1.1076	1.6632	1.8206	2.7629	3.8043	0.9330	1.3636	1.9537
C43	1.4022	1.7654	2.1540	0.7490	1.1076	1.6632	0.9756	1.4142	2.0148	0.6711	0.9642	1.4902

Criteria	C22			C23			C24			C25		
C11	0.6654	0.8265	1.0696	0.8531	1.0709	1.3808	0.8531	1.0709	1.3808	0.6507	0.8116	1.0532
C12	0.6507	0.8116	1.0532	0.9285	1.1614	1.5029	0.9285	1.1614	1.5029	0.6654	0.8265	1.0696
C13	0.4456	0.6762	1.0118	0.5610	0.8670	1.2973	0.5610	0.8670	1.2973	0.2629	0.3619	0.5493
C21	0.6507	1.0000	1.4251	0.5439	0.8360	1.2407	0.5439	0.8360	1.2407	0.1945	0.2453	0.3377
C22	1.0000	1.0000	1.0000	0.5330	0.7548	1.0960	0.5551	0.7768	1.1207	1.4200	1.8684	2.3144
C23	0.9124	1.3249	1.8760	1.0000	1.0000	1.0000	1.0718	1.5436	1.9977	0.7222	1.0371	1.4933
C24	0.8923	1.2873	1.8015	0.5006	0.6478	0.9330	1.0000	1.0000	1.0000	1.1161	1.4902	2.0123
C25	0.4321	0.5352	0.7042	0.6697	0.9642	1.3847	0.4969	0.6711	0.8960	1.0000	1.0000	1.0000
C31	0.4321	0.5352	0.7042	0.6697	0.9642	1.3847	0.9479	1.3259	1.6843	0.7832	1.0718	1.6174
C32	0.7995	1.1207	1.6141	0.4693	0.6084	0.7687	0.7017	1.0098	1.4758	1.4614	2.0939	3.0539
C33	0.8414	1.2011	1.8015	0.4693	0.6084	0.7687	0.5318	0.6881	1.0021	0.7832	1.0718	1.6174
C34	1.3195	2.0320	2.8772	0.4621	0.5974	0.7517	0.5318	0.6881	1.0021	1.4614	2.0939	3.0539
C41	0.6418	0.9103	1.3741	0.5345	0.7146	0.9502	0.5318	0.6881	1.0021	0.5574	0.7277	1.0740
C42	0.6418	0.9103	1.3741	0.3335	0.4234	0.5676	0.8394	1.1390	1.6174	0.7832	1.0718	1.6174
C43	1.2873	1.8541	2.5832	0.4512	0.5949	0.7628	0.8394	1.1390	1.6174	1.4614	2.0939	3.0539

Criteria	C31			C32			C33			C34		
C11	0.2280	0.2766	0.3502	0.6465	0.8083	1.0503	0.3253	0.3959	0.4998	0.6322	0.7937	1.0342
C12	0.3761	0.4955	0.6683	0.2374	0.3178	0.4190	0.9883	1.4420	1.8882	0.3243	0.4726	0.7364
C13	0.5032	0.6960	0.9541	0.3769	0.5428	0.7892	0.5394	0.7248	0.9819	0.2629	0.3619	0.5493
C21	0.4321	0.6520	0.9677	0.4321	0.6520	0.9677	0.4321	0.6520	0.9677	0.2629	0.3619	0.5493
C22	1.4200	1.8684	2.3144	0.6196	0.8923	1.2508	0.5551	0.8326	1.1885	0.3476	0.4921	0.7579
C23	0.7222	1.0371	1.4933	1.3010	1.6438	2.1308	1.3010	1.6438	2.1308	1.3303	1.6740	2.1639
C24	0.5937	0.7542	1.0549	0.6776	0.9903	1.4251	0.9979	1.4532	1.8805	0.9979	1.4532	1.8805
C25	0.6183	0.9330	1.2769	0.3274	0.4776	0.6843	0.6183	0.9330	1.2769	0.3274	0.4776	0.6843
C31	1.0000	1.0000	1.0000	0.6183	0.9330	1.2769	0.3274	0.4776	0.6843	0.6183	0.9330	1.2769
C32	0.7832	1.0718	1.6174	1.0000	1.0000	1.0000	1.0000	1.3830	1.8303	0.6084	0.8569	1.1548
C33	1.4614	2.0939	3.0539	0.5464	0.7231	1.0000	1.0000	1.0000	1.0000	0.2288	0.3026	0.4592
C34	0.7832	1.0718	1.6174	0.8659	1.1671	1.6438	2.1778	3.3051	4.3700	1.0000	1.0000	1.0000
C41	0.6711	0.9642	1.4902	0.5464	0.7231	1.0000	1.8206	2.7629	3.8043	1.0334	1.5337	2.3144
C42	0.6711	0.9642	1.4902	0.5464	0.7231	1.0000	1.0334	1.5337	2.3144	0.7017	1.0000	1.5368
C43	0.9883	1.4788	2.2442	1.1598	1.5332	2.0927	1.0334	1.5337	2.3144	0.5296	0.6790	0.9622

Criteria	C41			C42			C43		
C11	0.6322	0.7937	1.0342	0.6322	0.7937	1.0342	0.4642	0.5665	0.7132
C12	0.3243	0.4726	0.7364	0.6012	0.9029	1.3351	0.6012	0.9029	1.3351
C13	0.2629	0.3619	0.5493	0.2629	0.3619	0.5493	0.4963	0.7071	1.0250
C21	0.5119	0.7334	1.0718	0.5119	0.7334	1.0718	0.6711	1.0371	1.4902
C22	0.7277	1.0986	1.5582	0.7277	1.0986	1.5582	0.3871	0.5394	0.7768
C23	1.0524	1.3994	1.8708	1.7617	2.3618	2.9987	1.3110	1.6808	2.2162
C24	0.9979	1.4532	1.8805	0.6183	0.8780	1.1914	0.6183	0.8780	1.1914
C25	0.9311	1.3741	1.7941	0.6183	0.9330	1.2769	0.3274	0.4776	0.6843
C31	0.6711	1.0371	1.4902	0.6711	1.0371	1.4902	0.4456	0.6762	1.0118
C32	1.0000	1.3830	1.8303	1.0000	1.3830	1.8303	0.4778	0.6522	0.8622
C33	0.2629	0.3619	0.5493	0.4321	0.6520	0.9677	0.4321	0.6520	0.9677
C34	0.4321	0.6520	0.9677	0.6507	1.0000	1.4251	1.0392	1.4727	1.8882
C41	1.0000	1.0000	1.0000	0.2629	0.3619	0.5493	0.4321	0.6520	0.9677
C42	1.8206	2.7629	3.8043	1.0000	1.0000	1.0000	0.2629	0.3619	0.5493
C43	1.0334	1.5337	2.3144	1.8206	2.7629	3.8043	1.0000	1.0000	1.0000

Table A3. The integrated normalized fuzzy decision matrix of F-MARCOS.

Location	C11			C12			C13			C21		
	l	*m*	*u*	*l*	*m*	*u*	*l*	*m*	*u*	*l*	*m*	*u*
DMU-09	0.5603	0.7284	0.8401	0.1901	0.2050	0.2486	0.8521	1.0335	1.1144	0.8064	0.9780	1.0546
DMU-11	0.2922	0.4690	0.5746	0.5508	0.9963	1.0485	0.2126	0.3300	0.4956	0.2012	0.2012	0.3765
DMU-16	0.4618	0.6154	0.7466	0.3485	0.5796	0.6420	0.3655	0.4709	0.6502	0.3287	0.3459	0.5950
DMU-17	0.2777	0.5194	0.5556	0.7221	0.7997	1.1702	0.2649	0.2934	0.5489	0.1713	0.2507	0.2777
DMU-18	0.7290	0.8340	0.9780	0.2750	0.3425	0.4201	0.6186	0.7703	0.8813	0.4772	0.5854	0.7290
DMU-19	0.2945	0.4094	0.5654	0.6809	1.3061	1.3061	0.1622	0.3112	0.4326	0.1535	0.1535	0.2945
DMU-20	0.6262	0.7928	0.8770	0.3202	0.3732	0.5465	0.5677	0.6617	0.8377	0.3668	0.5372	0.6262
DMU-21	0.4736	0.5654	0.7409	0.4234	0.6809	0.7541	0.3112	0.5004	0.5974	0.2659	0.2945	0.4736
DMU-23	0.8340	0.9222	1.0815	0.1854	0.2174	0.2404	0.6186	0.7703	0.8813	0.1232	0.2134	0.3312
DMU-25	0.1447	0.1447	0.2593	0.6809	1.3061	1.3061	0.1622	0.3112	0.4326	0.1535	0.1535	0.2945
DMU-28	0.8626	1.0285	1.1090	0.2140	0.2366	0.3073	0.6893	0.8953	0.9900	0.8626	1.0285	1.1090
Location	C22			C23			C24			C25		
DMU-09	0.2896	0.3960	0.5277	0.4226	0.5824	0.7700	0.2511	0.2925	0.4000	0.2892	0.3955	0.5269
DMU-11	0.4976	0.9000	0.9472	0.2354	0.2478	0.4482	0.3900	0.5025	0.9089	0.4969	0.8987	0.9458
DMU-16	0.3148	0.5237	0.5800	0.3845	0.4405	0.7084	0.2973	0.3179	0.5288	0.3144	0.5229	0.5791
DMU-17	0.6523	0.7225	1.0572	0.2109	0.3087	0.3419	0.3521	0.6588	0.7296	0.6514	0.7215	1.0557
DMU-18	0.2485	0.3094	0.3795	0.5876	0.7208	0.8976	0.2193	0.2509	0.3125	0.2611	0.3089	0.4230
DMU-19	0.7662	1.1800	1.1800	0.1890	0.1890	0.3626	0.4468	0.7738	1.1916	0.6803	1.1783	1.4678
DMU-20	0.2893	0.3372	0.4938	0.4517	0.6614	0.7710	0.2307	0.2921	0.3405	0.3199	0.3367	0.6142
DMU-21	0.4269	0.6151	0.6813	0.3274	0.3626	0.5831	0.3235	0.4311	0.6212	0.4930	0.6142	1.1783
DMU-23	0.5469	0.8487	1.4699	0.1517	0.2628	0.4078	0.2193	0.2509	0.3125	0.2481	0.3255	0.3790
DMU-25	0.6151	1.1800	1.1800	0.1890	0.1890	0.2910	0.7055	1.2638	1.2638	0.6142	1.0638	1.1783
DMU-28	0.1933	0.2138	0.2777	0.8032	1.0432	1.1536	0.1649	0.1779	0.2121	0.1930	0.2135	0.2773
Location	C31			C32			C33			C34		
DMU-09	0.6609	0.7697	0.9342	0.3432	0.4573	0.6254	0.8521	1.0335	1.1144	0.8521	1.0335	1.1144
DMU-11	0.3846	0.4956	0.6725	0.1912	0.2012	0.3640	0.2021	0.2126	0.3846	0.2021	0.2126	0.3846
DMU-16	0.6079	0.6502	0.8738	0.3123	0.3459	0.5753	0.3300	0.3655	0.6079	0.3300	0.3655	0.6079
DMU-17	0.2934	0.5677	0.5871	0.1713	0.2507	0.2777	0.2498	0.3250	0.3476	0.1453	0.2373	0.2957
DMU-18	0.7703	0.7967	1.0335	0.4772	0.6927	0.7290	0.2649	0.4111	0.5489	0.4518	0.5542	0.7319
DMU-19	0.3112	0.4627	0.5974	0.1535	0.1535	0.2945	0.1796	0.1796	0.3328	0.2255	0.3136	0.5043
DMU-20	0.8521	1.0335	1.1144	0.8064	0.9780	1.0546	0.3250	0.5677	0.6279	0.2788	0.3658	0.5086
DMU-21	0.5004	0.6609	0.7829	0.2659	0.2945	0.4736	0.2911	0.3627	0.5346	0.2021	0.2498	0.4792
DMU-23	0.4792	0.5769	0.7448	0.4772	0.6927	0.7290	0.8813	0.9745	1.1428	0.8813	0.9745	1.1428
DMU-25	0.1529	0.1529	0.2740	0.1447	0.1447	0.2593	0.1302	0.1302	0.2255	0.2255	0.3136	0.5043
DMU-28	0.6893	0.8953	0.9900	0.8626	1.0285	1.1090	0.6893	0.8953	0.9900	0.2788	0.3658	0.5086
Location	C41			C42			C43					
DMU-09	0.3197	0.3447	0.4181	0.2211	0.2385	0.2892	0.7887	0.9185	1.1149			
DMU-11	0.7189	0.9263	1.6755	0.6407	1.1589	1.2197	0.4825	0.6326	0.8368			
DMU-16	0.5479	0.5861	0.9748	0.4054	0.6743	0.7468	0.7494	0.8300	1.0780			
DMU-17	0.6491	1.2143	1.3450	0.8400	0.9303	1.3613	0.4148	0.7494	0.7880			
DMU-18	0.4043	0.4625	0.5759	0.4887	0.8908	1.0928	0.6550	0.8035	0.9749			
DMU-19	0.7065	0.9823	1.5798	0.5185	0.6795	0.6795	0.3972	0.5522	0.7497			
DMU-20	0.5484	0.7316	1.0172	0.3725	0.4341	0.6358	0.7494	0.9997	1.0780			
DMU-21	0.7435	0.9192	1.7633	0.4157	0.5740	0.6358	0.6380	0.7887	0.9905			
DMU-23	0.4043	0.4625	0.5759	0.4490	0.5995	0.9303	0.6614	0.8735	0.9993			
DMU-25	0.7065	0.9823	1.5798	0.3203	0.3790	0.5223	0.8300	1.0169	1.1531			
DMU-28	0.3599	0.3979	0.5169	0.2489	0.2753	0.3575	0.6774	0.7896	0.9997			

References

1. Aleixandre-Tudó, J.L.; Castelló-Cogollos, L.; Aleixandre, J.L.; Aleixandre-Benavent, R. Renewable Energies: Worldwide Trends in Research, Funding and International Collaboration. *Renew. Energy* **2019**, *139*, 268–278. [CrossRef]
2. International Energy Agency [IEA]. 2022, p. 98. Available online: https://www.iea.org/reports/world-energy-outlook-2022 (accessed on 18 August 2022).

3. Secretary General of National Energy Council. 2019, p. 51. Available online: https://www.esdm.go.id/assets/media/content content-indonesia-energy-outlook-2019-english-version (accessed on 18 August 2022).
4. Asian Development Bank. 2020, pp. 17–18. Available online: https://www.adb.org/sites/default/files/publication/57562 /ado2020.pdf (accessed on 18 August 2022).
5. International Renewable Energy Agency (IRENA) 2017. Available online: https://www.irena.org/publications/2017/Jul Renewable-Energy-Statistics-2017 (accessed on 20 August 2022).
6. Rose, A.; Stoner, R.; Pérez-Arriaga, I. Prospects for Grid-Connected Solar PV in Kenya: A Systems Approach. *Appl. Energy* **2016** *161*, 583–590. [CrossRef]
7. Tang, J.; Ni, H.; Peng, R.-L.; Wang, N.; Zuo, L. A Review on Energy Conversion Using Hybrid Photovoltaic and Thermoelectric Systems. *J. Power Sources* **2023**, *562*, 232785. [CrossRef]
8. Ruiz, H.S.; Sunarso, A.; Ibrahim-Bathis, K.; Murti, S.A.; Budiarto, I. GIS-AHP Multi Criteria Decision Analysis for the Optima Location of Solar Energy Plants at Indonesia. *Energy Rep.* **2020**, *6*, 3249–3263. [CrossRef]
9. Wang, C.-N.; Dang, T.-T.; Nguyen, N.-A.-T.; Wang, J.-W. A Combined Data Envelopment Analysis (DEA) and Grey Based Multiple Criteria Decision Making (G-MCDM) for Solar PV Power Plants Site Selection: A Case Study in Vietnam. *Energy Rep.* **2022**, *8* 1124–1142. [CrossRef]
10. Al Garni, H.Z.; Awasthi, A. Solar PV Power Plants Site Selection. In *Advances in Renewable Energies and Power Technologies*; Elsevier Amsterdam, The Netherlands, 2018; pp. 57–75.
11. Deveci, M.; Cali, U.; Pamucar, D. Evaluation of Criteria for Site Selection of Solar Photovoltaic (PV) Projects Using Fuzzy Logarithmic Additive Estimation of Weight Coefficients. *Energy Rep.* **2021**, *7*, 8805–8824. [CrossRef]
12. Khan, M.F.; Pervez, A.; Modibbo, U.M.; Chauhan, J.; Ali, I. Flexible Fuzzy Goal Programming Approach in Optimal Mix of Power Generation for Socio-Economic Sustainability: A Case Study. *Sustainability* **2021**, *13*, 8256. [CrossRef]
13. Modibbo, U.M.; Hassan, M.; Ahmed, A.; Ali, I. Multi-Criteria Decision Analysis for Pharmaceutical Supplier Selection Problem Using Fuzzy TOPSIS. *Manag. Decis.* **2022**, *60*, 806–836. [CrossRef]
14. Jurasz, J.; Canales, F.A.; Kies, A.; Guezgouz, M.; Beluco, A. A Review on the Complementarity of Renewable Energy Sources Concept, Metrics, Application and Future Research Directions. *Sol. Energy* **2020**, *195*, 703–724. [CrossRef]
15. Burke, M.J.; Stephens, J.C. Political Power and Renewable Energy Futures: A Critical Review. *Energy Res. Soc. Sci.* **2018**, *35*, 78–93 [CrossRef]
16. Sindhu, S.; Nehra, V.; Luthra, S. Investigation of Feasibility Study of Solar Farms Deployment Using Hybrid AHP-TOPSIS Analysis: Case Study of India. *Renew. Sustain. Energy Rev.* **2017**, *73*, 496–511. [CrossRef]
17. Wang, C.-N.; Nguyen, N.-A.-T.; Dang, T.-T.; Bayer, J. A Two-Stage Multiple Criteria Decision Making for Site Selection of Solar Photovoltaic (PV) Power Plant: A Case Study in Taiwan. *IEEE Access* **2021**, *9*, 75509–75525. [CrossRef]
18. Doorga, J.R.S.; Rughooputh, S.D.D.V.; Boojhawon, R. Multi-Criteria GIS-Based Modelling Technique for Identifying Potential Solar Farm Sites: A Case Study in Mauritius. *Renew. Energy* **2019**, *133*, 1201–1219. [CrossRef]
19. Potić, I.; Golić, R.; Joksimović, T. Analysis of Insolation Potential of Knjaževac Municipality (Serbia) Using Multi-Criteria Approach. *Renew. Sustain. Energy Rev.* **2016**, *56*, 235–245. [CrossRef]
20. Liu, J.; Xu, F.; Lin, S. Site Selection of Photovoltaic Power Plants in a Value Chain Based on Grey Cumulative Prospect Theory for Sustainability: A Case Study in Northwest China. *J. Clean. Prod.* **2017**, *148*, 386–397. [CrossRef]
21. Gherboudj, I.; Ghedira, H. Assessment of Solar Energy Potential over the United Arab Emirates Using Remote Sensing and Weather Forecast Data. *Renew. Sustain. Energy Rev.* **2016**, *55*, 1210–1224. [CrossRef]
22. Watson, J.J.W.; Hudson, M.D. Regional Scale Wind Farm and Solar Farm Suitability Assessment Using GIS-Assisted Multi-Criteria Evaluation. *Landsc. Urban Plan.* **2015**, *138*, 20–31. [CrossRef]
23. Qolipour, M.; Mostafaeipour, A.; Shamshirband, S.; Alavi, O.; Goudarzi, H.; Petković, D. Evaluation of Wind Power Generation Potential Using a Three Hybrid Approach for Households in Ardebil Province, Iran. *Energy Convers. Manag.* **2016**, *118*, 295–305 [CrossRef]
24. Zoghi, M.; Houshang Ehsani, A.; Sadat, M.; javad Amiri, M.; Karimi, S. Optimization Solar Site Selection by Fuzzy Logic Model and Weighted Linear Combination Method in Arid and Semi-Arid Region: A Case Study Isfahan-IRAN. *Renew. Sustain. Energy Rev.* **2017**, *68*, 986–996. [CrossRef]
25. Wu, Y.; Geng, S.; Zhang, H.; Gao, M. Decision Framework of Solar Thermal Power Plant Site Selection Based on Linguistic Choquet Operator. *Appl. Energy* **2014**, *136*, 303–311. [CrossRef]
26. Jun, D.; Tian-tian, F.; Yi-sheng, Y.; Yu, M. Macro-Site Selection of Wind/Solar Hybrid Power Station Based on ELECTRE-II. *Renew Sustain. Energy Rev.* **2014**, *35*, 194–204. [CrossRef]
27. Ozdemir, S.; Sahin, G. Multi-Criteria Decision-Making in the Location Selection for a Solar PV Power Plant Using AHP. *Measurement* **2018**, *129*, 218–226. [CrossRef]
28. Vafaeipour, M.; Hashemkhani Zolfani, S.; Morshed Varzandeh, M.H.; Derakhti, A.; Keshavarz Eshkalag, M. Assessment of Regions Priority for Implementation of Solar Projects in Iran: New Application of a Hybrid Multi-Criteria Decision Making Approach. *Energy Convers. Manag.* **2014**, *86*, 653–663. [CrossRef]
29. Do, T.N.; Burke, P.J.; Baldwin, K.G.H.; Nguyen, C.T. Underlying Drivers and Barriers for Solar Photovoltaics Diffusion: The Case of Vietnam. *Energy Policy* **2020**, *144*, 111561. [CrossRef]

30. Rigo, P.D.; Rediske, G.; Rosa, C.B.; Gastaldo, N.G.; Michels, L.; Neuenfeldt Júnior, A.L.; Siluk, J.C.M. Renewable Energy Problems: Exploring the Methods to Support the Decision-Making Process. *Sustainability* **2020**, *12*, 10195. [CrossRef]
31. Uyan, M. GIS-Based Solar Farms Site Selection Using Analytic Hierarchy Process (AHP) in Karapinar Region, Konya/Turkey. *Renew. Sustain. Energy Rev.* **2013**, *28*, 11–17. [CrossRef]
32. Lee, A.; Kang, H.-Y.; Liou, Y.-J. A Hybrid Multiple-Criteria Decision-Making Approach for Photovoltaic Solar Plant Location Selection. *Sustainability* **2017**, *9*, 184. [CrossRef]
33. Al Garni, H.Z.; Awasthi, A. Solar PV Power Plant Site Selection Using a GIS-AHP Based Approach with Application in Saudi Arabia. *Appl. Energy* **2017**, *206*, 1225–1240. [CrossRef]
34. Seyed Alavi, S.M.; Maleki, A.; Khaleghi, A. Optimal Site Selection for Wind Power Plant Using Multi-Criteria Decision-Making Methods: A Case Study in Eastern Iran. *Int. J. Low-Carbon Technol.* **2022**, *17*, 1319–1337. [CrossRef]
35. Janke, J.R. Multicriteria GIS Modeling of Wind and Solar Farms in Colorado. *Renew. Energy* **2010**, *35*, 2228–2234. [CrossRef]
36. Sánchez-Lozano, J.M.; Henggeler Antunes, C.; García-Cascales, M.S.; Dias, L.C. GIS-Based Photovoltaic Solar Farms Site Selection Using ELECTRE-TRI: Evaluating the Case for Torre Pacheco, Murcia, Southeast of Spain. *Renew. Energy* **2014**, *66*, 478–494. [CrossRef]
37. Aragonés-Beltrán, P.; Chaparro-González, F.; Pastor-Ferrando, J.-P.; Pla-Rubio, A. An AHP (Analytic Hierarchy Process)/ANP (Analytic Network Process)-Based Multi-Criteria Decision Approach for the Selection of Solar-Thermal Power Plant Investment Projects. *Energy* **2014**, *66*, 222–238. [CrossRef]
38. Sánchez-Lozano, J.M.; García-Cascales, M.S.; Lamata, M.T. Evaluation of Suitable Locations for the Installation of Solar Thermoelectric Power Plants. *Comput. Ind. Eng.* **2015**, *87*, 343–355. [CrossRef]
39. Tavana, M.; Santos Arteaga, F.J.; Mohammadi, S.; Alimohammadi, M. A Fuzzy Multi-Criteria Spatial Decision Support System for Solar Farm Location Planning. *Energy Strategy Rev.* **2017**, *18*, 93–105. [CrossRef]
40. Anwarzai, M.A.; Nagasaka, K. Utility-Scale Implementable Potential of Wind and Solar Energies for Afghanistan Using GIS Multi-Criteria Decision Analysis. *Renew. Sustain. Energy Rev.* **2017**, *71*, 150–160. [CrossRef]
41. Akkas, O.P.; Erten, M.Y.; Cam, E.; Inanc, N. Optimal Site Selection for a Solar Power Plant in the Central Anatolian Region of Turkey. *Int. J. Photoenergy* **2017**, *2017*, 7452715. [CrossRef]
42. Rezaei, M.; Mostafaeipour, A.; Qolipour, M.; Tavakkoli-Moghaddam, R. Investigation of the Optimal Location Design of a Hybrid Wind-Solar Plant: A Case Study. *Int. J. Hydrog. Energy* **2018**, *43*, 100–114. [CrossRef]
43. Wu, Y.; Zhang, B.; Wu, C.; Zhang, T.; Liu, F. Optimal Site Selection for Parabolic Trough Concentrating Solar Power Plant Using Extended PROMETHEE Method: A Case in China. *Renew. Energy* **2019**, *143*, 1910–1927. [CrossRef]
44. Badi, I.; Pamucar, D.; Gigović, L.; Tatomirović, S. Optimal Site Selection for Sitting a Solar Park Using a Novel GIS- SWA'TEL Model: A Case Study in Libya. *Int. J. Green Energy* **2021**, *18*, 336–350. [CrossRef]
45. Heidary Dahooie, J.; Husseinzadeh Kashan, A.; Shoaei Naeini, Z.; Vanaki, A.S.; Zavadskas, E.K.; Turskis, Z. A Hybrid Multi-Criteria-Decision-Making Aggregation Method and Geographic Information System for Selecting Optimal Solar Power Plants in Iran. *Energies* **2022**, *15*, 2801. [CrossRef]
46. Jbaihi, O.; Ouchani, F.; Alami Merrouni, A.; Cherkaoui, M.; Ghennioui, A.; Maaroufi, M. An AHP-GIS Based Site Suitability Analysis for Integrating Large-Scale Hybrid CSP+PV Plants in Morocco: An Approach to Address the Intermittency of Solar Energy. *J. Clean Prod.* **2022**, *369*, 133250. [CrossRef]
47. Stanković, M.; Stević, Ž.; Das, D.K.; Subotić, M.; Pamučar, D. A New Fuzzy MARCOS Method for Road Traffic Risk Analysis. *Mathematics* **2020**, *8*, 457. [CrossRef]
48. Stević, Ž.; Pamučar, D.; Puška, A.; Chatterjee, P. Sustainable Supplier Selection in Healthcare Industries Using a New MCDM Method: Measurement of Alternatives and Ranking According to COmpromise Solution (MARCOS). *Comput. Ind. Eng.* **2020**, *140*, 106231. [CrossRef]
49. Wang, C.-N.; Nguyen, N.-A.-T.; Dang, T.-T.; Trinh, T.-T.-Q. A Decision Support Model for Measuring Technological Progress and Productivity Growth: The Case of Commercial Banks in Vietnam. *Axioms* **2021**, *10*, 131. [CrossRef]
50. Banker, R.D.; Charnes, A.; Cooper, W.W. Some Models for Estimating Technical and Scale Inefficiencies in Data Envelopment Analysis. *Manag. Sci.* **1984**, *30*, 1078–1092. [CrossRef]
51. Tone, K. A Slacks-Based Measure of Efficiency in Data Envelopment Analysis. *Eur. J. Oper. Res.* **2001**, *130*, 498–509. [CrossRef]
52. Božanić, D.; Tešić, D.; Kočić, J. Multi-Criteria FUCOM—Fuzzy MABAC Model for the Selection of Location for Construction of Single-Span Bailey Bridge. *Decis. Mak. Appl. Manag. Eng.* **2019**, *2*, 132–146. [CrossRef]
53. Agarwal, S.; Kant, R.; Shankar, R. Evaluating Solutions to Overcome Humanitarian Supply Chain Management Barriers: A Hybrid Fuzzy SWARA—Fuzzy WASPAS Approach. *Int. J. Disaster Risk Reduct.* **2020**, *51*, 101838. [CrossRef]
54. Ecer, F.; Pamucar, D. Sustainable Supplier Selection: A Novel Integrated Fuzzy Best Worst Method (F-BWM) and Fuzzy CoCoSo with Bonferroni (CoCoSo'B) Multi-Criteria Model. *J. Clean. Prod.* **2020**, *266*, 121981. [CrossRef]
55. Roszkowska, E.; Kacprzak, D. The Fuzzy Saw and Fuzzy TOPSIS Procedures Based on Ordered Fuzzy Numbers. *Inf. Sci. N. Y.* **2016**, *369*, 564–584. [CrossRef]

energies

MDPI

Article

Battery Energy Management System Using Edge-Driven Fuzzy Logic

Mustapha Habib [1,*], Elmar Bollin [2] and Qian Wang [1,3]

[1] Division of Building Technology and Design, Department of Civil and Architectural Engineering, KTH Royal Institute of Technology, 11428 Stockholm, Sweden; qianwang@kth.se
[2] Institute of Energy System Technology, Offenburg University of Applied Sciences, 77652 Offenburg, Germany; ebollin@hs-offenburg.de
[3] Uponor AB, Hackstavägen 1, 72132 Västerås, Sweden
* Correspondence: mushab@kth.se

Abstract: Building energy management systems (BEMSs), dedicated to sustainable buildings, may have additional duties, such as hosting efficient energy management systems (EMSs) algorithms. This duty can become crucial when operating renewable energy sources (RES) and eventual electric energy storage systems (ESSs). Sophisticated EMS approaches that aim to manage RES and ESSs in real time may need high computing capabilities that BEMSs typically cannot provide. This article addresses and validates a fuzzy logic-based EMS for the optimal management of photovoltaic (PV) systems with lead-acid ESSs using an edge computing technology. The proposed method is tested on a real smart grid prototype in comparison with a classical rule-based EMS for different weather conditions. The goal is to investigate the efficacy of islanding the building local network as a control command, along with ESS power control. The results show the implementation feasibility and performance of the fuzzy algorithm in the optimal management of ESSs in both operation modes: grid-connected and islanded modes.

Keywords: photovoltaic; electric battery; energy management system; fuzzy logic; edge computing

1. Introduction

Energy consumption in the global building sector has dramatically increased due to population growth and rapid urbanization. The global growth rate of electricity in buildings is about 2.5% per year, while the current global electricity use in the building sector is around 30% of the total final energy consumption and over 55% of the global electricity demand [1]. Accordingly, a significant rise in sustainable buildings has been noticed. Solar photovoltaics (PV) are among the most widely used renewable energy sources in buildings due to their zero operating noise and very low and ease-in maintenance [2,3]. However, PV systems heavily rely on energy storage systems (ESSs) to overcome their irregular power production nature. The most commonly adopted ESSs are electro-chemical batteries, due to their impact on the overall building energy management system (EMS) performance [4].

The need for energy flexibility in sustainable buildings is highly needed to reach an optimal power share between different distributed energy systems (DERs) in different operation conditions [5]. PV systems typically generate power according to the Maximum Power Point Tracking (MPPT) algorithm, which is usually implemented on all commercial PV inverters. Except for the curtailment function, PV inverters are commonly not controllable, and their operation point depends solely on weather conditions. In contrast to PV, ESSs can add high flexibility to the building local network. This may serve to provide a load peak shaving function [6] or primary frequency regulation function [7] or both [8]. ESSs can be integrated into the DC bus along with the PV system; in this case, the exchanged ESS power depends solely on the DC voltage regulation. However, AC-linked architecture has recently been preferred by many manufacturers due to some advantages, such as the ability to control the ESS independently from the PV system and to participate in grid frequency regulation [9]. In a residential building, the power demand side is mainly linked to the AC side of the energy hybrid system, with which the grid utility is also associated. A typical scenario is that the algebraic difference between PV generation and power demand is to be covered by a power combination of the ESS and the grid utility. In island mode, the ESS works as an energy buffer, trying to recover the PV surplus power, or as a secondary power source in higher peak demands; in this case, ESS is no longer controllable and can only be disconnected as a protection action in case of overcharging or over-discharging scenarios.

When it comes to EMS implementation, BEMS low-level controllers, such as programmable logic controllers (PLC), can host basic algorithms based on IF-THEN statements. Those algorithms operate the energy system based on predefined conditions. Such methods may not be able to drive the hybrid energy system optimally, as the control setpoints are selected manually. Recently, novel BEMS architectures have been aiming to push building owners or facility managers away from manually determining the different operational setpoints and give this mission to a higher supervisory layer, either using edge computing [10] or cloud computing technologies [11].

Fuzzy logic (FL) is a computing technique that can deal with information arising from computational perception and cognition, that is, information that is uncertain, imprecise, vague, partially true, or without sharp boundaries [12]. In energy management, the power of FL is its ability to act as an online decision-making tool that covers an infinity of operation conditions, e.g., whether the battery should be charged or discharged at a certain condition and at what rate. In this regard, fuzzy set theory offers a good resolution as a mathematical approach designed to model the vagueness and imprecision of a human cognitive process. In the case of energy systems, various FL-based approaches have been proposed and validated [13]. An intelligent multi-objective EMS for a microgrid is proposed and simulated in [14], in which FL is responsible for battery operation scheduling. The proposed method accomplished 1.35% and 5.76% cost savings and 2.96% and 6.1% of lower emissions compared to the heuristic flowchart and the conventional opportunity charging approaches, respectively. A similar approach is suggested and validated in [15] for the management of stand-alone wind turbines, which are PV/hydrogen/ESS hybrid systems. A total cost savings of 13% was achieved over a control state-based EMS in simulation. It has been noted in previous works that all FL-based EMS approaches take actions on the controllable energy generators/buffers in real time, either in stand-alone or grid-connected modes separately. Up to now, no FL approach has been designed to deal with both operation modes simultaneously. It has also been noticed that the most common way to validate FL approaches, as an EMS, was in the digital simulation stage only [16,17]. The authors of [18] validated a similar method for the energy management of a PV/Diesel generator/ESS hybrid ship based on experimental data issued from a BEMS; however, no real implementation was carried out. Moreover, to date, integration into an existing BEMS has not yet been investigated or validated.

This article addresses and validates a systematic approach to implementing a fuzzy EMS into a BEMS using edge computing technology. Along with the ESS charging and discharging control, the proposed FL-based energy manager uses the connectivity to the main grid utility as an additional control action. Therefore, the implemented fuzzy rules are designed with regard to the system constraints associated with both operation modes: grid-connected and island modes. The proposed method is hosted on an edge device, which is a Windows Personal Computer (PC), with which the communication with the BEMS low-level controller was established using a serial communication protocol. The remainder of this paper is organized into three main sections: Section 2 describes the proposed FL algorithm for PV/ESS management. In Section 3, the experimental validation setup is clarified, while Section 4 provides some results and discussions.

2. Materials and Methods

The proposed EMS is based on continuously performing control actions each cycle time after taking new measurement data. PV power supply data are collected, via Modbus protocol, from the PV inverter; batteries' status data (SOC, voltage and current) and voltage/power data from DC and AC sides are collected with a similar protocol from the ESS inverter/charger, while power consumption data are collected from the energy meter. Collected data are stored in a local database after being processed by a PLC. Starting from this point, Sugeno fuzzy rules are responsible for finding out, in real time, the optimal values for the decision variables, which are the ESS current setpoint to be sent to the ESS inverter/charger and the connection/disconnection command to be sent to the main grid relay. A simplified diagram of the hybrid energy system, showing the role of the proposed EMS, is presented in Figure 1 (PLC and many other data processing auxiliaries are not displayed here for simplification).

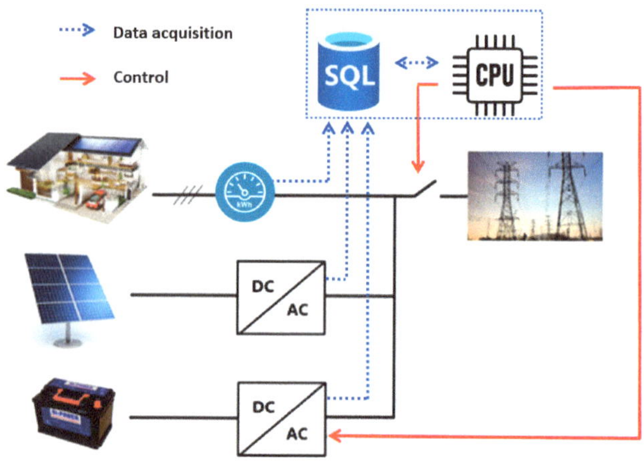

Figure 1. Power topology of AC-coupled ESS with the role of the energy manager.

2.1. Power Balance Equation

The power flow equation is formulated as below:

$$P_L = \eta_{PV} P_{PV} + \eta_B V_B I_B + \alpha P_g \tag{1}$$

where P_L is the electric load power; P_{PV} is the supplied PV power; V_B and I_B are the batteries bank voltage and current, respectively; P_g is the exchanged grid power; α is the grid relay ($\alpha \epsilon [0, 1]$); and η_{PV} and η_b are the efficiency of PV and the batteries bank system, respectively, including the power converters' efficiencies.

2.2. Battery State of Charge Equation

ESS SOC is a key parameter that should be supervised continuously, and it is determined with the equation formulated below:

$$SOC(t) = SOC(t_0) - 100.\frac{1}{C}\int I_B.dt \tag{2}$$

where *SOC*(*t*) is the actual battery SOC at time t in (%); *SOC*(t_0) is the initial SOC at time t_0 in (%); C is the battery nominal capacity in (Ah); and I_B is the battery charge/discharge current in (A), which is obtained using Equation (3).

$$I_B = \frac{P_B}{V_B} \tag{3}$$

where P_B is the algebraic value of the batteries' power. To reduce the algorithm complexity, V_B is chosen as constant all the time (48 V).

2.3. Fuzzy Logic Control Structure

As mentioned previously, the suggested FL energy manager uses real-time status data from the building local network to optimally adjust the power flow. In this article, three data inputs are required to build up optimal EMS decision variables:

- Algebraic difference between PV power supply and building power demand (ΔP).
- ESS SOC.
- Dynamic electricity price (EP).

With this control framework, the power flow in the network, the energy storage constraints, and the energy cost hare considered by taking an infinity of possible operation scenarios, which is the fundamental advantage of using the fuzzy logic approach in this study.

The structure of fuzzy logic signal processing stages is summarized in Figure 2. The purpose of fuzzification is to encode to precision input values into fuzzy linguistic values. The measurement values are always crisp in general. Therefore, they have to be translated to proper terms of the corresponding linguistic variables, and this process is called fuzzification or coding input. Fuzzy inference is a method that interprets the values in the input variables and, based on some set of rules, assigns values to the output. In fuzzy logic, the truth of any statement becomes a matter of a degree between 0 and 1. Defuzzification is the process of obtaining a single number from the output of the aggregated fuzzy set. It is used to transfer fuzzy inference results into a crisp output. In other words, defuzzification is realized by a decision-making algorithm that selects the best crisp value based on a fuzzy set.

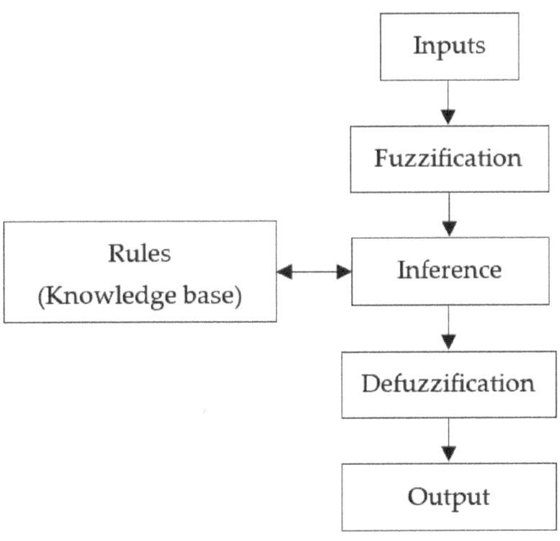

Figure 2. Fuzzy logic data processing steps.

Different triangle and trapezoidal membership functions are chosen to interpret the input variables. Based on the fuzzy rules, the controller can adjust the power flow in the building's local network using two parameters: the ESS current, which is controlled by the inverter/charging, and the external grid relay. Figure 3 shows a simplified structure of the proposed fuzzy controller, while Figure 4 displays the number and types of fuzzy membership functions of the input/output variables.

The fuzzy rules are designed for the following purposes:

- Decreasing the cost of energy imported from the grid utility taking into consideration the hourly electricity price.
- Maximizing the PV power share.
- Charging the batteries from the grid when the electricity price is low and from the excess PV power when it is high; the latter option is feasible by opening the external relay.
- Inject more power to the public grid when the electricity price is high.
- Keep SOC between the two upper and lower allowable limits.
- Maximize the use of PV power for load supply, especially when the power price is high.
- Operate the microgrid independently of the electrical grid as much as the system constraints allow.

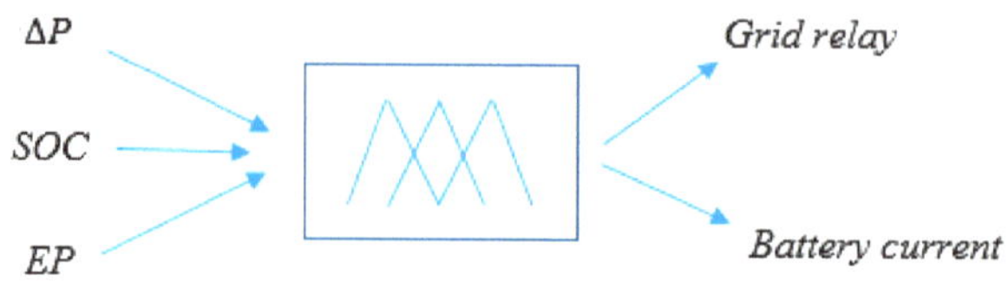

Figure 3. Figure 3. Proposed fuzzy energy manager.

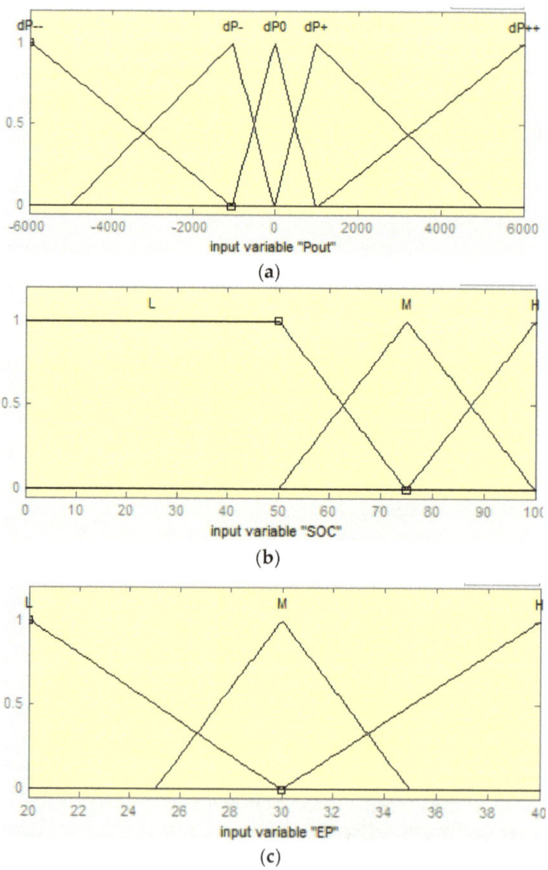

Figure 4. Membership functions of fuzzy controller inputs: (**a**) power difference Pout between PV supply and load (W), (**b**) ESS SOC level (%), and (**c**) electricity price EP (€/MWh).

In this context, 45 rules are created to manage and monitor the power flow in the building hybrid system, including 18 rules for ESS charging mode, 18 rules for grid feeding mode, and 9 rules for island mode, as listed in Appendix A (Table A1). Maximizing self-consumption is targeted because the energy selling prices are always lower than the purchasing ones; therefore, it is valuable to benefit from the local renewable energies rather than selling them to the grid utility owner. For this purpose, the microgrid islanding mode is mainly targeted. Physically, this is possible thanks to an electric relay called "grid external relay," which is already integrated in the ESS inverter/charger. This relay can connect the whole building's local network to the grid utility as well as disconnect it.

Indeed, islanding the building microgrid can lead to serious damages to the building's electric equipment in some situations, e.g., if a significant amount of extra PV power is locally supplied, this can lead to batteries overcharging in low power demand. Similarly, higher power demands cause an over-discharging scenario in the case of low PV supply. Luckily, power converter manufacturers for PV and battery systems are now taking these situations into consideration, i.e., the ESS inverter/charger is equipped with a frequency/voltage control mechanism that regulates the power fed to the local network according to the evolution of frequency and voltage at the connection point.

To show the FL energy manager response for different operation situations, Figure 5 displays the fuzzy surfaces generated based on the created rules and the variables membership functions. It is worth mentioning that the proposed FL energy manager cannot deliver exact Boolean values for the output R, which corresponds to the external grid relay command. Therefore, a rounding function is added at the corresponding output to fix this issue. The different command actions, which should be sent from the edge controller to the ESS inverter/charger using the FL algorithm, are displayed within the flowchart Figure A1 in Appendix B.

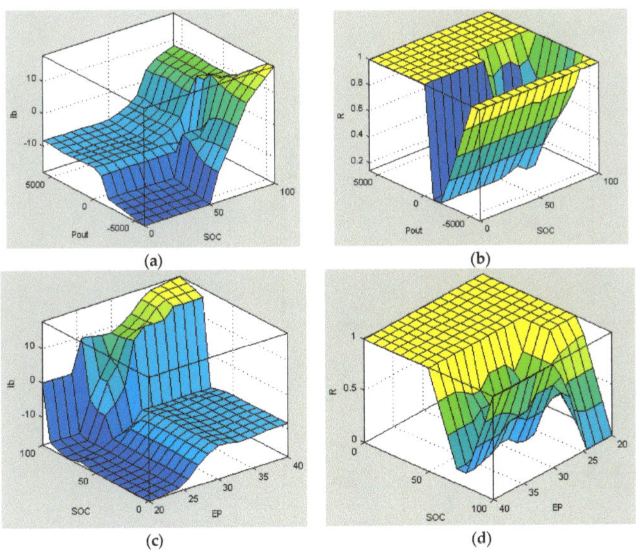

Figure 5. Fuzzy surfaces between inputs and outputs: (**a**) ESS current (Ib) as function of power difference (Pout) and SOC; (**b**) grid external relay (R) as a function of power difference (Pout) and SOC; (**c**) ESS current (Ib) as a function of SOC and electricity price (EP); and (**d**) grid external relay (R) as a function of SOC and electricity price (EP).

2.4. Constraints

The ESS operation limits are highly crucial when designing the fuzzy rules; in this context, two important parameters are to be considered when performing the control: the maximum operational power of the inverter/charger and the upper/lower limits of SOC, which are formulated in (4) and (5), respectively.

$$-P_{\max} \leq \eta_B P_B \leq P_{\max} \quad (4)$$

$$SOC_{\min} \leq SOC(t) - 100.\frac{P_B \Delta t}{V_B C} \leq SOC_{\max} \quad (5)$$

where $P_{\max}$ s the maximum allowed power supported by the ESS inverter/charger; SOC_{min} and SOC_{max} are the predefined minimum and maximum limits of ESS SOC, respectively; and ΔT is the cycling control time.

Note that, in island mode, the fuzzy controller is no longer able to control ESS current; in this case, the ESS operational point depends solely on the power balance in the local microgrid between PV generation and power demands. However, in island mode, the ESS current should be kept supervised during the cycling control time ΔT to satisfy the constraints in (4) and (5).

2.5. Baseline Method (Rule-Based EMS)

Rule-based EMS is a simple method that offers a real-time evaluation of the energy system's performance using pre-defined conditions (rules). In this study, a rule-based ESS management system based on real-time evaluation of SOC is developed. It defines the operation mode of the hybrid system according to the SOC level. The island mode is active only if the ESS constraints, formulated in (4) and (5), are satisfied. The flowchart of the proposed rule-based EMS is shown in Figure 6.

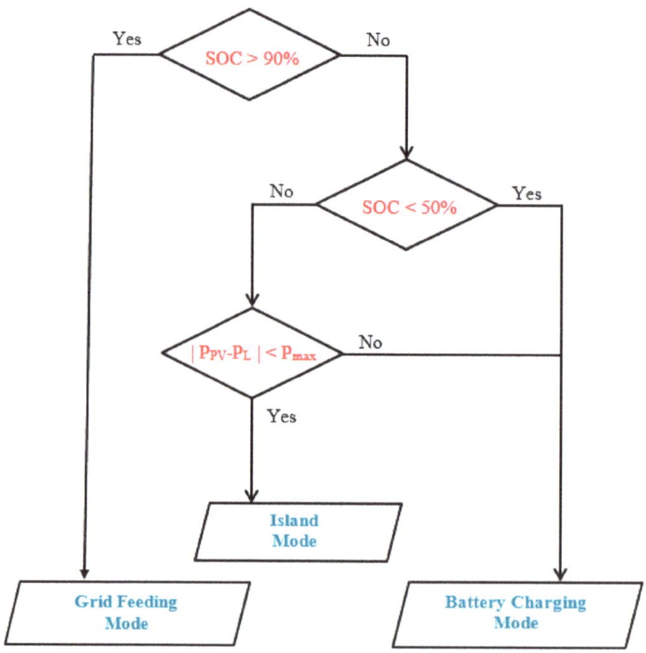

Figure 6. Rule-based EMS flowchart.

Rule-based EMS is an efficient approach when it comes to cost-effective implementation. The rules are designed to focus mainly on ESS SOC variation. Operating ESS between predefined upper and lower limits offers various advantages. The lower limit protects ESS from deep undercharging scenarios, which increases the batteries' life, and it also offers an energy backup in case any unexpected energy needs occur. The upper limit is to protect the batteries from overcharging issues, such as corrosion on the positive plates and excessive temperatures; the upper limit also ensures the energy recovery capacity of any sudden extra PV supply, particularly in island mode. The control commands used to ensure the targeted performance are the same as those used in the previous FL approach (external grid relay and ESS current). Rule-based methods can be performed online without requiring much computing time, which makes them suitable for real-time EMS.

3. Validation System Description

In this section, more details about the experimental setup and the implementation steps are given. The tests were carried out on the smart grid prototype of the Institute of Energy Systems Technologies (INES) at Offenburg University. This prototype makes it possible to demonstrate control and management policies using real industrial hardware, which makes the results replicable in any other application.

3.1. System Components

The experimental setup consists of three single-phase STUDER XTM 4000-48 Xtender inverter/charger devices in parallel to form a three-phase converter. This latter will control the exchange of power between 4.5 KW lead-acid batteries and the local building microgrid. The inverter/charger can also connect the whole hybrid system to the grid utility, or it can disconnect it to operate it as an island microgrid, as explained previously. The 6.3 KWp PV system is connected to the AC bus of the local network via three Sunny Boy 2500 HF inverters; these inverters are controlled to supply the maximum available power. The different system parameters are listed in Table 1.

Table 1. Hybrid System Parameters.

Component	Subcomponent	Parameter	Value
PV system	PV module	Power at MPP	240 Wp
		Voltage at MPP	30.0 V
		Current at MPP	8.1 A
		Open-circuit voltage	37.4 V
		Short-circuit current	8.6 A
		Temperature coefficient	−0.46%/K
		Module model	Bosch solar module c-Si M 60
	PV power plant	Number of modules	27
		Inclination	9 × 35° 18 × 30°
		Alignment	180° south
		Power	6.3 KWp
Batteries' system	Battery cell	Voltage	4 V
		Nominal capacity	546 Ah
		Battery model	Rolls Battery 4CS17P
	Batteries' bank	Number of cells in series	12
		Number of cells in parallel	1
		Power	4.5 KW
Programmable load	-	Nominal power	3.6 KW
		Load mode	Constant power
		Control mode	Remote
		Model	Chroma 63,803

ESS SOC data feedback is essential for the EMS algorithm; data are measured permanently via a battery status processor (BSP) device that offers real-time measurements of all battery parameters (SOC, voltage, current, and temperature). PV and load powers are other required signals that are collected via transmitters and treated by means of BECKHOFF CX2040 PLC. To simulate a residential building's power demand, three CHROMA 63,803 programmable loads are connected to the local network to form a three-phase load system. Those loads are controlled, remotely, to follow a real residential building power demand profile. All data are stored in real time in a local database. PLC communicates also with Labview software, version 14.0.0, which serves as a Human–Machine Interface (HMI) system, via Open Platform Communications United Architecture (OPC UA) to provide real-time data visualization and a user–system interaction tool.

The system was initially designed so the ESS current setpoint is to be generated continuously by PLC using a classical IF-THEN EMS algorithm (rule-based). Since our target is to apply a FL-based EMS, as explained earlier, a Windows PC, serving as an edge device, is responsible on generating the ESS current setpoint using a MATLAB code as a high-level programming language. At each cycle time, the system status data are queried from the database using MATLAB and Structured Query Language (SQL). Here, the FL algorithm can take over and map the system input data to the optimal outputs. In this case, PLC is bypassed when performing the control, and the edge device directly controls the ESS inverter/charger using a specific communication protocol called "Xtender Serial Protocol". For this purpose, Xcom-232i is needed as a communication module. The corresponding control parameter to be written (ESS current) is defined in the Remote Control Center RCC-02, which has a direct control action on the inverter/charger. The complete experimental system is represented in Figure 7. This process is being repeated continuously each control cycle time until the algorithm-stopping criteria are reached. Regarding the system dynamics, the chosen cycling time for the experiments is fixed at 10 min.

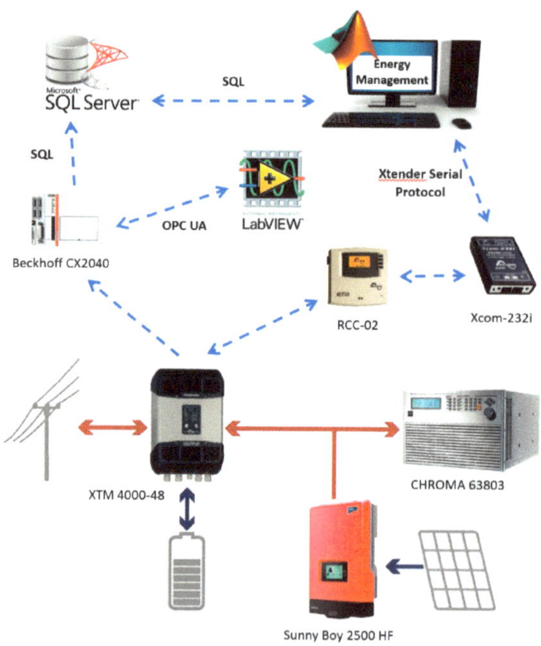

Figure 7. Experimental setup.

3.2. PC—Xtender Communication Protocol

The Xtender Serial Protocol is the communication path between Xcom-232i and the edge device (PC), which acts as a master, and the ESS power converter, which acts as a slave device. This protocol is highly similar to the industrial Modbus RTU; it consists of exchanging data frames composed of a header of 14 bytes, followed by a variable number of data bytes and 2 bytes of checksum. To facilitate the implementation of the protocol, a command line tool is used to communicate directly with the RCC-02, via Xcom-232i. As an example, to force the batteries to be charged with 12 A, the following command line statement can be built using the Windows command prompt:

>scom.exe –port=COM3 –verbose=3 write_property src_addr=1 dst_addr=101 object_type=2 object_id=1138 property_id=5 format=FLOAT value=12.0

Where write_property is the "Write" function; dst_addr = 101 is the device destination address, in this case, 101 for Xtender inverter/charger; object_id = 1138 is the "charging current" parameter ID; and value = 12.0 is the charging current value in Ampere.

To not overstate the content of this article, more information on the structure of the command lines, and on Xtender Serial Protocol in general, can be found in the documentation section of the manufacturer's website. Combining the command line tool with a high-level programming language, like MATLAB, facilitates the conception of advanced EMS algorithms by simply calling predefined functions, such as "evalfis" for the Sugeno fuzzy inference system.

One advantage of the fuzzy EMS is that it can be considered as an online control procedure, i.e., the system status data evaluation and control actions are performed in real time. Therefore, no significant calculation time is needed. This makes it a very suitable approach when the computational efficacy is targeted. However, the time delay related to the data acquisition through industrial communication protocols, like the one explained earlier, may not be negligible!

4. Results and Discussion

In this section, the performance of the proposed FL algorithm within the framework of edge computing is evaluated. As a baseline method, a simple rule-based EMS is developed and validated. For both EMS methods, the test is to be completed in 8 h, starting at 10:00 a.m. on two clear-sky days. The maximum allowed power for the inverter/charger is fixed to 4 KW, while the upper and lower ESS SOC limits are fixed at 90% and 50%, respectively.

4.1. Rule-Based EMS Test

Based on the testing day specifications, the control commands are defined as shown in Figure 8. The system operates accordingly in island and grid-connected modes. Although the ESS current setpoint, defined by the fuzzy management, is constant during the control cycling time (10 min), we see rapid current fluctuations in Figure 8a. This is due to the fact that the inverter/charger is designed to participate in the local grid voltage and frequency regulation by continuously adjusting the power fed to the grid. Nevertheless, those fluctuations are negligible compared to the constant setpoint defined by the energy manager.

As it was a sunny day, the amount of supplied PV power was relatively significant compared to the power demand (see Figure 9; therefore, the energy manager aims to keep SOC below the upper limit by connecting a hybrid system to the grid to feed extra power. When SOC is turned back inside the tolerated zone, the energy manager operates the system in island mode again, as this is the preferred operation mode. During the test, ESS SOC crossed the upper limit several times, as shown in Figure 10; this is due to the fact that the energy manager is totally offline during the cycling time (10 min). The control actions, in this case, are being updated only after the end of each cycle. To protect the batteries from overcharging scenarios, the energy manager feeds extra power to the grid with different AC currents, as shown in Figure 11. Despite the fact that, initially, one back deeding current was fixed in rule-based EMS (~6 A), the ESS inverter/charger bypassed the sent current setpoint for frequency/voltage regulation considerations, as they are prioritized over any EMS commands.

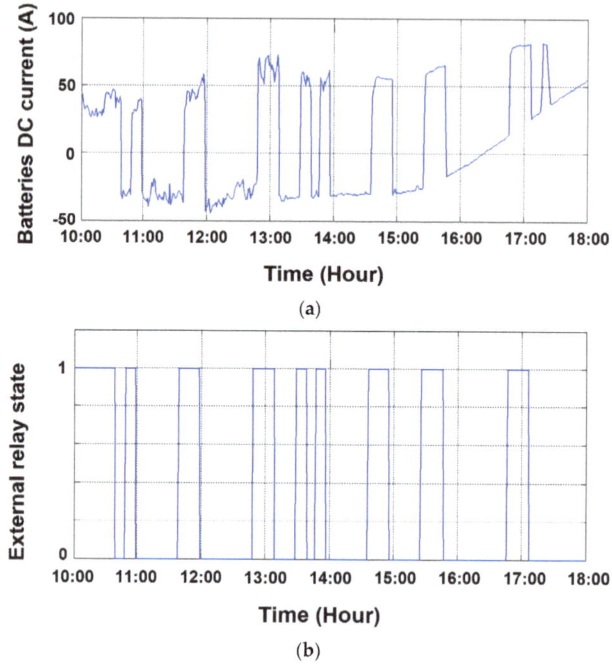

Figure 8. Rule-based EMS: (**a**) ESS DC current and (**b**) grid relay.

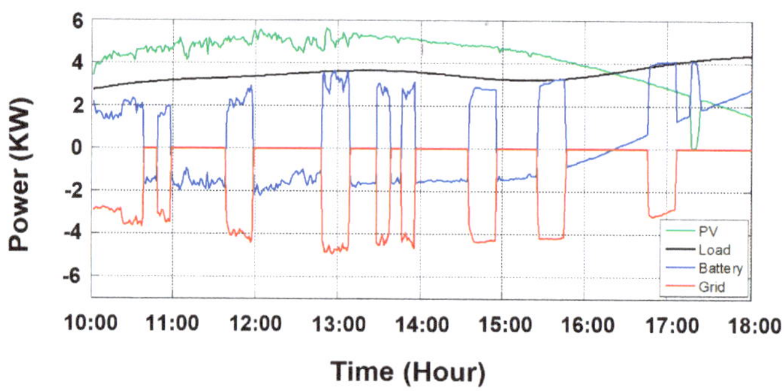

Figure 9. Rule-based EMS: power management of the hybrid system.

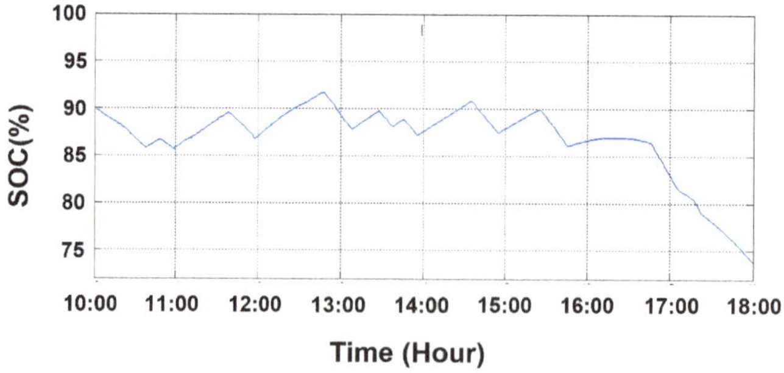

Figure 10. Rule-based EMS: ESS SOC.

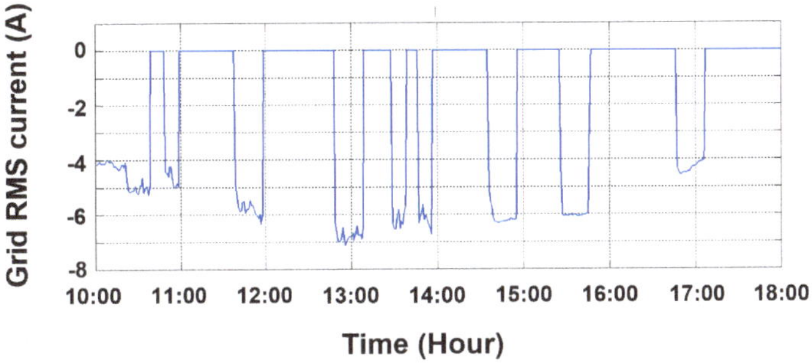

Figure 11. Rule-based EMS: grid RMS current.

4.2. *Fuzzy-Based EMS Test*

In contrast to rule-based EMS, fuzzy EMS integrates the dynamic electricity price as an additional input. During the test, the electricity price information was fetched online 24 h ahead thanks to an online service (nordpoolgroup.com) via the Application Programming Interface (API) (see Figure 12). Control commands generated during the test are displayed in Figure 13. The current fluctuations are due to the frequency/voltage regulation mechanism explained previously. Figure 13b shows that the grid-connected operation mode was mostly applied due to the fact that it was a partially cloudy day. In this operation condition, the supplied PV power is mostly less than the power demand (see Figure 14), which requires the connection of the grid as a secondary energy source. The grid-connected mode was also applied for SOC regulation and electricity price variation, which is going to be explained subsequently.

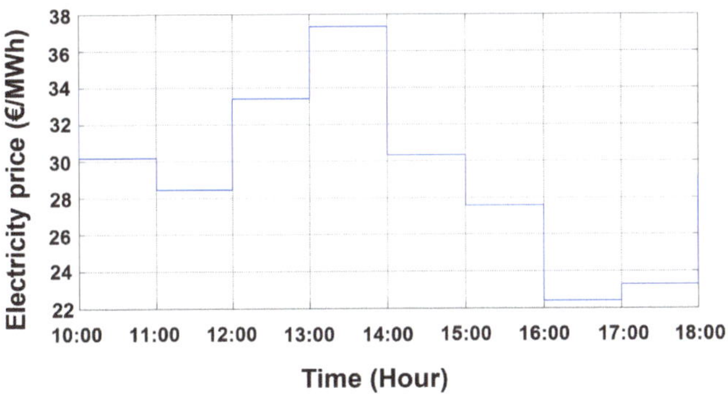

Figure 12. Electricity price hourly profile during the test period.

4.2.1. Partially Cloudy Day Test

The test outcomes presented in this section were obtained during a partially cloudy day, which is reflected in the supplied PV power level. After the test was completed, the graphs below were created based on the data fetched from the automation system database.

Despite the fact that the system constraints, formulated in (4) and (5), were respected during the 8 h test, the FL energy manager kept the hybrid system connected to the grid continuously when the electricity is not high. The reason for this is that the developed fuzzy rules aim to operate ESS with SOC values around 75% (see Figure 15). Moreover, since it was a partially cloudy day, the supplied PV power was lower than the power demand, which explains the currents imported from the grid (see Figure 16). Islanding the building microgrid in this situation may lead to excess ESS discharge scenarios. However, short islanding times are applied, mainly when the electricity price is high. In this situation, the power demand is satisfied by a combination of PV/ESS. In contrast to rule-based EMS, as validated previously, SOC control in fuzzy EMS is relatively smoother due to the infinity of situations considered during the fuzzification process.

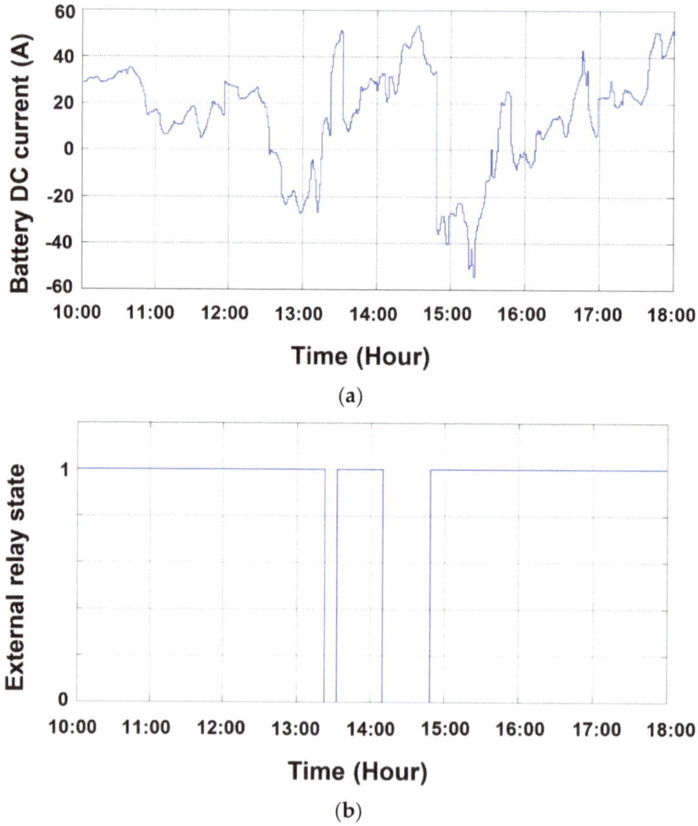

Figure 13. Fuzzy-based EMS in cloudy day: (**a**) ESS DC current and (**b**) grid relay.

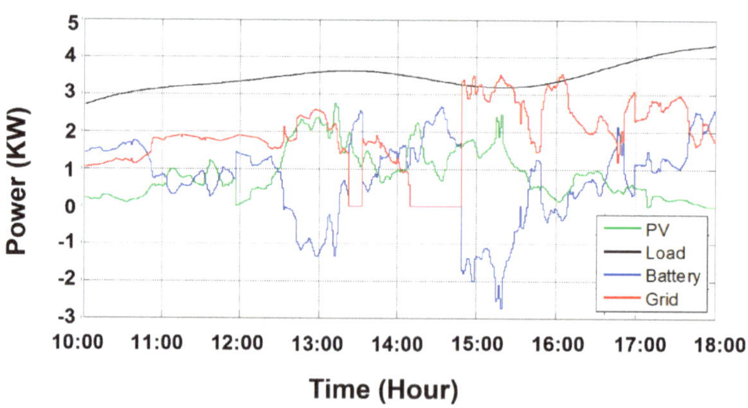

Figure 14. Fuzzy-based EMS in cloudy day: power management of the hybrid system.

In addition to the smooth control of SOC, the energy cost savings in fuzzy EMS are further targeted by the integration of the dynamic price of electricity. The fuzzy rules aim to increase self-consumption by profiting locally from the PV power produced. Since the electricity selling price to the grid utility is, generally speaking, much lower than the buying price, it is valuable to consume the PV power locally if the system constraints allow. Unlike the fuzzy EMS, the integration of supplementary rules into the rule-based EMS related to economic objectives makes it difficult to take into account all operational situations. This problem is naturally solved by the limitless number of possible use-cases covered by fuzzy membership functions.

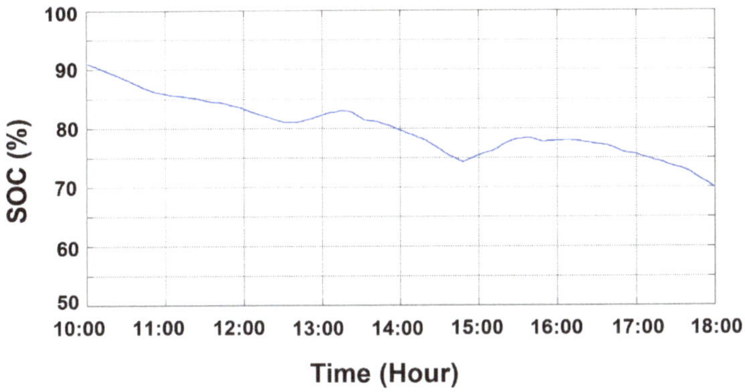

Figure 15. Fuzzy-based EMS in cloudy day: ESS SOC.

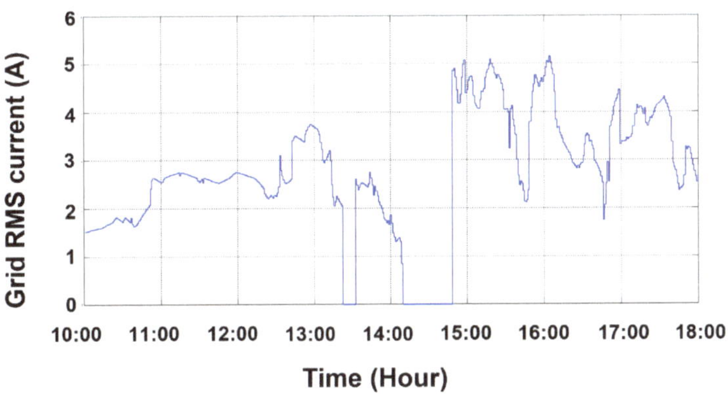

Figure 16. Fuzzy-based EMS in cloudy day: grid RMS current.

4.2.2. Sunny Day Test

In this test scenario, the day was mostly sunny, which is reflected in the supplied PV power. Therefore, PV power was generally higher than power demand with minor fluctuations (see Figure 17). This explains why SOC levels were varying around the upper limit (90%) during the first six hours, and why the fuzzy manager kept connecting the hybrid system to the grid for SOC regulation purposes (see Figure 18). However, SOC regulation in this case is relatively smoother compared to the case with the rule-based approach with similar weather conditions (see Figure 19). A significant drop in PV power supply was registered during the last two hours, which explains why the SOC was decreasing.

The drop in PV supply, during the last two hours, can also lead to ESS inverter/charger maximum power violation; therefore, the fuzzy energy manager connected the hybrid system to the grid as a preventive action to have additional support, which is reflected to the imported current shown in Figure 20 (the dashed red circle).

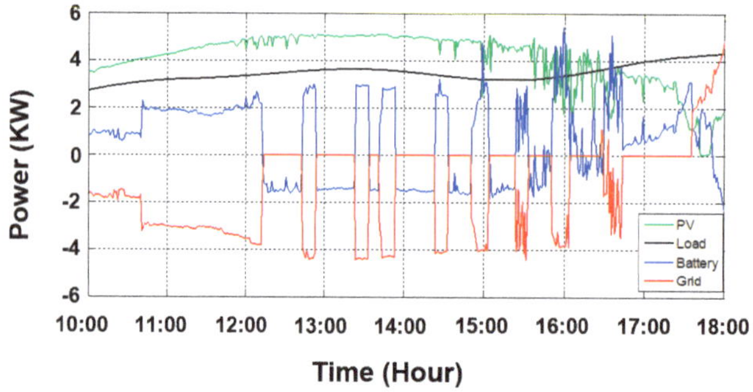

Figure 17. Fuzzy-based EMS in sunny day: power management of the hybrid system.

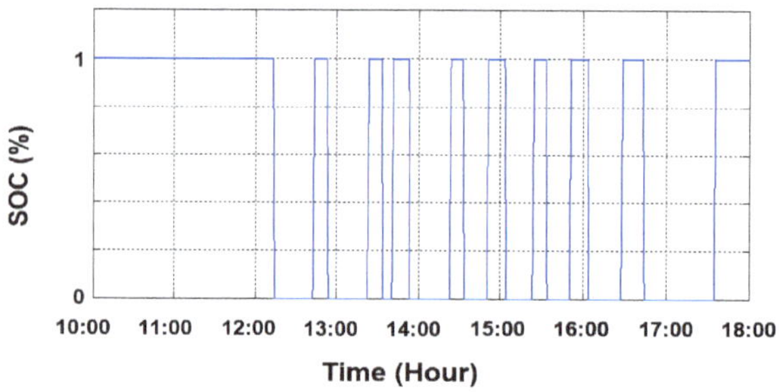

Figure 18. Fuzzy-based EMS in sunny day: grid relay.

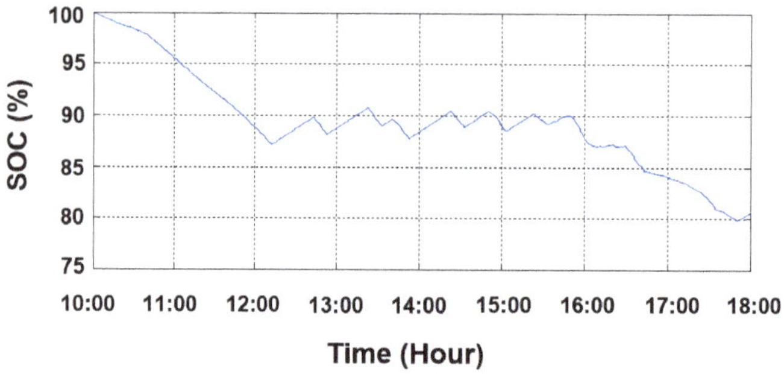

Figure 19. Fuzzy-based EMS in sunny day: ESS SOC.

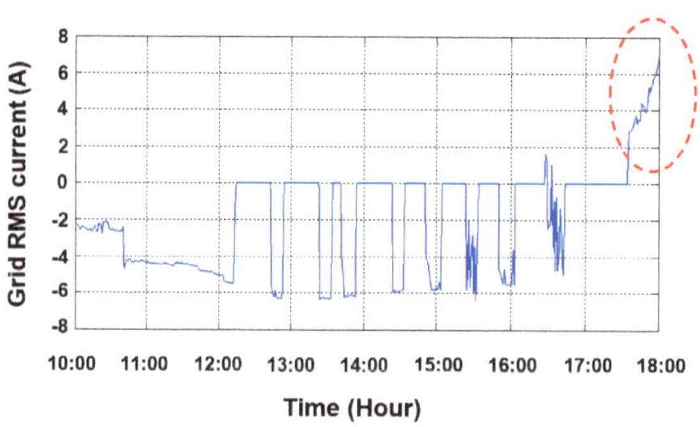

Figure 20. Fuzzy-based EMS in sunny day: grid RMS current.

5. Conclusions

This article addresses and validates an advanced edge-driven EMS approach. The technical feasibility of the implementation into an existing BEMS is mainly highlighted. For this, the fuzzy EMS algorithm was validated on two different climatic conditions. Thanks to the fuzzy data processing structure, an infinity of operation situations were considered during the control process. The efficacy of islanding the building microgrid as a control command was also demonstrated. The main features of the edge-driven fuzzy energy manager are as follows:

- An infinity of operation conditions can be considered during the evaluation of the system status data before performing control.
- Smooth control of ESS SOC.
- The ability to add various data inputs with less complexity compared to rule-based EMS approaches.
- Thanks to the edge communication interface, EMS commands can be sent via a low-level controller (PLC), which needs some additional software configurations, or directly to power converters without the need for any BEMS modifications. This last option is recommended only during the commissioning or test phase.
- Thanks to the high hardware resources of the edge device, a high-level programming language, combined with industrial communication protocols, makes it possible to implement advanced EMS algorithms in BEMS.

In future work, the edge-driven EMS is to be cascaded on top of an eventual Supervisory Control and Data Acquisition (SCADA) system. Within this architecture, edge-driven EMS will act as a management system that monitors an entire energy network including different DERs. The communication in this situation should be performed through the low-level control for more consistency and to take advantage of the security policies that have already been implemented.

Author Contributions: Conceptualization, M.H.; methodology, M.H.; software, M.H.; validation, M.H.; formal analysis, E.B. and Q.W.; investigation, E.B. and Q.W.; resources, E.B.; data curation, M.H.; writing—original draft preparation, M.H.; writing—review and editing, E.B. and Q.W.; visualization, M.H., E.B. and Q.W.; supervision, E.B.; funding acquisition, E.B. and Q.W. All authors have read and agreed to the published version of the manuscript.

Funding: This research was funded by Algerian Ministry of Higher Education and Scientific Research in the framework of national exceptional program. This research is also partially funded by EU H2020 program under Grant Agreement No. 101036656.

Data Availability Statement: Not applicable.

Conflicts of Interest: The authors declare no conflict of interest.

Appendix A

Table A1. Proposed fuzzy rules.

ΔP		dP++		dP+		dP0		dP–		dP– –	
EP-L	SOC–H	P+	R1	-	R0	-	R0	P+	R1	P+	R1
	SOC–M	P–	R1	P–	R1	P–	R1	P–	R1	P–	R1
	SOC–L	P– –	R1	P– –	R1	P– –	R1	P– –	R1	P– –	R1
EP-M	SOC–H	P+	R1	P+	R1	P+	R1	P+	R1	P++	R1
	SOC–M	P0	R1	P0	R1	-	R0	-	R0	P+	R1
	SOC–L	P–	R1	P–	R1	P–	R1	-	R0	P– –	R1
EL-H	SOC–H	P++	R1	P++	R1	P++	R1	P++	R1	P++	R1
	SOC–M	P+	R1	-	R0	-	R0	-	R0	P+	R1
	SOC–L	P–	R1	P–	R1	P–	R1	-	R0	P–	R1

Where EP-L, EP-M, and EL-H are the low, medium, and high values of the electricity price, respectively; SOC-L, SOC-M, and SOC-H are the low, medium, and high values of the batteries' SOC, respectively; dP++, dP+, dP0, dP−, and dP−− are the ordered values from a high positive power difference (P_{PV}-P_L) value to a high negative one, respectively. In Table A1, orange cells correspond to the grid feeding mode (ESS discharging) and blue ones correspond to ESS charging modes, while green ones correspond to island mode. Each cell is divided into two parts: the right one relates to the external relay status (R0: relay is opened; R1: relay is closed), while the left part is related to the ESS power reference, in which the values are ordered from the high negative value to high positive one according to the quantities P−−, P−, P0−, P+, and P++.

Appendix B

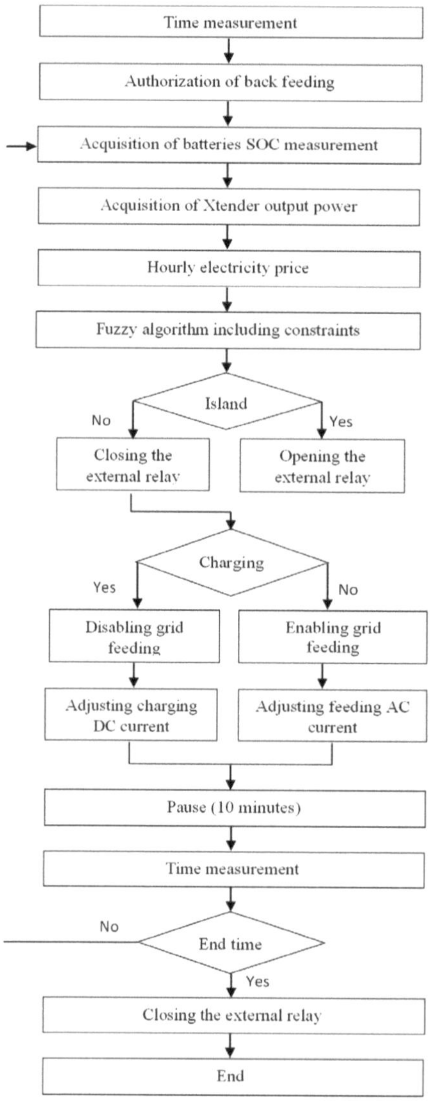

Figure A1. Flowchart of the fuzzy algorithm implementation.

References

1. International Energy Agency. *Energy Technology Perspectives 2012: Pathways to a Clean Energy System*; International Energy Agency: Paris, France, 2012.
2. Saadon, S.; Gaillard, L.; Giroux-Julien, S.; Menezo, C. Simulation study of a naturally-ventilated building integrated photovoltaic/thermal (BIPV/T) envelope. *Renew. Energy* **2016**, *87*, 517–531. [CrossRef]
3. Wang, W.L.; Liu, Y.S.; Wu, X.F.; Xu, Y.; Yu, W.Y.; Zhao, C.J.; Zhong, Y.B. Environmental assessments and economic performance of BAPV and BIPV systems in Shanghai. *Energy Build.* **2016**, *130*, 98–106. [CrossRef]
4. Qureshi, W.A.; Nair, N.-K.C.; Farid, M.M. Impact of energy storage in buildings on electricity demand side management. *Energy Convers. Manag.* **2011**, *52*, 2110–2120. [CrossRef]
5. Li, R.; Satchwell, A.J.; Finn, D.; Christensen, T.H.; Kummert, M.; Le Dréau, J.; Lopes, R.A.; Madsen, H.; Salom, J.; Henze, G.; et al. Ten questions concerning energy flexibility in buildings. *Build. Environ.* **2022**, *223*, 109461. [CrossRef]
6. Habib, M.; Ladjici, A.A.; Bollin, E.; Schmidt, M. One-day ahead predictive management ofbuilding hybrid power system improvingenergy cost and batteries lifetime. *IET Renew. Power Gener.* **2019**, *13*, 482–490. [CrossRef]
7. Habib, M.; Ladjici, A.A.; Khoucha, F. Frequency Control in Off-Grid Hybrid Diesel/PV/Battery Power System. In Proceedings of the International Conference on Electrical Engineering, Algiers, Algeria, 13–15 December 2015.
8. Habib, M.; Ladjici, A.A.; Harrag, A. Microgrid management using hybrid inverter fuzzy-based control. *Neural Comput. Applications* **2020**, *32*, 9093–9111. [CrossRef]
9. Long, B.; Jeong, T.W.; Lee, J.D.; Jung, Y.C.; Chong, K.T. Energy Management of a Hybrid AC–DC Micro-Grid Based on a Battery Testing System. *Energies* **2015**, *8*, 1181–1194. [CrossRef]
10. Ferrández-Pastor, F.-J.; Mora, H.; Jimeno-Morenilla, A.; Volckaert, B. Deployment of IoT Edge and Fog Computing Technologies to Develop Smart Building Services. *Sustainability* **2018**, *10*, 3832. [CrossRef]
11. Hashmi, S.A.; Ali, C.F.; Zafar, S. Internet of things and cloud computing-based energymanagement system for demand side managementin smart grid. *Int. J. Energy Res.* **2021**, *45*, 1007–1022. [CrossRef]
12. Singh, H.; Gupta, M.M.; Meitzler, T.; Hou, Z.-G.; Garg, K.K.; Solo, A.M.G.; Zadeh, L.A. Real-Life Applications of Fuzzy Logic. *Adv. Fuzzy Syst.* **2013**, *2013*, 581879. [CrossRef]
13. Suganthi, L.; Iniyan, S.; Samuel, A. Applications of fuzzy logic in renewable energy systems—A review. *Renew. Sustain. Energy Rev.* **2015**, *48*, 585–607. [CrossRef]
14. Chaouachi, A.; Kamel, R.M.; Andoulsi, R.; Nagasaka, K. Multiobjective Intelligent Energy Management for a Microgrid. *IEEE Trans. Ind. Electron.* **2013**, *60*, 1688–1699. [CrossRef]
15. Garcıa, P.; Torreglosa, J.P.; Fernandez, L.M.; Jurado, F. Optimal energy management system for stand-alone wind turbine/photovoltaic/hydrogen/battery hybrid system with supervisory control based on fuzzy logic. *Int. J. Hydrogen Energy* **2013**, *38*, 14146–14158. [CrossRef]
16. Abadlia, I.; Bahi, T.; Bouzeria, H. Energy management strategy based on fuzzy logic for compound RES/ESS used in stand-alone application. *Int. J. Hydrogen Energy* **2016**, *41*, 16705–16717. [CrossRef]
17. Al-Sakkaf, S.; Kassas, M.; Khalid, M.; Abido, M.A. An Energy Management System for Residential Autonomous DC Microgrid Using Optimized Fuzzy Logic Controller Considering Economic Dispatch. *Energies* **2019**, *12*, 1457. [CrossRef]
18. Yuan, Y.; Zhang, T.; Shen, B.; Yan, X.; Long, T. AFuzzyLogic Energy Management Strategy for a Photovoltaic/Diesel/Battery Hybrid Ship Based on Experimental Database. *Energies* **2018**, *11*, 2211. [CrossRef]

energies

Article

Algorithm for Energy Resource Selection Using Priority Degree-Based Aggregation Operators with Generalized Orthopair Fuzzy Information and Aczel–Alsina Aggregation Operators

Maria Akram [1], Kifayat Ullah [1,*], Goran Ćirović [2] and Dragan Pamucar [3]

[1] Department of Mathematics, Riphah International University, Lahore Campus, Lahore 54000, Pakistan
[2] Faculty of Technical Sciences, University of Novi Sad, Trg Dositeja Obradovica-6, 21000 Novi Sad, Serbia
[3] Department of Operations Research and Statistics, Faculty of Organizational Sciences, University of Belgrade, 11000 Belgrade, Serbia
* Correspondence: kifayat.khan.dr@gmail.com; Tel.: +92-334-9090225

Abstract: Many aggregation operators are studied to deal with multi-criteria group decision-making problems. Whenever information has two aspects, intuitionistic fuzzy sets and Pythagorean fuzzy sets are employed to handle the information. However, q-rung orthopair fuzzy sets are more flexible and suitable because they cover information widely. The current paper primarily focuses on the multi-criteria group decision-making technique based on prioritization and two robust aggregation operators based on Aczel–Alsina t-norm and t-conorm. This paper suggests two new aggregation operators based on q-rung orthopair fuzzy information and Aczel–Alsina t-norm and t-conorm, respectively. Firstly, novel q-rung orthopair fuzzy prioritized Aczel–Alsina averaging and q-rung orthopair fuzzy prioritized Aczel–Alsina geometric operators are proposed, involving priority weights of the information. Several related results of the proposed aggregation operators are investigated to see their diversity. A multi-criteria group decision-making algorithm based on newly established aggregation operators is developed, and a comprehensive numerical example for the selection of the most suitable energy resource is carried out. The proposed aggregation operators are compared with other operators to see some advantages of the proposed work. The proposed aggregation operators have a wider range for handling information, with priority degrees, and are based on novel Aczel–Alsina t-norm and t-conorm.

Keywords: prioritization; aggregation operators; Aczel–Alsina t-norm t-conorm; q-rung orthopair fuzzy sets; multi-criteria group decision making; energy resource management

1. Introduction

Multi-criteria group decision making (MCGDM) is a sophisticated approach in practical situations to deal with difficult and complex data. The MCGDM technique can provide scoring values for limited alternatives using the distinct characteristics of various possibilities. Uncertainty and imperfection are constant issues in real-world decision-making situations when one is examining data, especially large data. According to the notion of crisp sets, an object either belongs to a class or it does not. However, several phenomena in the real world cannot be presented on this scale. Zadeh [1] introduced the fuzzy set (FS) theory, where the membership grade (MG) is introduced to describe the belongingness of an element to a set.

The concept of FS is sometimes shown to be limited regarding its applicability. For example, whenever we have information about having two or more aspects, both of them are independent. To deal with such type of information, Atanassov [2] proposed the intuitionistic FS (IFS), a modified form of the FS that can accept complex and imprecise data with the help of an MG and a non-membership grade (NMG). The IFS theory has received lots of attention and has been used in various problems [3–5]. However, the IFS data set is constrained and depends on the irrational condition that the sum of MG and NMG must be contained within the unit interval, i.e., $[0, 1]$. To deal with complex and inaccurate information, Yager [6] proposed the concept of Pythagorean fuzzy sets (PyFS), a modified version of IFS. Similar to IFS, PyFS has a limited range and follows the condition that the sum of the squares of MG and NMG should lie within the interval $[0, 1]$. If the sum of the squares of the MG and NMG for a given Pythagorean fuzzy value (PyFV) becomes greater than the unit interval, for example, if MG is set at 0.5 and NMG is set as 0.9, then $(0.5, 0.9)$ cannot be considered as a PyFV. Yager [7] developed the q-rung orthopair fuzzy set (q-ROFS) to handle complex and uncertain conditions, including the abovementioned difficulty, to overcome this problem. A pair of MG and NMG requiring that the sum of the q powers of both of them should be within the unit interval is known as a q-ROF value (q-ROFV). The parameter q enables us to choose any MG and NMG from $[0, 1]$ as for every duplet (MG, NMG). we have a q, such that $0 \leq MG^q + NMG^q \leq 1$.

There are many applications of FSs and their generalizations, and one of the most widely discussed applications is MCGDM. To solve an MCGDM problem, we need some aggregation tools to give us collective preference value of information in decision making. A variety of aggregation operators (AOs) are very helpful in MCGDM approaches as mentioned in Table 1 below.

Table 1. Literature review concerning MCGDM problems.

Source	Results	Applications
Darko & Liang [8]	Hamacher Aggregation Operators	Mobile payment platform selection using EDAS method
Garg & Chen [9]	Neutrality-based Aggregation Operators	Selection of companies using neutrality AOs
Wei et al. [10]	Heronian mean Operators	MCGDM for enterprise resource planning system
Liu et al. [11]	Normalized bidirectional projection	Decision making with normalized bidirectional knowledge-based entropy measure
Garg & Rani [12]	Exponential AOs	Factors affecting the Indian stock exchange
Garg [13]	Trigonometric AOs	Decision maker preference toward the evaluation of the objects
Xia et al. [14]	Intuitionistic fuzzy AOs using Archimedean TN and TCN	Selection of manager by using Archimedean AOs
Wei & Zhao [15]	Induced interval-valued hesitant fuzzy AOs based on Einstein TN and TCN	MCGDM for technology commercialization
Seikh & Mandal [16]	q-ROF Frank Aggregation operators	Selection of government projects using MCGDM
Ali et al. [17]	Weighted interval-valued dual hesitant fuzzy AOs	Assessment of teaching quality using MCGDM
Liu et al. [18]	Complex q-ROF Muirhead mean operators	Analysis of investment policies using MCGDM
Aczél & Alsina [19]	AATN and AATCN	In this paper, novel Aczel–Alsina triangular norms are introduced

Table 1. *Cont.*

Source	Results	Applications
Senapati et al. [20]	Aczel–Alsina (A-A) AOs based on interval-valued intuitionistic fuzzy	Selection of research scientist using MCGDM
Hussain et al. [21]	PyF Aczel–Alsina AOs	Human resource management in multinational companies
Khan et al. [22]	q-ROF Aczel–Alsina AOs	Green supplier selection using MCGDM
Senapati [23]	Aczel–Alsina AOs with picture fuzzy information	Policy management using MCGDM
Hussain et al. [24]	T-spherical fuzzy AOs based on AATN and AATCN	Assessments of project based on AOs of TSF information
Ahmmad et al. [25]	Intuitionistic Fuzzy Rough Aczel–Alsina Average Aggregation Operators	Medical diagnosis based on AATN and AATCN
Ali & Naeem [26]	Complex Q-Rung Orthopair Fuzzy Aczel–Alsina Aggregation Operators	Analysis of factors effecting Pakistan stock exchange

Various circumstances that frequently happen in daily life require the application of a mathematical function that may reduce a collection of numbers into a single number. The examination of AOs has a big impact on MCGDM issues. In recent years, many researchers have concentrated on how to aggregate data because of their extensive application in various sectors. However, there are many situations where the data that need to be aggregated have a strict relationship in prioritizing. Assume a scenario where we are choosing a motorcycle for our child based on price and security considerations. In this case, we cannot permit an expense to fix a safety-related loss. Therefore, the criteria are the types that are prioritized. The priority is more for security. Choosing between different priority orders to determine priority degrees expands the scope of the prioritized operators. To deal with MCGDM problems, several prioritized AOs have been investigated in various real-life fields. The concept of prioritized AOs was first proposed by Yager [27,28]. Later, this concept was further extended to many fuzzy frameworks, and Yan et al. [29] discussed prioritized weighted AOs for MCGDM. Chen [30] developed the conception of prioritized AOs in the Atanassov intuitionistic fuzzy environment. Arora and Garg [31] discussed the significance of prioritized AOs using intuitionistic fuzzy soft sets. Some other recent work on prioritization-based AOs in several fuzzy settings can be seen in [32–36].

As discussed earlier, MCGDM algorithms and techniques have been used to deal with several real-life and energy-related problems. Akram et al. [37] investigated the applications of interval-valued T-spherical fuzzy Bonferroni means for selecting solar cells based on the MCGDM algorithm. Baumann et al. [38] presented a systematic review of energy storage systems for grid applications using the techniques and algorithms of MCGDM. The problem of offshore wind farm site selection was analyzed by Deveci et al. [39] based on the CoCoSo method and q-ROF information. Haiyun et al. [40] analyzed some strategies in the energy industry for Green Supply Chain Management using intuitionistic fuzzy details based on the QFD-based hybrid decision approach. Naseem et al. [41] studied some power Maclaurin symmetric mean operators to study their application in the assessment of smart grids for electricity. Some more recent work on the theory and application of MCGDM approaches on energy systems can be found in [42–45].

Previously, Senapati et al. [20] proposed Aczel–Alsina AOs for IFSs, and Hussain et al. [21] proposed Aczel–Alsina AOs for PyFSs. These AOs deal with uncertain information, but there are certain restrictions on them. Khan et al. [22] proposed improved AOs with a larger range using q-rung orthopair fuzzy details. However, these discussed AOs do not consider prioritization to be a critical factor in decision-making problems. Farahbod and Eftekhari [46] have shown the significance of using Aczel–Alsina t-norm and t-conorm with the help of a classification problem. Due to the significance of Aczel–Alsina AOs, prioritization, and the diverse nature of q-ROF information, this paper aims to develop the theory of prioritized AOs based on q-ROF information and Aczel–Alsina t-norm (AATN) and Aczel–Alsina t-Conorm (AATCN). The novelty of the proposed approach is based on the following facts:

1. AATN and AATCN generalize other triangular norms and provide more accuracy, as suggested by [46].
2. The framework of q-ROFS provides a wide range for describing uncertain information with no limitations.
3. To solve the energy-related problems, prioritization phenomena are associated with the proposed AOs.

The structure of this article is as follows: The core concepts of AATN and AATCN and q-ROFPSs are presented in Section 1. Aczel–Alsina operational laws for q-ROFPVs are described in Section 2. In Section 3, q-ROFPAAA and q-ROFPAAG operators are proposed, and some of their desirable characteristics and exceptional cases are demonstrated. Section 4 constructs an MCGDM framework for handling the problem of energy resource selection using q-ROFP information, where attributes experts are prioritized. An application of the proposed approach is demonstrated in a practical example in Section 5. Section 6 compares a variety of proven methods to show the effectiveness of the suggested method. The article is concluded in Section 7.

2. Preliminaries

To help readers understand the work, we recall the novel Aczel–Alsina t-norm, Aczel–Alsina t-norms, and some fundamentals of q-ROFSs in this section.

Definition 1. *Let X be any non-empty set. Then a q-ROFS T is dined as:*

$$T = \{(m_T(x), n_T(x))|x \in X\} \tag{1}$$

where $m_T : X \to [0,1]$ *and* $n_T : X \to [0,1]$ *denote the MG and NMG of* $x \in X$*,respectively, provided that* $0 \le m_T^q(x) + n_T^q(x) \le 1$*. Moreover, the term* $\widehat{\mathbf{r}}_T(x) = \left(\sqrt[q]{1 - \left(m_T^q(x) + n_T^q(x)\right)}\right)$*,* $\widehat{\mathbf{r}}_T(x) \in [0,1]$ *is considered to be a hesitancy degree, and* $(m_T(x),\ n_T(x))$ *is known as q-ROFV.*

Definition 2. *For any q-ROFV* $T = (m_T(x), n_T(x))$*, the scoreunction is defined as:*

$$\acute{S}c(T) = m_T^q(x) - n_T^q(x), \acute{S}c(T) \in [-1,1] \tag{2}$$

Definition 3. *The A-A TN and TCN are defined respectively as folls:* $\forall,\ 0 \le \text{ꞁ} \le +\infty$*:*

$$T_A^{\eta} = \begin{cases} T_D(a,b)\ if\ \eta = 0 \\ min(a,b)\ if\ \eta = \infty \\ e^{\left((-loga)^{\eta}+(-logb)^{\eta}\right)^{1/\eta}} \quad otherwise \end{cases} \quad and\ S_A^{\eta} = \begin{cases} S_D(a,b)\ if\ \eta = 0 \\ max(a,b)\ if\ \eta = \infty \\ 1 - e^{\left((-loga)^{\eta}+(-logb)^{\eta}\right)^{1/\eta}} \quad otherwise \end{cases}$$

In the next section, we aim to consider Aczel–Alsina AOs with prioritization degrees, which helps in modeling the opinion of experts.

3. q-Rung Orthopair Fuzzy Prioritized Aczel–Alsina Operators

This section contains some core concepts of q-ROFPAA operators based on A-A TN and A-A TCN. These AOs include averaging and geometric operators and involve the prioritization degree experts and attributes for decision-making problems. We also studied the fundamental features of proposed AOs.

Definition 4. *If we suppose* $T_j = \left(m_{T_j}(x), n_{T_j}(x)\right)$ *is the collection of q-ROFVs, where* $j = 1, 2, 3, \ldots, k$*, then, the q-ROFPAAA operator is defined as:*

$$q - ROFPAAA(T_1, T_2, \ldots, T_k) = \oplus_{j=1}^{k}\left(\frac{T_j}{\sum_{j=1}^{k} T_j}(T_j)\right) \tag{3}$$

Here, $\frac{T_j}{\sum_{j=1}^{k} T_j}$ *is the priority degree, which works as a weight of q-ROFV* T_j*. Based on the operational laws of the q-ROFVs, we obtain the succeeding theorem.*

Theorem 1. *If we suppose* $T_j = \left(m_{T_j}(x), n_{T_j}(x)\right)$ *is the collection of q-ROFVs, then, the q-ROFPAAA operator is given by:*

$$q - ROFPAAA(T_1, T_2, \ldots, T_k) = \left(\begin{array}{c} \sqrt[q]{1 - e^{-\left(\sum_{j=1}^{k}\left(\frac{T_j}{\sum_{j=1}^{n} T_j}\right)\left(-ln\left(1-m_{T_j}^{q}\right)\right)^{\eta}\right)^{\frac{1}{\eta}}}}, \\ e^{-\left(\sum_{j=1}^{k}\left(\frac{T_j}{\sum_{j=1}^{k} T_j}\right)\left(-ln\left(n_{T_j}\right)\right)^{\eta}\right)^{1/\eta}} \end{array}\right) \tag{4}$$

The proof is given in Appendix B.

In the following few theorems, we aim to discuss how q-ROFPAAA operators satisfy the basic characteristics of aggregation. These features include idempotency, monotonicity, and boundedness. Further, in the next sections, $j = 1, 2, 3, \ldots, k$ shall be used for indexing purposes.

Theorem 2. *Consider any number of q-ROFVs* $T_j = \left(m_{T_j}(x), n_{T_j}(x)\right)$*. If we let* $T_j = T = (m_T, n_T)$*, then*

$$q - ROFPAAA(T_1, T_2, \ldots, T_k) = T \tag{5}$$

Proof. Since

$$q - ROFPAAA(T_1, T_2, \ldots, T_k) = \left(\begin{array}{c} \sqrt[q]{1 - e^{-\left(\sum_{j=1}^{k} \frac{T_j}{\sum_{j=1}^{k} T_j}\left(-ln\left(1-m_{T_j}^{q}\right)\right)^{\eta}\right)^{\frac{1}{\eta}}}} \\ e^{-\left(\sum_{j=1}^{k} \frac{T_j}{\sum_{j=1}^{k} T_j}\left(-ln\left(n_{T_j}\right)\right)^{\eta}\right)^{1/\eta}} \end{array}\right) = (m_T, n_T) = T$$

□

Theorem 3. *Consider any number of q-ROFVs* $T_j = \left(m_{T_j}(x), n_{T_j}(x)\right)$*. If* $T^- = min(T_1, T_2, \ldots, T_k)$ *and* $T^+ = max(T_1, T_2, \ldots, T_k)$*, then,*

$$T^- \leq q - ROFPAAA(T_1, T_2, \ldots, T_k) \leq T^+ \tag{6}$$

For proof see Appendix C.

Theorem 4. *It we consider* $T_j = \left(m_{T_j}(x), n_{T_j}(x)\right)$ *and* $T_j' = \left(m_{T_j}'(x), n_{T_j}'(x)\right)$ *as the two collections of q-ROFVs. If* $T_j \leq T_j'$, *then*

$$q - ROFPAAA(T_1\ , T_2, T_3, \ldots, T_j) \leq q - ROFPAAA\left(T_1', T_2', T_3', \ldots, T_j'\right) \quad (7)$$

Proof. The proof is straightforward. □

Theorem 5. *Let* $T_j = \left(m_{T_j}(x), n_{T_j}(x)\right)$ *be a collection of q-ROFVs,* $T_j = \prod_{k=1}^{j-1} S(T_k)$. $T_1 = 1$ *and* $S(T_k)$ *are the scores of q-ROFVs* T_k. *If* $\beta = (a, b)$ *is a q-ROFV, then*

$$q - ROFPAAA(T_1 \oplus \beta, T_2 \oplus \beta, \ldots, T_j \oplus \beta) = q - ROFPAAA(T_1, T_2, \ldots, T_j) \oplus \beta \quad (8)$$

For proof see Appendix D.

Theorem 6. *Let* $T_j = \left(m_{T_j}(x), n_{T_j}(x)\right)$ *be a collection of q-ROFVs,* $T_j = \prod_{k=1}^{j-1} S(T_k)$. $T_j = 1$ *and* $S(T_k)$ *are the scores of q-ROFV* T_k. *If* $\varphi > 0$, *then:*

$$q - ROFPAAA(\varphi T_1, \varphi T_2, \ldots, \varphi T_j) = \varphi q - ROFPAAA(T_1, T_2, \ldots, T_j) \quad (9)$$

For proof see Appendix E.

Theorem 7. *Let* $T_j = \left(m_{T_j}(x), n_{T_j}(x)\right)$ $(j = 1, 2, 3, \ldots, k)$ *be a collection of q-ROFVs,* $T_j = \prod_{k=1}^{j-1} S(T_k)$. $T_j = 1$ *and* $S(T_k)$ *are the scores of q-ROFV* T_k *if* $\varphi > 0$, $\beta = (a, b)$ *is a q-ROFV, then*

$$q - ROFPAAA(\varphi T_1 \oplus \beta, \varphi T_2 \oplus \beta, \ldots, \varphi T_j \oplus \beta) = \varphi q - ROFPAAA(T_1, T_2, \ldots, T_j) \oplus \beta \quad (10)$$

Proof. Straightforward. □

Theorem 8. *Let* $T_j = \left(m_{T_j}(x), n_{T_j}(x)\right)$ *and* $\beta_j = \left(a_{T_j}(x), b_{T_j}(x)\right)$ $(j = 1, 2, 3, \ldots, k)$ *be two collection of q-ROFVs,* $T_j = \prod_{k=1}^{j-1} S(T_k)$. $T_1 = 1$ *and* $S(T_k)$ *are the scores of q-ROFV* T_k, *then:*

$$\begin{gathered} q - ROFPAAA(T_1 \oplus \beta_1, T_2 \oplus \beta_2, \ldots, T_k \oplus \beta_k) \\ = q - ROFPAAA(T_1, T_2, \ldots, T_k) \oplus q - ROFPAAA(\beta_1, \beta_2, \ldots, \beta_k) \end{gathered} \quad (11)$$

Proof. Similar. □

Definition 5. *If we suppose* $T_j = \left(m_{T_j}(x), n_{T_j}(x)\right)$ *is the collection of q-ROFVs where* $j = 1, 2, 3, \ldots, k$, *then, the q-ROFPAAG operator is defined as:*

$$q - ROFPAAA(T_1, T_2, \ldots, T_P) = \otimes_{j=1}^{k}\left((T_j)^{\frac{T_j}{\sum_{j=1}^{k} T_j}}\right) \quad (12)$$

Here, $\frac{T_j}{\sum_{j=1}^{k} T_j}$ *is the priority degree, which works as a weight of q-ROFV* T_j. *We obtain the succeeding theorem based on the operational laws of the q-ROFVs.*

Theorem 9. *If we suppose* $T_j = \left(m_{T_j}(x), n_{T_j}(x)\right)$ *is the collection of q-ROFVs, then, the q-ROFPAAG operator is given by:*

$$q - ROFPAAG(T_1, T_2, \ldots, T_k) = \left(\begin{array}{c} e^{-\left(\sum_{j=1}^{k}\left(\frac{T_j}{\sum_{j=1}^{k} T_j}\right)\left(-ln\left(m_{T_j}\right)\right)^{\eta}\right)^{\frac{1}{\eta}}}, \\ \sqrt[q]{1 - e^{-\left(\sum_{j=1}^{k}\left(\frac{T_j}{\sum_{j=1}^{k} T_j}\right)\left(-ln\left(1-n_{T_j}^{q}\right)\right)^{\eta}\right)^{1/\eta}}} \end{array} \right) \tag{13}$$

Proof. Similar to Theorem 1. □

Remark 1: *The q-ROFPAAG AOs satisfy the aggregation properties as stated in Theorems 2–4.*

Theorem 10. *Let* $T_j = \left(m_{T_j}(x), n_{T_j}(x)\right)$ *be a collection of q-ROFVs,* $T_j = \prod_{k=1}^{j-1} S(T_k)$. $T_1 = 1$ *and* $S(T_k)$ *are the scores of q-ROFVs* T_k. *If* $\beta = (a, b)$ *is a q-ROFV, then*

$$q - ROFPAAG(T_1 \otimes \beta, T_2 \otimes \beta, \ldots, T_k \otimes \beta) = q - ROFPAAG(T_1, T_2, \ldots, T_k) \otimes \beta \tag{14}$$

Proof. Straightforward. □

Theorem 11. *Let* $T_j = \left(m_{T_j}(x), n_{T_j}(x)\right)$ *be a collection of q-ROFVs,* $T_j = \prod_{k=1}^{j-1} S(T_k)$. $T_j = 1$ *and* $S(T_k)$ *are the scores of q-ROFV* T_k. *If* $\varphi > 0$, *then:*

$$q - ROFPAAG((T_1)^{\varphi}, (T_2)^{\varphi}, \ldots, (T_k)^{\varphi}) = (q - ROFPAAG(T_1, T_2, \ldots, T_k))^{\varphi} \tag{15}$$

Proof. Straightforward. □

Theorem 12. *Let* $T_j = \left(m_{T_j}(x), n_{T_j}(x)\right)$ *be a collection of q-ROFVs,* $T_j = \prod_{k=1}^{j-1} S(T_k)$. $T_j = 1$ *and* $S(T_k)$ *are the scores of q-ROFV* T_k, *if* $\varphi > 0$, $\beta = (a, b)$ *is a q-ROFV, then:*

$$q - ROFPAAG((T_1)^{\varphi} \otimes \beta, (T_2)^{\varphi} \otimes \beta, \ldots, (T_k)^{\varphi} \otimes \beta) = (q - ROFPAAG(T_1, T_2, \ldots, T_k))^{\varphi} \otimes \beta \tag{16}$$

Proof. Straightforward. □

Theorem 13. *Let* $T_j = \left(m_{T_j}(x), n_{T_j}(x)\right)$ *and* $\beta_j = \left(a_{T_j}(x), b_{T_j}(x)\right)$ *be two collections of q-ROFVs,* $T_j = \prod_{k=1}^{j-1} S(T_k)$. $T_1 = 1$ *and* $S(T_k)$ *are the scores of q-ROFV* T_k, *then:*

$$\begin{aligned} q - ROFPAAG(T_1 \otimes \beta_1, T_2 \otimes \beta_2, \ldots, T_k \otimes \beta_k) \\ = q - ROFPAAG(T_1, T_2, \ldots, T_k) \otimes q \\ -ROFPAAG(\beta_1, \beta_2, \ldots, \beta_k) \end{aligned} \tag{17}$$

Proof. Straightforward. □

4. Algorithm for Multi-Criteria Group Decision Making

This section utilizes the proposed AOs in an MCGDM in a q-ROF environment. In a group decision-making problem, suppose $\alpha = (\alpha_1, \alpha_2, \alpha_3, \ldots, \alpha_m)$ is the set of alternatives. Let $\beta = (\beta_1, \beta_2, \beta_3, \ldots, \beta_n)$ be a collection of criteria/attributes, and there is a prioritization between the criteria expressed by the linear ordering $\beta_1 > \beta_2 > \beta_3, \ldots > \beta_n$, which indicate criteria β_j has a higher priority, then β_i if $j < i$, and $\varepsilon = (\varepsilon_1, \varepsilon_2, \varepsilon_3, \ldots, \varepsilon_k)$ is the set of decision makers, and there is a prioritization between the decision makers expressed by the linear ordering $\varepsilon_1 > \varepsilon_2 > \varepsilon_3, \ldots > \varepsilon_k$, which indicates that expert ε_σ has a higher priority than expert e_τ if $\sigma < \tau$ does. Let $K^{(q)} = \left(k_{ij}^{q}\right)_{m\times n}$ be a q-ROF decision matrix and q-ROFV $k_{ij}^{(q)} = \left(m_{T_j}^{(q)}, n_{T_j}^{(q)}\right)$ is the information of the experts about the alternatives under given attributes, where $\left[m_{T_j}^{(q)}\right]$ indicates the degree range, and the alternative α_i satisfies the attribute β_j, and ε_q, $\left[n_{T_j}^{(q)}\right]$ indicates the degree range, and the alternative α_i does not satisfy the attribute β_j expressed by the decision maker ε_q, such that: $m_{T_j} \in [0,1]$, $n_{T_j} \in [0,1], 0 \le m_{T_j}^{(q)} + n_{T_j}^{(q)} \le 1$, $i = 1, 2, \ldots, m$.

If the criteria $\beta_j' s$ have same nature, the information is not necessarily normalized; otherwise $K^{(q)} = \left(k_{ij}^{(q)}\right)_{m\times n}$ into $R^{(q)} = \left(x_{ij}^{(q)}\right)_{m\times n}$ where:

$$x_{ij}^{(q)} = \begin{cases} k_{ij}^{(q)} & for\ benefit\ attribute\ \beta_j \\ \acute{k}_{ij}^{(q)} & for\ cost\ attribute\ \beta_j \end{cases}$$

where $\acute{k}_{ij}^{(q)}$ is the complement of $k_{ij}^{(q)}$, such that $\acute{k}_{ij}^{(q)} = \left(n_{T_j}^{(q)},\ m_{T_j}^{(q)}\right)$. The complete steps of the MCGDM algorithm are as follows:

Step 1: Formation of decision matrices using the information of experts in the form of q-ROFVs.

Step 2: Normalization of decision matrices (if needed).

Step 3: Calculate the value of $T_{ij}^{(q)}$, based on the following equations:

$$T_{ij}^{(q)} = \sqcap_{k=1}^{q-1} S\left(x_{ij}^{q}\right)(q = 2, \ldots, k),\ T_{ij}^{1} = 1$$

Step 4: Utilize the q-ROFPAAA or q-ROFPAAG operator, given below, to aggregate the individual preferences of the decision-makers and form a collective decision matrix.

$$x_{ij} = q - ROFPAAA\left(x_{ij}^{(1)}, x_{ij}^{(2)}, x_{ij}^{(3)}, \ldots, x_{ij}^{(k)}\right) = \left(\begin{bmatrix} \sqrt[q]{1 - e^{-\left(\sum_{j=1}^{k+1} \frac{T_j}{\sum_{j=1}^{n} T_j}(-ln\ (1 - m_{T_j}^{q}))^{\eta}\right)^{\frac{1}{\eta}}}} \\ e^{-\left(\sum_{j=1}^{k+1} \frac{T_j}{\sum_{j=1}^{n} T_j}(-ln(n_{T_j}))^{\eta}\right)^{1/\eta}} \end{bmatrix}\right)$$

Or the q-ROFPAAG operator:

$$x_{ij} = q - ROFPAAG\left(x_{ij}^{(1)}, x_{ij}^{(2)}, x_{ij}^{(3)}, \ldots, x_{ij}^{(k)}\right) = \left(\begin{bmatrix} e^{-\left(\sum_{j=1}^{k+1} \frac{T_j}{\sum_{j=1}^{n} T_j}(-ln(n_{T_j}))^{\eta}\right)^{\frac{1}{\eta}}}, \\ \sqrt[q]{1 - e^{-\left(\sum_{j=1}^{k+1} \frac{T_j}{\sum_{j=1}^{n} T_j}(-ln\ (1 - m_{T_j}^{q}))^{\eta}\right)^{\frac{1}{\eta}}}} \end{bmatrix}\right)$$

Step 5: Calculate the values of T_{ij} based on the following equations:

$$T_{ij} = \prod_{k=1}^{j-1} S(x_{ik}) \text{ where } i = 1, 2, \ldots, m,\ T_{1j} = 1.$$

Step 6: Aggregating the collective information against each x_{ij} for each alternative T_i by using q-ROFAAA (or q-ROFAAG) operator:

$$q - ROFPAAA(x_{i1}, x_{i2}, \ldots, x_{in}) = \left(\left[\sqrt[q]{1 - e^{-\left(\sum_{j=1}^{k+1} \frac{T_j}{\sum_{j=1}^{n} T_j} \left(-ln\left(1 - m_{T_j}^{q}\right)\right)^{\eta}\right)^{\frac{1}{\eta}}}}, e^{-\left(\sum_{j=1}^{k+1} \frac{T_j}{\sum_{j=1}^{n} T_j} \left(-ln\left(n_{T_j}\right)\right)^{\eta}\right)^{1/\eta}} \right] \right)$$

Or

$$q - ROFPAAG(x_{i1}, x_{i2}, \ldots, x_{in}) = \left(\left[e^{-\left(\sum_{j=1}^{k+1} \frac{T_j}{\sum_{j=1}^{n} T_j} \left(-ln\left(n_{T_j}\right)\right)^{\eta}\right)^{1/\eta}}, \sqrt[q]{1 - e^{-\left(\sum_{j=1}^{k+1} \frac{T_j}{\sum_{j=1}^{n} T_j} \left(-ln\left(1 - m_{T_j}^{q}\right)\right)^{\eta}\right)^{\frac{1}{\eta}}}} \right] \right)$$

Step 7: Rank all the alternatives by using the score function.

$$S(x) = \left(m_{T_j}\right)^q - \left(n_{T_j}\right)^q$$

5. Application

Energy is one of the most critical factors for achieving advancement and comfort in everyday life. Due to the improvement in living standards, population increase, and global economic growth, the energy demand has been steadily increasing over the years. But on the other hand, natural gas supplies are rapidly growing, raising the price of these resources. Water energy and thermal energy are also facing deficiencies. Managing energy resources in efficient power systems presents significant hurdles for today's decision makers. Determining the efficiency and reliability of energy systems is important. These systems are affected by several parameters, and due to the uncertainty in real-life situations, determining the efficiency of energy resource systems is challenging. As a result, it is essential to develop efficient and practical techniques for managing successful energy systems at various social and biological levels. Well-known and widely utilized techniques address various energy management and efficiency issues. When one is dealing with complicated, ambiguous, imprecise, and multi-objective challenges such as the management control of efficient energy, decision support systems are typically designed under fuzzy logic.

In the below example, we aim to analyze an energy resource selection problem, where we consider some energy resources and try to evaluate the most efficient resource among a finite list of energy sources. The main feature of this algorithm is that it involves the priority preference of the experts and attributes during decision-making problems. The prioritization allows us to take the expert's opinion about any energy resource, considering all the parameters that affect the energy resource's efficiency.

Example 1. *We define several criteria to include technical, economic, environmental, and social issues in the management of energy resources when one is comparing different energy resources selection. Four criteria are selected from the research for this purpose to evaluate energy sources using the MCGDM approach. The cost (C_1) criteria include all the expenses and costs associated with establishing the generation of energy, including those related to land, machinery, labor, installation, and infrastructure. The energy information management agency offered capital prices, as well as operations and maintenance expenses, for renewable energy technology alternatives. Energy cost (C_2) denotes the expected cost of the energy (electricity) a plant will obtain from renewable energy technology alternatives during its lifespan. Capacity (C_3) denotes how quickly a renewable energy system transforms its fundamental energy source into electricity. Resources that can be used to create power utilizing renewable energy technologies are represented by (C_4). The team of decision makers evaluates the four energy resources, where $\mathbf{X_1}$: coal; $\mathbf{X_2}$: petroleum; $\mathbf{X_3}$: natural gas; $\mathbf{X_4}$: wind energy; $\mathbf{X_5}$: solar energy, as given in* Figure 1.

Figure 1. Different energy resources.

Three experts evaluate these five energy resources under four attributes; the information is expressed as q-ROFVs in Step 1. The expert's evaluation of the energy resources is given in Tables 2–4*, respectively.*

Step 1: Formation of decision matrix.

Table 2. Expert e_1 about energy resources under the given criteria.

	C_1		C_2		C_3		C_4	
X_1	0.7	0.6	0.9	0.5	0.7	0.6	0.9	0.5
X_2	0.8	0.7	0.8	0.6	0.8	0.7	0.8	0.6
X_3	0.9	0.6	0.7	0.6	0.9	0.5	0.8	0.7
X_4	0.9	0.3	0.8	0.4	0.8	0.6	0.9	0.4
X_5	0.8	0.7	0.9	0.5	0.6	0.5	0.8	0.6

Table 3. Expert e_2 about energy resources under the given criteria.

	C_1		C_2		C_3		C_4	
X_1	0.9	0.6	0.8	0.4	0.9	0.5	0.9	0.4
X_2	0.8	0.4	0.9	0.6	0.8	0.7	0.8	0.5
X_3	0.8	0.7	0.7	0.5	0.7	0.6	0.7	0.6
X_4	0.8	0.6	0.9	0.6	0.8	0.6	0.8	0.6
X_5	0.9	0.5	0.7	0.5	0.9	0.3	0.9	0.5

Table 4. Expert e_3 about energy resources under the given criteria.

	C_1		C_2		C_3		C_4	
X_1	0.8	0.5	0.9	0.6	0.9	0.5	0.9	0.6
X_2	0.9	0.4	0.8	0.5	0.8	0.6	0.8	0.7
X_3	0.8	0.3	0.9	0.7	0.7	0.6	0.7	0.6
X_4	0.7	0.6	0.8	0.6	0.8	0.6	0.8	0.5
X_5	0.8	0.7	0.9	0.5	0.9	0.5	0.9	0.4

Step 2: In the current example, we have two attributes as cost attributes. To unify all the attributes, we normalize the decision matrices as follows in Tables 5–7, respectively.

Table 5. Expert e_1 about energy resources under given criteria (after normalization).

	C_1		C_2		C_3		C_4	
X_1	0.6	0.7	0.5	0.9	0.7	0.6	0.9	0.5
X_2	0.7	0.8	0.6	0.8	0.8	0.7	0.8	0.6
X_3	0.6	0.9	0.6	0.7	0.9	0.5	0.8	0.7
X_4	0.3	0.9	0.4	0.8	0.8	0.6	0.9	0.4
X_5	0.7	0.8	0.5	0.9	0.6	0.5	0.8	0.6

Table 6. Expert e_2 about energy resources under given criteria (after normalization).

	C_1		C_2		C_3		C_4	
X_1	0.6	0.9	0.4	0.8	0.9	0.5	0.9	0.4
X_2	0.4	0.8	0.6	0.9	0.8	0.7	0.8	0.5
X_3	0.7	0.8	0.5	0.7	0.7	0.6	0.7	0.6
X_4	0.6	0.8	0.6	0.9	0.8	0.6	0.8	0.6
X_5	0.5	0.9	0.5	0.7	0.9	0.3	0.9	0.5

Table 7. Expert e_3 about energy resources under given criteria (after normalization).

	C_1		C_2		C_3		C_4	
X_1	0.5	0.8	0.6	0.9	0.9	0.5	0.9	0.6
X_2	0.4	0.9	0.5	0.8	0.8	0.6	0.8	0.7
X_3	0.3	0.8	0.7	0.9	0.7	0.6	0.7	0.6
X_4	0.6	0.7	0.6	0.8	0.8	0.6	0.8	0.5
X_5	0.7	0.8	0.5	0.9	0.9	0.5	0.9	0.4

Step 3: Calculate the values of T_{ij}^1, T_{ij}^2, and T_{ij}^3 using Step 3 of the algorithm as follows.

$$T_{ij}^1 = \begin{pmatrix} 1 & 1 & 1 & 1 \\ 1 & 1 & 1 & 1 \\ 1 & 1 & 1 & 1 \\ 1 & 1 & 1 & 1 \\ 1 & 1 & 1 & 1 \end{pmatrix}$$

$$T_{ij}^2 = \begin{pmatrix} 0.127 & 0.604 & 0.127 & 0.604 \\ 0.169 & 0.296 & 0.169 & 0.296 \\ 0.513 & 0.127 & 0.604 & 0.169 \\ 0.702 & 0.448 & 0.296 & 0.665 \\ 0.169 & 0.604 & 0.091 & 0.296 \end{pmatrix}$$

$$T_{ij}^3 = \begin{pmatrix} 0.0651551 & 0.270592 & 0.076708 & 0.40166 \\ 0.075712 & 0.151848 & 0.028561 & 0.114552 \\ 0.086697 & 0.027686 & 0.076708 & 0.021463 \\ 0.207792 & 0.229824 & 0.087616 & 0.19684 \\ 0.102076 & 0.131672 & 0.063882 & 0.178784 \end{pmatrix}$$

Step 4: Utilize the q-ROFPAAA operator to aggregate the q-ROF decision matrix $R^q = \left(x_{ij}^q\right)_{4x5} (q = 1, 2, 3)$ into the collective q-ROF decision matrix $R = \left(x_{ij}\right)_{5x4}$, as given in Table 8.

Table 8. Collective preferences using q-ROFAAA of expert's information given in Tables 5–7.

	C_1		C_2		C_3		C_4	
X_1	0.6417	0.5941	0.8200	0.4777	0.6591	0.5818	0.8538	0.4849
X_2	0.7274	0.6271	0.7532	0.5886	0.7155	0.6974	0.7155	0.5848
X_3	0.8137	0.6072	0.5973	0.5903	0.7824	0.5383	0.6987	0.6829
X_4	0.7935	0.4174	0.7635	0.4712	0.7155	0.6000	0.8026	0.4734
X_5	0.7407	0.6694	0.7945	0.5000	0.5658	0.4803	0.7721	0.5507

Step 5: Calculate the values of $T_{ij}, (i = 1,2,\ldots m,\ j = 1,2,\ldots n)$ based on the equation given in Step 3 of the algorithm.

$$T_{ij} = \begin{pmatrix} 1 & 0.0546 & 0.0242 & 0.002 \\ 1 & 0.1383 & 0.0309 & 0.001 \\ 1 & 0.3150 & 0.0024 & 0.001 \\ 1 & 0.4268 & 0.1453 & 0.022 \\ 1 & 0.1065 & 0.0401 & 0.003 \end{pmatrix}$$

Step 6: Utilize the q-ROFPAAA operator to aggregate all the preference values $x_i (i = 1,2,\ldots 5)$ given in Table 8. The overall aggregated values are given in Table 9 below.

Table 9. Collective preference information.

	Aggregated Information	
X_1	0.6417	0.5941
X_2	0.7274	0.6271
X_3	0.8137	0.6072
X_4	0.7935	0.4174
X_5	0.7407	0.6694

Step 7: Calculate the scores of $x_i(1,2,\ldots,5)$, respectively, in Table 10 as given below.

Table 10. The score values of the aggregated information.

Alternatives	Scores	Ranking
X_1	−0.0511	
X_2	0.0001	
X_3	0.1089	$S_4 > S_3 > S_2 > S_5 > S_1$
X_4	0.2379	
X_5	−0.0047	

Thus, the best alternative is X_4 and X_3 are the most suitable energy resources, respectively, according to the q-ROFPAAA operator. Now, we apply the same algorithm to classify the energy resources using the q-ROFPAAG operator, and the main steps are given below. (The first three steps have already been completed.)

Step 4: Utilize the q-ROFPAAG operator to aggregate the q-ROF decision matrix $R^q = \left(x_{ij}^q\right)_{4x5} (q = 1,2,3)$ into the collective q-ROF decision matrix $R = \left(x_{ij}\right)_{5x4}$ as given in Table 11.

Table 11. Collective preferences using q-ROFAAG of expert's information given in Tables 5–7.

	C_1		C_2		C_3		C_4	
X_1	0.7243	0.4597	0.866485	0.346201	0.730414	0.448658	0.9	0.355645
X_2	0.8058	0.5437	0.819498	0.454883	0.80000	0.583288	0.80000	0.457335
X_3	0.8611	0.5005	0.704231	0.458071	0.812901	0.403812	0.78309	0.569349
X_4	0.8386	0.3495	0.825559	0.3587	0.8000	0.464758	0.852244	0.357274
X_5	0.8126	0.5635	0.824634	0.353553	0.63353	0.343001	0.830917	0.425587

Step 5: Calculate the values of $T_{ij}, (i = 1, 2, \ldots m,\ j = 1, 2, \ldots n)$ based on the equation given in Step 3 of the algorithm.

$$T_{ij} = \begin{pmatrix} 1 & 0.2828 & 0.17224 & 0.051563 \\ 1 & 0.3624 & 0.165322 & 0.051837 \\ 1 & 0.5132 & 0.129912 & 0.061231 \\ 1 & 0.5471 & 0.2825683 & 0.116314 \\ 1 & 0.3577 & 0.184798 & 0.039532 \end{pmatrix}$$

Step 6: Utilize the q-ROFPAAA operator to aggregate all the preference values $x_i (i = 1, 2, \ldots 5)$ given in Table 8. The overall aggregated values are given in Table 12 below.

Table 12. Collective preference information.

	Aggregated Information	
X_1	0.7554	0.2905
X_2	0.8081	0.3846
X_3	0.8042	0.3383
X_4	0.8300	0.2290
X_5	0.7924	0.3634

Step 7: Calculate the score of $x_i(1, 2, \ldots, 5)$, respectively, in Table 13, as given below.

Table 13. The score values of the aggregated information.

Alternatives	Scores	Ranking
X_1	0.486197	
X_2	0.505076	
X_3	0.532325	$S_4 > S_3 > S_2 > S_5 > S_1$
X_4	0.636522	
X_5	0.495845	

Thus, the best alternatives X_4 and X_3 are the most appropriate energy resources, respectively, using the q-ROFPAAG operator. Tables 10 and 13 shows that the outcomes using q-ROFPAAA and q-ROFPAAG operators are the same. However, the results may vary and may not always be the same. The choice of the AOs is up to the decision makers. The ranking results obtained using q-ROFAAA and q-ROFAAG operators, as given in Tables 10 and 13, are geometrically expressed, as shown in Figure 2 below.

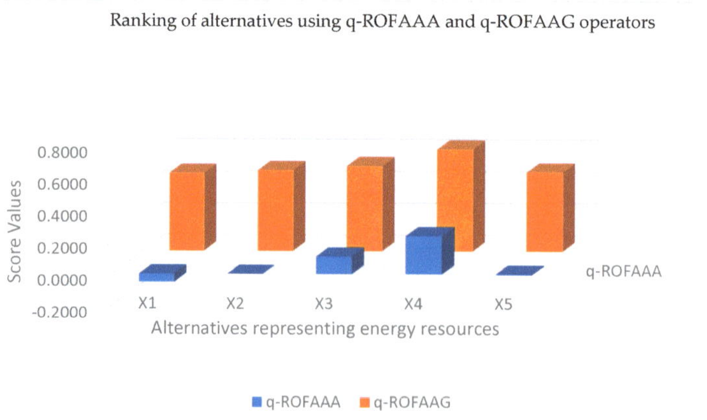

Figure 2. Representation of ranking results using q-ROFAA operators.

The above-discussed results are reliable and significant because of the prioritization of experts and attributes. If we keep all the experts and characteristics at the same level, then the proposed operators reduce to previous traditional AOs. As prioritization is a more realistic approach, using q-ROFPAAA and q-ROFPAAG operators is essential.

6. Comparative Study

This section will compare the aggregated results achieved using q-ROFPAAA and q-ROFPAAG operators with various other AOs based on q-ROF information. For this purpose, we applied averaging and geometric AOs of the q-ROFSs [22], q-ROF Hamacher operators [8], and q-ROF Dombi operators [47]. We also show the comparison with the AOs in some other frameworks [21,48], which shows the superiority of the proposed work. The aggregated results are portrayed in Table 14 below.

Table 14. The comparison of current and previous approaches.

Aggregation Operator	Operator	Ranking Result
Proposed Work	Averaging	$T_4 > T_3 > T_2 > T_5 > T_1$
	Geometric	$T_4 > T_3 > T_2 > T_5 > T_1$
Khan et al. [22]	Averaging	$T_4 > T_3 > T_2 > T_5 > T_1$
	Geometric	$T_4 > T_3 > T_2 > T_5 > T_1$
Jana et al. [47]	Averaging	$T_4 > T_3 > T_2 > T_5 > T_1$
	Geometric	$T_4 > T_3 > T_2 > T_5 > T_1$
Darko and Liang [8]	Averaging	$T_4 > T_3 > T_2 > T_5 > T_1$
	Geometric	$T_4 > T_3 > T_2 > T_5 > T_1$
Hussain et al. [21]	Averaging	Not Applicable
	Geometric	Not Applicable
Senapati et al. [48]	Averaging	Not Applicable
	Geometric	Not Applicable

From the data in Table 14, we noticed that the theory of Hussain et al. [21] was proposed based on Pythagorean fuzzy sets. The theory of Senapati et al. [48] is based on intuitionistic fuzzy sets, which failed to evaluate the considered data because these concepts are the special cases of the proposed work. The comparison results of proposed q-ROFPAAA and q-ROFPAAG operators with other AOs shown in Table 14 are geometrically described in Figure 3 below.

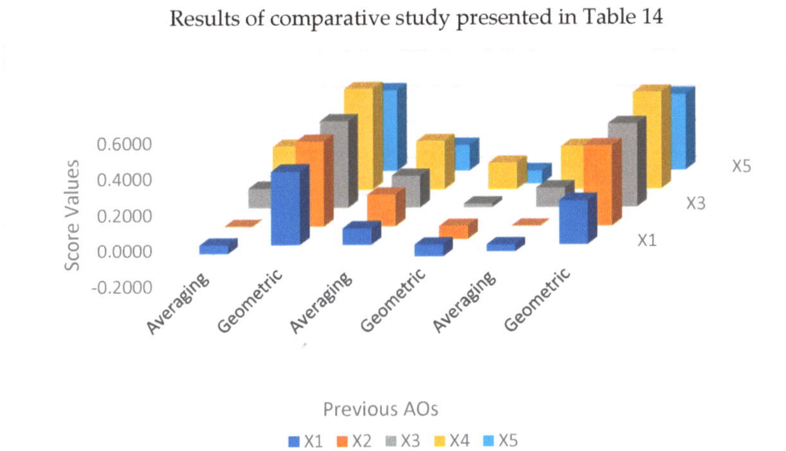

Figure 3. Score values using Khan et al. [23], Jana et al. [49] and Darko and Liang [8].

The analysis of Table 14 shows the result of the MCGDM problems considered in Example 1 and using some previous approaches. From the study, we conclude that the results were obtained using previous AOs. However, they solved the current example, but did not utilize prioritization, proving the proposed approach's worth. Further, some AOs established in the framework of PyFSs and IFSs cannot solve the given problem showing the diverse nature of q-ROFSs and the proposed q-ROFPAAA and q-ROFPAAG operators.

7. Conclusions

In this paper, we introduced the conception of the prioritization of AATN and AATCN-based AOs using q-ROF information. Prioritization is eminent in decision-making problems for prioritizing the attributes and experts and is similar to real-life phenomena. We introduced two types of AOs, q-ROFPAAA, and q-ROFPAAG operators, and noticed their basic features. We provided some interesting additional results for aggregation operators. Based on the proposed AOs, we developed an MCGDM algorithm, which was further applied to examine a real-life problem of energy resource selection. Comparing the proposed work with existing work shows its feasibility and applicability. Some key findings and advantages of the proposed work are given:

1. q-ROFPAA operators consider the relation of prioritization while they are aggregating information, while existing AOs do not have such a feature.
2. q-ROFPAA operators can be applied to a more extensive range of information, whereas other information is not used.
3. The proposed AOs generalize the previous AOs.

We aim to study the present concept in some well-known methods [49–51] involving unknown weights of the attributes, where weights are obtained using the information of experts. We also aim to develop power AOs [52] associated with q-ROFPAA operators to see their impact on real-life problems.

Author Contributions: Conceptualization, M.A. and K.U.; Formal analysis, G.Ć.; Investigation, M.A., G.Ć. and D.P.; Project administration, K.U. and G.Ć.; Software, M.A., K.U. and D.P.; Supervision, K.U. and D.P.; Validation, K.U.; Visualization, M.A.; Writing—original draft, M.A., K.U., G.Ć. and D.P.; Writing—review and editing, M.A., K.U., G.Ć. and D.P. All authors have read and agreed to the published version of the manuscript.

Funding: This research received no external funding.

Data Availability Statement: Not applicable.

Conflicts of Interest: The authors declare no conflict of interest.

Appendix A

Definition A1. *For any q-ROFV* $T = (m_T(x), n_T(x))$, *the accuracy function is defined as:*

$$cc(T) = m_T^q(x) + n_T^q(x), cc(T) \in [0,1]$$

Definition A2. *Suppose any three q-ROFVs* $T = (m_T(x), n_T(x))$, $T_1 = (m_{T_1}(x), n_{T_1}(x))$, *and* $T_2 = (m_{T_2}(x), n_{T_1}(x))$, *where* $\eta > 0$ *is any real number. Then,*

$$1. \rightarrow T_1 \oplus T_2 = \left(\sqrt[q]{1 - e^{-\left(\left(-ln\,(1-m_{T_1}^q)\right)^{\eta} + \left(-ln\,(1-m_{T_2}^q)\right)^{\eta}\right)^{\frac{1}{\eta}}}}, \; e^{-\left(\left(-ln(n_{T_1})\right)^{\eta} + \left(-ln(n_{T_2})\right)^{\eta}\right)^{1/\eta}} \right)$$

$$2. \rightarrow T_1 \otimes T_2 = \left(\frac{e^{-((-ln(m_{T_1}))^{\eta}+(-ln(m_{T_2}))^{\eta})^{\frac{1}{\eta}}}}{\sqrt[q]{1-e^{-((-ln\,(1-n^q_{T_1}))^{\eta}+(-ln\,(1-n^q_{T_2}))^{\eta})^{1/\eta}}}}, \right)$$

$$3. \rightarrow \varphi T = \left(\sqrt[q]{1-e^{(-\varphi((-ln\,(1-m^q_T))^{\eta})^{1/\eta})}}, e^{-(\varphi(-ln(n_T))^{\eta})^{1/\eta}} \right)$$

$$4. \rightarrow T^{\varphi} = \left(e^{-(\varphi(-ln(m_T))^{\eta})^{1/\eta}}, \sqrt[q]{1-e^{(-\varphi((-ln\,(1-n^q_T))^{\eta})^{1/\eta})}} \right)$$

Appendix B

Proof of Theorem 1. By using the mathematical induction and basic Aczel–Alsina operations given in Appendix A, we prove this theorem as follows:

Case 1. Consider $k = 2$, then

$$\frac{T_1}{\sum_{j=1}^{2} T_j} m_{T_1} = \left(\sqrt[q]{1-e^{-(\frac{T_1}{\sum_{j=1}^{2} T_j}(-ln\,(1-m^q_{T_1}))^{\eta})^{1/\eta}}}, e^{-(\frac{T_1}{\sum_{j=1}^{2} T_j}(-ln(n_{T_1}))^{\eta})^{1/\eta}} \right)$$

$$\frac{T_2}{\sum_{j=1}^{2} T_j} m_{T_2} = \left(\sqrt[q]{1-e^{-(\frac{T_2}{\sum_{j=1}^{2} T_j}(-ln\,(1-m^q_{T_2}))^{\eta})^{1/\eta}}}, e^{-(\frac{T_1}{\sum_{j=1}^{2} T_j}(-ln(n_{T_2}))^{\eta})^{1/\eta}} \right)$$

Then,

$$q-ROFPAAA(T_1, T_2) = \frac{T_1}{\sum_{j=1}^{2} T_j}(T_1) \oplus \frac{T_2}{\sum_{j=1}^{2} T_j}(T_2)$$

$$= \left(\begin{array}{c} \left(\sqrt[q]{1-e^{-(\frac{T_1}{\sum_{j=1}^{2} T_j}(-ln\,(1-m^q_{T_1}))^{\eta})^{\frac{1}{\eta}}}}, e^{-(\frac{T_2}{\sum_{j=1}^{2} T_j}(-ln(n_{T_1}))^{\eta})^{\frac{1}{\eta}}} \right) \\ \oplus \left(\sqrt[q]{1-e^{-(\frac{T_2}{\sum_{j=1}^{2} T_j}(-ln\,(1-m^q_{T_2}))^{\eta})^{1/\eta}}}, e^{-(\frac{T_1}{\sum_{j=1}^{2} T_j}(-ln(n_{T_2}))^{\eta})^{1/\eta}} \right) \end{array} \right)$$

$$= \left(\begin{array}{c} \sqrt[q]{1-e^{-(\frac{T_1}{\sum_{j=1}^{2} T_j}(-ln\,(1-m^q_{T_1}))^{\eta}+\frac{T_2}{\sum_{j=1}^{2} T_j}(-ln\,(1-m^q_{T_2}))^{\eta})^{\frac{1}{\eta}}}} \\ e^{-(\frac{T_2}{\sum_{j=1}^{2} T_j}(-ln(n_{T_1}))^{\eta}+\frac{T_2}{\sum_{j=1}^{2} T_j}(-ln(n_{T_2}))^{\eta})^{1/\eta}} \end{array} \right)$$

$$= \left(\sqrt[q]{1-e^{-(\frac{T_1}{\sum_{j=1}^{2} T_j}(-ln\,(1-m^q_{T_j}))^{\eta})^{\frac{1}{\eta}}}}, e^{-(\frac{T_1}{\sum_{j=1}^{2} T_j}(-ln(n_{T_j}))^{\eta})^{1/\eta}} \right)$$

Clearly, for $k = 2$, Equation (9) works.

Case 2. Consider that for $k = n$, Equation (9) is satisfied and

$$q-ROFPAAA(T_1, T_2, \ldots, T_n) = \left(\sqrt[q]{1 - e^{-\left(\sum_{j=1}^{n} \frac{T_j}{\sum_{j=1}^{n} T_j}(-ln\ (1-m_{T_j}^{q}))^{\text{ๆ}}\right)^{\frac{1}{\text{ๆ}}}}}, e^{-\left(\sum_{j=1}^{n} \frac{T_j}{\sum_{j=1}^{n} T_j}(-ln(n_{T_j}))^{\text{ๆ}}\right)^{1/\text{ๆ}}} \right)$$

Case 3. When we take $k = n + 1$, we obtain,

$$q-ROFPAAA(T_1, T_2, \ldots, T_n, T_{n+1}) = \oplus_{j=1}^{n}\left(\frac{T_j}{\sum_{j=1}^{n} T_j}(T_j)\right) \oplus \frac{T_{n+1}}{\sum_{j=1}^{n+1} T_j}(T_{n+1})$$

$$= \left(\sqrt[q]{1 - e^{-\left(\sum_{j=1}^{n} \frac{T_j}{\sum_{j=1}^{n} T_j}(-ln\ (1-m_{T_n}^{q}))^{\text{ๆ}}\right)^{\frac{1}{\text{ๆ}}}}} \\ e^{-\left(\sum_{j=1}^{k} \frac{T_j}{\sum_{j=1}^{k} T_j}(-ln(n_{T_k}))^{\text{ๆ}}\right)^{1/\text{ๆ}}} \right) \oplus \left(\sqrt[q]{1 - e^{-\left(\frac{T_{k+1}}{\sum_{j=1}^{k+1} T_j}(-ln\ (1-m_{k+1}^{q}))^{\text{ๆ}}\right)^{\frac{1}{\text{ๆ}}}}} \\ e^{-\left(\frac{T_{k+1}}{\sum_{j=1}^{k} T_j}(-ln(n_{k+1}))^{\text{ๆ}}\right)^{1/\text{ๆ}}} \right)$$

$$= \left(\sqrt[q]{1 - e^{-\left(\sum_{j=1}^{k+1} \frac{T_j}{\sum_{j=1}^{k+1} T_j}(-ln\ (1-m_{T_j}^{q}))^{\text{ๆ}}\right)^{\frac{1}{\text{ๆ}}}}}, e^{-\left(\sum_{j=1}^{k+1} \frac{T_j}{\sum_{j=1}^{k+1} T_j}(-ln(n_{T_j}))^{\text{ๆ}}\right)^{1/\text{ๆ}}} \right)$$

Thus, Equation (9) works for all k values. □

Appendix C

Proof of Theorem 3. For any q-ROFVs $T_j = \left(m_{T_j}(x), n_{T_j}(x)\right)$, let $T^- = \left(\min_j m_{T_j}(x), \max_j m_{T_j}(x)\right)$, $T^+ = \left(\max_j m_{T_j}(x), \min_j m_{T_j}(x)\right)$

$$= \left(\sqrt[q]{1 - e^{-\left(\sum_{j=1}^{k} \frac{T_j}{\sum_{j=1}^{k} T_j}(-ln\ (1-m_{T_j}^{-q}))^{\text{ๆ}}\right)^{\frac{1}{\text{ๆ}}}}} \leq \sqrt[q]{1 - e^{-\left(\sum_{j=1}^{k} \frac{T_j}{\sum_{j=1}^{k} T_j}(-ln\ (1-m_{T_j}^{q}))^{\text{ๆ}}\right)^{\frac{1}{\text{ๆ}}}}} \leq \sqrt[q]{1 - e^{-\left(\sum_{j=1}^{k} \frac{T_j}{\sum_{j=1}^{k} T_j}(-ln\ (1-m^{+}{}_{T_j}^{q}))^{\text{ๆ}}\right)^{\frac{1}{\text{ๆ}}}}} \right)$$

and

$$e^{-\left(\sum_{j=1}^{k} \frac{T_j}{\sum_{j=1}^{k} T_j}(-ln(n_{T_j}^{-q}))^{\text{ๆ}}\right)^{1/\text{ๆ}}} \geq e^{-\left(\sum_{j=1}^{k} \frac{T_j}{\sum_{j=1}^{k} T_j}(-ln(n_{T_j}^{q}))^{\text{ๆ}}\right)^{1/\text{ๆ}}} \geq e^{-\left(\sum_{j=1}^{k} \frac{T_j}{\sum_{j=1}^{k} T_j}(-ln(n_{T_j}^{+q}))^{\text{ๆ}}\right)^{1/\text{ๆ}}}$$

This shows that

$$T^- \leq q-ROFPAAA(T_1, T_2, \ldots, T_j) \leq T^+$$

□

Appendix D

Proof of Theorem 5. According to Definition 5 and Theorem 1.

$$T_1 \oplus T_2 = \left(\sqrt[q]{1 - e^{-\left((-ln\,(1-m_{T_1}^q))^{\eta} + (-ln\,(1-m_{T_2}^q))^{\eta}\right)^{1/\eta}}},\ e^{-\left((-ln(n_{T_1}))^{\eta} + (-ln(n_{T_2}))^{\eta}\right)^{1/\eta}} \right)$$

Also $q-ROFPAAA(T_1, T_2, \ldots, T_k) = \left(\begin{array}{c} \sqrt[q]{1 - e^{-\left(\sum_{j=1}^{k}\left(\frac{T_j}{\sum_{j=1}^{n} T_j}\right)(-ln\,(1-m_{T_j}^q))^{\eta}\right)^{\frac{1}{\eta}}}}, \\ e^{-\left(\sum_{j=1}^{k}\left(\frac{T_j}{\sum_{j=1}^{k} T_j}\right)(-ln(n_{T_j}))^{\eta}\right)^{1/\eta}} \end{array} \right)$

$$q-ROFPAAA(T_1 \oplus \beta, T_2 \oplus \beta, \ldots, T_j \oplus \beta)$$

$$= \left(\begin{array}{c} \sqrt[q]{1 - e^{-\left(\sum_{j=1}^{k}\left(\frac{T_j}{\sum_{j=1}^{k} T_j}\right)\left(-\ln\left(1-\left(\sqrt[q]{1-e^{-\left((-\ln(1-m_{T_1}^q))^{\eta} + (-\ln(1-a))^{\eta}\right)^{\frac{1}{\eta}}}}\right)^{q}\right)\right)^{\eta}\right)^{\frac{1}{\eta}}}}, \\ e^{-\left(\sum_{j=1}^{k}\left(\frac{T_j}{\sum_{j=1}^{k} T_j}\right)\left(-\ln\left(e^{-\left((-\ln(n_{T_1}))^{\eta} + (-\ln(b))^{\eta}\right)^{\frac{1}{\eta}}}\right)\right)^{\eta}\right)^{\frac{1}{\eta}}} \end{array} \right)$$

$$= \left(\begin{array}{c} \sqrt[q]{1 - e^{-\left(\sum_{j=1}^{k}\left(\frac{T_j}{\sum_{j=1}^{k} T_j}\right)\left(\left((-ln\,(1-m_{T_1}^q))^{\eta} + (-ln\,(1-a))^{\eta}\right)^{\frac{1}{\eta}}\right)^{\eta}\right)^{\frac{1}{\eta}}}}, \\ e^{-\left(\sum_{j=1}^{k}\left(\frac{T_j}{\sum_{j=1}^{k} T_j}\right)\left(\left((-ln(n_{T_1}))^{\eta} + (-ln(b))^{\eta}\right)^{1/\eta}\right)^{\eta}\right)^{1/\eta}} \end{array} \right)$$

Now, consider $q-ROFPAAA(T_1, T_2, \ldots, T_j) \oplus \beta$.

$$T_1 \oplus \beta = \left(\sqrt[q]{1 - e^{-\left((-ln\,(1-m_{T_1}^q))^{\eta} + (-ln\,(1-a))^{\eta}\right)^{1/\eta}}},\ e^{-\left((-ln(n_{T_1}))^{\eta} + (-ln(b))^{\eta}\right)^{1/\eta}} \right)$$

$$= \left(\begin{array}{c} \sqrt[q]{1 - e^{-\left(\left(-ln\,\left(1-\left(\sqrt[q]{1-e^{-\left(\sum_{j=1}^{k}\left(\frac{T_j}{\sum_{j=1}^{k} T_j}\right)(-ln\,(1-m_{T_j}^q))^{\eta}\right)^{\frac{1}{\eta}}}}\right)^{q}\right)\right)^{\eta} + (-ln\,(1-a))^{\eta}\right)^{\frac{1}{\eta}}}}, \\ e^{-\left(\left(-ln\left(e^{-\left(\sum_{j=1}^{k}\left(\frac{T_j}{\sum_{j=1}^{k} T_j}\right)(-ln(n_{T_j}))^{\eta}\right)^{\frac{1}{\eta}}}\right)\right)^{\eta} + (-ln(b))^{\eta}\right)^{\frac{1}{\eta}}} \end{array} \right)$$

$$= \left(\begin{array}{c} \sqrt[q]{1 - e^{-\left(\left(\sum_{j=1}^{k}\left(\frac{T_j}{\sum_{j=1}^{k} T_j}\right)(-ln\,(1-m_{T_j}^q))^{\eta}\right) + (-ln\,(1-a))^{\eta}\right)^{\frac{1}{\eta}}}}, \\ e^{-\left(\sum_{j=1}^{k}\left(\frac{T_j}{\sum_{j=1}^{k} T_j}\right)(-ln(n_{T_j}))^{\eta} + (-ln(b))^{\eta}\right)^{1/\eta}} \end{array} \right)$$

Hence,

$$q-ROFPAAA(T_1 \oplus \beta, T_2 \oplus \beta, \ldots, T_j \oplus \beta) = q-ROFPAAA(T_1, T_2, \ldots, T_j) \oplus \beta$$

□

Appendix E

Proof of Theorem 6. According to Theorem 1 and Definition 5:

$$q-ROFPAAA(T_1,T_2,\ldots,T_j)=\left(\sqrt[q]{1-e^{-\left(\sum_{j=1}^{k}\frac{T_j}{\sum_{j=1}^{k}T_j}\left(-ln\left(1-m_{T_j}^{q}\right)\right)^{\eta}\right)^{\frac{1}{\eta}}}},\ e^{-\left(\sum_{j=1}^{k}\frac{T_j}{\sum_{j=1}^{k}T_j}\left(-ln\left(n_{T_j}\right)\right)^{\eta}\right)^{\frac{1}{\eta}}}\right)$$

$$\varphi T=\left(\sqrt[q]{1-e^{\left(-\varphi\left(\left(-ln\left(1-m_T^{q}\right)\right)^{\eta}\right)\right)^{1/\eta}}},\ e^{-\left(\varphi\left(-ln\left(n_T\right)\right)^{\eta}\right)^{1/\eta}}\right)$$

$$q-ROFPAAA(\varphi T_1,\varphi T_2,\ldots,\varphi T_P)=\left(\begin{array}{c}\sqrt[q]{1-e^{-\left(\sum_{j=1}^{k}\frac{T_j}{\sum_{j=1}^{k}T_j}\left(-ln\left(1-\left(\sqrt[q]{1-e^{\left(-\varphi\left(\left(-ln\left(1-m_{T_j}^{q}\right)\right)^{\eta}\right)\right)^{\frac{1}{\eta}}}}\right)^{q}\right)\right)^{\eta}\right)^{\frac{1}{\eta}}}},\\ e^{-\left(\sum_{j=1}^{k}\frac{T_j}{\sum_{j=1}^{k}T_j}\left(-ln\left(e^{-\left(\varphi\left(-ln\left(n_{T_j}\right)\right)^{\eta}\right)^{1/\eta}}\right)\right)^{\eta}\right)^{1/\eta}}\end{array}\right)$$

$$q-ROFPAAA(\varphi T_1,\varphi T_2,\ldots,\varphi T_P)=\left(\begin{array}{c}\sqrt[q]{1-e^{-\left(\sum_{j=1}^{k}\frac{T_j}{\sum_{j=1}^{k}T_j}\left(-ln\left(1-1-e^{\left(-\varphi\left(\left(-ln\left(1-m_{T_j}^{q}\right)\right)^{\eta}\right)\right)^{\frac{1}{\eta}}}\right)\right)^{\eta}\right)^{\frac{1}{\eta}}}},\\ e^{-\left(\sum_{j=1}^{k}\frac{T_j}{\sum_{j=1}^{k}T_j}\left(\left(\varphi\left(-ln\left(n_{T_j}\right)\right)^{\eta}\right)\right)\right)^{1/\eta}}\end{array}\right)$$

$$q-ROFPAAA(\varphi T_1,\varphi T_2,\ldots,\varphi T_P)=\left(\begin{array}{c}\sqrt[q]{1-e^{-\left(\sum_{j=1}^{k}\frac{T_j}{\sum_{j=1}^{k}T_j}\left(\left(\varphi\left(-ln\left(1-m_{T_j}^{q}\right)\right)^{\eta}\right)\right)\right)^{\frac{1}{\eta}}}},\\ e^{-\left(\sum_{j=1}^{k}\frac{T_j}{\sum_{j=1}^{k}T_j}\left(\left(\varphi\left(-ln\left(n_{T_j}\right)\right)^{\eta}\right)\right)\right)^{1/\eta}}\end{array}\right)$$

$$q-ROFPAAA(\varphi T_1,\varphi T_2,\ldots,\varphi T_P)=\left(\begin{array}{c}\sqrt[q]{1-e^{-\left(\sum_{j=1}^{k}\frac{T_j}{\sum_{j=1}^{k}T_j}\left(\varphi\left(-ln\left(1-m_{T_j}^{q}\right)^{\eta}\right)\right)\right)^{\frac{1}{\eta}}}},\\ e^{-\left(\sum_{j=1}^{k}\frac{T_j}{\sum_{j=1}^{k}T_j}\left(\varphi\left(-ln\left(n_{T_j}\right)^{\eta}\right)\right)\right)^{1/\eta}}\end{array}\right)$$

Now, consider

$$\varphi q-ROFPAAA(T_1,T_2,\ldots,T_P)=\varphi\left(\begin{array}{c}\sqrt[q]{1-e^{-\left(\sum_{j=1}^{k}\frac{T_j}{\sum_{j=1}^{k}T_j}\left(-ln\left(1-m_{T_j}^{q}\right)\right)^{\eta}\right)^{\frac{1}{\eta}}}},\\ e^{-\left(\sum_{j=1}^{k}\frac{T_j}{\sum_{j=1}^{k}T_j}\left(-ln\left(n_{T_j}\right)\right)^{\eta}\right)^{\frac{1}{\eta}}}\end{array}\right)$$

$$=\left(\begin{array}{c}\sqrt[q]{1-e^{-\left(\varphi\left(-ln\left(1-\left(\sqrt[q]{1-e^{-\left(\sum_{j=1}^{k}\frac{T_j}{\sum_{j=1}^{k}T_j}\left(-ln\left(1-m_{T_j}^{q}\right)\right)^{\eta}\right)^{\frac{1}{\eta}}}}\right)^{q}\right)\right)^{\eta}\right)^{\frac{1}{\eta}}}},\\ e^{-\left(\varphi\left(-ln\left(e^{-\left(\sum_{j=1}^{k}\frac{T_j}{\sum_{j=1}^{k}T_j}\left(-ln\left(n_{T_j}\right)\right)^{\eta}\right)^{\frac{1}{\eta}}}\right)\right)^{\eta}\right)^{\frac{1}{\eta}}}\end{array}\right)$$

$$= \left(\sqrt[q]{1 - e^{-\left(\varphi\left(-ln\left(1-\left(1-e^{-\left(\sum_{j=1}^{k} \frac{T_j}{\sum_{j=1}^{k} T_j}\left(-ln\left(1-m_{T_j}^{q}\right)\right)^{\eta}\right)^{\frac{1}{\eta}}}\right)\right)\right)^{\eta}\right)^{\frac{1}{\eta}}}}, \; e^{-\left(\varphi\left(\left(\sum_{j=1}^{k} \frac{T_j}{\sum_{j=1}^{k} T_j}\left(-ln\left(n_{T_j}\right)\right)^{\eta}\right)\right)\right)^{1/\eta}} \right)$$

$$= \left(\sqrt[q]{1 - e^{-\left(\varphi\left(\left(\sum_{j=1}^{k} \frac{T_j}{\sum_{j=1}^{k} T_j}\left(-ln\left(1-m_{T_j}^{q}\right)\right)^{\eta}\right)\right)\right)^{\frac{1}{\eta}}}}, \; e^{-\left(\varphi\left(\left(\sum_{j=1}^{k} \frac{T_j}{\sum_{j=1}^{k} T_j}\left(-ln\left(n_{T_j}\right)\right)^{\eta}\right)\right)\right)^{1/\eta}} \right)$$

$$\varphi q - ROFPAAA(T_1, T_2, \ldots, T_J) = \left(\sqrt[q]{1 - e^{-\left(\varphi\left(\left(\sum_{j=1}^{k} \frac{T_j}{\sum_{j=1}^{k} T_j}\left(-ln\left(1-m_{T_j}^{q}\right)\right)^{\eta}\right)\right)\right)^{\frac{1}{\eta}}}}, \; e^{-\left(\varphi\left(\left(\sum_{j=1}^{k} \frac{T_j}{\sum_{j=1}^{k} T_j}\left(-ln\left(n_{T_j}\right)\right)^{\eta}\right)\right)\right)^{1/\eta}} \right)$$

Thus,

$$q - ROFPAAA(\varphi T_1, \varphi T_2, \ldots, \varphi T_j) = \varphi q - ROFPAAA(T_1, T_2, \ldots, T_j)$$

□

References

1. Zadeh, L.A. Fuzzy Sets. *Inf. Control* **1965**, *8*, 338–353. [CrossRef]
2. Atanassov, K. Intuitionistic Fuzzy Sets. *Fuzzy Sets Syst.* **1986**, *20*, 87–96. [CrossRef]
3. Atanassov, K.T. More on Intuitionistic Fuzzy Sets. *Fuzzy Sets Syst.* **1989**, *33*, 37–45. [CrossRef]
4. Atanassov, K.T. Intuitionistic Fuzzy Sets. In *Intuitionistic Fuzzy Sets*; Springer: Berlin/Heidelberg, Germany, 1999; pp. 1–137.
5. Ali, M.; Tamir, D.E.; Rishe, N.D.; Kandel, A. Complex Intuitionistic Fuzzy Classes. In Proceedings of the 2016 IEEE International Conference on Fuzzy Systems (FUZZ-IEEE), Vancouver, BC, Canada, 24–29 July 2016; pp. 2027–2034.
6. Yager, R.R. Pythagorean Fuzzy Subsets. In Proceedings of the 2013 Joint IFSA World Congress and NAFIPS Annual Meeting (IFSA/NAFIPS), Edmonton, AB, Canada, 24–28 June 2013; pp. 57–61.
7. Yager, R.R. Generalized Orthopair Fuzzy Sets. *IEEE Trans. Fuzzy Syst.* **2016**, *25*, 1222–1230. [CrossRef]
8. Darko, A.P.; Liang, D. Some Q-Rung Orthopair Fuzzy Hamacher Aggregation Operators and Their Application to Multiple Attribute Group Decision Making with Modified EDAS Method. *Eng. Appl. Artif. Intell.* **2020**, *87*, 103259. [CrossRef]
9. Garg, H.; Chen, S.-M. Multiattribute Group Decision Making Based on Neutrality Aggregation Operators of Q-Rung Orthopair Fuzzy Sets. *Inf. Sci.* **2020**, *517*, 427–447. [CrossRef]
10. Wei, G.; Gao, H.; Wei, Y. Some Q-Rung Orthopair Fuzzy Heronian Mean Operators in Multiple Attribute Decision Making. *Int. J. Intell. Syst.* **2018**, *33*, 1426–1458. [CrossRef]
11. Liu, Z.; Wang, X.; Li, L.; Zhao, X.; Liu, P. Q-Rung Orthopair Fuzzy Multiple Attribute Group Decision-Making Method Based on Normalized Bidirectional Projection Model and Generalized Knowledge-Based Entropy Measure. *J. Ambient Intell. Humaniz. Comput.* **2021**, *12*, 2715–2730. [CrossRef]
12. Garg, H.; Rani, D. New Prioritized Aggregation Operators with Priority Degrees among Priority Orders for Complex Intuitionistic Fuzzy Information. *J. Ambient Intell. Humaniz. Comput.* **2021**, *14*, 1373–1399. [CrossRef]
13. Garg, H. A Novel Trigonometric Operation-Based q-Rung Orthopair Fuzzy Aggregation Operator and Its Fundamental Properties. *Neural Comput. Appl.* **2020**, *32*, 15077–15099. [CrossRef]
14. Xia, M.; Xu, Z.; Zhu, B. Some Issues on Intuitionistic Fuzzy Aggregation Operators Based on Archimedean T-Conorm and t-Norm. *Knowl.-Based Syst.* **2012**, *31*, 78–88. [CrossRef]
15. Wei, G.; Zhao, X. Induced Hesitant Interval-Valued Fuzzy Einstein Aggregation Operators and Their Application to Multiple Attribute Decision Making. *J. Intell. Fuzzy Syst.* **2013**, *24*, 789–803. [CrossRef]
16. Seikh, M.R.; Mandal, U. Q-Rung Orthopair Fuzzy Frank Aggregation Operators and Its Application in Multiple Attribute Decision-Making with Unknown Attribute Weights. *Granul. Comput.* **2021**, *7*, 709–730. [CrossRef]
17. Ali, J.; Bashir, Z.; Rashid, T. Weighted Interval-Valued Dual-Hesitant Fuzzy Sets and Its Application in Teaching Quality Assessment. *Soft Comput.* **2021**, *25*, 3503–3530. [CrossRef]
18. Liu, P.; Mahmood, T.; Ali, Z. Complex Q-Rung Orthopair Fuzzy Schweizer–Sklar Muirhead Mean Aggregation Operators and Their Application in Multi-Criteria Decision-Making. *J. Intell. Fuzzy Syst.* **2021**, *40*, 11287–11309. [CrossRef]

19. Aczél, J.; Alsina, C. Characterizations of Some Classes of Quasilinear Functions with Applications to Triangular Norms and t Synthesizing Judgements. *Aequ. Math.* **1982**, *25*, 313–315. [CrossRef]
20. Senapati, T.; Chen, G.; Mesiar, R.; Yager, R.R. Novel Aczel–Alsina Operations-Based Interval-Valued Intuitionistic Fuzz Aggregation Operators and Their Applications in Multiple Attribute Decision-Making Process. *Int. J. Intell. Syst.* **2021**, *3* 5059–5081. [CrossRef]
21. Hussain, A.; Ullah, K.; Alshahrani, M.N.; Yang, M.-S.; Pamucar, D. Novel Aczel–Alsina Operators for Pythagorean Fuzzy Set with Application in Multi-Attribute Decision Making. *Symmetry* **2022**, *14*, 940. [CrossRef]
22. Khan, M.R.; Wang, H.; Ullah, K.; Karamti, H. Construction Material Selection by Using Multi-Attribute Decision Making Base on q-Rung Orthopair Fuzzy Aczel–Alsina Aggregation Operators. *Appl. Sci.* **2022**, *12*, 8537. [CrossRef]
23. Senapati, T. Approaches to Multi-Attribute Decision-Making Based on Picture Fuzzy Aczel–Alsina Average Aggregatio Operators. *Comput. Appl. Math.* **2022**, *41*, 40. [CrossRef]
24. Hussain, A.; Ullah, K.; Yang, M.-S.; Pamucar, D. Aczel-Alsina Aggregation Operators on T-Spherical Fuzzy (TSF) Informatio with Application to TSF Multi-Attribute Decision Making. *IEEE Access* **2022**, *10*, 26011–26023. [CrossRef]
25. Ahmmad, J.; Mahmood, T.; Mehmood, N.; Urawong, K.; Chinram, R. Intuitionistic Fuzzy Rough Aczel-Alsina Average Aggrega tion Operators and Their Applications in Medical Diagnoses. *Symmetry* **2022**, *14*, 2537. [CrossRef]
26. Ali, J.; Naeem, M. Complex Q-Rung Orthopair Fuzzy Aczel–Alsina Aggregation Operators and Its Application to Multipl Criteria Decision-Making with Unknown Weight Information. *IEEE Access* **2022**, *10*, 85315–85342. [CrossRef]
27. Yager, R.R. Prioritized Aggregation Operators. *Int. J. Approx. Reason.* **2008**, *48*, 263–274. [CrossRef]
28. Yager, R.R. Prioritized OWA Aggregation. *Fuzzy Optim. Decis. Mak.* **2009**, *8*, 245–262. [CrossRef]
29. Yan, H.-B.; Huynh, V.-N.; Nakamori, Y.; Murai, T. On Prioritized Weighted Aggregation in Multi-Criteria Decision Making. *Exper Syst. Appl.* **2011**, *38*, 812–823. [CrossRef]
30. Chen, T.-Y. A Prioritized Aggregation Operator-Based Approach to Multiple Criteria Decision Making Using Interval-Value Intuitionistic Fuzzy Sets: A Comparative Perspective. *Inf. Sci.* **2014**, *281*, 97–112. [CrossRef]
31. Arora, R.; Garg, H. Prioritized Averaging/Geometric Aggregation Operators under the Intuitionistic Fuzzy Soft Set Environmen *Sci. Iran.* **2017**, *25*, 466–482. [CrossRef]
32. Ali, Z.; Mahmood, T.; Aslam, M.; Chinram, R. Another View of Complex Intuitionistic Fuzzy Soft Sets Based on Prioritize Aggregation Operators and Their Applications to Multiattribute Decision Making. *Mathematics* **2021**, *9*, 1922. [CrossRef]
33. Gao, H. Pythagorean Fuzzy Hamacher Prioritized Aggregation Operators in Multiple Attribute Decision Making. *J. Intell. Fuzz Syst.* **2018**, *35*, 2229–2245. [CrossRef]
34. Mahmood, T.; Ali, Z. Prioritized Muirhead Mean Aggregation Operators under the Complex Single-Valued Neutrosophic Setting and Their Application in Multi-Attribute Decision Making. *J. Comput. Cogn. Eng.* **2022**, *10*, 280.
35. Riaz, M.; Farid, H.M.A.; Shakeel, H.M.; Aslam, M.; Mohamed, S.H.; Riaz, M.; Farid, H.M.A.; Shakeel, H.M.; Aslam, M.; Mohamed S.H. Innovative Q-Rung Orthopair Fuzzy Prioritized Aggregation Operators Based on Priority Degrees with Application t Sustainable Energy Planning: A Case Study of Gwadar. *AIMS Math.* **2021**, *6*, 12795–12831. [CrossRef]
36. Sarfraz, M.; Ullah, K.; Akram, M.; Pamucar, D.; Božanić, D. Prioritized Aggregation Operators for Intuitionistic Fuzzy Informatio Based on Aczel–Alsina T-Norm and T-Conorm and Their Applications in Group Decision-Making. *Symmetry* **2022**, *14*, 2655 [CrossRef]
37. Akram, M.; Ullah, K.; Pamucar, D. Performance Evaluation of Solar Energy Cells Using the Interval-Valued T-Spherical Fuzz Bonferroni Mean Operators. *Energies* **2022**, *15*, 292. [CrossRef]
38. Baumann, M.; Weil, M.; Peters, J.F.; Chibeles-Martins, N.; Moniz, A.B. A Review of Multi-Criteria Decision Making Approache for Evaluating Energy Storage Systems for Grid Applications. *Renew. Sustain. Energy Rev.* **2019**, *107*, 516–534. [CrossRef]
39. Deveci, M.; Pamucar, D.; Cali, U.; Kantar, E.; Kolle, K.; Tande, J.O. A Hybrid Q-Rung Orthopair Fuzzy Sets Based CoCoSo Mode for Floating Offshore Wind Farm Site Selection in Norway. *CSEE J. Power Energy Syst.* **2022**, *8*, 5. [CrossRef]
40. Haiyun, C.; Zhixiong, H.; Yüksel, S.; Dinçer, H. Analysis of the Innovation Strategies for Green Supply Chain Management in the Energy Industry Using the QFD-Based Hybrid Interval Valued Intuitionistic Fuzzy Decision Approach. *Renew. Sustain. Energ Rev.* **2021**, *143*, 110844. [CrossRef]
41. Naseem, A.; Ullah, K.; Akram, M.; Božanić, D.; Ćirović, G. Assessment of Smart Grid Systems for Electricity Using Powe Maclaurin Symmetric Mean Operators Based on T-Spherical Fuzzy Information. *Energies* **2022**, *15*, 7826. [CrossRef]
42. Ijadi Maghsoodi, A.; Ijadi Maghsoodi, A.; Mosavi, A.; Rabczuk, T.; Zavadskas, E.K. Renewable Energy Technology Selection Problem Using Integrated H-SWARA-MULTIMOORA Approach. *Sustainability* **2018**, *10*, 4481. [CrossRef]
43. Ilbahar, E.; Cebi, S.; Kahraman, C. A State-of-the-Art Review on Multi-Attribute Renewable Energy Decision Making. *Energ Strategy Rev.* **2019**, *25*, 18–33. [CrossRef]
44. Liu, Z.; Mohammadzadeh, A.; Turabieh, H.; Mafarja, M.; Band, S.S.; Mosavi, A. A New Online Learned Interval Type-3 Fuzzy Control System for Solar Energy Management Systems. *IEEE Access* **2021**, *9*, 10498–10508. [CrossRef]
45. Riaz, M.; Sałabun, W.; Athar Farid, H.M.; Ali, N.; Wątróbski, J. A Robust Q-Rung Orthopair Fuzzy Information Aggregation Using Einstein Operations with Application to Sustainable Energy Planning Decision Management. *Energies* **2020**, *13*, 2155. [CrossRef]
46. Farahbod, F.; Eftekhari, M. Comparison of Different T-Norm Operators in Classification Problems. *Int. J. Fuzzy Log. Syst.* **2012**, *2* 33–39. [CrossRef]

47. Jana, C.; Muhiuddin, G.; Pal, M. Some Dombi Aggregation of Q-Rung Orthopair Fuzzy Numbers in Multiple-Attribute Decision Making. *Int. J. Intell. Syst.* **2019**, *34*, 3220–3240. [CrossRef]
48. Senapati, T.; Chen, G.; Yager, R.R. Aczel–Alsina Aggregation Operators and Their Application to Intuitionistic Fuzzy Multiple Attribute Decision Making. *Int. J. Intell. Syst.* **2022**, *37*, 1529–1551. [CrossRef]
49. Ali, Z.; Mahmood, T.; Yang, M.-S. TOPSIS Method Based on Complex Spherical Fuzzy Sets with Bonferroni Mean Operators. *Mathematics* **2020**, *8*, 1739. [CrossRef]
50. Wang, H.; Zhang, F.; Ullah, K. Waste Clothing Recycling Channel Selection Using a CoCoSo-D Method Based on Sine Trigonometric Interaction Operational Laws with Pythagorean Fuzzy Information. *Energies* **2022**, *15*, 2010. [CrossRef]
51. Wang, H.; Ullah, K. T-Spherical Uncertain Linguistic MARCOS Method Based on Generalized Distance and Heronian Mean for Multi-Attribute Group Decision-Making with Unknown Weight Information. *Complex Intell. Syst.* **2022**, 1–33. [CrossRef]
52. Garg, H.; Ullah, K.; Mahmood, T.; Hassan, N.; Jan, N. T-Spherical Fuzzy Power Aggregation Operators and Their Applications in Multi-Attribute Decision Making. *J. Ambient Intell. Humaniz. Comput.* **2021**, *12*, 9067–9080. [CrossRef] [PubMed]

MDPI AG
Grosspeteranlage 5
4052 Basel
Switzerland
Tel.: +41 61 683 77 34

Energies Editorial Office
E-mail: energies@mdpi.com
www.mdpi.com/journal/energies

www.ingramcontent.com/pod-product-compliance
Lightning Source LLC
Chambersburg PA
CBHW041403210926
51850CB00013B/3161